P9-CLR-313

THE CRITICAL HERITAGE SERIES

GENERAL EDITOR: B. C. SOUTHAM, M.A., B.LITT.(OXON)
Formerly Department of English, Westfield College, University of London

For a list of books in the series see the back end paper

H. G. WELLS

THE CRITICAL HERITAGE

Edited by
PATRICK PARRINDER
Fellow of King's College, Cambridge

ROUTLEDGE & KEGAN PAUL LONDON AND BOSTON

First published 1972
by Routledge & Kegan Paul Ltd
Broadway House, 68–74 Carter Lane,
London EC4V 5EL and
9 Park Street,
Boston, Mass. 02108, U.S.A.
© Patrick Parrinder 1972
No part of this book may be reproduced in
any form without permission from the
publisher, except for the quotation of brief
passages in criticism
Library of Congress Catalog Card Number: 72–83659
ISBN 0 7100 7387 9

Printed in Great Britain
by W & J Mackay Limited, Chatham

General Editor's Preface

The reception given to a writer by his contemporaries and near-contemporaries is evidence of considerable value to the student of literature. On one side we learn a great deal about the state of criticism at large and in particular about the development of critical attitudes towards a single writer; at the same time, through private comments in letters, journals or marginalia, we gain an insight upon the tastes and literary thought of individual readers of the period. Evidence of this kind helps us to understand the writer's historical situation, the nature of his immediate reading-public, and his response to these pressures.

The separate volumes in the *Critical Heritage Series* present a record of this early criticism. Clearly, for many of the highly productive and lengthily reviewed nineteenth- and twentieth-century writers, there exists an enormous body of material; and in these cases the volume editors have made a selection of the most important views, significant for their intrinsic critical worth or for their representative quality— perhaps even registering incomprehension!

For earlier writers, notably pre-eighteenth century, the materials are much scarcer and the historical period has been extended, sometimes far beyond the writer's lifetime, in order to show the inception and growth of critical views which were initially slow to appear.

In each volume the documents are headed by an Introduction, discussing the material assembled and relating the early stages of the author's reception to what we have come to identify as the critical tradition. The volumes will make available much material which would otherwise be difficult of access and it is hoped that the modern reader will be thereby helped towards an informed understanding of the ways in which literature has been read and judged.

B.C.S.

Contents

CONTENTS

CONTENTS

CONTENTS

Preface

Wells's critical reception has already been exhaustively studied by Ingvald Raknem in *H. G. Wells and his Critics* (1962). I am indebted to Dr Raknem's volume generally and in particular to his excellent bibliography of reviews and articles on Wells. The amount of contemporary material on Wells is so great, however, that in preparing this book I have read over two hundred items not previously listed, and inevitably more must remain to be found. My principles of selection are described in the first part of the Introduction.

Acknowledgments

Careful attempts have been made to locate the owners of all copyright material included in this volume. Acknowledgments are due to the following: the *Spectator* for Nos 2, 6, 16, 37, 50, 55 and 87; Professor Oliver Zangwill for No. 4; the *New Statesman* for Nos 8, 9, 12, 17, 25, 54 and 63; *Nature* for No. 20; the Estate of H. G. Wells for Nos 21 and 55(b); the British Library of Political and Economic Science for Nos 27, 49 and 59; the Society of Authors as the literary representative of the Estate of Havelock Ellis for No. 30, and as the literary representative of the Estate of John Middleton Murry for No. 91; Miss D. Collins and the Bodley Head Ltd for No. 34; the Fabian Society for Nos 35 and 45; Lady Rothschild for No. 36; Mrs Dorothy Cheston Bennett, Rupert Hart-Davis and the University of Illinois Press for No. 42, and Mrs Bennett and Doubleday for No. 51; the Directeur Général of the *Revue des Deux Mondes* for No. 46; the Trustees of the Estate of H. L. Mencken for Nos 58 and 82; the *Atlantic Monthly* for No. 65 (Margaret Sherwood) and No. 80 (Conrad Aiken); Dame Rebecca West for No. 66; Mr Walter Lippmann for No. 71; Gladys Brooks for No. 72 (extract from the book *The World of H. G. Wells* by Van Wyck Brooks); the Estate of Virginia Woolf, the Hogarth Press and Harcourt Brace Jovanovich Inc. for No. 76 (copyright © 1965 by Leonard Woolf Estate); the Trustees of the Estate of E. M. Forster for No. 77; Lesley Milne for No. 79; the *Saturday Review of Literature* for No. 81 (Mary M. Colum); the Keynes Trustees for No. 83; Mr Lance Sieveking for No. 85; the *Nation* for No. 86 (Freda Kirchwey); Dr F. R. Leavis for No. 88; Valerie Eliot for No. 89; the editor of the *The Times Literary Supplement* for No. 90; University of Texas Press for No. 92; William Heinemann Ltd for extract from *Joseph Conrad: Life and Letters*, ed. G. Jean-Aubry (No. 14); The Artemis Press Ltd for No. 69.

I should like to thank Eric Homberger for his advice, Lesley Milne for her translation and my wife for her help with preparing the text. I am also indebted to the long-suffering staffs of several of our national libraries, to Mr C. J. Allen of the British Library of Political and Economic Science and to the Librarians of the *New Statesman* and *Spectator* for their identification of authors of unsigned reviews.

Introduction

There are many sides to H. G. Wells. Today he belongs to literary history and is best known as a novelist—the author of romantic social comedies, the bold and opinionated critic of Edwardian England, and the creator of modern science fiction. His political and sociological books, his Utopias, encyclopaedias and prophecies once had an immense impact but are now largely unread. Wells was a prolific and versatile writer, the author of over a hundred books as well as pamphlets and journalism, who attempted to give a complete commentary on the world in which he lived. He came to prominence as a novelist, and much of his commentary came through fiction, but a mere glance at the extent of his contemporary influence shows that 'novelist' is too narrow a classification for him. For Wells during his lifetime provoked as large a volume of criticism and discussion as any writer who has ever lived.

His first works were scientific romances, and for all their originality these books were based on orthodox beliefs about the imaginative autonomy of fiction. In common with much writing of the 1890s (the great period of the romance and the short story) they were far closer to pure entertainment than to pure didacticism. Their immediate success brought Wells into a literary milieu where he was welcomed as a fellow-artist by George Gissing, Henry James, Joseph Conrad and others. He found the role of the literary artist increasingly restrictive, and became something broader and less easy to define—a journalist, a social prophet, a great educator and communicator. Given that in later life he repeatedly affirmed his commitment to journalism and public debate as against the disciplines of art, it may seem paradoxical that he continued to write novels and remained essentially a man of letters. He began publishing fiction in 1895, and the last of his novels for which his admirers could make major claims was *The World of William Clissold* in 1926. The dates are suggestive when we recall that the future Lord Northcliffe founded the *Daily Mail* in 1896, while the British Broadcasting Corporation was constituted in 1927. These thirty years represent the first phase of modern mass communications and mass entertainment in Britain, during which the written word had yet to be challenged by film, radio and television. The dedicated literary artists of Wells's acquaintance viewed the emergence of fiction as a mass medium with defensive mistrust, and resigned themselves to addressing a small minority audience untouched by the general 'vulgarity'. But Wells lacked their firm aesthetic convictions and saw the huge potential audience for fiction, and the number and variety of newspapers and magazines which reviewed or serialized it, as an opportunity and not a threat. With Chesterton and Bernard Shaw as his only rivals, he set out to influence the thoughts, the feelings, the morals and politics of the new public. Whatever their concrete achievements, these three came to represent a new (and possibly short-lived) type of the democratic man of letters. Moving freely between literature and journalism, they augmented creative gifts with the earnest commitment of the political ideologist and the professional showmanship of the television personality.

There was no ready-made audience for Wells. He was essentially a provocative, crusading writer, whose conscious purpose was not to give the public what it wanted but what it needed. In political terms he declared himself a socialist, a scientific materialist and an advocate of sexual freedom and of world unity; and as he did so some of his early admirers deserted him. His public was at first rather specialized, as he ruefully wrote to his publisher in 1904, in a letter suggesting where review copies of his latest romance might be sent: 'My public is a peculiar one, and the electro-technical publications, scholastic papers and especially the *Schoolmaster*, medical and nursing publications—the *Positivist Review*—truck up sections of it. The women don't read me.'[1] This was written before his politics became widely known; yet a few years later he had both become more outspoken and achieved a much broader readership. 'Back in the nineteen-hundreds it was a wonderful experience for a boy to discover H. G. Wells', George Orwell later wrote (1941).[2] After *Ann Veronica* this manifestly applied to girls as well. Discovering Wells was a romantic and liberating experience, a revelation of the vast possibilities of individual experience in the immediate future. It is difficult to separate his role as a teacher in this from his role as a visionary. What he taught was the necessity and imminence of social change. Technology was bringing the human race into an era of unimagined dangers and opportunities, and the old conventions and ideas of Western society must undergo drastic revision. To those willing to emancipate themselves from traditional beliefs Wells expounded a modern world-view opening out to a Utopian vision of the new social order. This world-view was notable for its intellectually synthetic character and for the basis in the natural sciences (particularly evolutionary biology) which gave it a widely influential position in twentieth-century popular thought. Wells saw the scientific spirit as the motive force of human progress, and he became the foremost missionary of modern science. The elaboration of his world-view led him from the science fiction and the social novels with which he made his reputation to excursions into ethics, politics, history, sociology, theology, metaphysics, education and film. There was little system in these excursions, and the zigzags of Wells's literary career reveal a mercurial energy which treated each book as an intellectual gamble, a staking of perpetual repetition of his beliefs against perpetual self-renewal. While the sheer difficulty of keeping up with Wells was one of his attractions, another was the creative gift which made his attempted synthesis far more an imaginative feat than a rigorously intellectual construction. The world-view he expounded was contagious not merely on account of its scientific character, but also because it was a vision of repressed individual energies—energies which must be released from social restriction and cast into a new form as man's only hope of survival. Tales like *The Invisible Man* and *The War of the Worlds* are concerned with the immense resources of untapped human energy and the perils of exploiting them; and the result of applying this speculative insight to the realities of contemporary society can be seen in *Tono-Bungay* and *The New Machiavelli* where the powerful cognitive instincts and sexual drives of the Wellsian hero are engaged in a relentless struggle with existing social forms. While in the overcrowded and post-Freudian culture of today we are exhorted to find self-realization in the 'inner space' of personal experience, the psychic resources Wells depicts express themselves outwardly, in the exploration of time and space and the construction of new societies; they look for their fulfilment to the idea of Utopia. Hence the range of his work and the profound ambiguity of the response it evoked, for although his sociological books invariably involved a creed and some suggestions for immediate action, they were far more effective as visionary works than as political exhortations. Wells's attempts to engage in direct political activity, most notably his campaign to reform the Fabian Society, often ended in fiasco. He wished to influence the praxis of the twentieth century, but his real contribution was to its dreams. And so it is his novels that remain both the essential introduction to his mind and its more durable products.

The range of contemporary comment which might in principle have been considered for this volume is very wide indeed. Among those who listened to Wells, read some of his books and expressed opinions about him are scientists and theologians, economists and politicians—who included Stalin, Lenin, Roosevelt and Churchill. Like other famous modern writers, the record of his reception includes gossip and scandal, moral outrage and political abuse. My intention has not been to make the most of his place in the history of his times, but rather to show the reception of his more important books as they appeared and the emergence of understanding and critical judgment of his work. Thus a reasonable standard of critical responsibility has been required of the items included (some more sensational material is cited in this Introduction). While a selection of the most significant notices of Wells's nonfiction has been included, neither these books nor their reviews have tended to wear very well. Political controversy and discussions of specific Wellsian prophecies have been omitted, and there is nothing in this volume which is not 'literary criticism' in the catholic sense I believe this term demands. Indeed, much of it is very orthodox in method and approach: and if further justification for concentrating upon Wells's literary reception is needed, it must be sought in the quality of the contemporary response itself. Although Wells eventually defied literary orthodoxy in the person of Henry James, and presented himself as a new kind of communicator adapting the fictional medium to his own ends, few of the critics could follow him in this. The majority continued to judge him primarily as a creative writer answerable to existing critical standards. The image persisted despite his efforts to belittle the merely imaginative portion of his work, and it now seems unlikely to be challenged. The present volume traces the growth of an understanding of his work and of a field of argument about it which have not indeed been essentially altered or superseded in the quarter-century since his death.

EARLY PUBLICATION

Wells came from the lower-middle class, and his childhood struggles are told in his *Experiment in Autobiography* and reflected in many of his novels. He escaped from his early environment by means of a scholarship to the Normal School of Science in South Kensington, where he trained as a science teacher (1884–7). His first book was a *Textbook of Biology* (1893), and he joined the reviewing staff of the scientific periodical *Nature* in the following year. His biology book had been based upon the course that he taught for the University Correspondence College, but already in 1893 he had abandoned teaching under the stress of ill-health for the risks of a career in journalism. He began writing humorous sketches for the *Pall Mall Gazette*, which had just been revitalized under the editorship of Harry Cust. Despite his social and literary inexperience, he was soon serving a brief period as Cust's theatre critic (1895), and a longer one as fiction reviewer on Frank Harris's *Saturday Review* (1895–7). Harris was another member of the flamboyant new generation of editors in the 1890s, and, like Cust, had just replaced a whole staid and respectable staff with bright young men of whom Wells was one. As his humorous sketches were followed by short stories and then scientific romances, Wells, after years of poverty, quickly became prosperous and socially successful. In November 1893 he received £14 13s. for a month's contributions to the *Pall Mall Gazette*; but his income for 1894 totalled nearly £600, and by 1896, when he exceeded £1,000 a year, he was firmly established as a professional writer.

After 1896 the bulk of his earnings came from fiction, and he only wrote occasional pieces of journalism. His initial anxiety to launch himself as a creative writer independent of journalism is recorded in his *Autobiography*,[3] and it is evidenced by the fact that he published no fewer than four books in 1895, the year in which he first became known to the general public. They were put out by four different publishers, all newly established—Methuen, John Lane, Heinemann and Dent; his prolific output and his impatience and opportunism meant that throughout his life Wells would continually be changing his publishers. These books earned him very moderate sums: a £20 advance for *The Stolen Bacillus* (short stories), £50 for *The Time Machine* and £75 for *The Wonderful Visit*. What really enabled him to devote himself to fiction in the 1890s was the ease of serial publication and the publicity it yielded. In 1894, at the invitation of W. E. Henley, he contributed a series of 'Time Traveller' articles to the *National Observer*. The articles derived from 'The Chronic Argonauts', a serial he had published six years earlier in the college magazine he had edited while a student. Shortly afterwards Henley lost editorial control of the *National Observer* and took over a monthly, the *New Review*, to which Wells was again asked to contribute a story about time-travelling. He was now paid £100 for the serial rights of *The Time Machine*, which soon became the most talked-about feature of Henley's magazine. It was published in book form in July 1895 and had sold 6,000 copies by Christmas.

The *New Review* under Henley combined political articles with a list of literary contributors who included Stevenson, Kipling and Yeats.

Wells contributed occasional pieces to other leading reviews and magazines, including the *Yellow Book*, which printed his story 'A Slip under the Microscope'. But once his name was known, he found the main outlet for his scientific romances and stories in the new popular fiction magazines like *Pearson's* (which paid £200 for *The War of the Worlds*) and *Today*. Some observers identified him with the 'suburban' and 'half-educated' reader to whom these magazines reputedly appealed. The *Athenaeum* reviewer (No. 17 below) who spoke of the vulgarity and 'young man from Clapham attitude' manifested in *The War of the Worlds* was probably reacting to the manner of its publication as much as to its literary style. The demand for stories and serials in the magazines certainly encouraged Wells to maintain his extremely prolific output in the 1890s. When he later turned to the social novel, he continued to seek for serial publication but this no longer represented a large proportion of his income. There was no question of his struggling to complete his monthly instalments as Dickens had done; the serial rights were not usually sold until book publication had been arranged and the text was virtually complete. They were offered to the magazines through literary agents, and negotiations with cautious publishers were often protracted. In the case of *The War of the Worlds*, for example, *Pearson's* refused to close with their offer until they saw how the story ended.[4]

Many of Wells's sociological books and almost all his novels up to the 1920s appeared first in serial form. His early sociological books *Anticipations* (1901), *Mankind in the Making* (1903) and *A Modern Utopia* were published in the *Fortnightly Review*. His novels alternated between popular magazines and even daily newspapers, and the leading intellectual reviews such as the *New Republic*, the *Nation* and the *English Review* (which took *Tono-Bungay* and *The New Machiavelli*). *The Outline of History* was published by Newnes in fortnightly parts (1919–20), and as late as 1936 Wells was able to serialize *The Anatomy of Frustration* in the *Spectator*. In addition, the most common sets of Wells's works today are still those produced by the newspaper companies during the circulation wars of the 1920s.

By 1900 he was prosperous enough to have commissioned a house from the fashionable architect C. F. A. Voysey on the cliffs at Sandgate. The terms he was able to get for his books, first with Harper and later with Macmillan, were a £500 advance on 25 per cent royalties. Yet when Macmillan became his publisher in 1903, none of his books had sold more than 10,000 copies.[5] Wells anxiously followed his sales, scanning the reviews to see how they would boost his reputation and pestering his new publisher with promotional schemes. *Kipps* sold 12,000 in a few months in 1905, and by 1910 it had reached 60,000 in a cheaper edition. From this time on, a new book by Wells commanded the leading notice in any journal which carried fiction reviews. His sales were further stimulated by cheap reprint editions, and by the controversies over *Ann Veronica* and *The New Machiavelli*. In addition to the press attacks on these novels, they were both rejected on moral grounds by Frederick Macmillan, who was under contract to publish them. The appearance of *The New Machiavelli* in the *English Review* was followed by six months of delay during which it was rumoured that publishers were boycotting the novel, which was finally brought out by John Lane early in 1911. Wells claimed at the time that the result of the campaign against him in the conservative press had been to bring him an 'enormous, unpremeditated popularity' and an 'artificial and exaggerated importance'.[6] At any rate, *The New Machiavelli* had sold 17,000 copies by the end of April, and Macmillan was ready to offer him an advance of £1,500 for his next novel, *Marriage*.

All Wells's earlier books were published in America, but he remained virtually unknown there until the period of *Kipps*. Long before this, however, his works began to be translated into the major European languages. The first of Henry D. Davray's long series of translations for the French market appeared in 1899; *The Invisible Man* appeared in Italian and French in 1900, and already Wells was thought important enough for the English edition of *Love and Mr. Lewisham* to merit a ten-page review in the *Revue des Deux Mondes*.[7] The reception that greeted Wells in France was so enthusiastic that an advertising leaflet, 'M. H. G. Wells et la Critique Française', was issued by Macmillan in 1904 in an attempt to boost his English reputation. By 1905 his works had also appeared in German, Italian, Polish, Czech, Swedish and Dutch. But the most impressive record of all is that of translations into Russian. *The War of the Worlds* appeared in a St Petersburg journal in 1898, and thereafter virtually every new novel and story by Wells appeared in Russian in the year of its English publication. The novels must have been translated direct from the English periodicals before they appeared in book form. Some of them, such as *The Food of the Gods* and *In the Days of the Comet*, were serialized twice; as Russia was not a signatory to the Berne Convention, they were presumably pirated. In addition, up to 1966 there had been no fewer than seven sets of 'Collected Works' published in Russian. The first of these appeared in St Petersburg in 1901, and the second (in thirteen volumes) in 1908, while the third, begun in 1918 under the editorial direction of Zamyatin, was among the first foreign-language publishing ventures in the new Soviet state. In England a collected edition of Wells did not become available until the 1920s. While the translation of novels on a large scale had begun in the early nineteenth century, and Scott, Dickens, Zola and Tolstoy had built up a wide European influence, Wells's reputation spread throughout Europe with a speed which was perhaps unprecedented. His scientific romances particularly lent themselves to transplantation. Wells vigorously protested over a pirated version of *The War of the Worlds* in the Boston *Post* in 1898, in which the Martians were made to land in New England; and a more famous American adaptation caused a nationwide panic when it was broadcast by Orson Welles in 1938. As early as 1906, Wells made arrangements for the simultaneous publication of his romance *In the Days of the Comet* in English, French, German, Italian and Dutch, and it may be said that he had become the prototype of the modern international writer.

THE SCIENTIFIC ROMANCES 1895–1900

The Time Machine, Wells's first scientific romance, was a brilliant literary invention which could scarcely avoid attracting comment. The first notices appeared while it was still being serialized in five parts in the *New Review*, and its author was acclaimed in the *Review of Reviews* as a 'man of genius' after the third instalment (No. 1). Its appearance in book form in July was largely ignored, yet such reviews as it did get were generous and detailed. It was Wells's ideas and not the aesthetic qualities of his story which were felt to invite analysis. Israel Zangwill tackled the notion of time-travelling itself (No. 4), while R. H. Hutton, the veteran *Spectator* critic and Christian apologist, challenged some of the arguments about social evolution on which Wells's vision of the world of Eloi and Morlocks is based (No. 2). The reviewer in *Nature* saw it as a useful lesson in applied scientific reasoning:[8]

Apart from its merits as a clever piece of imagination, the story is well worth the attention of the scientific reader, for the reason that it is based so far as possible on scientific data, and while not taking it too seriously, it helps one to get a connected idea of the possible results of the ever-continuing processes of evolution.

The notion of 'science fiction' did not yet exist, and Wells would not be seen as pioneering a new genre until much later. Yet from the beginning his stories were recognized as appealing to the 'scientific reader'. They continued to be reviewed in *Nature*, and their scientific basis was sometimes the subject of expert discussion. At the same time readers were warned against taking them too seriously. While *The Time Machine* attracted attention by means of its startling ideas, the reviewers of Wells's romances can be divided into those who read them as moral allegory and the majority who judged them as light entertainment. Following the success of Stevenson, Kipling and Rider Haggard, the entertaining romance or short story was one of the main critical demands of the 1890s. Aesthetes and popular journalists were united in their dislike of the moral seriousness and sordidly factual approach of the realistic novelists. This was the period of the fireside tale of mystery or adventure, of ghost stories (even Henry James wrote *The Turn of the Screw*) and of children's classics. The earliest notice of *The Time Machine* (No. 1) spoke of Wells as a successor of Poe, and adjectives such as 'gruesome', 'weird' and 'horrible' abounded in the reviews. The first substantial critical article on Wells described him as a 'professor of the gruesome' and a 'past master in the art of producing creepy sensations' (No. 15). His brilliant combination of creepiness and scientific subject-matter gave Wells a growing prominence among the young romancers of the time.

In 1895 Wells had yet to discover that the 'gruesome' extolled by the reviewers was only a titillating form of entertainment. In the following year he published *The Island of Doctor Moreau*, the story of a vivisectionist who synthesizes human beings from animals on a Pacific island. The savage scenes on the island and in the laboratory anticipate twentieth-century history and fiction; and most of the critics who tried to elicit the book's allegorical meaning found it alarming and even blasphemous. Man's descent from the apes was still a highly emotive subject, and this macabre fantasy by a former biology teacher caused widespread shock and offence. *The Times* called it 'perverse', 'loathsome' and 'repulsive', and like several other papers warned that it should be kept away from young people and those with weak nerves. The *Critic*, no doubt remembering the story of Frankenstein, warned that it might prove dangerous 'even for physicians and scientific men—especially those of an experimental turn of mind'.[9] Other reviewers showed some ingenuity in linking Wells with the disreputable school of the realists. Chalmers Mitchell in the *Saturday Review* spoke of Wells's 'zeal of a sanitary inspector probing a crowded graveyard' (No. 5), and the reviewer in the

Speaker associated the book's 'gruesome horror' with that of the sexual problem-novelists of the day (No. 8). Grant Allen's novel *The Woman Who Did* had appeared in 1895, and Wells himself had given one of the few favourable reviews to *Jude the Obscure* in February 1896.

To some extent *The Island of Doctor Moreau* may have been the victim of a general climate of moral suppression epitomized by the Wilde trial of 1895. But few of the reviewers were personally vindictive, and several were frankly puzzled. Grant Richards suggested plausibly enough that 'Mr. Wells has an unusually vivid imagination, which sometimes runs away with him'.[10] In retrospect, this was Wells's first appearance as the 'unpleasant' and subversive writer who was to invite more malicious attacks with books like *In the Days of the Comet* and *Ann Veronica*; at the time, however, it seemed that he was prepared to submit to the reviewers' standards and that *Doctor Moreau* was an aberration. Much could be pardoned a young writer whose next book, which began as a serial in the following month, was *The Wheels of Chance*. Although it now seems a pale and conventional forerunner of *Kipps* and *Mr. Polly*, this 'bicycling romance' was the book in which Wells first revealed his gift for romantic comedy. The timid adventures of Hoopdriver, the Cockney shop assistant on a cycling tour, were wholly innocuous and very much in the taste of the times. In addition, *The Wheels of Chance* provided one element which an appreciable section of reviewers found to be sadly lacking in the scientific romances—'human interest'. What one writer called the 'gigantic, mail-clad, sexless' Martians of *The War of the Worlds*[11] were not everyone's idea of good entertainment, and for some years *The Wheels of Chance* was the Wells favourite among those readers who preferred the domestic to the scientific.

As *The Island of Doctor Moreau* was followed by *The Invisible Man* and *The War of the Worlds*, the literary status of the scientific romance was increasingly debated by the critics. The academically-minded Edmund Gosse noted Wells's debt to Huxley and Tyndall, the great Victorian philosophers of science, but lamented his addiction to 'little horrible stories about monsters'.[12] Wells was defended by Clement Shorter, one of the new generation of popular journalists: far from wasting his talent, Shorter wrote, his concern with scientific fairy-tales made him an 'imperative product of his age' (No. 13). Other critics, while remaining cautious about taking Wells's tales too seriously, pointed to his literary antecedents, and to Poe and Stevenson there were added Swift and the Defoe of *A Journal of the Plague Year* (No. 16). Wells later recalled that the quickest way to literary respectability in the 1890s was to be acclaimed a ' "second"—somebody or other' (No. 21). The model most commonly attributed to him was, of course, his predecessor in science fiction Jules Verne. Verne was rated as a boys' writer and a mere popular entertainer, and when in 1902 Wells justifiably complained of his poor early reception in America, he stated that 'the English Jules Verne is my utmost glory'.[13] Yet although the comparison with Verne is a perennial item of Wells criticism, the majority of these comparisons were from the beginning highly favourable to the English writer. He was judged to have greater imaginative gifts, a deeper and more philosophical understanding of science, and a more vividly realistic style than his predecessor. French critics no less than the English were convinced of Wells's superiority, and in the end the only vigorous dissentient was Verne himself (No. 33). While Verne complained of the implausibility of Wells's romances, their skilful blend of realism and fantasy was widely admired. Reviewers commented on the paradox of a fantasy which was 'concrete and specific' (No. 16), and Joseph Conrad christened Wells the 'Realist of the Fantastic' in a brief paragraph on his technique which would have been endorsed by most of his early admirers (No. 14). What impressed such readers was not the lack of verisimilitude or human interest in these stories, but their insight and emotional power.

Wells reached the peak of his reputation for scientific romance with *The War of the Worlds*. One of its most striking features today is its anticipation of twentieth-century total war—the experiences of *Blitzkrieg*, civilian terror, mass evacuation and the destruction of cities. Despite its power to terrify radio listeners forty years later, Wells's tale did not frighten its early readers unduly. In the devastation of England by extra-terrestrial forces they merely found a successful combination of the enjoyable and the gruesome. Wells's subsequent romances, however, contained less far-fetched versions of modern war. The fighter pilot is shown defying totalitarian repression at the end of *When the Sleeper Wakes* (1899), the air fleets of the great powers destroy civilization in *The War in the Air* (1908) and Europe is torn by atomic warfare in *The World Set Free* (1914). I. F. Clarke has pointed out in *Voices Prophesying War* (1966) that Wells's books were only the best-known examples of a whole genre of prophetic war and invasion novels in the years up to 1914. Yet for the most part Wells's stories in this genre were read solely for amusement, and where some deliberate prophetic warning was suspected, reviewers were quick to disapprove. The 'forecast novel' was variously derided as commonplace, tiresome and profitless, and Wells's prophetic essays and treatises were received with far more respect. A special irony attaches to the reviews of *The World Set Free*, which appeared in the spring of 1914. Many belaboured Wells's propagandism and 'materialism', while barely mentioning the book's opening scenes of world war. Those that did mention them asked the old questions—was it artistically convincing? did it have human interest? The *Spectator* talked jauntily of his 'habit of scrapping civilisation every two years or so', and the *New Statesman* opined that 'we all like a good catastrophe when we get it'.[14] Clearly the romance with its premium on the 'gruesome' was not the best place for the serious investigation of the future to which Wells increasingly inclined.

NOVELIST, PROPHET AND FABIAN 1900-9

Reading Wells today it is easy to regret that the scientific romances were left so quickly behind and that their author had so little regard for them. A few readers had recognized them as unique works of genius, and many more would do so in the next few years as he became the most debated figure in Edwardian literature. Yet we have seen that the majority of reviewers treated the romances as light entertainment, and Wells himself did not question that the realistic novel was a more serious and challenging artistic form. This belief is explicit in his own fiction reviews of 1895–7, with their discriminating praise of Hardy, Turgenev, Meredith and Gissing. During these years he began writing *Love and Mr. Lewisham*, and in 1898 he made a start on *Kipps*. *Mr. Lewisham* appeared in 1900, and its reception was encouraging. This story of a science student's experiences was seen as an ambitious project demanding considerably more than the 'cleverness' sufficient for scientific romances. Moreover, it came out at an opportune moment in the debate about 'realism'. While the reviewer in the *Saturday Review* (No. 24) called it morbid, sordid and decadent—the familiar adjectives which had been hurled at Zola, Hardy and Gissing—the *Atlantic Monthly* spoke for the majority when it placed Wells among the 'school of healthy realists'.[15] The one-sidedness of the naturalistic novel with its spectacles of dehumanization and self-destruction was a critical commonplace, and Wells's more genial, optimistic outlook was found reassuring. A healthily 'realistic' novel soothed its readers rather than disturbing them; it was comedy rather than tragedy. *Love and Mr. Lewisham* ends with Lewisham gladly accepting the humdrum lower-class life to which his susceptibility to love and domesticity has condemned him. This note convinced many of the critics, although Wells himself later admitted its falsity. In general, *Love and Mr. Lewisham* was felt to have elevated his literary status from that of a successful entertainer to a serious novelist of promise, and the writer of an article in the *Academy* (1900) went so far as to declare that 'Modern fiction will be regenerated by these faithful seizures of neglected types.'

Wells was not interested in winning acceptance as a 'healthy realist'. The epithet is far more aptly applied to his friend Arnold Bennett (whose first novel, *A Man from the North*, had been published in 1898), and *Love and Mr. Lewisham* is the most Bennett-like of Wells's novels. Where it had a modest success, *Anticipations*, which followed in 1901, caused an intellectual sensation. *Anticipations* was the first of his essays in social prophecy: it presented a skilful mixture of forecasts of the future social effects of technology, and ideological advocacy of a rationalized technocratic state he called the New Republic. If Wells needed any encouragement to take himself seriously in his role as a social thinker, the reception of this book and its successor *Mankind in the Making* (1903) certainly provided it. Put in discursive form, his speculations about the future could not be dismissed as an idle amusement, and most of the papers reviewed Wells's sociological books at a length which only the most established novelist could command. His emergence as a prophet of the twentieth century was appropriately timed, and his forecasts were treated more as news than as subjects for critical judgment. William Archer, the translator of Ibsen and one of the leading literary journalists of the time, suggested that Wells might be publicly endowed in his capacity as a prophet.[16] It was some time before a more detached assessment of Wells's social outlook became possible. Even Havelock Ellis, reviewing *Mankind in the Making* in 1904 (No. 30), restricted himself on the whole to acute criticisms of points of detail, and it perhaps took the robust intelligence of a G. K. Chesterton to begin to put the new Wells in his place (No. 34).

Anticipations and *Mankind in the Making* brought Wells into the world of politics and public affairs. The Webbs took an interest in him, and he joined the Fabian Society. Soon his political acquaintance broadened further, to include such men as Haldane and Grey, Milner and L. S. Amery. By 1906, when he visited America for the first time, he was well known enough to get an interview with the President, Theodore Roosevelt—and to discuss *The Time Machine* with him. This visit marks the entry of the Wells who was for thirty years an international celebrity, and was later to obtain well-publicized meetings with Franklin Roosevelt, Lenin and Stalin.

The growth of his reputation in America had in fact been surprisingly slow. The tone of transatlantic literary journalism before Mencken was genteel and academic, and critics, like William Morton Payne of the *Dial* (No. 40), who looked to Europe for cultural refinement were shocked by Wells's Cockneyism and the social vulgarity it revealed. Many of the early reviews were frigid in the extreme. The Boston *Literary World* dismissed *Anticipations* as the work of 'a very cocksure person' (No. 28), and the New York *Critic* dealt with *Mankind in the Making* in twenty-nine words.[17] The scientific romances were treated as cheap potboilers. Wells had some justification for his complaint to Arnold Bennett in 1902 that 'At present no decent article on me, no decent criticism (not a column of reviewing even) has ever appeared about me in America. The great American public has for the most part never heard of me.'[18] Always the obliging friend, Bennett helped to supply this deficiency with a long descriptive article in the *Cosmopolitan Magazine* (1902), but it was not until the publication of *Kipps* in 1905 that Wells was treated as a writer of any standing.

In Europe it was very different. The demand for translations has already been mentioned, but his intellectual impact was no less striking, particularly in France, where the immediate vogue for his prophecies soon began to influence his English reputation; predictably enough, one reviewer of *Anticipations* adduced it as evidence that his habits of thought were too logical and mechanical for the English mind.[19] From the French point of view, Wells's scientific outlook redeemed him from the insularity of the English and made him a true cosmopolitan (No. 32). One French article which had a direct impact in England was an attack on Wells's style by Frank Blunt in the *Nouvelle Revue* (1904). Blunt accused Wells of elementary grammatical and stylistic blunders which would make his works intolerable to French readers had they not been touched up by the translator. The article was discussed in the *Westminster Gazette* (1904) and provoked some correspondence. The carelessness of Wells's writing, indeed, was the subject of reviewers' complaints throughout his life. But if Blunt's intention was to warn his countrymen against an over-credulous response to a foreign author, his article had little effect. Critics like Henri Ghéon (No. 31) and Augustin Filon (Nos 11 and 32) discovered philosophical implications in Wells's romances which had largely been overlooked by the English reviewers. Expositions of Wells's social ideas abounded, and for many years he remained the prime representative of modern English literature in France.

When *Kipps* and *A Modern Utopia* appeared in 1905, Wells's prominence was secured at home and abroad, and it seemed for a brief moment that his genius could excel both in the art of fiction and in prophecy. *Kipps* was Wells's first large-scale novel, combining romantic comedy with the first of his broad satirical exposures of English society. His portrayal of the lower-class world of the drapery was praised on all sides; and while the novel's social criticism was enthusiastically welcomed by C. F. G. Masterman in the *Daily News* (No. 38), it was not sufficiently obtrusive to upset the politically unsympathetic critics of the more conservative papers. Some admirers, including Masterman and the novelist W. D. Howells (No. 41), expressed misgivings about Wells's use of direct exhortations to the reader in the narrative; yet after all Henry James, in a letter of lavish praise which marks the high point of his appreciation of Wells, grandly disdained to notice these. In his view, the lower-middle class was portrayed in *Kipps* with a freedom from 'interference' which neither Dickens nor George Eliot had achieved (No. 39). This is a curiously misleading comment, for there is no attempt at artistic impersonality in the novel, and passages such as the didactic reflection on 'The stupid little tragedies of these clipped and limited lives' are notorious. Wells's social philosophy unquestionably pervades the narrative of *Kipps*, although its presence is modulated by the ironic comedy.

Widespread doubts about the compatibility of Wellsian propaganda and art were not expressed until the reviews of his next novel, *In the Days of the Comet* (1906). It was a hasty and rather muddled book, but the reviewers scarcely noticed this—for the first time they attacked and defended it on uniformly political grounds. Wells had boldly decided to present his vision of contemporary life not through conventional narrative irony, as in *Kipps*, but from the imagined viewpoint of a Utopian future. The result was an avowedly socialist novel, which created far more of a stir than *Kipps* and was eagerly seized upon as a way of discrediting the entire socialist movement. Controversy was sparked off by *The Times Literary Supplement*, which ended a mild review with the remark that 'Socialistic men's wives, we gather, are, no less than their goods, to be held in common. Free love, according to Mr Wells, is to be of the essence of the new social contract.' This reference to the resolution of sexual jealousy in Wells's Utopia was picked up the following day by the *Daily Express*, which was running a series of articles entitled 'The Fraud of Socialism'. The paper's leading article on 15 September 1906 proclaimed that free love was now revealed as one of the socialists' aims, and 'for any guarantee they can offer to the contrary, it may become the predominating Socialistic doctrine in the near future'. Wells, who was never the most judicious of controversialists, tried to rebut this unfalsifiable charge, so providing several days' worth of free copy for an editor who a week later was able to come out with the following alarming headline:

EVERYTHING 'FREE'
AMAZING PROGRAMME OF LONDON SOCIALISTS[20]

The story underneath was merely a report on the Labour programme in the London County Council elections.

The reception of *In the Days of the Comet* revealed the opportunities and dangers of Wells's position as a leading Edwardian communicator. In most (though not all) of the Conservative papers the novel was condemned for its propagandist tinge, but the Liberal press was overwhelmingly favourable. Progressives like C. F. G. Masterman and the reviewers in the *Tribune* and *Clarion* praised its art and discreetly commended it as a political weapon.[21] Leslie Haden Guest in *Fabian News* did not even pretend to judge it on literary merit (No. 45). Wells was now active in the Fabian Society, and had shown himself ready to write books and pamphlets in the cause; he was seen as a heaven-sent missionary on their behalf to the great British public. Henceforth in the popular press Wells was frequently an artist to his ideological friends and a propagandist to his enemies, and at all levels of criticism his emergence as a committed and, so to speak, as a 'socialist realist' novelist prescribed the terms of debate. Some early supporters like Clement Shorter and Frank Harris (who was to describe *Tono-Bungay* in *Vanity Fair* as 'five hundred pages of tenth-rate twaddle')[22] now turned against him; the new popular journalists of the 1890s had mostly become staunch Conservatives. And it was at this time that fellow-novelists such as Arnold Bennett (No. 42), Henry James and Ford Madox Hueffer began to wonder if Wells was really one of their company. Hueffer knew Wells through Joseph Conrad and arranged for the serialization of *Tono-Bungay* in the *English Review* during his brief editorship of that journal (1908–9). But in 1909 he also published a series of articles on current English literature under the title 'The Critical Attitude', in which Wells was introduced as an object-lesson of the dangers surrounding an artist who set out to occupy the position of a 'man of intellect'. The artist's domain, in Hueffer's account, was confined to the subjective: 'His business is to register a truth as he sees it, and no more than Pilate can he, as a rule, see the truth as it is.' While admitting Wells's intellectual influence and hold over the young, Hueffer implied that he had all the faults and none of the virtues of the imaginative writer:[23]

Outside the circle of those who work consciously at a conscious art Mr Wells is also the most prominent novelist that we have. He has his bad moments and he has his astonishingly good ones. Probably he cannot tell the one from the other. ... Mr Wells is the disciple of no technical school. He produces a British novel along the lines of his national temperament. He trusts to his personality, he revels in it. And, as each new thing interests him, he makes a book of it. Aesthetically he is the child of artless writers like Dickens, and by the young men of our generation he is regarded with an affection as great as that the whole nation affords to Mr Barrie. A wayward person, his writing is at times astonishingly good, at times astonishingly slipshod. But young Oxford, young Cambridge, the young men and women of the medical schools and of the provincial universities discuss his ideas with the avidity that their forefathers accorded to Mr Ruskin. To what ends of thought he will conduct them we have no means of knowing.

Even if we overlook the reference to Dickens, it is not difficult to recognize this as a critical caricature. Hueffer's tactic is to present Wells as the type of the amateur in fiction. For him, as later for Pound and Eliot, artistic self-respect demands that one sees oneself as a specialist in a world of specialists. The freebooting, eclectic approach represented by Wells became deeply suspect. Hueffer argues that an artist should not set up as a 'man of intellect' because to compete with the experts in fields like ethics or sociology must inevitably put him at a disadvantage; he should stick to his last. This is to take the artist's responsibility to his subject-matter as his sole concern, whereas Wells saw himself as a communicator, charged with conveying certain kinds of knowledge and certain modes of feeling and thought to an audience—and the possession of this audience was for him the novelist's main privilege. Yet he could claim with some justice that he was merely updating the mixture of journalism, instruction and entertainment endemic in the English novel from Defoe to Dickens, and which Hueffer and the school of Conscious Artists wished to eradicate.

The problematic of 'art versus propaganda' which emerged in Wells criticism at this period has tended to dominate it ever since. It was crystallized in the quarrel with Henry James, in which Wells himself avowed that 'I had rather be called a journalist than an artist.' The episode began with his satirical parody of James in *Boon* (1915)—an attempt to take the offensive against the doctrine of Conscious Art and to hold its most eminent practitioner up to ridicule. It ended with his abandoning the word 'artist' to the literary specialists. In *Experiment in Autobiography* he goes over the arguments again in the course of discussing 'Whether I am a novelist', a question he answers mainly in the negative. As both the aggrieved party in the quarrel and the defender of artistic values, James has received the overwhelming support of commentators on this affair. Yet although James's single-minded dedication to art was a wonderfully resourceful response to the pressures of his age, Wells's view of the ethos of Conscious Art as being academic and restrictive can find ample sanction in literary history. The issues here are highly complex. James was a successor of Flaubert and the Romantics in seeking an impregnable social position for the artist, whose lofty calling and integrity gave him an essential superiority over the herd of his contemporaries. The whole history of high-bourgeois art from Wordsworth onwards can be seen as a search for some privileged kind of cultural authority which cannot be challenged in the realm of ordinary discourse. If this is so, what makes the Wells-James quarrel so illustrative is that Wells had declared (in a manifesto on 'The Contemporary Novel', 1911) that the novel should be deliberately controversial and should aim to provoke discussion about moral behaviour. Such discussion in the public arena was the last thing that James and Hueffer wished to provoke; it would have compromised their special status as 'artists'. Both sides in the quarrel are united by the modern mystique of the expert. The aesthetic of Hueffer and James was founded upon it, while Wells contributed directly to it through his glorification of science.

The ready dualism of art and propaganda has been a frequent source of schematic judgments of Wells's work. On the other hand, the belief that 'all art is propaganda' has had its adherents. The enthusiasm for Wells as a socialist artist expressed in 1915 by Van Wyck Brooks (No. 72)—and later outgrown by him—would (but for the changing definitions of socialism) have been a highly respectable approach in the 1930s and 1960s, and anathema in the 1920s and 1950s. The literary climate of the Edwardian years, however, was one which valued the appearance of 'high seriousness' whether artistic or persuasive. Wells satisfied these criteria amply for the most part, until he wrote *The History of Mr. Polly* (1910). *Mr. Polly* was very far from gaining instant recognition. It failed to address itself to any burning topical issue, and its mixture of romance and farce could not be squared with orthodox ideas about the Novel; it was neither a contemporary discussion novel nor an example of painstaking or healthy realism. To the reviewer in the *Field*, it seemed positively unhealthy—a story of lower-class vulgarity unredeemed by the artistic seriousness with which Zola and Maupassant had treated such subjects: 'It is the prevailing stench of stagnant mire to which we object most strongly.'[24] He was almost alone among the early critics in feeling strongly about *Mr. Polly* at all. With one notable exception, H. L. Mencken (No. 58), the reviewers were offhand and patronizing about it. In fact *Mr. Polly* was an imaginative work of genuinely popular appeal, which became a classic by stealth. Like *The Invisible Man* and *The War of the Worlds*, it was initially treated not as Art or Propaganda but as light entertainment.

THE CONTEMPORARY REALIST 1909–15

Tono-Bungay, Ann Veronica and *The New Machiavelli* confirmed Wells's place as the most controversial novelist of his generation. For many, perhaps the majority, he was the leading novelist. Some of the criticism of these novels took the form of detached appraisal of his informal and unorthodox artistry from the standpoint of existing literary convention, but such detachment was extremely difficult to maintain. His books had an immediate and imperative power. With their half-imaginative, half-argumentative dissection of Edwardian commerce, politics, family and sexual relationships, *Tono-Bungay* and its successors had a unique combination of topicality and psychological intimacy. Many readers, swept away by the directness of Wells's exploration of contemporary experience, were willing to credit his new kind of realism with total candour and authenticity. He seemed an intensely modern writer. His novels were highly emotive and contentious events, and those whom they did not convert or enlighten were often moved to anger and derision. It might be loosely said that Wells's books became a kind of religion; for some ardent admirers they would always remain so.

    Tono-Bungay offered itself as a panoramic critique of English society. The scope of its ambition was recognized by almost every reviewer— here was Wells attempting a major novel at last. Perhaps the most impressive endorsement of its claims comes in the book by the leading Liberal journalist and politician C. F. G. Masterman, *The Condition of England*, published in the same year. As we have seen, Masterman had been an enthusiastic advocate of Wells's books for some years. In *The*

Condition of England, not only does he make prominent use of *Tono-Bungay* for illustrative purposes, but his whole account of the state of England bears an unmistakably Wellsian stamp. Summarizing the theme of Wells's novel, he writes (pp. 234–5) that

The hero of his greatest novel reveals an experience fragmentary and disconnected in a tumultuous world. Mr Wells can show that world in its rockings and upheavals, until beneath the seeming calm and conventionality of the surface view, is heard the very sound of the fractures and fallings; an age in the headlong rush of change.

Masterman himself describes society in exactly these terms, which are those of the incipient 'modernism' of the advanced intellectual of 1909. Another enthusiastic reader of *Tono-Bungay* was the young D. H. Lawrence, who was later to express his own sense of the 'fractures and fallings' of a tumultuous age in *Women in Love.* Social change in *Tono-Bungay* is not simply an external process. It is embodied in the uncertain narrator, George Ponderevo, who surveys his life with a mixture of urgency and bewilderment, positiveness and hesitation, pragmatism and candour. The result is utterly different from the calm narrative authority exercised in such representative Edwardian novels as *The Man of Property, The Old Wives' Tale, Howards End* and *Kipps.* Experience is more random and disjointed, so that social analysis appears a more necessary and conscious process; society itself becomes more illusory and less solidly 'there'. A remarkably forward-looking novel in some respects, *Tono-Bungay* was also Wells's artistic turning-point; he would never expend such pains on a work of fiction again. Its subjectivity and its apocalyptic social vision did meet with a response from Masterman, Lawrence and others. It was very much less to the taste of another significant group of Wells's readers, the Fabians. He had now left the Society and quarrelled bitterly with its leaders, but from the dislike of the novel expressed by both Hubert Bland and Beatrice Webb (Nos 47 and 49) we can see that their personal quarrels revealed fundamental ideological differences. The leading Fabians, after all, believed in an orderly and methodical approach to social problems. The transition to socialism was to be brought about by gradual reforms determined by positivistic sociology within a fixed constitutional framework. To these industrious public servants the mental attitude exhibited in Wells's novel, with its fusion of sociology and impressionism, its submission to the 'rush of change' and its ebullient relativism, must have seemed the very pitch of anarchy.

Beatrice Webb's diary reveals a moral distrust of Wells as man and novelist; others were ready to bring the attack upon his morality out into the open once more. Robertson Nicoll denounced the sexual realism and permissiveness of *Tono-Bungay* in the Nonconformist *British Weekly*,[25] but worse was to come with the publication of *Ann Veronica* later in the year. This was a very topical study of a girl who rebelled against her family and asserted her right to live independently. Wells's full endorsement of his outspoken heroine was highly provocative. Once again the Liberal papers praised the book, but *T.P.'s Weekly* called it a 'dangerous novel' (No. 53) and the Conservative *Saturday Review* spoke of 'realism run mad and into unpleasant places'.[26] The main attack, however, did not come until seven weeks after publication, when John St Loe Strachey pilloried it in the *Spectator* as a 'Poisonous Book' (No. 55a). Strachey was editor and proprietor of the *Spectator*, and an active supporter of the National Social Purity Crusade which was then at its peak. His violent attack upon *Ann Veronica* formed part of a campaign for formal literary censorship to be exercised by the circulating libraries.[27] Wells must have expected something like this: his novel had already been turned down in breach of contract by Macmillan, and gossip about its real-life basis in his love-affair with Amber Reeves was widespread. His 'immoral' brand of socialism had made him heartily disliked among the Conservative establishment, but there was and could be no concerted campaign to suppress his work. The impure targets against which Strachey thundered were a random lot which included not only Wells, as the representative of the modern novel, but also the 'mischievous new development' of scouting for girls.

Wells's cardinal sin in *Ann Veronica* was that of allowing his heroine to acknowledge the existence of sexual desire and gratification (she was not, of course, shown experiencing these things). The fuss over the novel was a mild anticipation of the twentieth-century censorship battles which later so deeply affected Joyce and Lawrence. Wells suffered a certain amount of social ostracism and a period of waiting while it was rumoured that his next novel, *The New Machiavelli*, would not find a publisher. On publication it was ignored by the *Spectator* and *Westminster Gazette*—but elsewhere it was widely recognized as a masterpiece. Wells wrote in triumph that he had inadvertently become 'a symbol against the authoritative, the dull, the presumptuously established, against all that is hateful and hostile to youth and tomorrow'.[28] What in fact he had done was to establish his right to treat sexual themes in the novel with impunity. In *The New Machiavelli* he had made some concessions to orthodox fictional convention: Remington espouses Wells's ideas as a Tory politician, so that the actual balance of political forces is only obliquely reflected, and his adultery with Isabel Rivers has the highly moral result of terminating his career. But Wells was also able to give one of his chapters the title 'The Besetting of Sex'. This is indicative of the way sex is presented in his novels—as a *problem*, an all-powerful force or temptation unexpectedly bearing down on the rational individual. Sexual morality became the major theme of his subsequent novels; and the fact that he remained a symbol of 'youth and tomorrow' indicates the resonance of his characters' explicit and high-minded questioning of the place of sex in modern life.

It was now that his English reputation reached, and passed, its peak. The more discerning critics had begun to perceive his artistic limitations as a contemporary realist, and although impressed by *The New Machiavelli*, they identified certain damaging weaknesses. It was pointed out that the hero's political philosophy was bogus and the implied comparison with Machiavelli absurd. The transparent caricatures of real political figures in the book elicited much discussion, and a superb reaction from the principal victim, Beatrice Webb (No. 59). But these aspects were really only symptomatic of Wells's deep-rooted habit of transcribing personal experience and observation into his novels. Reviewers such as Francis Hackett (No. 62) remarked on the extreme subjectivity of *The New Machiavelli*, and the solipsistic effect of its intrusive first-person narration. What Wells actually revealed in contemporary life was beginning to seem less important than his singular mode of presenting it. Henry James, whose letters to Wells amount to a series of confidential reviews of many of his books, begged Wells to abandon the confessional narrative mode (No. 64). But when he read Wells's next novel, *Marriage*, written in the third person, he had to acknowledge that the solipsism was far more than could be expunged by a change of narrative convention. The story itself had become merely secondary—it was the projection of Wells himself as the experiencing narrator which focused all the energy and vitality of the novel (No. 67). James's mounting disapproval of what he saw as the abandonment of artistic standards by the new wave of English novelists, led by Wells and Bennett and including D. H. Lawrence in the 'dusty rear', was publicly expressed in an uncharacteristically sweeping and petulant essay, 'The Younger Generation', which appeared in *The Times Literary Supplement* (1914).

We have seen that Wells's declared intention at this time was to write novels which would provoke immediate discussion on social and moral issues. But while he thought of using fiction as a medium of mass communication, rather than as art or entertainment, the discussion novel in his hands tended to become a virtuoso performance by a central character expounding his total view of life. However vigorous and unpredictable, this Wellsian commentary was bound to lose its attraction in the end. It is remarkable that its popularity was sustained for so long. A whole series of topical discussion novels followed *The New Machiavelli* in the years leading up to the First World War. The reviews of *The Passionate Friends* in this volume represent the differing views of these books. Their faults were widely realized: the tone was too hectoring, the characters had no life and Wells had said it all before. Equally, however, there were always reviewers ready to declare that each book was a new departure and perhaps the finest novel Wells had written; even Ford Madox Hueffer can be found doing this.[29] In America, where his reputation was still growing, Van Wyck Brooks published *The World of H. G. Wells*, an acute but neglected critical study, in 1915. Brooks interpreted Wells's books as the products of a quintessentially 'socialist' imagination (No. 72); he also described his role as a social prophet as that of a latter-day Matthew Arnold. Stuart P. Sherman, the conservative critic of the New York *Nation*, replied that Wells was no Arnold but an irresponsible and anarchic Shelley (No. 73). Sherman was also the author of a brilliant polemic on Wells and Bennett (1915), which sparked off weeks of controversy in the *Nation*. For Sherman Bennett was the mature and orthodox writer, while Wells had become the heretical apostle of the 'young lions and lionesses of radicalism'. The spectacle of critics younger than Wells attacking him as the spokesman of the younger generation was by now a familiar one. At the same time, the first suggestions that he was no longer in the van of progressive thought can be heard from 1912 onwards; notably in Rebecca West's scathing attack on his reactionary portrayal of women in *Marriage* (No. 66). Disenchantment with the Wells of the discussion novels was also strongly expressed by A. R. Orage, the influential editor of the *New Age* (No. 69), and to the tiny avant-garde of Pound, Hulme and Wyndham Lewis who were numbered among its contributors he already seemed an anachronism. Yet Rebecca West, who quickly became the leading young radical critic of the day, was soon a close friend of Wells and an ardent champion of his subsequent novels. His period as a symbol of 'youth and tomorrow' had some years to go.

WELLS IN THE MODERN PERIOD 1915-46

In the long run, the growth of modernism in the arts after 1912, with the emergence of Joyce, Lawrence and Virginia Woolf as novelists, was the major force which led to the repudiation of Wells's methods and influence. As the 'modern', with its cultivation of dissonance, subjectivity and technical experimentation, replaced the 'contemporary', Wells came to be seen as an artistic reactionary. But this was a gradual process. When Virginia Woolf reviewed *Joan and Peter* in 1918 (No. 76), she deplored his sacrifice of his career as a novelist to the interests of the younger generation or, as she put it, the 'rights of youth'. We can sense in this a clearer distinction than had previously been made between the broad section of youth to whom Wells spoke, and the young artistic avant-garde. But it was not until her essays 'Modern Fiction' and 'Mr Bennett and Mrs Brown' (1924) that she felt confident enough to write off Wells, Bennett and Galsworthy as Edwardian novelists whose glib surface realism was now being superseded by a more advanced fiction. These essays do not contain any very close discussion of Wells's work, and the primary target of their hostile analysis is Arnold Bennett. Their importance in the present context is that they established the grouping of Wells, Bennett and Galsworthy as the representatives of a kind of 'middlebrow fiction' which was no longer intellectually respectable. For it is a crucial fact that all three Edwardian novelists maintained and indeed increased their popularity during the 1920s, and the animosity which they, as successful writers, aroused among the supporters of the avant-garde at this time still affects their reputations today.

Although left stranded by the dynamism of the modernist movement, Wells had his own kind of resilience and bouncing energy which continued to fascinate readers. In 1916 he published *Mr. Britling Sees It Through,* a novel now mainly read for its picture of his own life at Easton Glebe in Essex and for its historical record of early reactions to the war. At the time its publication was an intensely moving event, as the reviews make clear, and it became the most widely-read serious novel of the war years. *The Times Literary Supplement* noted the 'unfailing distinction of tone' with which it reproduced the wartime experience (No. 74), and another reviewer said that 'it actually makes one glad to be a man and to be alive in the year 1916'.[30] For Wells's regular readers, however, the most striking feature of the book was not its morale-boosting effect but the new departure this marked in Wells's thought: Mr Britling came through his ordeal by believing in a Finite God. Wells's attempt to invent a new theology lasted for the duration of the war and caused a heated (and now very tedious) debate. His opponents were quick to point out the moral and intellectual weaknesses which this hasty 'conversion' revealed. Among them were the veteran Positivist Frederic Harrison, who wrote a dialogue (1917) in which a junior fellow of an Oxford college, returning from the war as a hot-headed Wellsian, is trounced by a mature Comtian rationalist; and H. L. Mencken, who in a blistering attack on *Joan and Peter* (1918) called Wells a 'hawker of sociological liver-pills' and accused him of a 'messianic delusion'. Mencken was certainly not alone in attributing the deterioration of Wells's thought to his obsession with his role as prophet and sage. Wells's quasi-religious phase was in fact a disastrous departure from his normal standards of intellectual integrity, which it would be charitable to attribute to wartime stress. At any rate, he eventually repudiated it categorically.

No sooner did he discard the Finite God than he launched upon a far more fruitful enterprise, the writing of *The Outline of History*. Begun in the expectation of financial loss, the *Outline* had an enormous popular success and over two million copies were sold. While the critics pointed out numerous mistakes found it a deeply, and Wells and Belloc exchanged abusive pamphlets, most impressive achievement. The *Outline* embarked Wells on a new mission as a public educator, propagating the scientific world-view to which he had long adhered by means of a new presentation of the basic elements of human knowledge in encyclopaedic form. This mission had itself grown out of his involvement in the League of Nations Union towards the end of the War, and for the rest of his life he also became an advocate of world government maintaining a running commentary on international politics. He was a bitter critic of the Treaty of Versailles and of the rise of Fascism and Nazism, and later served on the Sankey Committee on Human Rights. As a campaigner in education and world affairs he continued to enjoy the support of many people (notably the members of the Bloomsbury Group) who had written him off as an artist.

He remained a productive novelist, and one last attempt to embody his ideas in major fiction was *The World of William Clissold* (1926). It was subtitled 'A Novel at a New Angle' and began with an angry preface directed at the reviewers. Wells defended the space given to his hero's opinions and the introduction of real people into the narrative, and asserted sharply that his book was fiction rather than disguised auto-biography. The accusation that Wells was only capable of self-portrayal was by now a familiar one. It is implicit in James's comments on *Marriage*, and it can be traced back at least to 1909, when Frank Harris wrote splenetically that 'he is utterly incapable of creating any character which is not a side of himself, or a pretty fair likeness of himself, such as Kipps'.[31] John Holms's article in the 'Scrutinies' series for the *Calendar of Modern Letters* (No. 85) shows that there was a serious critical case to be made about Wells's limitation to self-portrayal. While the resem-blance of, say, Mr Polly to Kipps should not be exaggerated—it is far more in the *de haut en bas* attitude of the comic narrative than in the characters themselves—Holms was certainly justified in pointing to the very narrow range of comic types in Wells compared to Dickens. Yet Wells was only briefly a comic novelist in the Dickens mode, and a large number of his novels adopt the special, subjective viewpoint which has become the norm of twentieth-century fiction. If they were wrong to object to the presence of an autobiographical element as such, the reviewers can hardly be blamed for treating the characters in his later novels as ventriloquists' dummies when they so constantly served as propagandists for his political and social opinions. The publishers' advertisement for *The World of William Clissold*, indeed, hinted that the book was not primarily a literary event at all. They suggested that it might 'prove epoch-making in the literal sense—that it may have a power to shape and mould the future of our world which will make it for future historians the most important literary work of the twentieth century'. The reviewers were impressed neither by this nor by the self-defensive preface, and the book was widely and scornfully condemned. Only those sufficiently under the sway of its ideas, such as H. L. Mencken (No. 82) and J. M. Keynes (No. 83), were prepared to take Wells's side. In this division of opinion the seeds of the 'two cultures' debate of thirty-five years later can already be detected. Clissold himself is a scientific business man who would like to turn universities into research institutes. Men like Keynes, Julian Huxley, Kingsley Martin and (in the 1930s) C. P. Snow were representative 'Wellsians' who believed in the importance of his ideas however they were expressed. The hostility of their contemporaries in the literary world was most sharply expressed in the new critical reviews, the *Calendar of Modern Letters* and *Scrutiny*. Beside Holms's article, the *Calendar* printed a bored review of *William*

Clissold by D. H. Lawrence,[32] and F. R. Leavis reviewed Wells in the first number of *Scrutiny* (No. 88). Leavis later made 'crass Wellsianism' one of his targets in the 1962 Richmond Lecture on Snow and the 'two cultures'. In his role as prophet of technological progress, Wells could unhappily now be presented as the enemy of literature and the embodiment of the modern Philistine.

Very little of interest was written on Wells during the 1930s. The sales of his books fell steeply, and his ideas lost their appeal. *Scrutiny* did not return to him, and in the new left-wing journals such as *Partisan Review* he was totally ignored; only Christopher Caudwell, in *Studies in a Dying Culture* (1938), bothered to submit his 'petit-bourgeois' imagination to Marxist analysis. Wells was now outmoded, a figure from the Edwardian past. Those who, like Freda Kirchwey (No. 86), remembered his impact twenty years earlier wrily concluded that he had remained stationary while they had moved on. When younger writers reviewed his books (now usually relegated to the routine batch of 'New Fiction') they did so mechanically, as a literary chore. His scientific materialism seemed the faith of an altogether more confident and less ominous historical period: Malcolm Cowley neatly described him in his own favoured evolutionary idiom as 'the survivor of a prehistoric time, a warm, ponderous, innocent creature ill adapted to the Ice Age in which we live'.[33] Precisely the same point, that Wells was too innocent to understand the age of dictators, was made by George Orwell, in an essay, 'Wells, Hitler and the World State' (1941) which was felt to be too well known to include in the present book. To a largely sympathetic critic like Orwell, Wells's internationalist and anti-militarist attitudes were as obvious as they were ineffectual. But Wells himself went on, revising and updating his world outlook, and plunging into one-sided polemic. If his abandonment of art for the direct communication of ideas had led him to bore his critics at last, he could not perhaps legitimately complain. His *Experiment in Autobiography* (1934) had a dull reception, although this now appears as the masterpiece of his later years and the most durable book he had written since before the war. Two years later he passed his seventieth birthday, and the quirkiness and irascibility of some of his later books reveals the strain of keeping a hold on his public. Yet tedious as it was to the literary intellectuals, Wells's voice continued to be heard. As is evidenced by his 1944 doctoral thesis for London University on the one hand, and by his Penguin Specials and his contributions to Watts' Thinkers' Library on the other, his efforts to influence the mainstream of contemporary opinion continued to the end. When he died in 1946, Middleton Murry, in the finest of the obituary articles, called him 'the last prophet of bourgeois Europe' (No. 91).

As an artist he had been a historical figure for over twenty years. A number of retrospective articles on his fiction appeared in the 1920s, together with a bibliography, a scholarly study of his thought and Geoffrey West's biography (1930). West was perhaps the most perceptive among several critics who investigated his failure to fulfil his artistic promise (No. 84). *Mr. Polly* was now widely seen as his most permanent book, while *Tono-Bungay* was taken as the decisive turning-point in his writing. With Wells thus established as a figure in English literature on the strength of his Edwardian novels, his earlier short stories and scientific romances could also be rediscovered and rescued from the imputation of being mere entertainment. The symbolic or mythopoeic quality of these books was pointed out in passing by Edward Shanks (1923), and many other writers testified to their high place among Wells's artistic achievements. The scientific romances were not only accepted by the critics: unlike his other works, they also profoundly influenced later novelists, from the whole school of science-fiction writers to Huxley, Orwell, Golding, Nabokov and Borges (No. 92). One important critical document records the transmission of this influence—the essay on Wells by Evgenii Zamyatin (No. 79), author of the anti-Utopian novel *We* (1920–1) which was the earliest of the post-Wellsian visions of a totalitarian, technocratic society of the future. Zamyatin, an unorthodox ex-Bolshevik who had been trained as an engineer, saw Wells as a writer of urban fairy-tales based on a quintessentially modern combination of science and a heretical socialism. His essay is a direct evocation of the liberating excitement of Wells's books. Unlike the English critics with their rigid separation of art from propaganda, Zamyatin was able to see the unity of Wells's work as a whole and to move quite naturally from the romances to an admittedly vague and general discussion of his social ideas. Although it has its own context in the brief creative outburst of post-revolutionary Russia, Zamyatin's essay expresses an emotion which was far more widely known during what Middleton Murry called Wells's 'intoxicating progress' through the earlier twentieth century. For it may perhaps be said that while he was not a revolutionary writer in any politically 'correct' sense, Wells had at his peak the rarer gift of arousing the energies which revolutionaries attempt to harness. Thus it is that no writer in the modern English-speaking world has surpassed his ability to combine a strictly imaginative appeal with an intense political and ideological relevance.

While little of fundamental importance has been added to the views which emerged during his lifetime, the more recent tendencies of Wells criticism may be briefly summarized here. Despite the efforts of the H. G. Wells Society (founded in 1960 under the auspices of Julian Huxley, Philip Noel-Baker, Bertrand Russell, C. P. Snow and others) to keep his social thought alive, serious interest in his work is now almost entirely confined to the literary field. Whereas Malcolm Cowley wrote of him as an innocent dinosaur 'ill adapted to the Ice Age in which we live', recent critics have performed this adaptation somewhat drastically by their reinstatement of the pessimistic Wells of the scientific romances. Anthony West and Bernard Bergonzi have gone so far as to suggest that pessimism was the deepest intuition of Wells's art, and that his later career as reformist and educator might be seen as a prolonged essay in self-suppression. As yet there has been no nearer approach to a total revaluation of his work than this rather one-sided theory, and despite Bergonzi's demonstration of the imaginative richness of the scientific romances in *The Early H. G. Wells* (1961), concentration upon these works has had the unintended result of confirming his somewhat peripheral status in modern literary studies. However, a recent revival of interest in his social novels has been stimulated by the publication of material from the Wells archive at the University of Illinois. A great deal is now known about the development of his literary theory and practice and his relationships with other writers in his formative period, although no full-scale critical biography is as yet available. The vagaries of critical fashion may also now be working in Wells's favour. A generation ago Mark Schorer's essay 'Technique as Discovery', an influential manifesto for a formalist approach to the novel, used *Tono-Bungay* as a textbook example of slipshod composition. It is significant that recent work has included both a substantial defence of Wells's novel in formalist terms (by David Lodge), and a number of historically-orientated studies of the late Victorian and Edwardian periods in which Wells is allotted a major role. As for his later novels, Edward Shanks presciently wrote (1923) that future students would 'read them in order to declare that no one else need do so'. The small group of romances and novels which had already been singled out by critics in the 1920s continues to enjoy a wide popularity. Wells indeed doubted whether a character like Mr Polly had 'that sort of vitality which endures into new social phases',[34] but then he sometimes entertained the same doubt of humanity itself.

NOTES

1 Letter to Frederick Macmillan, 26 September 1904, in British Museum (Macmillan Archive).
2 Where the date of an article on Wells is cited in parentheses, full bibliographical details will be found in the Appendix.
3 *Experiment in Autobiography* (1934), ii, p. 530.
4 See Wells's 'picshua' in *Autobiography*, ii, p. 555.
5 Lovat Dickson, *H. G. Wells: His Turbulent Life and Times* (1969), p. 135. The figure must be taken as referring to the original English editions.
6 'My Lucky Moment', *View* (29 April 1911), i, 212.
7 *Revue des Deux Mondes* (15 August 1900), clx, 936–46 (T. de Wyzewa).
8 *Nature* (18 July 1895), lii, 268.
9 *The Times* (17 June 1896), 17; *Critic* (25 July 1896), n.s. xxvi, 55–6.
10 *Academy* (30 May 1896), xlix, 443–4.
11 *The Times* (18 April 1898), 7.
12 'Ten Years of English Literature', *North American Review* (August 1897), clxv, 145.
13 Letter to Bennett, 8 February 1902, in *Arnold Bennett and H. G. Wells* (1960), ed. Harris Wilson, p. 73.
14 *Spectator* (16 May 1914), cvii, 837; *New Statesman* (30 May 1914), iii, 249.
15 *Atlantic Monthly* (January 1901), lxxxvii, 62–3.
16 'Study and Stage', *Morning Leader* (8 March 1902), 4.
17 *Critic* (September 1904), xlv, 287.
18 *Arnold Bennett and H. G. Wells*, p. 73.
19 *Athenaeum* (7 December 1901), 766–7.
20 *The Times Literary Supplement* (14 September 1906), 314; *Daily Express* (21 September 1906), 2.
21 Masterman, review in *Daily News* (14 September 1906), 4; *Tribune* (14 September 1906), 2; *Clarion* (21 September 1906), 4.
22 *Vanity Fair* (3 March 1909), lxxxii, 263.
23 *English Review* (November 1909), iii, 666–8.
24 *Field* (23 April 1910), cxv, 721. Wells was stung by this sentence into proposing a libel action, with Macmillan and other respected literary men to appear as witnesses.
25 *British Weekly* (18 February 1909), xlv, 549.
26 *Saturday Review* (9 October 1909), cviii, 444–5.
27 For a full account of the *Ann Veronica* episode in connection with the Purity

Crusade, see Samuel Hynes, *The Edwardian Turn of Mind* (1968), pp. 293ff.

28 *View* (29 April 1911).

29 *Outlook* (27 September 1913), xxxii, 415 (review of *The Passionate Friends*).

30 *North American Review* (December 1916), cciv, 939.

31 *Vanity Fair* (3 March 1909).

32 This is reprinted in his *Selected Literary Criticism* (1961), ed. Anthony Beal, pp. 133–8.

33 *New Republic* (14 November 1934), lxxxi, 23 (review of *Experiment in Autobiography*).

34 *Experiment in Autobiography*, ii, 499.

The materials printed in this volume follow the original texts in all important respects. Where quotations from the works of H. G. Wells and simple plot-summaries of his novels have been omitted, these omissions are clearly indicated in the text. Typographical errors in the originals have been silently corrected and the form of reference to titles has been regularized. Footnotes are by the editor unless otherwise specified.

THE TIME MACHINE

July 1895

---

1. Unsigned notice, 'A Man of Genius', *Review of Reviews*

March 1895, xi, 263

The author is either W. T. Stead (1849–1912), editor and founder of the *Review of Reviews*, or his assistant Grant Richards (1872–1948). Both were later to claim the credit for discovering Wells. Richards, who became a well-known publisher, wrote 'I think that notice was mine, and, even if it wasn't, it was I who made "W.T.S." read the story' (*Memories of a Misspent Youth*, 1932, 331).

H. G. Wells, who is writing the serial in the *New Review*, is a man of genius. His invention of the Time Machine was good, but his description of the ultimate evolution of society into the aristocrats and the capitalists who live on the surface of the earth in the sunshine, and the toilers who are doomed to live in the bowels of the earth in black darkness, in which they learn to see by the evolution of huge owl-like eyes, is gruesome and horrible to the last point. The story is not yet finished, but he has written enough to show that he has an imagination as gruesome as that of Poe.

2. R. H. Hutton, unsigned review in *Spectator*

13 July 1895, lxxv, 41–3

Richard Holt Hutton (1826–97), eminent critic and literary editor of the *Spectator* from 1861. His earnest criticism of Wells from a Christian standpoint suggests how habitually forecasts of human evolution were used as a means of moral propaganda in the post-Darwinian period.

Mr. H. G. Wells has written a very clever story as to the condition of this planet in the year 802,701 A.D., though the two letters A.D. appear to have lost their meaning in that distant date, as indeed they have lost their meaning for not a few even in the comparatively early date at which we all live. The story is one based on that rather favourite speculation of modern metaphysicians which supposes *time* to be at once the most important of the conditions of organic evolution, and the most misleading of subjective illusions. It is, we are told, by the efflux of time that all the modifications of species arise on the one hand, and yet Time is so purely subjective a mode of thought, that a man of searching intellect is supposed to be able to devise the means of travelling in time as well as in space, and visiting, so as to be contemporary with, any age of the world, past or future, so as to become as it were a true 'pilgrim of eternity.' This is the dream on which Mr. H. G. Wells has built up his amusing story of *The Time Machine*. A speculative mechanician is supposed to have discovered that the 'fourth dimension,' concerning which mathematicians have speculated, is Time, and that with a little ingenuity a man may travel in Time as well as in Space. The Time-traveller of this story invents some hocus-pocus of a machine by the help of which all that belongs or is affixed to that machine may pass into the Future by pressing down one lever, and into the Past by pressing down another. In other words, he can make himself at home with the society of hundreds of thousands of centuries hence, or with the chaos of hundreds of thousands of centuries past, at his pleasure. As a matter of choice, the novelist very judiciously chooses the Future only in which to disport himself. And as we have no means of testing his conceptions of the Future, he is of course at liberty to imagine what he pleases. And he is rather ingenious in his choice of what to imagine. Mr. Wells supposes his Time-traveller to travel forward from A.D. 1895 to A.D. 802,701, and to make acquaintance with the people inhabiting the valley of the Thames (which has, of course, somewhat changed its channel) at that date. He finds a race of pretty and gentle creatures of silken organisations, as it were, and no particular interests or aims, except the love of amusement, inhabiting the surface of the earth, almost all evil passions dead, almost all natural or physical evils overcome, with a serener atmosphere, a brighter sun, lovelier flowers and fruits, no dangerous animals or poisonous vegetables, no angry passions or tumultuous and grasping selfishness, and only one object of fear. While the race of the surface of the earth has improved away all its dangers and embarrassments (including, apparently, every trace of a religion), the race of the underworld,—the race which has originally sprung from the mining population,—has developed a great dread of light, and a power of vision which can work and carry on all its great engineering operations with a minimum of light. At the same time, by inheriting a state of servitude it has also inherited a cruel contempt for its former masters, who can now resist its attacks only by congregating in crowds during the hours of darkness, for in the daylight, or even in the bright moonlight, they are safe from the attacks of their former serfs. This beautiful superior race of faint and delicate beauty is wholly vegetarian. But the inferior world of industrious dwellers in the darkness has retained its desire for flesh, and in the absence of all other animal life has returned to cannibalism; and is eager to catch unwary members of the soft surface race in order to feed on their flesh. Moreover, this is the one source of fear which disturbs the gentle pastimes of the otherwise successful subduers of natural evils. Here is Mr. Wells's dream of the two branches into which the race of men, under the laws of evolution, had diverged:—

[Quotes ch. 10 'I grieved to think' to 'I give it to you'.]

The central idea of this dream is, then, the unnerving effect of a too great success in conquering the natural resistance which the physical constitution of the world presents to our love of ease and pleasure. Let a race which has learned to serve, and to serve efficiently, and has lost its physical equality with its masters by the conditions of its servitude, coexist with a race that has secured all the advantages of superior organisation, and the former will gradually recover, by its energetic habits, at least some of the advantages which it has lost, and will unite with them the cruel and selfish spirit which servitude breeds. This is, we take it, the warning which Mr. Wells intends to give:—'Above all things avoid sinking into a condition of satisfied ease; avoid a soft and languid serenity; even evil passions which involve continuous effort, are not so absolutely deadly as the temperament of languid and harmless playfulness.' We have no doubt that, so far as Mr. Wells goes, his warning is wise. But we have little fear that the languid, ease-loving, and serene temperament will ever paralyse the human race after the manner he supposes, even though there may be at present some temporary signs of the growth of the appetite for mere amusement.

In the first place, Mr. Wells assumes, what is well-nigh impossible, that the growth of the pleasure-loving temperament would not itself prevent that victory over physical obstacles to enjoyment on which he founds his dream. The pleasure-loving temperament soon becomes both selfish and fretful. And selfishness no less than fretfulness poisons all enjoyment. Before our race had reached anything like the languid grace and frivolity of the Eloi (the surface population), it would have fallen a prey to the many competing and conflicting energies of Nature which are always on the watch to crush out weak and languid organisations, to say nothing of the uncanny Morlocks (the envious subterranean population), who would soon have invented spectacles shutting out from their sensitive eyes the glare of either moon or sun. If the doctrines as to evolution have any truth in them at all, nothing is more certain than that the superiority of man to Nature will never endure beyond the endurance of his fighting strength. The physical condition of the Eloi is supposed, for instance, so to have accommodated itself to external circumstances as to extinguish that continual growth of population which renders the mere competition for food so serious a factor in the history of the globe. But even supposing such a change to have taken place, of which we see no trace at all in history or civilisation, what is there in the nature of frivolity and love of ease, to diminish, and not rather to increase, that craving to accumulate sources of enjoyment at the expense of others, which seems to be *most* visible in the nations whose populations are of the slowest growth, and which so reintroduces rivalries and war. Let any race find the pressure of population on its energies diminishing, and the mutual jealousy amongst those who are thus placed in a position of advantage for securing wealth and ease, will advance with giant strides. The hardest-pressed populations are not the most, but on the whole the least, selfish.

In the next place Mr. Wells's fancy ignores the conspicuous fact that man's nature needs a great deal of hard work to keep it in order at all, and that no class of men or women are so dissatisfied with their own internal condition as those who are least disciplined by the necessity for industry. Find the idlest class of a nation and you certainly find the most miserable class. There would be no tranquillity or serenity at all in any population for which there were not hard tasks and great duties. The Eloi of this fanciful story would have become even more eager for the satisfaction of selfish desires than the Morlocks themselves. The nature of man must have altered not merely accidentally, but essentially, if the devotion to ease and amusement had left it sweet and serene. Matthew Arnold wrote in his unreal mood of agnosticism:—

> We, in some unknown Power's employ,
> Move on a rigorous line;
> Can neither, when we will, enjoy,
> Nor, when we will, resign.

But it is not in some 'unknown Power's employ' that we move on this 'rigorous line.' On the contrary, it is in the employ of a Power which has revealed itself in the Incarnation and the Cross. And we may expect with the utmost confidence that if the earth is still in existence in the year 802,701 A.D., either the A.D. will mean a great deal more than it means now, or else its inhabitants will be neither Eloi nor Morlocks. For in that case evil passions will by that time have led to the extinction of races spurred and pricked on by conscience and yet so frivolous or so malignant. Yet Mr. Wells's fanciful and lively dream is well worth reading, if only because it will draw attention to the great moral and religious factors in human nature which he appears to ignore.

3. Unsigned review, *Daily Chronicle*

27 July 1895, 3

No two books could well be more unlike than *The Time Machine* and *The Strange Case of Dr. Jekyll and Mr. Hyde*, but since the appearance of Stevenson's creepy romance we have had nothing in the domain of pure fantasy so bizarre as this 'invention' by Mr. H. G. Wells. For his central idea Mr. Wells may be indebted to some previously published narrative suggestion, but if so we must confess ourselves entirely unacquainted with it, and so far as our knowledge goes he has produced in fiction that rarity which Solomon declared to be not merely rare but non-existent—a 'new thing under the sun.'

The narrative opens in the dining-room of the man who is known to us throughout simply as the Time Traveller, and who is expounding to his guests a somewhat remarkable theory in esoteric mathematics.

[Quotes ch. 1 'You know' to 'our lives'.]

By this Poe-like ingenuity of whimsical reasoning the Time Traveller leads up to his great invention—nothing less than a machine which shall convey him through time, that fourth dimension of space, with even greater facility than men are conveyed through the other three dimensions by bicycle or balloon. He can go back either to the days of his grandsires or to the days of creation; he can go forward to the days of his grandsons, or still further to that last *fin de siècle*, when earth is moribund and man has ceased to be. The one journey of which we have a record is a voyage into far futurity, and when after a wild flight through the centuries the Time Traveller stops the machine the dial register tells him that he is in or about the year 802,000 A.D. Man is still existent, but a remarkable change has passed upon him. The fissure of cleavage between the classes and the masses instead of being bridged over or filled up has become a great gulf. In centuries of centuries the environment of the more favoured has become so exquisitely adapted to all their needs, and indeed to all their desires, that the necessity for physical or mental activity is so many generations behind them that it does not survive even as a memory; the powers of body and mind which are distinctively manly have perished in ages of disuse, and they have become frail, listless, pleasure-loving children. The workers, on the other hand, have become brutalised, bleached, ape-like creatures, who live underground and toil for their effeminate lords, taking their pay, when they can, by living upon them literally in a horrible canni-balistic fashion. The adventures of the Time Traveller among the Eloi and the Morlocks are conceived in the true spirit of fantasy—the effect of remoteness being achieved much more successfully than in such a book, for example, as Lord Lytton's *The Coming Race*. Still more weird are the further wanderings in a future when man has gone, and even nature is not what it was, because sun, moon, stars, and earth are tottering to their doom. The description of the seacoast of the dying ocean, still embracing a dying world, and of the huge, hideous creeping things which are the last remains of life on a worn-out planet has real impressiveness—it grips the imagination as it is only gripped by genuinely imaginative work. It is in what may be described literally as the 'machinery' of the story that Mr. Wells's imagination plays least freely and convincingly. He constantly forgets—or seems to forget—that his Traveller is journeying simply through *time*, and records effects which inevitably suggest travel through *space*. Why, for example, should the model of the machine vanish from sight when in the second chapter it is set in motion? Why, in the last chapter, should the machine itself disappear when the Traveller has set out on his final journey; why on his progress through the centuries should it jar and sway as if it were moving through the air; why should he write of 'slipping like a vapour through the interstices of intervening substance,' or anticipate sudden contact with some physical obstacle? To these questions Mr. Wells will probably reply that it is unfair to blame an artist for not surmounting difficulties which are practically insurmountable; but the obvious rejoinder is that it is unwise to choose a scheme from which such difficulties are inseparable. Still, when all deductions are made *The Time Machine* remains a strikingly original performance.

4. Israel Zangwill on time-travelling

September 1895

Extracts from Zangwill's column 'Without Prejudice', *Pall Mall Magazine*, vii, 153–5.

Israel Zangwill (1864–1926), author of *Children of the Ghetto*, *Ghetto Tragedies* and other novels.

Countless are the romances that deal with other times, other manners; endless have been the attempts to picture the time to come. Sometimes the future is grey with evolutionary perspectives, with previsions of a post-historic man, bald, toothless and fallen into his second infancy; sometimes it is gay with ingenuous fore-glimpses of a renewed golden age of socialism and sentimentality. In his brilliant little romance *The Time Machine* Mr. Wells has inclined to the severer and more scientific form of prophecy—to the notion of a humanity degenerating inevitably from sheer pressure of physical comfort; but this not very novel conception, which was the theme of Mr. Besant's *Inner House*, and even partly of Pearson's *National Life and Character*, Mr. Wells has enriched by the invention of the Morlocks, a differentiated type of humanity which lives underground and preys upon the softer, prettier species that lives luxuriously in the sun, a fine imaginative creation worthy of Swift, and possibly not devoid of satirical reference to 'the present discontents.' There is a good deal of what Tyndall would have called 'scientific imagination' in Mr. Wells' further vision of the latter end of all things, a vision far more sombre and impressive than the ancient imaginings of the Biblical seers. The only criticism I have to offer is that his Time Traveller, a cool scientific thinker, behaves exactly like the hero of a commonplace sensational novel, with his frenzies of despair and his appeals to fate, when he finds himself in danger of having to remain in the year eight hundred and two thousand seven hundred and one, into which he has recklessly travelled; nor does it ever occur to him that in the aforesaid year he will have to repeat these painful experiences of his, else his vision of the future will have falsified itself—though how the long dispersed dust is to be vivified again does not appear. Moreover, had he travelled backwards, he would have reproduced a Past which, in so far as his own appearance in it with his newly invented machine was concerned, would have been *ex hypothesi* unveracious. Had he recurred to his own earlier life, he would have had to exist in two forms simultaneously, of varying ages—a feat which even Sir Boyle Roche would have found difficult. These absurdities illustrate the absurdity of any attempt to grapple with the notion of Time; and, despite some ingenious metaphysics, worthy of the inventor of the Eleatic paradoxes, Mr. Wells' *Time Machine*, which traverses time (viewed as the Fourth Dimension of Space) backwards or forwards, much as the magic carpet of *The Arabian Nights* traversed space, remains an amusing fantasy. That Time is an illusion is one of the earliest lessons of metaphysics; but even if we could realise Time as self-complete and immovable, a vast *continuum* holding all that has happened and all that will happen, an eternal Present, even so to introduce a man travelling through this sleeping ocean is to re-introduce the notion of Time which has just been expelled. There is really more difficulty in understanding the Present than the Past or the Future into which it is always slipping; and those old Oriental languages which omitted the Present altogether displayed the keen metaphysical instinct of the East. And yet there is a sense in which the continued and continuous existence of all past time, at least, can be grasped by the human intellect without the intervention of metaphysics. The star whose light reaches us to-night may have perished and become extinct a thousand years ago, the rays of light from it having so many millions of miles to travel that they have only just impinged upon our planet. Could we perceive clearly the incidents on its surface, we should be beholding the Past in the Present, and we could travel to any given year by travelling actually through space to the point at which the rays of that year would first strike upon our consciousness. In like manner the whole Past of the earth is still playing itself out—to an eye conceived as stationed to-day in space, and moving now forwards to catch the Middle Ages, now backwards to watch Nero fiddling over the burning of Rome. . . .

. . . In verity, there is no Time Traveller, Mr. Wells, save Old Father Time himself. Instead of being a Fourth Dimension of Space, Time is perpetually travelling through Space, repeating itself in vibrations farther and farther from the original point of incidence; a vocal panorama moving through the universe across the infinities, a succession of sounds and visions that, having once been, can never pass away, but only on and on from point to point, permanently enregistered in the sum of things, preserved from annihilation by the endlessness of Space, and ever visible and audible to eye or ear that should travel in a parallel movement. It is true the scientists allege that only light can thus travel through the infinities, sound-waves being confined to a material medium and being quickly dissipated into heat. But light alone is sufficient to sustain my fantasy, and in any case the sounds would be æons behind the sights. Terrible, solemn thought that the Past can never die, and that for each of us Heaven or Hell may consist in our being placed at the point of vantage in Space where we may witness the spectacle of our past lives, and find bliss or bale in the panorama. How much ghastlier than the pains of the pit, for the wicked to be perpetually 'moved on' by some Satanic policeman to the mathematical point at which their autobiography becomes visible, a point that moves back-wards in the infinite universe each time the green curtain of the grave falls over the final episode, so that the sordid show may commence all over again, and so *ad infinitum*. Pascal defined Space as a sphere whose centre is everywhere and whose circumference is nowhere. This brilliant figure helps us to conceive God as always at the centre of vision, receiving all vibrations simultaneously, and thus beholding all Past time simul-taneously with the Present. We can also conceive of Future incidents being visible to a spectator, who should be moved forward to receive the impressions of them æons earlier than they would otherwise have reached him. But these 'futures' would only be relative; in reality they would already have happened, and the absolute Future, the universe of things that have *not* happened, would still elude our vision, though we can very faintly imagine the Future, interwoven inevitably with the Past, visible to an omniscient Being somewhat as the evolution of a story is to the man of genius upon whom past and future flash in one conception. Mr. Wells might have been plausibly scientific in engineer-ing his Time Machine through Space and stopping at the points where particular periods of the world's past history became visible: he would then have avoided the fallacy of mingling personally in the panorama. But this would not have suited his design of 'dealing in futures.' For there is no getting into the Future, except by waiting. You can only sit down and see it come by, as the drunken man thought he might wait for his house to come round in the circulation of the earth; and if you lived for an eternity, the show would only be 'just about to begin.'

THE ISLAND OF DOCTOR MOREAU

April 1896

5. Chalmers Mitchell, review in *Saturday Review*

11 April 1896, lxxxi, 368–9

Sir Peter Chalmers Mitchell, F.R.S. (1864–1945), zoologist, Secretary of the Zoological Society of London from 1903 to 1935 and author of a biography of T. H. Huxley (1900). Mitchell and Wells were then colleagues on the staff of the *Saturday Review*.

Those who have delighted in the singular talent of Mr. Wells will read *The Island of Doctor Moreau* with dismay. We have all been saying that here is an author with the emotions of an artist and the intellectual imagination of a scientific investigator. He has given us in *The Time Machine* a diorama of prophetic visions of the dying earth, imagined with a pitiless logic, and yet filled with a rare beauty, sometimes sombre and majestic, sometimes shining with fantastic grace. He has brought down among us the angel of our dreams, and, while using the faculties a naturalist would employ in studying the new habitat of a species, he has made us laugh and weep, flush with an unsuspected shame, hug a discovered virtue.* Behind these high gifts, behind the simple delight of his story-telling, there has seemed to lie a reasoned attitude to life, a fine seriousness that one at least conjectures to be the background of the greater novelists. When the prenatal whispers of *The Island of Doctor Moreau* reached me, I rejoiced at the promise of another novel with a scientific basis, and I accepted gladly the opportunity given me to say something of it, from the scientific point of view, as well as from that of a devoted novel-reader. But, instead of being able to lay my little

* In *The Wonderful Visit* (1895).

wreath at the feet of Mr. Wells, I have to confess the frankest dismay.

For Mr. Wells has put out his talent to the most flagitious usury. His central idea is a modelling of the human frame and endowment of it with some semblance of humanity, by plastic operations upon living animals. The possibilities of grafting and moulding, of shaping the limbs and larynx and brain, of transfusing blood, of changing physiological rhythm, and vague suggestions of hypnotizing dawning intelligence with the elemental rules of human society—these would seem to offer a rich vein to be worked by Mr. Wells's logical fancy. They are, indeed, finely imagined, and the story of the hero, suddenly brought into an island peopled with such nightmare creatures, is vivid and exciting to the last degree. To realize them, you must read of the bewilderment and horror of the hero, while he thinks the creatures are men outraged and distorted: of his fear for his own fate at the hands of the artificer of the unnatural: of his gradual acquaintance with the real nature of the monsters: of his new horror at the travesties of human form and mind: of the perils that begin when the 'stubborn beast-flesh' has overcome the engrafted humanity, and the population has risen in rebellion against its creator. All this is excellent; but the author, during the inception of his story, like his own creatures, has tasted blood. The usurious interest began when the author, not content with the horror inevitable in his idea, and yet congruous with the fine work he has given us hitherto, sought out revolting details with the zeal of a sanitary inspector probing a crowded graveyard.

You begin with a chromolithographic shipwreck, and three starving survivors playing odd-man-out for a cannibal feast. The odd man breaks faith, and, in the resulting struggle, the hero is left alone in a blood-bespattered boat. When he is rescued, a drunken doctor, no doubt disinclined to change the supposed diet, restores him with a draught of iced blood. When the island is reached he is not allowed by Mr. Wells to land until, refused hospitality by Dr. Moreau and cast adrift by the drunken captain, he has again meditated upon starvation, this time without any mates for whose blood he may pass halfpence. Dr. Moreau himself is a *cliché* from the pages of an anti-vivisection pamphlet. He has been hounded out of London because a flayed dog (you hear the shuddering ladies handing over their guineas) has been liberated from his laboratory by a spying reporter. It is the blood that Mr. Wells insists upon forcing on us; blood in the sink 'brown and red,' on the floor, on the hands of the operators, on the bandages that swathe the creatures or that they have left hanging on the bushes—physically disgusting details inevitable in the most conservative surgery; but still more unworthy of restrained art, and, in this case, of scientific *vraisemblance*, is the insistence upon the terror and pains of the animals, on their screams under the knife, and on Dr. Moreau's indifference to the 'bath of pain' in which his victims were moulded and recast. Mr. Wells must know that the delicate, prolonged operations of modern surgery became possible only after the introduction of anæsthetics. Equally wrong is the semi-psychological suggestion that pain could be a humanizing agency. It may be that the conscious subjection to pain for a purpose has a desirable mental effect; pain in itself, and above all continuous pain inflicted on a struggling, protesting creature, would produce only madness and death. Mr. Wells will not even get his hero out of the island decently. When Dr. Moreau has been killed by his latest victim— a puma become in the laboratory 'not human, not animal, but hellish, brown, seamed with red branching scars, red drops starting out upon it'—Mr. Wells must needs bring in an alien horror. The 'boat from the machine' drifts ashore with two dead men in it—men 'dead so long that they fell in pieces' when the hero dumped them out for the last of the island monsters to snarl over.

It may be that a constant familiarity with the ways and work of laboratories has dulled my sense of the aesthetic possibilities of blood— anatomists, for the most part, wash their hands before they leave their work—and that a public attuned to Mr. Rider Haggard's view of the romantic may demand the insertion of details physically unpleasant; but, for my own part, I feel that Mr. Wells has spoiled a fine conception by greed of cheap horrors. I beg of him, in the name of many, a return to his sane transmutations of the dull conceptions of science into the living and magical beauty he has already given us. We that have read his earlier stories will read all he chooses to write; but must he choose the spell of Circe?

There remains to be said a word about the scientific conceptions underlying Dr. Moreau's experiments. I quite agree that there is scientific basis enough to form the plot of a story. But in an appended note, Mr. Wells is scaring the public unduly. He declares:—'There can be no denying that whatever amount of scientific credibility attaches to the detail of this story, the manufacture of monsters—and perhaps even of *quasi*-human monsters—is within the possibilities of vivisection.' The most recent discussion of grafting and transfusion experiments is to be found in a treatise by Oscar Hertwig, a translation of which Mr. Heinemann announces. Later investigators have failed to repeat the grafting experiments of Hunter, and a multitude of experiments on skin and bone grafting and on transfusion of blood shows that animal-hybrids cannot be produced in these fashions. You can transfuse blood or graft skin from one man to another; but attempts to combine living material from different creatures fail.

6. R. H. Hutton, unsigned review in *Spectator*

11 April 1896, lxxvi, 519–20

Hutton's review is a curious exception to the chorus of denunciations of *The Island of Doctor Moreau*. A veteran opponent of scientific materialism, he misinterprets the book as an anti-vivisectionist tract.

The ingenious author of *The Time Machine* has found in this little book a subject exactly suited to his rather peculiar type of imagination. When he tried to conceive the idea of making a man of the nineteenth century *travel* in time, so that he was at the same moment both contemporary with and far removed from the people of a prehistoric age, he conceived an idea which was really quite too self-contradictory to be worked out with any sort of coherence. But in this little book he has worked out a notion much less intrinsically incoherent, and though impossible, yet not so impossible as to be quite inconceivable. In other words, the impossibility is of a less unworkable order, though it is also much more gruesome. He has taken a few of the leading methods of the modern surgery and exaggerated them in the hands of an accomplished vivisector into a new physiological calculus that enables its professor to transmute various animals into the semblance of man,—after a fashion of which he gives us a notion in the passage we are just about to extract.

[Quotes ch. 14 'You forget' to '*L'homme qui rit*'.]

46

Of course, the real value for literary purposes of this ghastly conception depends on the power of the author to make his readers realise the half-way stages between the brute and the rational creature, with which he has to deal. And we must admit that Mr. Wells succeeds in this little story in giving a most fearful vividness to his picture of half-created monsters endowed with a little speech, a little human curiosity, a little sense of shame, and an overgrown dread of the pain and terror which the scientific dabbler in creative processes had inflicted. There is nothing in Swift's grim conceptions of animalised man and rationalised animals more powerfully conceived than Mr. Wells's description of these deformed and malformed creations of Dr. Moreau, repeating the litany in which they abase themselves before the physiological demigod by whom they have been endowed with their new powers of speech, their new servility to a human master, and their profound dread of that 'house of pain' in which they have been made and fashioned into half-baked men. The hero of the story, who has been thrown into Dr. Moreau's grisly society, comes suddenly on the huts of these spoiled animals who have been fashioned into a bad imitation of men, and hears them proclaim their new law in the following creed:—

[Quotes ch. 12 'The Ape Man looked' to 'stars in the sky'.]

Our readers may gain from this passage some faint idea of the power with which this grim conception of the mauling and maiming of brutes into bad imitations of human beings has been worked out by Mr. Wells. It is, of course, a very ingenious caricature of what has been done in certain exceptional efforts of human surgery,—a caricature inspired by the fanaticism of a foul ambition to remake God's creatures by confusing and transfusing and remoulding human and animal organs so as to extinguish so far as possible the chasm which divides man from brute. Mr. Wells has had the prudence, too, not to dwell on the impossibilities of his subject too long. He gives us a very slight, though a very powerful and ghastly, picture, and may, we hope, have done more to render vivisection unpopular, and that contempt for animal pain, which enthusiastic physiologists seem to feel, hideous, than all the efforts of the societies which have been organised for that wholesome and beneficent end. Dr. Moreau is a figure to make an impression on the imagination, and his tragic death under the attack of the puma which he has been torturing so long, has a kind of poetic justice in it which satisfies the mind of the reader. Again, the picture of the rapid reversion to the brute, of the victims which Dr. Moreau had so painfully fashioned, so soon as the terrors of his 'house of pain' are withdrawn, is very impressively painted. Altogether, though we do not recommend *The Island of Doctor Moreau* to readers of sensitive nerves, as it might well haunt them only too powerfully, we believe that Mr. Wells has almost rivalled Swift in the power of his very gruesome, but very salutary as well as impressive, conception.

7. Unsigned review, *Manchester Guardian*

14 April 1896, 4

In *The Island of Doctor Moreau* Mr. H. G. Wells gains our attention at once by the closeness and vigour of his narrative style and by his terse and natural dialogue. His realism of detail is, in fact, the sign of imagination. It is full of skilful and subtle touches, and, harrowing as is the whole effect, he cannot be accused of forcing the note beyond the limits of his conception by any irrelevant accumulation of horrors. But this curious fantasy, with its quasi-scientific foundation, in which a doctor upon a remote island practises vivisection in the spirit of a modern and unsentimental Frankenstein, is intrinsically horrible. The impressions should not be put to the test of analysis or reflection. As it is, they grip the mind with a painful interest and a fearful curiosity. The mysteries of the forbidden enclosure; the cries of the tortured puma; the pursuit through the dark wood by the leopard man; the strange litany of the beast folk; Prendick's flight and frantic apprehensions; the revolt of the beast folk—such scenes and incidents crowd upon us with a persistent fascination. Absolute success in such a narrative is impossible; to play these curious tricks with science is not the highest art; it might even be contended that this is no legitimate subject for art at all; but in its kind Mr. Wells has achieved a success unquestionable and extraordinary. There must be, of course, a weak place where science and fantasy join. To obscure this plausibly is the great difficulty, and we think that here, as too in *Dr. Jekyll and Mr. Hyde*, there is some little creaking of the machinery. But if the chapter 'Dr. Moreau Explains' brings us dangerously near a too critical habit of mind, it is full of striking things—the masterful, overbearing manner of the Doctor, his dreadful plausibility in maintaining his impossible position, his perfect devotion to investigation, the fine contempt for both pleasure and pain which enables him to make the effective counterstroke of accusing his opponent of materialism. 'The study of nature makes a man at last as remorseless as nature,' he says, and with Prendick we are thrown on our resources to combat this appalling inversion. Here is the picture of the terrible Doctor:—

[Quotes ch. 14 'I looked at him' to 'comfortable old gentleman'.]

But though the reader of this book must sup full of horrors, it must not be supposed that there are no mitigations and no relief. There is a grotesque pathos about the beast folk which redeems them, and Montgomery, a character very much in Mr. Stevenson's manner, is reassuring and quite human in his vulgarity. The effect of the final chapter, 'The Man Alone', is admirable, and that he should find solace and a 'sense of infinite peace and protection' in the study of the stars is one of the many points that differentiate Mr. Wells from the mere sensational story-spinner. Yet, great as is the ability and pronounced as is the success of this book, we are convinced that Mr. Wells is too strong and original a writer to devote himself exclusively to fantastic themes.

8. Unsigned review, *Speaker*

18 April 1896, xiii, 429–30

A typical example of the moral denunciations which greeted the book.

We should have thought it impossible for any work of fiction to surpass in gruesome horror some of the problem-novels relating to the great sexual question which have been recently published, if we had not read the *Island of Doctor Moreau*, by H. G. Wells. Having read it, we are bound to admit that there are still lower depths of nastiness, and still cruder manifestations of fantastic imbecility than any attained by the ladies who have been so much with us in recent years. Mr. Wells is a very clever person, who has written one or two stories which have had the merit of originality. In these stories he has shown that he possesses distinct gifts as a writer of fiction, and that he could interest a reader, even if his theme was comparatively commonplace. But the commonplace is evidently hateful to him, and he makes it his first business, when sitting down to write a story, to hit upon an idea that shall startle everybody by its extravagance and novelty. In the present instance he has achieved originality at the expense of decency (we do not use the word in its sexual significance) and common sense. He introduces us to a remote islet in the Pacific where a notorious professor of vivisection, with the aid of a drunken Scotch doctor, is engaged in a series of hideous experiments upon living animals. The object of these experiments is to create something having the semblance of man out of the lower creatures. We need not go further into the details of this delectable theme. Mr. Wells, as we have said, has talent, and he employs it here for a purpose which is absolutely degrading. It is no excuse that he should have made his book one that sends a thrill of horror through the mind of the reader. After all, even among writers of fiction, talents are accompanied by responsibilities—a fact which Mr. Wells seems to have forgotten.

9. Basil Williams, unsigned review in *Athenaeum*

9 May 1896, 615–16

Basil Williams (1867–1950) became a historian and was professor of history at Edinburgh from 1925 to 1937.

The horrors described by Mr. Wells in his latest book very pertinently raise the question how far it is legitimate to create feelings of disgust in a work of art. It is undeniable that details of horror and disgust sometimes appear perfectly legitimate methods of arousing the emotions, and add to the beauty of a tragedy and to the pleasure to be derived therefrom. The *Philoctetes* is perhaps an extreme instance of this, for there the loathsomeness of the details of Philoctetes's suffering is as great as it can be, and yet it is never revolting. But in this book the details of suffering so elaborately set forth by Mr. Wells simply have a nauseating effect. The distinction between legitimate and illegitimate use of horror seems to lie not in the form of the horror, but in the purpose for which it is used. The repulsive details in the *Philoctetes* are merely used to give verisimilitude to a tragedy which would be tragic without them; the case of Philoctetes, quite apart from his particular form of suffering, arouses pity, and his special sufferings are adventitious, and not of the essence of the tragedy. But in Mr. Wells's story, which may be taken as a type of many others tainted with the same fault, the tragedy, such as it is, merely consists in the details of the form of horror chosen; the disgusting descriptions arouse loathing without any equivalent personal interest. The sufferings inflicted in the course of the story have absolutely no adequate artistic reason, for it is impossible to feel the slightest interest in any one of the characters, who are used as nothing but groundwork on which to paint the horrors. In fact, these horrors have not even the merit of penny-a-lining descriptions of police-court atrocities, for in them there is at least some human interest, but here, without the actual form of horror described, the book would be quite irrational. It has, we observe, been suggested in some quarters* that Mr. Wells was animated by a desire to expose the repulsive aspect of vivisection, but we do not believe it. At least, it is singularly ineffective from that point of view, and would be about as valuable for such a purpose as a pornological story in suppressing immorality; and even if that were the object, it would be no defence for artistic failure.

10. Unsigned review, *Guardian*

3 June 1896, 871

The reviewer in this Anglican weekly suggests that *The Island of Doctor Moreau* comes close to blasphemy. But his reading of the book as a parody of divine creation apparently met with Wells's approval. In an interview he gave in the following year, Wells said: 'I should say that *The Island of Doctor Moreau*, although it was written in a great hurry and is marred by many faults, is the best work I have done. It has been stupidly dealt with—as a mere shocker—by people who ought to have known better. The *Guardian* critic seemed to be the only one who read it aright, and who therefore succeeded in giving a really intelligent notice of it' (*Young Man*, August 1897, xi, 256).

The Island of Doctor Moreau is an exceedingly ghastly book; of which it is not altogether easy to divine the intention. Dr. Moreau is a vivisectionist who has the strange and horrible ambition to manufacture men out of animals by means of hideous operations. He lives on an island with an entirely human confederate and a rout of semi-human attendants and subjects of his own manufacturing, until accident throws in his way a ship-wrecked man, who very much against his own will finds himself obliged to stay also on the island. This man is supposed to write

* See No. 6 above.

the story of the horrors he is compelled to witness, and very repulsive much of his story is. Sometimes one is inclined to think the intention of the author has been to satirise and rebuke the presumption of science; at other times his object seems to be to parody the work of the Creator of the human race, and cast contempt upon the dealings of God with His creatures. This is the suggestion of the exceedingly clever and realistic scenes in which the humanised beasts recite the Law their human maker has given them, and show very plainly how impossible it is to them to keep that law. The inevitable reversion of these creatures to bestiality is very well described; but it ought to have been shown that they revert inevitably because they are only man-made creatures. The book is one no one could have the courage to recommend, and we are not inclined to commend it either. It is certainly unpleasant and painful, and we cannot find it profitable. But it is undoubtedly a clever, original, and very powerful effort of imagination.

11. Augustin Filon, article in *Revue des Deux Mondes*

1 December 1904, xxiv, 584–6

Pierre Marie Augustin Filon (1841–1916), Anglophile scholar and critic.

Filon's discussion of *The Island of Doctor Moreau* is extracted from a long article on Wells as 'Novelist, Prophet and Reformer'. He was the earliest critic to reveal a genuine understanding of Wells's purposes in *Doctor Moreau*, interpreting it as a parable of civilization ironically balanced between 'human' and 'bestial' states. Filon identifies this as the characteristic irony of Wells's romances, and the extract is introduced by a brief discussion of *The War of the Worlds*.

Mr. Wells has seen the thawing of the air which is breathed by the Selenites during their day which lasts a fortnight of ours; he has seen London terrorized by a score of fantastic beings projected from another planet and armed with means of destruction unknown to ours. He has seen millions of men and women passing before him in a desperate and inexpressible confusion, bewildered, frantic, and rushing straight ahead like a flock of sheep pursued by a hurricane of panic, or—still tinier— like the water-drops of a flood. . . . Among our author's compatriots, I wonder if there is one who has been able to give such an intense impression of the confusion of a great catastrophe. One book only comes to mind: the *Journal of the Plague Year* by Daniel Defoe, who was like Wells not only in being a Londoner and a child of the petty bourgeoisie, but also in being a Utopian with a vivid imagination, a reformer in the guise of a novelist. I do not think I am exaggerating the severe and sombre grandeur of these two books, the *Journal of the Plague Year* and *The War of the Worlds*, published nearly two centuries apart. The Calvinism of the one and the determinism of the other coincide on the same ground to show us the human will and energy of a whole people abdicating when faced with a cataclysm; but one feels that in both cases, the abdication will be brief and that the need to hope, to believe and to act will again assert itself with the unconquerable optimism of the race. When, having left England ruined, gasping and disfigured at their feet, the matchless and invulnerable Martians are killed by microbes, Defoe would have applauded this dénouement, and would have recognised and worshipped in it a providential design. For Mr. Wells, it is only the irony of things—the humour of Destiny, the final reversal which his philosophy, inherited from Darwin and Schopenhauer, suggests to him.

I have sought for this philosophy in Mr. Wells's books, and it can be glimpsed in *The Island of Doctor Moreau*. After a shipwreck and some thrilling adventures, an English traveller is stranded on an almost unknown Pacific islet. Once there, he is reluctantly given shelter by two Englishmen who have set up a curious scientific institute on the island. One is Dr. Moreau, who has been obliged to throw up a distinguished position on account of the horror excited by his experiments in vivisection. The other, Montgomery, his assistant, has gone into exile because of a serious offence, probably committed under the influence of alcoholism. Moreau has recommenced his experiments in this isolated spot, where his victims' cries will reach neither sensitive souls nor journalists in search of copy. His absurd and sublime dream is that of condensing the innumerable slow stages of evolution into a few weeks or a few months. In his laboratory he manufactures men out of beasts. The operation is not explained. How could it be? Dr. Moreau discusses the possibilities of the enterprise with Prendick, his guest. 'But the instincts?' objects the latter. 'The instincts can be modified. As educators we are doing no more than that. Have we not trained pugnacity into courageous self-sacrifice, and sexual urges into chastity?' 'But you are inflicting terrible pain.' 'Pain will disappear one day. But it has been and is still necessary to warn us of danger. It is the necessary condition of progress and, if modern man is degenerating instead of advancing, he owes it to this cowardly fear of pain which governs our societies.'*

Soon we get to know the bestial humanity which he has created around him and endowed, at the price of frightful tortures, with rudiments of speech and thought. The Beast Folk continually repeat the prescriptions of the code he has instilled into them in order to hold in check their savage inclinations. Their worship of their executioner is expressed in a characteristic chant: '*His* are the stars in the sky. . . . *His* is the Hand that wounds. *His* is the hand that heals. . . .' In this nascent

* This is a rough paraphrase of Moreau's argument in ch. 14.

55

society, this artificial semi-humanity which is but a day old, there are already rebels and hypocrites. An apparent order and methodical activity reign, but all this is felt to be strangely precarious. Let but a single drop of blood touch the tip of the tongue of that bear which has been taught to chant and snuffle, and it will drop back onto its four spiked paws and its carnivorous desires will be unleashed once again. 'I had before my eyes,' Prendick observes, 'the epitome of human history, the action and reaction of forces which intersect and collide or coalesce: instinct, reason, destiny.'

Moreau is killed by one of his victims which has broken its bonds and escaped from the laboratory. We then witness the deplorable relapse of these beings into the bestiality from which they had been so abruptly and violently raised to a higher existence. They carry with them Moreau's colleague, Montgomery, and if Mr. Wells had not been writing for a fussy and easily shockable public, the spectacle of this orgy, with its combination of bestial instinct and civilised vice, might have taken on all the breadth and the atrocious reality which it demands. But perhaps it is better from a moral as well as an artistic point of view that these things should be merely suggested.

After undergoing indescribable suffering and dangers, Prendick returns to England, where he is haunted by terrible memories which make the sight and the society of his fellows odious to him. The men and women around him seem themselves to be no more than animals. Their primitive instincts try to get the upper-hand again and secretly undermine the artificial law of duty which oppresses them and contradicts their very nature. Thus virtue is a struggle, and what is the use of this struggle?

Such is the substance of this book which has had very little recognition from the English public, whether because of the repulsive details with which it abounds, or because an anti-Christian symbolism was discovered in it. The author himself, whose point of view has changed, as we shall see, seems prepared to consign this work to oblivion, since it has not been reprinted with his other works. That is why I thought I should stop for a moment to draw attention to the frame of mind which it reveals.

THE PLATTNER STORY
AND OTHERS

May 1897

12. Basil Williams, unsigned review in *Athenaeum*

26 June 1897, 837

Mr. H. G. Wells has happily given up the exaggerated horrors of *The Island of Doctor Moreau* for stories quite in his best vein. He has all Jules Verne's convincing *insouciance* in telling the most wildly improbable stories. This result is largely gained by a solemn precision in the preliminary and unimportant details of the story. Thus in 'The Plattner Story,' as in 'The Apple,' 'The Argonauts of the Air,' and, in fact, all the stories dealing with the marvellous, the reader is prepared to accept anything after the minute description of the principal characters' commonplace vulgarity or the inglorious dulness of their surroundings. There is hardly any mystery left in their adventures, for one feels that it is almost impossible for anything out of the way to have happened to such people. This effect is heightened by a rigid avoidance of any attempt to dwell on the marvellous character of the prodigy described, be it a flying machine, or the fruit of the tree of knowledge, or what not. Precision in the unessential and vagueness in the essential are really the basis of Mr. Wells's art, and convey admirably the just amount of conviction. In his more possible stories he shows that his constant choice of commonplace characters is no fortuitous matter; all his characters would in themselves be fearfully dull, but by catching and crystallizing the point of reality which is to be found everywhere, in showing the individuality which underlies the veneer of gross conventionality, he often makes such stories of a most seizing interest.

THE INVISIBLE MAN

September 1897

13. Clement Shorter, review in *Bookman*

October 1897, viii, 19–20

Clement King Shorter (1857–1926), journalist and editor of
Illustrated London News from 1891 to 1900 and *Sphere* from 1900
to 1926. The critic whose words are quoted at the beginning of the
review is Edmund Gosse (see Introduction).

A critic of great discernment has recently mourned over the decay of
serious literature. We are all too steadily bent on the writing and the
reading of fiction, most of it bad, most of it certainly ephemeral.
Scientific philosophy, for example, has been neglected since Huxley
and Tyndall died. 'The class of writers which they represented, the
pioneer in physical discovery, who is also a splendid popular exponent,
combining accurate research with the exercise of imagination and style,
has ceased to exist in England. Mr. Wells might have risen in it to the
highest consideration, but he prefers to tell horrible little stories about
monsters. On all sides we may see, and we ought not to see without
acute alarm, the finer talents being drawn from the arduous exercises to
which nature intended to devote them, to the facile fields of fiction.'
One hardly knows which most to admire—the alliteration of this last
line or the splendid assumption that some of our prosperous latter-day
novelists, whose chief glory is their rate per thousand words, have the
making in them of Huxleys and Tyndalls. There is little reason to
suppose, for example, that Mr. Wells, had he made science his life-work,
would have come off better than any one of a dozen smart young men
turned out by the Science and Art Department annually. We probably
lost a quite indifferent man of science to gain the really able author of

The Time Machine and *The Invisible Man*. So far from being an accident of misdirected talent, Mr. Wells is an imperative product of his age. Phantasy has always been with us, and has conceived of people preternaturally masters of time and space. Dreamers have carried us back to the Ichthyosaurus and forward to the Golden Age. The cap which makes for the invisible is familiar enough in fairy tales. But Mr. Wells has not obtained a smattering of science for naught. It was Huxley and Tyndall who made him possible, although both would have loathed his conclusions; and he gives us a fairy tale with a plausible scientific justification. The imagination is everything, the science is nothing; but the end of the century, which shares Mr. Wells's smattering of South Kensington, prefers the two together; and I sympathise with the end of the century. *The Time Machine* and *The Invisible Man*—Mr. Wells's first and last books—make capital reading, and one is the complement to the other. *The Time Machine* pictured the effects of physical experiments which should be able to transport one into other ages, separated by æons, it may be, from our own. We have heard of these future ages before. Two at least of our great Victorian poets have dreamt of them. Tennyson believed, at one time at least, that it meant the widening of the thoughts of men and 'the federation of the world.' Morris conceived of a social life fragrant with the love of man for man. This optimism has left us. Mr. Wells's future is a world in which men have harked back to cannibalism and intellectual life is dead. Similar pessimism follows Mr. Wells into his new book. Scientific experiment never makes the world any better or happier. Mr. Wells's 'Invisible Man'—Griffin is his name—has succeeded in rendering his body invisible, although it retains its corporeal character. Yet what misery this 'triumph of science' entails on its discoverer will be learned by many an eager reader. Griffin had thought to lord it over all his race. To have 'a good time' was the motive of his experiments, but one misfortune follows upon another until the wretched man hates his fellows and becomes fiendish in his attempts to war with them. Scientific research is indeed vanity if we are to accept Mr. Wells as a guide. That is only one interpretation of his book. The important thing to note is that the author has conceived of his creation with a splendid mastery of detail. Point after point helps to fix Griffin in his wanderings vividly upon the imagination, and at every turn we learn most realistically how disastrous his new power must be to him. Only children, for example, to whom life offers no mysteries, would have followed the footprints of the hunted man. But to write all this is perhaps to treat the matter too seriously. The story, which is bound to be popular, has not a suspicion of preaching about it, and in a quite unpretentious way will help to pass an amusing hour or so. I have not been so fascinated by a new book for many a day.

14. Joseph Conrad's impression

4 December 1898

Extract from letter to Wells in *Joseph Conrad: Life and Letters* (1927), ed. G. Jean-Aubry, i, pp. 259–60.

Conrad had gained his first literary recognition through Wells's enthusiastic review of *Almayer's Folly* (*Saturday Review*, 15 June 1895, xxix, 797). Their correspondence began as a result of this, and as near-neighbours on the Kent coast from 1898 their relations were cordial if never intimate. Conrad later dedicated *The Secret Agent* to Wells (1907), and its subtitle, 'A Simple Tale', echoes that of *Kipps*.

Frankly—it is uncommonly fine. One can always *see* a lot in your work—there is always a 'beyond' to your books—but into this (with due regard to theme and length) you've managed to put an amazing quantity of effects. If it just misses being tremendous, it is because you didn't make it so—and if you didn't, there isn't a man in England who could. As to b—— furriners they ain't in it at all.

I suppose you'll have the common decency to believe me when I tell you I am always powerfully impressed by your work. Impressed is *the* word, O Realist of the Fantastic! whether you like it or not. And if you want to know what impresses me it is to see how you contrive to give over humanity into the clutches of the Impossible and yet manage to keep it down (or up) to its humanity, to its flesh, blood, sorrow, folly. *That* is the achievement! In this little book you do it with an appalling completeness.

15. W.T. Stead on the Wellsian 'Gruesome'

April 1898

Extract from 'The Latest Apocalypse of the End of the World', *Review of Reviews*, xvii, 389–96.

One of Wells's earliest admirers (see No. 1), Stead responded to the publication of *The War of the Worlds* with a long and enthusiastic article summarizing all Wells's fiction up to that date. In this passage he discusses *The Invisible Man* and 'The Star'.

Mr. Wells, as a novelist, cannot be said to deal in pleasant themes. He is a professor of the gruesome, a past master in the art of producing creepy sensations. I leave out of account his book *The Island of Doctor Moreau*, which ought never to have been written, and which Mr. Wells would consult his own reputation by withdrawing from circulation. But that is only an extreme instance of the note of the horrible, the weird and the uncanny which characterise all his writings. There is his story of *The Invisible Man*, for instance, the subject of which is a discovery by which it was possible for man to render himself absolutely invisible while retaining his body and all his faculties. The hero of this novel having possessed himself of this extraordinary gift, finds it a very dubious advantage. His invisibility did not extend to his raiment, and it was therefore necessary for him either to go stark naked, if he would be completely invisible, or else sacrifice the advantages of his invisibility without securing the ordinary commonplace advantages of visibility by dressing himself, and concealing the invisible void where the face should have been seen. The story is worked out with much ingenuity; but as if by irresistible gravitation towards the unpleasant, the invisible man passes through a series of disastrous experiences, until finally he goes mad, and is beaten to death as the only way of putting an end to a homicidal maniac with the abnormal gift of invisibility.

But Mr. Wells is a seer of gruesome visions. He spends his life imagining what would happen if one of the laws of Nature were altered just a little—with terrifying results. One of the latest of his tales, which appeared in the Christmas number of the *Graphic*, described the devastation that was wrought by the swoop of a blazing star so near the earth that its heat melted the snow on the Himalayas and swept hundreds of millions to sudden death. He has caught the trick of describing events which only exist in his imagination with the technical precision of a newspaper reporter. Leaving to the ordinary journalist the chronicling of the happenings of every day, he soars into space of Four Dimensions, and exults in nothing so much as in readjusting the familiar environment of daily life to the circumstances of a world altered, it may be only in one important particular, from that in which we live. Stories work out in his brain as a kind of mathematical problem. If human nature under such conditions evolved such results, what results would be evolved if this, that, or the other condition were revolutionised? And it must be admitted that Mr. Wells works out his problems with a skill which leaves all his rivals far behind.

THE WAR OF THE WORLDS

January 1898

16. St Loe Strachey, unsigned review in *Spectator*

29 January 1898, lxxx, 168–9

John St Loe Strachey (1860–1927), editor and proprietor of the *Spectator* from 1898 to 1925, and leader of the campaign against Wells's *Ann Veronica* in 1909.

In *The War of the Worlds* Mr. Wells has achieved a very notable success in that special field of fiction which he has chosen for the exercise of his very remarkable gift of narration. As a writer of scientific romances he has never been surpassed. Poe was a man of rare genius, and his art was perhaps greater than Mr. Wells's, though Mr. Wells has a well-cultivated instinct for style. But in Poe there is a certain vein of pedantry which makes much of even his best work tame and mechanical. The logical method which he invented, or at any rate perfected, is too clearly visible in his stories, and appears to cramp his imagination. Besides, in Poe there is always a stifling hothouse feeling which is absent from Mr. Wells's work. Even when Mr. Wells is most awful and most eccentric, there is something human about his characters. The Invisible Man is in many ways like one of Poe's creations; but yet we feel that Poe would have stiffened the invisible man into a splendidly ingenious automaton, not left him a disagreeable, but still possible, medical student. Both Poe and Mr. Wells are, of course, conscious or unconscious followers of Swift, but Mr. Wells keeps nearest to the human side of the author of Gulliver. In manner, however, as in scheme and incident, Mr. Wells is singularly original, and if he suggests any one in externals it is Defoe. There are several passages in *The War of the Worlds* which seem to recall the *History of the Plague*. Nevertheless, we should not be surprised to hear that Mr. Wells had never read Defoe's immortal book. In any case, the resemblance comes, we are certain, not from imitation, but from the parallel action of two very acute and sincere intelligences. Each had to get into something like the same mental attitude towards the things to be related, and hence the two narrations are something akin. We say 'sincere intelligences' advisedly. We feel that in spite of the wildness of Mr. Wells's story it is in no sort of sense a 'fake.' He has not written haphazard, but has imagined, and then followed his imagination with the utmost niceness and sincerity. To this niceness and sincerity Mr. Wells adds an ingenuity and inventiveness in the matter of detail which is beyond praise. Any man can be original if he may be also vague and inexpressive. Mr. Wells when he is most giving wings to his imagination is careful to be concrete and specific. Some sleights of chiaroscuro, some tricks of perspective, some hiding of difficult pieces of drawing with convenient shadows,—these there must be in every picture, but Mr. Wells relies as little as possible on such effects. He is not perpetually telling us that such-and-such things could not be described by mortal pen.

Mr. Wells's main design is most original. As a rule, those who pass beyond the poles and deal with non-terrestrial matters take their readers to the planets or the moon. Mr. Wells does not 'err so greatly' in the art of securing the sympathy of his readers. He brings the awful creatures of another sphere to Woking Junction, and places them, with all their abhorred dexterity, in the most homely and familiar surroundings. A Martian dropped in the centre of Africa would be comparatively endurable. One feels, with the grave-digger in *Hamlet*, that they are all mad and bad and awful there, or, if not, it is no great matter. When the Martians come flying through the vast and dreadful expanses of inter- planetary space hid in the fiery womb of their infernal cylinders, and land on a peaceful Surrey common, we come to close quarters at once with the full horror of the earth's invasion. Those who know the valleys of the Wey and the Thames, and to whom Shepperton and Laleham are familiar places, will follow the advance of the Martians upon London with breathless interest. The vividness of the local touches, and the accuracy of the geographical details, enormously enhance the horror of the picture. When everything else is so true and exact, the mind finds it difficult to be always rebelling against the impossible Martians. We shall not attempt here—it would not be fair to Mr. Wells's thrilling book— to tell the story of the Martian war. We may, however, mention one point of detail. Many readers will be annoyed with Mr. Wells for not having made his Martians rather more human, and so more able to receive our sympathy of comprehension, if not of approbation. A little reflection will, we think, show that this was impossible. This is the age of scientific speculation, and scientific speculation, rightly or wrongly, has declared that if there are living and sentient creatures on Mars they will be very different from men. Mr. Wells, whose knowledge of such speculations is obviously great, has followed the prevailing scientific opinion, and hence his appalling Martian monster—a mere brain surrounded by a kind of brown jelly, with tentacles for hands—a creature which, by relying upon machinery, has been able to dispense with almost everything connected with the body but the brain. Mr. Wells has made his Martians semi-globular and bisexual. Had he, we wonder, in his mind the passage in Plato's *Symposium* which describes how man was once two sexes in one, and had a round body? If he was not relying upon Plato's legend, it is curious to note how the scientific imagination has twice produced a similar result.

In Mr. Wells's romance two things have been done with marvellous power. The first is the imagining of the Martians, their descent upon the earth and their final overthrow. They were terribly difficult figures to bring on and keep on the stage, but the difficulty of managing their exit with a reasonable deference to the decencies of fictional probability was nothing but colossal. Yet Mr. Wells turns this difficulty triumphantly, as our readers will discover for themselves. The second thing which Mr. Wells has done with notable success is his description of the moral effects produced on a great city by the attack of a ruthless enemy. His account of the stampede from London along the great North Road is full of imaginative force.

[Quotes Bk I, ch. 16 'So much as they could see' to ' "The Martians are coming!" ']

That is a most remarkable piece of literary workmanship, and therefore we quote it, though far more sensational is the account of how the Martians turned their heat-ray on their victims, how they fed themselves by sucking into their own veins the blood of the men and women they caught, how they threw the canisters of black powder that blasted half London, and how they died in the end because they were not, like men, the descendants of those who have survived after millions of years of struggle with the bacteria that swarm in air, earth, and water. These, however, we must leave our readers to read about by themselves. That they will read with intense pleasure and interest we make no sort of doubt, for the book is one of the most readable and most exciting works of imaginative fiction published for many a long day. There is not a dull page in it, and virtually no padding. One reads and reads with an interest so unflagging that it is positively exhausting. *The War of the Worlds* stands, in fact, the final test of fiction. When once one has taken it up, one cannot bear to put it down without a pang. It is one of the books which it is imperatively necessary to sit up and finish. We will add one word of personal comment. Our readers may remember that some three or four months ago we tried to work out, *à propos* of Mr. Wells's book, which was then appearing serially, the possible results on mankind of a Martian invasion. Mr. Wells enters upon a similar inquiry, though on somewhat different lines. And now, before we leave Mr. Wells's book, we will add our one piece of adverse criticism. Why did he cumber his page with such a hopelessly conventional figure as the poor, mouthing, silly curate? A weak-minded curate of this kind is the sort of lay figure that any second-rate novelist might have borrowed out of a fictional costumier's cupboard. Mr. Wells should have been above so poor and strained a device. If it was necessary for him to use a stalking-horse of this kind, why not an editor, a publisher, an author, or an architect? Even a rector would have been a little fresher. One has had so many serio-comic curates in fiction that the mind really refuses to bite upon them.

17. Basil Williams, unsigned review in *Athenaeum*

5 February 1898, 178

A view of Wells's 'Cockneyism' from above.

Mr. Wells has evidently studied and attempted to imitate the methods of Jules Verne in this account of an attack from Mars on the earth. But while perceiving that Jules Verne's plausibility comes largely from a scrupulous exactitude in matter-of-fact details, he has not seen that matter-of-fact details need not necessarily be vulgar and commonplace. There is too much of the young man from Clapham attitude about the book; the narrator sees and hears exciting things, but he has not the gift of making them exciting to other people. He reminds one of the man of whom it was said that he had travelled to more interesting places and talked with more clever people than the rest of the world, but had really seen and heard nothing for himself. The idea of the invasion from Mars—which, by-the-by, Mr. Wells says he owes to somebody else*— is magnificent, and the machines and weapons used by the Martians for devastating the earth must have been stupendous; but the whole business fizzles away in the most disappointing fashion. For example, what a splendid opportunity is lost in the description of the exodus from London! One thinks what a writer with a great eye for poetical effect like Mr. Meredith would have made of such an idea; whereas Mr. Wells is content with describing the cheap emotions of a few bank clerks and newspaper touts, and the jostling in the road which might very well do for an account of a Derby crowd going to Epsom. Mr. Wells must look carefully to his writing; he began well, but he evidently writes too much now, and is too apt to trust solely to the effect of his blood-curdling ideas, without taking the trouble to give them distinction.

* This is a reference to his dedication of *The War of the Worlds* 'To my brother, Frank Wells, this rendering of his idea'.

18. Unsigned review, *Critic*

23 April 1898, n.s. xxix, 282

One of the earliest American reviews.

Following in the wake of the sciences for half a century is a new species of literary work, which may be called the quasi-scientific novel. From M. Verne's prophetic submarine boat to Mr. Waterloo's prehistoric caveman, one could classify a score of romances which try to put into imaginative form the latest results in science and mechanics. Like all literature, too, the new novel is not content with presenting living embodiments of truth, but is fain to make guesses at the future. It is as yet experimental, and is quite too young to have produced an enduring masterpiece. The whole group can claim nothing that will live very far into the next century. It is hopelessly doomed, not more by its lack of artistic breadth of treatment than by its slipshod style, which betrays all the haste of the daily 'leader' to get into type.

Had Mr. Wells not been forestalled by Mr. Du Maurier, he would probably have called the novel before us *The Martians*.* It is the story of the invasion of our earth by a company of intelligent beings from Mars. Kepler furnishes an appropriate motto: 'But who shall dwell in these worlds, if they be inhabited? Are we or they Lords of the World? And how are all things made for man?' Having created an atmosphere of reality for his story, the author proceeds in journalistic style to tell of the coming of the first cylinder. 'Flying swiftly and steadily towards me across that incredible distance, came the thing they were sending us.' Though the mysterious projectile fell near London, its arrival did not cause the sensation that an ultimatum to Spain would have done. Ten cylinders, each thirty yards in diameter and containing five Martians, arrived at intervals of twenty-four hours.

The war which ensues is melodramatic and shamefully one-sided. The strangers fight in vast spider-like engines, a hundred feet high, which stride along with the speed of a limited express. In each of these

---

* Du Maurier's *The Martian* was published in 1896.

'boilers on stilts' sat the guiding intelligence of the machine, smothering cities with seas of poisonous black smoke, and wiping out of existence artillery and battleships with his heat-ray, a sort of search-light which burned. As the gunner said, it was soon all up with humanity; we were beaten by superior mechanical genius. After completely subjugating humanity, the Martians are attacked from an unexpected quarter, and fall victims to our invisible allies, the bacteria. This is highly satisfactory and the happiest stroke in the plot.

Mr. Wells's conception of the Martians is not only daring as a piece of imaginative work, but interesting for its deduction from biological laws. He, in common with Mr. Du Maurier and Miss Corelli, is evidently a close student of M. Camille Flammarion. The highest intelligence in Mars, through the processes of evolution, is embodied in what is scarcely more than a huge round head with large protruding eyes, and a mouth surrounded by sixteen whip-like tentacles—a kind of octopus that is all brain. The complex apparatus of digestion is dispensed with, for he injects directly into his veins the blood of living creatures, including man. The interest of Mr. Wells's work is divided between the excitement of the story and speculations on the differentiated forms of life on this and other planets.

The author has written an ingenious and original work. Now and again in the intervals of a colloquial or hysterical style, one comes upon passages of sweetness and virility. The book has the tone of intense modernity, with notes of convincing realism and morbid horror. One misses the simplicity of Gulliver and the epic impressiveness of the stories of Sodom and Mt. Carmel. It is an Associated Press dispatch, describing a universal nightmare.

19. Unsigned review, *Academy*

29 January 1898, liv, 121–2

The two parts into which this review is divided were headed 'The Story' and 'Mr. Wells's Science' respectively.

I

Mr. Wells has done good work before, but nothing quite so fine as this. He has two distinct gifts—of scientific imagination and of mundane observation—and he has succeeded in bringing them together and harmoniously into play. Upon the scientific imagination depends the structure, the plot, of the whole thing. The worlds are Mars and the Earth. The Martians, whose planet, older, further from the sun than ours, was becoming uncomfortably cool, planned a descent upon a new abiding-place. Their extraordinary mechanical development enabled them to accomplish this. Projected with stupendous velocity in cylinders they alighted upon Woking Common. Here is Mr. Wells's description of one of them:

[Quotes Bk I, ch. 4 'A big greyish, rounded bulk' to 'shadow of the aperture'.]

The narrator is a student of moral philosophy living at Maybury Hill, and he becomes an eye-witness of many of the strange events that follow: of the construction by the Martians of their fighting-machines, of their advance upon London, of the rout of the military and flight of the populace, and of the ultimate and remarkable collapse by which the world is freed from the invaders. The course of evolution on Mars has been very different to ours: the Martians have all gone to brain. Here they move heavily because the gravitational force of the earth is greater than they are accustomed to. But their mechanical appliances are irresistible. They mount themselves upon vast walking tripods.

[Quotes Bk I, ch. 10 'Seen nearer' to 'it was gone'.]

With the accuracy of Mr. Wells's speculative science we deal elsewhere. It is extraordinarily detailed, and the probable departures from possibility are, at least, so contrived as not to offend the reader who has but a small smattering of exact knowledge. The consistency and definiteness of the descriptions create an adroit illusion. And, in any case, given the scientific hypotheses, the story as a whole is remarkably plausible. You feel it, not as romance, but as realism. Mr. Wells's art lies, we fancy, in the fact that, while his monsters are sufficiently like mankind to be terrible, his human beings are throughout so completely human. The inhabitants of Chertsey and Woking behave, in presence of the Martians, precisely as a Surrey suburban population would. Mr. Wells never relaxes his hold on the commonplace, everyday life, against which his marvels stand out so luridly. A thousand deft and detailed touches create an atmosphere of actuality, bring the marvels into the realistic plane. The moral philosopher himself is thoroughly natural from beginning to end. So is the drunken artilleryman, who devises a brilliant scheme for living the life of a rat in a London subject to the invaders. He is not sure that it will not be better than civilisation. On the other hand, the imbecile and greedy curate with whom the narrator foregathers, and whom he is reluctantly compelled to slay, seems to us to introduce a needlessly farcical element. Mr. Wells must have suffered from curates lately, we should think.

As a crowning merit of the book, beyond its imaginative vigour and its fidelity to life, it suggests rather than obtrudes moral ideas. The artilleryman with his scorn of the 'damn little clerks' who would willingly be fattened for Martian dietary, and might even be trained to hunt their wilder fellows, has some truth on his side. In the light of the imagined cataclysm certain follies and meannesses of our civilisation stand out. Our smallness, after all, in the universe receives its illustration. It is a thoughtful as well as an unusually vivid and effective bit of workmanship.

II

Mr. H. G. Wells has probably a greater proportion of admirers among people actively engaged in scientific work than among any other section of the reading public. It is not difficult to understand the reason of this. Nothing irritates a man of science more than incorrect assertions with reference to natural facts and phenomena; and the writer who essays to use such material must obtain information from Nature herself, or he will provoke the derision of better informed readers. Mr. Wells has a practical familiarity with the facts of science, and this knowledge, combined with his imaginative mind, enables him to command the attention of readers who are not usually interested in romance.

The fact that Mr. Wells has been able to present the planet Mars in a new light is in itself a testimony to originality. The planet has been brought within the world of fiction by several writers, but in the *War of the Worlds* an aspect of it is dealt with altogether different from what has gone before. We have had a number of stories of journeys to Mars, but hitherto, so far as we remember, the idea of an invasion by inhabitants of Mars has not been exploited. Astronomers can make out just enough of the planet's surface to justify the conclusion that water and ice or snow exist there, and that the land areas are at times traversed by a network of canals or channels more or less enigmatical in origin. According to Mr. Percival Lowell, who made an exhaustive study of Mars in 1894, these canals are really belts of fertilised land, and are the only habitable tracts on Mars, the remainder of the land surface being desert. The view that the Martians—it is less unreasonable to think that Mars is inhabited than that it is not—would look towards our earth with longing eyes is thus quite within the bounds of legitimate speculation; and the fact that Mr. Wells put it forward before Mr. Lowell had brought before the attention of British astronomers the reasons for thinking that Mars at the present time is mostly a dreary waste from which all organic life has been driven, is a high testimony to his perceptive faculties. In other words, the reasons given for the invasion of the Earth by Mars are perfectly valid from a scientific point of view, and are supported by the latest observations of the nature of the planet's surface.

Then, as to the intellectual status of whatever inhabitants there may be on Mars, there is every reason for thinking that it would be higher than that of man. On this matter the following words, written by a distinguished observer of Mars—M. E. M. Antoniadi—in July last, give evidence to the view of the Martians presented by Mr. Wells. Referring to the origin of the canal systems, M. Antoniadi wrote:

Perhaps the least improbable—not to say the most plausible—clue to the mystery still attaches to the overbold and almost absurd assumption that what we are witnessing on Mars is the work of rational beings immeasurably superior to man, and capable of dealing with thousands and thousands of square miles of grey and yellow material with more ease than we can cultivate or destroy vegetation in a garden one acre in extent.

Naturally, the view that beings immeasurably superior to man exist upon Mars is repugnant, but we see by the words quoted that astronomers are being forced to accept it as the easiest method of explaining the phenomena observed. Mr. Wells's idea of the invasion of the earth by emigrants of a race possessing more effective fighting machinery than we have is thus not at all impossible; and the verisimilitude of the narrative appeals more strongly, perhaps, to scientific readers than to others not so familiar with accepted opinion upon the points deftly introduced.

The most striking characteristic of the work is not, however, the description of the Martians, but the way they are disposed of after they had invaded the Earth. We venture to assert that scientific material has never been more cleverly woven into the web of fiction than it is in the epilogue of this story. The observations of Pasteur, Chaveau, Buchner, Metschnikoff, and many others, have made the germ theory of disease an established truth. In the struggle for existence man has acquired, to a certain extent, immunity against the attacks of harmful micro-organisms, and there is little doubt that any visitors from another planet would not be able to resist these insidious germs of disease. The Earth itself furnishes analogous instances: Englishmen who migrate to the West Coast of Africa, or the strip of forest land in India known as the Terai, succumb to malarial disease, and the Pacific Islander who comes to reside in London or another large British city, almost certainly perishes from tuberculosis. Mr. Wells expresses the doctrine of acquired immunity so neatly that not to quote his words would be to do him an injustice.

[Quotes Bk II, ch. 8 'These germs of disease' to 'die in vain'.]

The book contains many other paragraphs which happily express scientific views, but we must refrain from quoting them. Not for an instant, however, do we think that Mr. Wells owes his success to mere correctness of statement. Science possesses a plethora of facts and ideas, yet not once in a generation does a writer arise competent to make use of them for purposes of romance. Already Mr. Wells has his imitators, but their laboured productions, distinguished either by prolixity or inaccuracy, neither excite the admiration of scientific readers nor attract the attention of the world in general.

20. R. A. Gregory, review in *Nature*

10 February 1898, lvii, 339–40

Sir Richard Gregory, F.R.S. (1864–1952) had been a fellow student of Wells at the Normal School of Science and became a lifelong friend. He was editor of *Nature* (1919–39) and is described in the *Dictionary of National Biography* as 'the greatest scientific journalist of his day'.

Many writers of fiction have gathered material from the fairy-land of science, and have used it in the construction of literary fabrics, but none have done it more successfully than Mr. H. G. Wells. It is often easy to understand the cause of failure. The material may be used in such a way that there appears no connection between it and the background upon which it is seen; it may be so prominent that the threads with which it ought to harmonise are thrown into obscurity; or (and this is the worst of all) it may be employed by a writer whose knowledge of natural phenomena is not sufficient to justify his working with scientific colour. Mr. Wells makes none of these mistakes. Upon a groundwork of scientific fact, his vivid imagination and exceptional powers of description enable him to erect a structure which intellectual readers can find pleasure in contemplating.

The Time Machine—considered by the majority of scientific readers to be Mr. Wells's best work—showed at once that a writer had arisen who was not only familiar with scientific facts, but who knew them intimately enough to present a view of the future. *The Island of Doctor Moreau*, though decried by some critics, is a distinctly powerful work, and the worst that can be said of it is that the pabulum it provides is too strong for the mental digestion of sentimental readers. But in several respects *The War of the Worlds* is even better than either of these contributions to scientific romance, and there are parts of it which are more stimulating to thought than anything that the author has yet written.

The invasion of the earth by inhabitants of Mars is the idea around which the present story is constructed. The planet is, as Mr. Percival Lowell puts it, older in age if not in years than the earth; and it is not unreasonable to suppose that if sentient beings exist upon it they would regard our world as a desirable place for occupation after their own globe had gone so far in the secular cooling as to be unable to support life. Mr. Wells bring the Martians to the earth in ten cylinders discharged from the planet and precipitated in Surrey. The immigrants are as much unlike men as it is possible to imagine, and only a writer familiar with the lines of biological development could conceive them. The greater part of their structure was brain, which sent enormous nerves to a pair of large eyes, an auditory organ, and sixteen long tactile tentacles arranged about the mouth; they had none of our complex apparatus of digestion, nor did they require it, for instead of eating they injected into their veins the fresh living blood of other creatures. Their organisms did not sleep any more than the heart of man sleeps; they multiplied by budding; and no bacteria entered into the scheme of their life. When they came to the earth they brought with them a means of producing a ray of intense heat which was used in connection with a heavy vapour to exterminate the inhabitants of London and the neighbourhood.

This bald outline does not, however, convey a good idea of the narrative, which must be read before the ingenuity which the author displays in manipulating scientific material can be appreciated. The manner in which the Martians are disposed of is undoubtedly the best instance of this skill. As the Martians had eliminated micro-organisms from their planet, when they came to the earth their bodies were besieged by our microscopic allies, and they were destroyed by germs to which natural selection has rendered us immune. This is a distinctly clever idea, and it is introduced in a way which will allay the fears of those who may be led by the verisimilitude of the narrative to expect an invasion from Mars. Of course, outside fiction such an event is hardly worth consideration; but that the possibility of it can be convincingly stated, will be conceded after reading Mr. Wells' story. A remarkable case of the fulfilment of fiction is furnished by the history of the satellites of Mars. When Dean Swift wrote *Gulliver's Travels* (published in 1726), he made the astronomers on the island of Laputa not only observe two satellites, but caused one of these to move round the planet in less time than the planet itself takes to rotate on its axis. As every student of astronomy knows, the satellites were not discovered until 1877, and one of them actually does revolve round Mars three times while the planet makes a rotation. The coincidence is remarkable; but it is to be hoped, for the sake of the peace of mind of terrestrial inhabitants, that Mr. Wells does not possess the prophetic insight vouchsafed to Swift.

In conclusion, it is worth remark that scientific romances are not without a value in furthering scientific interests; they attract attention to work that is being done in the realm of natural knowledge, and so create sympathy with the aims and observations of men of science.

21. H. G. Wells on reviewers in the 1890s

1934

Extract from *Experiment in Autobiography*, ii, pp. 507–8.

Wells recalls that the 1890s were an 'extraordinarily favourable time for new writers. . . . New books were being demanded and fresh authors were in request.' Criticism, however, remained hidebound by precedent.

Literary criticism in those days had some odd conventions. It was still either scholarly or with scholarly pretensions. It was dominated by the mediaeval assumption that whatever is worth knowing is already known and whatever is worth doing has already been done. Astonishment is unbecoming in scholarly men and their attitude to newcomers is best expressed by the word 'recognition.' Anybody fresh who turned up was treated as an aspirant Dalai Lama is treated, and scrutinized for evidence of his predecessor's soul. So it came about that every one of us who started writing in the nineties, was discovered to be 'a second'—

somebody or other. In the course of two or three years I was welcomed
as a second Dickens, a second Bulwer Lytton and a second Jules Verne.
But also I was a second Barrie, though J.M.B. was hardly more than
my contemporary, and, when I turned to short stories, I became a
second Kipling. I certainly, on occasion, imitated both these excellent
masters. Later on I figured also as a second Diderot, a second Carlyle
and a second Rousseau. . . .

Until recently this was the common lot. Literature 'broadened down
from precedent to precedent.' The influence of the publisher who wanted
us to be new but did not want us to be *strange*, worked in the same
direction as educated criticism. A sheaf of second-hand tickets to literary
distinction was thrust into our hands and hardly anyone could get a
straight ticket on his own. These second-hand tickets were very convenient as admission tickets. It was however unwise to sit down in the
vacant chairs, because if one did so, one rarely got up again. Pett Ridge
for instance pinned himself down as a second Dickens to the end of his
days. I was saved from a parallel fate by the perplexing variety of my
early attributions.

LOVE AND MR. LEWISHAM

June 1900

22. Unsigned review, *Daily Telegraph*

6 June 1900, 11

In this and the following review the 'healthy' realism of *Love and Mr. Lewisham* is contrasted with the decadence of the 1890s.

Take a young man with the highest ideals and a lamentable lack of appreciation of the world as it is, give him a generous supply of vaulting ambition, and place him in circumstances against which fate has not fitted him to fight, and you get the keynote of a tragedy. Hence we wonder whether it is tragedy or comedy with which Mr. Wells is dealing in his latest novel. His method is in direct opposition to the so-called realistic spirit of modern literature. He has an infinite tenderness for the ordinary, a tenderness almost maternal, were it not for the fact that mothers, as a class, have no sense of humour—the rose-coloured glass through which Mr. Wells sees what others find merely vulgar or sordid. He does not, however, idealize the commonplace. He lifts it on to a different plane, and as the springs of humour and pathos lie very close together, the two often melt into one another so indefinably that the touch which will raise a smile in one reader will bring to others a tear.

A curious wave of what one might call domestic sentiment seems to be sweeping over the novelist of today, and the storm-tossed hero and heroine now find salvation, not in each other's love, but rather in the foundation of a family. This is a surprising outcome of our supposed decadence. ' "The future is the Child. The Future. What are we—any of us—but servants or traitors to that? . . ." ' And so Mr. Lewisham, student at the Royal College of Science, buries his dreams of a Career—

with a very big C—in the cradle of his first-born. Love teaches him a few things, life teaches him many. And so, though he frankly recognizes in his farewell interview with his platonic friend that the two have far more in common, and have far more sympathy with one another than he can hope to find in his matrimonial relations, he goes back to his wife cheerfully, nay lovingly, because ' "this way is happiness . . . must be. There can be no other. . . . To last a lifetime, that is." ' It is the family affection that endures, and Mr. Lewisham realizes that there is no finer career than that of a father.

The story is hardly more than a sequence of events, following on the romance of a very ordinary young man, who marries more or less in haste, and who would repent at leisure, but for his determination to break down the barrier which incompatibility of temperament—almost worse than that of temper—aided by the constant wear-and-tear of sordid troubles, builds up in a few months between him and his wife. The scene wherein he faces the difficulties of the matrimonial situation and suddenly resolves to wipe out the past and get back to the old footing is one of the truest in the book. But how to get back? He passes a florist's, with the window full of roses. The flowers express his emotions, they shall cut the knotty problem. And so they do, though not exactly on the lines designed by him. One can never quite get back, but Mr. Lewisham retraces a considerable portion of his steps at a bound, and the dividing paths once more converge. With his genius for the commonplace, Mr. Wells manages to secure a very large amount of sympathy and interest for his underbred, loveable hero, endowed with a somewhat useless catalogue of 'ologies' and 'ographies,' and an infinite ignorance of the ways of the world. The pretty, affectionate, foolish wife is, perhaps, less loveable, but no less cleverly drawn, while one of the characters which takes very firm hold of us is the friend, Alice Heydinger, the pathos of whose life lies in the knowledge of all she might have done for the man she loves but for her own physical unattractiveness and the intervention of another woman's pretty face. Mr. Wells is possessed of two entirely separate and opposite imaginations: with a gift for the uncanny, which is as fascinating as it is rare, he combines a wonderful talent for the depiction of the commonplace. Enthusiasts for *When the Sleeper Wakes*, *The War of the Worlds* and *The Time Machine* will not recognize their favourite author in the creator of Mr. Lewisham. He has once more adopted his 'Hoopdriver' manner, and his new novel is a successor to *The Wheels of Chance* rather than to any of his more imaginative works. In *Love and Mr. Lewisham*, however he strikes a deeper note than heretofore, and though the book begins very brightly, it ends in a minor key. Nevertheless, it will by many be regarded as by far the most fascinating piece of work he has given us.

23. Unsigned review, *Daily Chronicle*

14 June 1900, 3

In this, his latest story, Mr. Wells is at his very best. When we read *The Wheels of Chance* we felt pretty sure that it was in that *genre*, and not in the extra-scientific romance, that Mr. Wells would find his true métier. Now we are quite convinced of it. When he brings to bear upon human character the close, accurate observation which has been cultivated by his scientific studies, he produces first-class work.

Mr. Wells looks at the same type of people, the same social class, that Mr. Gissing and Mr. Anstey look at, but he looks at them through other eyes and through a different temperament. In our opinion those eyes of his are more true-sighted, his temperament a finer, because a more genial, one than theirs. In the lower, or, to be quite accurate, in the poorer, middle-class Mr. Anstey sees only subjects for his wit, and right excellent fun he makes of them; Mr. Gissing sees only their griminess, their sordidness, sometimes their sorrow, he takes the gray-tragic view; Mr. Wells, like a real man of science, and a true artist too, sees all there is to see, and presents it with care and craft.

In *Love and Mr. Lewisham* Mr. Wells portrays the life of the fifth-rate assistant master, the one who has no university degree, no high skill in 'games' to recommend him, but only his certificates from South Kensington. And it is wonderfully well done. For the moment we cannot think of anything better of its sort. Our sympathies are enlisted at once for poor Lewisham, with his small capacities, his meagre opportunities and his vaulting ambitions. So many other authors would have compelled us only to a kind of good-natured contempt. We have seldom read a better presentation of young, budding love than is given us in that walk in the country of Mr. Lewisham's with Ethel—with Ethel who was destined to scatter his ambitions, to break up his career, and to hold down his life on the lower planes. In that little scene is struck the motive of the book. Love came to Mr. Lewisham as a destroyer, an annihilator, the while he fondly imagined him to be an inspirer, a helper to greatness. But after all—and herein is manifested the author's temperament—Love the Destroyer did not destroy everything. He left much behind, and much that was right well worth having. A Career (Mr. Lewisham always spelled it with a capital letter) was ended before it was well begun; examinations which should have been passed triumphantly were hopelessly 'muffed'; those pamphlets 'in the Liberal interest' which were to have elevated and revolutionised politics were never written; the new socialist party was never formed and never found its leader, but there was still Ethel and the Child. As Mr. Lewisham said:

[Quotes ch. 32 'Come to think' to 'only a sort of play'.]

The married life of the man (he married on a pound a week and with fifty pounds in the bank) is made intensely interesting to us. For one moment we are positively harrowed because we feel that poverty having entered the door Love is really about to fly out of the window, as he undoubtedly would have flown had Mr. Gissing had anything to do with it. But he doesn't. He never gets further than the window-ledge. He remains, though he is the only good thing that does remain. As bits of delineation Mr. Lewisham, Ethel and Miss Heydinger are excellent; but Chaffery, Ethel's stepfather, is masterly. He is a delightful, humorous, and searching analysis of the Fraud. But he is something more than an analysis, a dissection, because only the dead can be effectively dissected, and Chaffery is alive to his villainous and most adroit finger tips. His defence of cheating is a whole rogue's philosophy done in a couple of pages. And a philosophy that is tenable, too, against a good many forms of attack.

The literary style of Mr. Wells has vastly improved. There is no stumbling here, and fewer words for whose meaning one has to search the latest dictionary. The descriptive pages are charming, the dialogue real and bright.

24. Unsigned review, *Saturday Review*

16 June 1900, lxxxix, 752–3

From Mr. Wells, novel-readers have come to expect a startling original plot and a breezy atmosphere. What then must be their disappointment when they turn to his latest narrative and find neither monsters nor machinery, not the minutest deviation from the sloughs of monotonous mediocrity, never even the promise of a surprise. Mr. Wells must suffer from that yearning for versatility, which has so often affected great men too. He is evidently coquetting with the decadent school and may be deemed an apt pupil, for a more morbid, sordid, hopelessly dull and depressing dissection of characters it were difficult to conceive. We wallow in gloom from cover to cover amid a succession of dreary episodes and when we reach the end the clouds remain as thick as ever, no dramatic climax, whether of relief or disaster, is foreshadowed, and we come away with a choking sensation as from the worst stations of the underground railway. No doubt Mr. Wells would retort that here is a tribute to his art in depicting the sordid hopelessness of the life of the lower middle classes; but to do that, he should have created a hero and heroine capable of arousing sympathy for undeserved sufferings. Whether or no he meant to teach, he has certainly failed to interest or amuse, and we can only hope that he may quickly return to those old fields, where the Pegasus of his imagination roamed uncurbed.

25. Unsigned review, *Speaker*

16 June 1900, n.s. ii, 312–13

Mr. H. G. Wells's new book, with the distressing title *Love and Mr. Lewisham*, is the work of the author of *Select Conversations with an Uncle*,* not of the author of *The Time Machine*. In a sense this is a relief. We were getting tired of the mechanical reproduction of pessimistic prophecy, and were ready to welcome a clever psychological problem, such as Mr. Wells knows so well how to propound, in a less gloomy atmosphere. Unfortunately we must admit a disappointment. *Love and Mr. Lewisham*, though its theme is the triumph of love over ambition and friendship, is permeated with that air of weary disillusionment which has spoiled the artistic effect of so much of Mr. Wells's later works. It is hard to determine what is the cause of this falling off, whether it is over-production or something radically wrong in the author's art. We cannot believe that the author of *The Time Machine* is altogether without a sense of style, yet it is hard to excuse such clap-trap as the following, which ends the most emotional chapter [ch. 29] of the book:—

> He drew her closer to him.
> He kissed her neck. She pressed him to her.
> Their lips met.
> The expiring candle streamed up into a tall flame, flickered, and was suddenly extinguished. The air was heavy with the scent of roses.

The fault lies deeper than in the mere arrangement of words and sentences. We have noticed in many of Mr. Wells's earlier and more promising works a disproportionate realism that almost amounted to vulgarity. He has allowed this to develop at the expense of his finer imagination, and has left little in its place to clothe his naked cleverness.

For clever Mr. Wells undoubtedly is, perhaps the cleverest of living novelists, and, if we did not believe that he was something more, we should not trouble to find fault when there is so much to praise. This study of a fairly commonplace young student's life, with its struggles,

* The collection of newspaper sketches he published in 1895.

ambition, failures, and final engulfment in a devouring love is a master-piece of critical analysis. But there is a side character in this book in which Mr. Wells has displayed his keen intellect at its best. It is, perhaps, the most original character he has created. This is Mr. Chaffery, the cheating medium, whose intellectual gymnastics are as entertaining as anything we have read for a long time and full of new and suggestive ideas. Take, for example, his remarks on a spiritualist whom he has just robbed:—

[Quotes ch. 30 'I marvel at that man' to 'alleged man of Chelsea!']

Love and Mr. Lewisham is distinctly one of the most amusing and read-able books of the year. We only wish that Mr. Wells had not written it.

ANTICIPATIONS AND MANKIND IN THE MAKING

November 1901 September 1903

26. Unsigned review, *Westminster Gazette*

12 November 1901, 1

If any of our readers want relief from current politics, we can scarcely advise them to do better than devote a few hours to Mr. H. G. Wells's *Anticipations*, which have interested the readers of the *Fortnightly Review* for several months past, and were published yesterday in book form. We should like to see this little book widely circulated among business-men and politicians, not by any means because we agree with everything that is in it, but because it applies a useful explosive to the conventional, acquiescent, complacent frame of mind which Lord Rosebery told us the other day was our besetting sin. Here at all events is an open mind busily engaged in criticising the present, by the standard of a possible future. Mr. Wells starts from the assumption not that whatever is is best, but that whatever is is certain to give place to better. It takes some courage to be a prophet, and our present prophet begins frankly by revising his own past predictions. He wrote a dismal romance a very few years ago which pictured the city of the future as packed with an intolerable crowd, the less fortunate of whom were driven into the bowels of the earth, while the more fortunate found air and light at the top of monstrous buildings of immense altitude.* This he now admits to be a mistaken idea. The modern city, as recent census-returns have shown, is thinning out from its centre, and we may permissibly think of the city of the future as half country and half town, spreading out as the means of locomotion improve, and organising itself according to types of character and occupation. Our prophet, therefore, is not infallible, and when he passes from the material to the moral we often

* 'A Story of the Days to Come'.

fail to follow him. In assuming, for instance, that the moral changes of the next hundred years will be on the same scale as the mechanical changes of the last hundred years, he seems to us greatly to underrate the conservatism of human nature. Opinion does not advance steadily; it is subject to reactions which arrest its progress, and even take it back to an earlier stage. If anyone at the end of the eighteenth century could have predicted the immense mechanical changes of the nineteenth century, he would, we think, have presumed a much greater moral change than has actually taken place. Mr. Wells makes too little allowance, it seems to us, for that romantic and mystical element in human nature which continues to move on its own plane in spite of all the developments of material science.

However, with Mr. Wells's main thesis we are disposed to agree. The successful society of the future will depend in the main on an intelligent, scientific middle-class, strenuous, efficient, serious, and highly educated. Aristocracy and plutocracy there will still be, but since in the scientific states of the future training and efficiency will count for everything, those who rely on money and birth cannot play the part that they played in simpler organisations. They will tend more and more to supply the decorative, non-efficient side of life, unless, indeed, luxury and ease spoil them for any serious purpose whatever. The efficient, professional, engineering scientific people will be recruited from the best of the wealthy and the best of the working-class, and they will be to human society what the working-bee is to the hive. In the main, we say, we believe this is true. Wealth and aristocracy are breaking down as governing forces before our eyes. The demand for secondary education which every day grows louder is, in effect, the demand for a class which shall save the country in industry and in administration, just as the aristocracy of a previous period saved it in war and high politics. But Mr. Wells paints his efficient class in rather drab colours. It is distinctly a dull class, as he presents it to us. It is segregated and special-ised; it lives wholly for its serious pursuits, feeds on Blue-books and biscuits, passes its learned and scientific periodicals from door to door, has no time to play the fool, or to relax its strained attention. It will deserve our respect and our gratitude, but we fear at this rate it will never be popular. Frankly, we do not believe it will fall out thus. Human beings will never be segregated into these classes of the serious and the frivolous, the decorative and the efficient. Happily there is no incompatibility between the two. A mathematician may also be a musician; indeed, frequently is a very good one.

Mr. Wells contrives very skilfully to make us ashamed of our conservatism. How little we realise the changes that are going on and how stubbornly we resist them! We hate the motor-car as our grandfathers hated the railway. Think of the police in rural districts being drawn off all their ordinary duties in order to time motor-cars, as if safety depended on speed, and not on the capacity of the driver to guide, stop, and control his vehicle; and as if an incompetent driver could not do all the possible damage at twelve miles an hour. We work on the false analogy of the horse and probably shall continue to do so for a generation, but the consequence, of course is that the automobile trade goes to France and America. Think, again, of the stupidity of the ordinary domestic house, its absence of lifts and automatic sanitary appliances which would at once relieve domestic servants of the worst half of their labours. Think, again, of the art of war and the stubborn reluctance of military men to adjust themselves to scientific appliances. Whether or not the future will be as Mr. Wells imagines, he certainly makes us feel that we have hardly as yet begun to realise what it may be. Have we all lived too soon?

27. Beatrice Webb's reaction

December 1901

Diary entry, published in *Our Partnership* (1948), p. 226.

Beatrice Webb (1858–1943) and her husband Sidney invited Wells to join the Fabian Society after reading *Anticipations* and *Mankind in the Making*. As Wells recalled it, 'They appeared riding very rapidly upon bicycles, from the direction of London, offering certain criticisms of my general forecast and urging me to join and stimulate the Fabians. . . . Their essential criticism of *Anticipations* was that I did not sufficiently recognize the need and probability of a specialized governing class' (Introduction to 1914 edn, p. xi).

The most remarkable book of the year: a powerful imagination furnished with the data and methods of physical science, working on social problems. The weak part of Wells' outfit is his lack of any detailed knowledge of social organisation—and this, I think, vitiates his capacity—for foreseeing the future machinery of government and the relation of classes. But his work is full of luminous hypotheses and worth careful study by those who are trying to look forward. Clever phrases abound, and by the way proposals on all sorts of questions—from the future direction of religious thought, to the exact curve of the skirting round the wall of middle class abodes.

28. Unsigned notice, *Literary World*

1 August 1902, 118

If anyone wishes to know what a very cocksure person, 'well up' in two or possibly three of the natural sciences, but comprehensively ignorant of history, ethics and the social sciences in general, thinks mankind will be and do in the year 2000 A.D., this is the book for him. The author is a well-known novelist who has dealt extensively with the possible future of men after the manner of fiction, and his novels have had a certain attractiveness for many. Certainly they deserve a wider reading than these *Anticipations*, which are not put in the form of fiction, but seem as purely the construction of a single brain working narrowly and arbitrarily as any novel could well be.

The work is placed before us as a very sober and coldly reasoned sketch of the actual society of a century from now. As such it invites criticism most of all from the historian. Let such a one compare any two periods of human history a hundred years apart and he will certainly find no such lack of continuity as Mr. Wells imagines between the society of today and the society of 2000 A.D. This society is ruled by the men of science and the shareholders, an aristocracy of a pattern yet unknown. Morally the future society is at loose ends, and politically it is reversion to the time before democracy; religiously it is indifferent to all forms of creed.

One must be free to remark that this picture throws more light upon the limitations of Mr. Wells's own culture than it does upon the probable evolution of society. It is no more reliable than the countless novels of the future unhappily so familiar in recent years and so profitless. The book is a travesty of possibilities.

29. Unsigned review of *Mankind in the Making*, *Academy and Literature*

26 September 1903, lxv, 285–6

We may briefly distinguish the present volume from Mr. Wells's previous work by characterising it as thought rather than imagination. That fundamental psychological process known as the 'association of ideas' is doubtless at the basis of both thought and imagination, nor do we wish to draw any untenable and rigid distinction; but we recommend those who have been amused or interested by the imaginative aspect of Mr. Wells's mind, closely to study this new book, wherein the more untrammelled associative process has been subordinated to that logical, self-critical and orderly concatenation of ideas which may be perfectly distinguished as thought, and which is, probably, in its highest development, the essential factor in the production of philosophic genius.

Having first stated, then, our belief that these essays constitute a serious contribution to modern thought on the most instant and important of all topics, it may perhaps be fitting to make a somewhat personal comment thereupon. To put it in the vulgar phrase, Mr. Wells has now given the show away. He has repeatedly been suspected of being a serious person, and now he has put the matter beyond a doubt. He tells us that he has 'aspired to creative art,' nor do we mean it to be inferred that his previous work in fiction is not serious, worthy, and brilliant. Its value in our eyes—enlightened by the promise of this latest volume—is indirect, however. The satisfactory thing is not that, in conceiving, say, *The Time Machine*, Mr. Wells has done a new thing, nor is it that, as M. Jules Verne approached the limits of his fruitful period, a young man should arise, who might continue the work of beguiling the many-headed into some faint perception of the vistas and the high hopes and grave warnings of modern science, but rather it is that all his past work has served to shape and stimulate Mr. Wells's mind, and, most important of all, has given him an assured public to whom, in what we expect to be a long and fruitful career of serious, useful and brilliant thought, Mr. Wells may certainly appeal and whom he will certainly influence. For he is now in this position: he has revealed his possession of intellect as distinguished from artistic power. He is, therefore, on the principles of the New Republican whom he has conceived for us in this book, bound to use not only the latter, but both, in the service of the ideal which, with all thoughtful and sensitive souls, he has at heart: and there lies upon him the further responsibility that he is certain of his audience, that to many of the younger generation he will speak as one having authority, and that so much the greater is his already grave responsibility.

This book contains so many new ideas, and those of such magnitude and such complex inter-relation with a thousand others, that it would be quite impertinent to the function of this review to deal with the essays seriatim. The problems of sociology are, in the nature of the case, more complex than those of any other science. Each suggestion in these pages must be discussed in a thousand connections, and though we have followed them as they appeared in serial form in the *Fortnightly*, to have arrived at dogmatic conclusions would be to have arrived at none worth recording. For Mr. Wells has no fear. With the future of civilisation as his topic there were numberless main and side issues to attack, and he has his courageous and—as it seems to us—often immature opinions about them all. Immature, we say, not incorrect or indefensible. And here we come to what, perhaps, may be the best use of our space. We might, whilst indicating praise and pleasure, have entered into a series of criticisms upon those points of fact or of logic which seemed to us hardly impeccable. It might be worth while, for instance, to assert the indisputable existence of that hereditary disease which he questions in one essay, on the ground of the collective silence of a great body of specialists. Elsewhere, also, we might find occasion to point the view that Mr. Wells has been somewhat superficial in his thought and hasty in his conclusions, though no other instance is so conspicuous as that above referred to, as in it Mr. Wells has gone over the oldest of ground—remembering Moses, we may almost rigidly defend the word oldest—and has arrived, with an air of original finality, at very old and very plausible and hopelessly impracticable conclusions.

But our special point is this, that, having now written one semi-serious and one wholly serious—yet withal brilliant and vastly amusing —volume on Sociology, and having concerned himself with the formation of the Sociological Society which is to be born before the year is out, it behoves Mr. Wells to read, and read largely, the works of his few but great predecessors in the same field. If he will but read, he will certainly do so with a balanced judgment, a vigour of imagination, and a nice sense of discrimination that will make him as good ground as ever these sowers sowed their seed upon; he will yield not thirty-fold but an hundred-fold; but read he must. And, for reasons which we think we can present and justify, he really must read his Spencer. For here are some surprising facts to be gathered from these essays. To begin with, the name of the man who applied the central truth of evolution to sociology, and who is, by reason of that fact if of no other, the first and indispensable mentor of all young sociologists, occurs *only once* in Mr. Wells's four hundred pages! Enumerating somewhat scornfully those writers whose views on education have made an 'uproar,' Mr. Wells mentions Spencer, whose name is sandwiched between those of Tolstoi and Ruskin—of all persons whatever—and, in every other line, this book which is based, begun and ended on the Spencerian theory, is without an allusion to his name, and without a solitary quotation from his works. That this is no accident Mr. Wells shows by falling into many errors of suggestion and assumption, from which a proper knowledge of Spencer would have saved him. Having studied biology, Mr. Wells must needs begin with the conception of evolution, and he pays his respects to Darwin. He then applies the 'Darwinian' theory to the current problems of society, apparently unaware that—in *Social Statics*, if we are not mistaken—Mr. Spencer outlined more than half a century ago the very principles in question. As we read the individual papers we wondered why this or that consideration was ignored, this or that pregnant and familiar truth stated as virgin and novel, but the preface which now appears in the bound volume solves our doubts. This book, says Mr. Wells—

is an attempt to deal with social and political questions in a new way and from a new starting-point, viewing the whole social and political world as aspects of one universal evolving scheme, and placing all social and political activities in a defined relation to that.

'New!' Why, it dates from 1851. True, vital, central—certainly; but new—certainly not. The sentence we have quoted defines the pre-eminent achievement of Spencer's thought on Sociology. Then, again, what of this quotation from 'The Problem of the Birth Supply' (Chap. II.)? It constitutes the gist of the chapter and the text of the entire book:—

It seemed to me then that to prevent the multiplication of people below a certain standard, and to encourage the multiplication of exceptionally superior people, was the only real and permanent way of mending the ills of the world. I think that still.

But why not have gone to the fountain head and refer to the Spencerian dictum that the most detrimental result of any social action is 'to encourage the production of the unworthy at the expense of the worthy'? The whole theory of the New Republic is centred about this conception of the child: the great spout, which no man can stop, discharging a child, every eight seconds, into a hall where all thinkers and doers are assembled. Our thanks to Mr. Wells for that excellent image. Similarly, in his first essay, Mr. Wells says, with dubious grammar—

the point of view which will be displayed in relation to a number of wide questions in these pages is primarily that of the writer's,

—which is really an astonishing illusion. And in the delightfully plain-spoken and wise remarks on schooling (we must remind Mr. Wells, by the way, that 'triennial' does not mean 'three times a year') much immaturity and haste of thought might have been averted if Mr. Wells had really studied those educational views to which he makes that single and cursory allusion. He would have learnt, for instance, from a series of papers written by Spencer three decades ago, that almost the first thing to fight for in educational reform is the instruction of the teacher as to the manner in which knowledge is received and assimilated by the learner's mind; and from the tract on *Education*, a dozen years older, he would have learnt enough to suppress his contemptuous and most unthoughtful condemnation of elementary physiological truths as 'absurdly unsuitable' for teaching in schools. Similarly a wider reading would have averted his hasty dismissal of the piano in education. 'To have half learnt anything is a lesson in failure,' he says. Well, we ourselves can recall only two executants who had wholly learned the piano, and we know dozens of instances where a most imperfect knowledge of the instrument has been a foe to ennui, depression and insanity, or a source of fine and unending pleasure to many a hearing ear.

But what invaluable and perdurable thought Mr. Wells will turn out a quarter of a century hence.

30. Havelock Ellis, review in
Weekly Critical Review

19 February 1904

This review is taken from *Views and Reviews: First Series* (1932), 204–12, where it is said to have first appeared in the *Weekly Critical Review*.

Henry Havelock Ellis (1859–1939), critic and sexual psychologist.

Although prophets are nowadays rare among us, Mr. Bernard Shaw is not absolutely alone. We have others, and among them not one is better worth listening to than Mr. H. G. Wells. As we have seen, a prophet may be defined as a person who is something of a scientist and something of an artist and altogether a moralist. In science, while Mr. Shaw has occupied himself with political economy, Mr. Wells has had the advantage of a training in physical and biological work; as in art, just as Mr. Shaw has amused himself with writing plays, Mr. Wells has developed a singularly original kind of fiction, and thereby attained a wide reputation, not only in England, but also in France, being indeed the only Englishman so far assigned a place in the 'Célébrités d'Aujourd'-hui' series. As a moralist, Mr. Shaw is more brilliant and accomplished, for from the outset he has clearly held before him this most conspicuous part of the prophet's duty. Mr. Wells has here been somewhat shy and reticent; though he has frequently put a certain amount of morality into his fiction he has usually been anxious that it should only be visible to those who know how to find it; even a prophet must live, he seems to have said to himself; it is only within the last few years, in the maturity of his power and reputation, that he has boldly stepped into the public arena conspicuously enfolded in the prophet's mantle. With these points of resemblance in the two men there are yet very marked differences, founded on essential divergences of temperament. If the analogy of the bull-fight were not too irreverent for the occasion, it might be said that

Mr. Shaw performs his prophetic functions in the spirit of the banderil-lero; he approaches the stolid British bull with graceful bravado, not anxious to conceal from us the tremendous personal risks he is running, he brandishes his darts before the creature's eyes, and having adroitly planted them in its hide he retires, well satisfied that he has goaded it to fury and precipitated its final destruction. Mr. Wells, on the other hand, it is evident, emulates the methods of the matador; there is no airy aggressiveness here (unless, indeed, when he takes the animal before him to stand for the British schoolmaster), his manner is simple, seemingly placable, he holds his weapon behind his back, and he seeks to make the stroke of it direct, downright, decisive. Then let the New Republic be proclaimed forthwith! It is thus that Mr. Wells comes before us in his recent and extremely able book, *Mankind in the Making*.

It scarcely seems to me that this 'New Republic' of Mr. Wells's is quite a happy term. He uses it in no genuinely political sense, while its literary associations, from Plato to Mr. Mallock, do not greatly help him. The 'New Republic' of Mr. Wells has no relation to any existing party or faction. The New Republican has absorbed the modern conception of evolution, and the only social and political movements in which he is interested are those that 'make for sound births and sound growth.' His creed is thus expressed: 'We are here to get better births and a better result from the births we get; each one of us is going to set himself immediately to that, using whatever power he finds to his hand.' We live in a land, as Mr. Wells puts it, into which there may be said to be a spout discharging a baby every eight seconds. All our statesmen, philanthropists, public men, parties and institutions are engaged in a struggle to deal with the stream of babies which no man can stop. 'Our success or failure with that unending stream of babies is the measure of our civilisation.'

The problem with which Mr. Wells seeks to deal—whether or not we care to adopt the 'New Republican' label—is certainly of the first importance. To those few of us who reached this same standpoint many years back, and are trying to work towards the elucidation of the problem, it is a genuine satisfaction to find this question brought into the market-place so vigorously, so sanely, so intelligently. If a few critical comments have occurred to me as I followed Mr. Wells in his discussion of this tremendous problem, I set them down with no ungracious wish to minimise the value of his services in the cause he has undertaken to preach, which is, after all, the cause of all of us.

To survey life and to reorganise it, on so broad and sweeping a scale as Mr. Wells attempts, necessarily brings him into a great many fields which have been appropriated by specialists. Mr. Wells quite realises the dangers he thus runs, but it can by no means be said that he has altogether escaped them. In this way he sometimes seems to be led into unnecessary confusions and contradictions. One may observe this in the discussion of heredity which is inevitably a main part of his theme. Mr. Francis Galton has proposed that we should seek to improve the human race as we improve our horses and dogs, by careful breeding, in order to develop their best qualities. Mr. Wells argues, quite soundly in my opinion, that this will not work out, that we do not know what qualities we want to breed, nor how we are to get them. But Mr. Wells rushes to the other extreme when, without exactly proposing it, he suggests that there may be nothing unreasonable in mating people of insane family with 'dull, stagnant, respectable people,' in the hope that the mixture will turn out just right. We do certainly know that as a rule mad people are most decidedly not examples of 'genius out of hand,' but, on the contrary, people who have got into a monotonous rut that they cannot lift themselves out of; they are far more dull and stagnant than the respectable people, and the suggested mixture is scarcely hopeful. Again, Mr. Wells argues that, before we can make progress with this question of breeding desirable qualities, we require to be able to weed out those human qualities which are 'pre-eminently undesirable,' and then he proceeds to cast contempt on the study of criminology. But criminals represent exactly those stocks in the community which possess most of the pre-eminently undesirable qualities, and if we wish to weed such qualities out we cannot study criminology too carefully. It is certainly true that many foolish things have been said in the name of criminal anthropology, but so sagacious a thinker as Mr. Wells can have no difficulty in realising that it is unnecessary to pour away the baby with the bath.

Another more fundamental criticism occurs as we read Mr. Wells's pages, and one that more closely touches his prophetic mission. He appears before us as the apostle of Evolution; he states briefly, as a self-evident proposition, that 'man will rise to be overman'; the New Republican is always to bear that in mind. But while such a belief is certainly an aid to an inspiring gospel of life, it can by no means be admitted that it is self-evident. On the contrary, from an evolutionary point of view, there is not the slightest reason to suppose that man will ever rise to be overman. Evolution never proceeds far in a straight line, and while it is undoubtedly true that intelligence is a factor in evolution, it is by no means true that a very high degree of intelligence is specially likely to lead to the evolution of its possessor, it may even hinder it. Many species of ants are highly intelligent and 'civilised'—in some respects more so than various human peoples—yet we do not hear of the 'super-ant,' nor is it likely that we shall. As regards man it might be plausibly maintained that the typical Man reached his fullest and finest all-round development, as the highest zoological species, in the Stone Age some ten thousand years ago, that the Superman really began to arise with the discovery of writing, the growth of tradition and the multiplication of inventions some six or eight thousand years ago, and that we have now reached, not the beginning of the Superman but the beginning of the end of him. All we know of the 'evolution' of man in historical times is that each nation in turn has had its rise and its fall, breaking like a wave on the sands of time, but no man can say that the tide itself is clearly rising; as likely as not it is at the turn, for there are not many new nations left. We only know that there is movement, a little constant oscillation, that for all we know may be backwards and forwards in equal measure. No man can definitely say that France has produced finer persons than Greece, or England than Rome. We have all had a good conceit of ourselves; each of us in turn has believed that 'we are the people.' It is a belief that has helped us to make the best of ourselves.

And here we are led to the only remaining criticism of the New Republic that I have to offer. One feels throughout Mr. Wells's prophesyings a certain note of what I may perhaps venture to call without offence, parochialism. The evolution of man, if it means anything, must affect the whole species, and not a single section. Mr. Wells confines himself exclusively to the English-speaking lands, and through a great part of his book he is very much occupied with tinkering at some of our cherished English institutions. The preacher who set out by proclaiming salvation for mankind invites us to contribute to the fund for the new organ. Not only is Mr. Wells's 'mankind' thus narrowly limited, he even objects to the study of other nations. Ancient languages he taboos altogether; a knowledge of modern languages he regards as 'a rather irksome necessity, of little or no educational value.' He rightly insists that the pressing business of education is 'to widen the range of intercourse,' yet he fails to see that the possession of a key to the unfamiliar thoughts and feelings of an unknown people is the one effectual method by which such an end can be attained. It is vain to say that of most good books there are more or less good translations. The educational value of a language lies less in the statements contained in its literature than in its own untranslatable atmosphere, which brings us into a new sphere of influences and places us at a fresh point of view. The contradiction in Mr. Wells's attitude is still further emphasised by the fact that he very rightly insists on the importance of a thorough knowledge of the English language and literature. Yet it may safely be said that, putting aside a very few exceptional men of genius, there have been no great masters of English who were without insight and knowledge as regards at least one or two foreign languages, while the people whose ill-treatment of English arouses Mr. Wells's indignation will rarely indeed be found to know any language but their own. It could scarcely be otherwise, for the man who can never look at his own language from the outside and estimate by comparison its exact structure and force is unlikely ever to become a master of it. Mr. Wells carries his insularity so far that he will not even admit any decency or virtue to the lower human races; the savage, he says, is simply a creature who smells and rots and starves. Mr. Wells is scornful of his 'untravelled' fellow-prophets in the eighteenth century, who held up the savage for imitation. But our travelled modern prophet has been a little unfortunate in his experiences, nor was the eighteenth century by any means un-travelled. It was, indeed, the opening up of the Pacific at that time and the quaint accurate narratives of Cook, Bougainville and the other great navigators that enabled Rousseau and Diderot to use the Polynesian for the purposes of edification as effectively as Tacitus used the German.

If, however, Mr. Wells is sometimes led into unwarrantable extremes of statement, it is generally easy to see that he is so led by his moralising purpose, and that he is legitimately exercising the prophetic function. How admirable a moralist he is may be clearly seen in the chapter entitled 'The Cultivation of the Imagination.' Here he deals with the question of the methods by which the boy or girl should be initiated into the knowledge of all that makes manhood and womanhood. It is a delicate question, but it could not well be discussed in a more sane, wholesome, frank, and yet reticent manner. In such a discussion Mr. Wells is at his best; he enables us to realise that we are perhaps advancing beyond 'that age of nasty sentiment, sham delicacy, and giggles,' as he calls the Victorian era; it is here that he shows how significant a prophet he is of the twentieth century.

EARLY FRENCH RESPONSES

1901–3

---

31. Henri Ghéon on Wells and Verne

December 1901

Review of *The First Men in the Moon* in *L'Ermitage* (December 1901), xxiii, 471–2.

Henri Ghéon [Henri Vangeon] (b. 1875), critic, playwright and friend and associate of André Gide.

In speaking of Wells, it is usual to mention Edgar Poe and Jules Verne—a curious juxtaposition. Poe is too much; Jules Verne not enough. I would not speak ill of the French author who delighted my earliest infancy, but I think he is in fact too infantile to be reread at my age. Starting from the same point of view—science and imagination—Wells seems to write rather more for grown-ups, and hence his superiority; not in that he aspires to this, but in the fact that he succeeds. Jules Verne wanted to but could not manage it. I would hesitate to compare the inventive gifts of these two writers. Those of Wells must be richer and rarer—undoubtedly. But I hold that it is as a philosopher, and even as a psychologist, that one principally sees him. Whether he puts his earthly heroes on and even in the moon, or in the intangible dimensions of time, he allows them to retain a body, a soul and a mind; he imagines what a man may become in these fictitious circumstances and fancied atmospheres, and sometimes he gives us the precise sensation of it. The interest moves continually from the external to the internal; this is the source of drama and irony, and also of the Swiftian satirical intention of certain descriptive passages, deliberately strange and calculated in their absurdity, which parody and ridicule our terrestrial reality. And nowhere has more accurate mockery been combined with livelier entertainment than in *The First Men in the Moon*, translated by Davray with an agile pen. The words of the Grand Lunar are to be reread and pondered over. Starting out from the good Jules Verne, are we now so very far from the terrible Nietzsche?

32. Augustin Filon on the metropolitan imagination

19 March 1902

Extract from review of *Anticipations* in *Journal des Débats* (19 March 1902), 1.

In the omitted sections of this review, Filon contrasts Wells and Verne and speculates on the future shape of London.

Mr. Wells is the great realist of a non-existent world. He is present at the death-agony of our planet: beside half-frozen seas, in the icy twilight of the world's end, he sees 'foul, slow-stirring monsters,' the last living creatures to be nourished by the earth; he sees them as clearly, indeed much more clearly than I am now seeing the lawn and trees in my garden. And he has another visionary faculty besides this, in the activity of thought by which he traces the sensations produced by these visions, and observes their effect upon the feelings. He never loses sight of the reciprocal evolution of Science and Humanity. Men create science, and science in its turn remakes mankind. That seems to me to be the dominant idea of Mr. Wells's work.

Wells represents a special new type of thinker and writer which could not have emerged and come into its own in the intellectual atmosphere of thirty years ago. He is a product of the Royal College of Science, a great democratic institution, preserving none of the old university traditions. Afterwards, he knew the difficulties of the life of an apprentice teacher. And all this was in the thick of the great whirlpool of London, where one is forced to speak little, think quickly and keep constantly on the move, and where the individual is reduced to the point of deafness to his own cries and insensibility to his own suffering. Not in his books are to be found the scents of the meadow and the forest, which so delightfully permeate the musings of the solitary; instead, in each word you will sense the clamour of six million beings, and the vibration of a million buildings, you will have the feeling of the noise, the crowd, and, as Maurice de Guérin put it so well in *Le Centaure*, 'of life inflamed and come to a head.' With many other causes of which I am ignorant, London and science have contributed to the formation of Mr. Wells's mind. It is because of this, no doubt, that it would be difficult to apply to him either of the labels which correspond to the two usual forms of the English mind—imperialism and insularity. His books could have been written by an American settler in England; they could even, at a pinch, have been conceived originally in German or in French.

33. Jules Verne interviewed

9 October 1903

Extract from *T.P.'s Weekly*, ii, 589. The interviewer was Robert H. Sherard.

It was inevitable, as Jules Verne remarked, that I should speak to him about Wells.

'*Je pensiez bien que vous alliez me demander cela*,' he said. 'His books were sent to me, and I have read them. It is very curious, and, I will add, very English. But I do not see the possibility of comparison between his work and mine. We do not proceed in the same manner. It occurs to me that his stories do not repose on very scientific bases. No, there is no *rapport* between his work and mine. I make use of physics. He invents.

I go to the moon in a cannon-ball, discharged from a cannon. Here there is no invention. He goes to Mars in an airship, which he constructs of a metal which does away with the law of gravitation. *Ça c'est très joli*,' cried Monsieur Verne in an animated way, 'but show me this metal. Let him produce it.'

THE FOOD OF THE GODS

September 1904

34. G. K. Chesterton in *Heretics*

1905

Extract from 'Mr. H. G. Wells and the Giants', *Heretics* (1905), pp. 76–88.

Chesterton (1874–1936) and Wells were friends and lifelong adversaries. In this influential essay Chesterton, the romantic conservative and Catholic, makes out a robust case against Wells's scientific Fabianism.

Mr. H. G. Wells exists at present in a gay and exhilarating progress of conservativism. He is finding out more and more that conventions, though silent, are alive. As good an example as any of this humility and sanity of his may be found in his change of view on the subject of science and marriage. He once held, I believe, the opinion which some singular sociologists still hold, that human creatures could successfully be paired and bred after the manner of dogs or horses. He no longer holds that view. Not only does he no longer hold that view, but he has written about it in *Mankind in the Making* with such smashing sense and humour, that I find it difficult to believe that anybody else can hold it either. It is true that his chief objection to the proposal is that it is physically impossible, which seems to me a very slight objection, and almost negligible compared with the others. The one objection to scientific marriage which is worthy of final attention is simply that such a thing could only be imposed on unthinkable slaves and cowards. I do not know whether the scientific marriage-mongers are right (as they say) or wrong (as Mr. Wells says) in saying that medical supervision would produce strong and healthy men. I am only certain that if it did, the first act of the strong and healthy men would be to smash the medical supervision.

The mistake of all that medical talk lies in the very fact that it connects the idea of health with the idea of care. What has health to do with care? Health has to do with carelessness. In special and abnormal cases it is necessary to have care. When we are peculiarly unhealthy it may be necessary to be careful in order to be healthy. But even then we are only trying to be healthy in order to be careless. If we are doctors we are speaking to exceptionally sick men, and they ought to be told to be careful. But when we are sociologists we are addressing the normal man, we are addressing humanity. And humanity ought to be told to be recklessness itself. For all the fundamental functions of a healthy man ought emphatically to be performed with pleasure and for pleasure; they emphatically ought not to be performed with precaution or for precaution. A man ought to eat because he has a good appetite to satisfy, and emphatically not because he has a body to sustain. A man ought to take exercise not because he is too fat, but because he loves foils or horses or high mountains, and loves them for their own sake. And a man ought to marry because he has fallen in love, and emphatically not because the world requires to be populated. The food will really renovate his tissues as long as he is not thinking about his tissues. The exercise will really get him into training so long as he is thinking about something else. And the marriage will really stand some chance of producing a generous-blooded generation if it had its origin in its own natural and generous excitement. It is the first law of health that our necessities should not be accepted as necessities; they should be accepted as luxuries. Let us, then, be careful about the small things, such as a scratch or a slight illness, or anything that can be managed with care. But in the name of all sanity, let us be careless about the important things, such as marriage, or the fountain of our very life will fail.

Mr. Wells, however, is not quite clear enough of the narrower scientific outlook to see that there are some things which actually ought not to be scientific. He is still slightly affected with the great scientific fallacy; I mean the habit of beginning not with the human soul, which is the first thing a man learns about, but with some such thing as protoplasm, which is about the last. The one defect in his splendid mental equipment is that he does not sufficiently allow for the stuff or material of men. In his new Utopia he says, for instance, that a chief point of the Utopia will be a disbelief in original sin. If he had begun on himself—he would have found original sin almost the first thing to be believed in. He would have found, to put the matter shortly, that a permanent possibility of selfishness arises from the mere fact of having a self, and not from any accidents of education or ill-treatment. And the weakness of all Utopias is this, that they take the greatest difficulty of man and assume it to be overcome, and then give an elaborate account of the overcoming of the smaller ones. They first assume that no man will want more than his share, and then are very ingenious in explaining whether his share will be delivered by motor-car or balloon. And an even stronger example of Mr. Wells's indifference to the human psychology can be found in his cosmopolitanism, the abolition in his Utopia of all patriotic boundaries. He says in his innocent way that Utopia must be a world-state, or else people might make war on it. It does not seem to occur to him that, for a good many of us, if it were a world-state we should still make war on it to the end of the world. For if we admit that there must be varieties in art or opinion what sense is there in thinking there will not be varieties in government? The fact is very simple. Unless you are going deliberately to prevent a thing being good, you cannot prevent it being worth fighting for. It is impossible to prevent a possible conflict of civilizations, because it is impossible to prevent a possible conflict between ideals. If there were no longer our modern strife between nations, there would only be a strife between Utopias. For the highest thing does not tend to union only; the highest thing tends also to differentiation. You can often get men to fight for the union; but you can never prevent them from fighting also for the differentiation. This variety in the highest thing is the meaning of the fierce patriotism, the fierce nationalism of the great European civilization. It is also, incidentally, the meaning of the doctrine of the Trinity.

But I think the main mistake of Mr. Wells's philosophy is a somewhat deeper one, one that he expresses in a very entertaining manner in the introductory part of the new Utopia. His philosophy in some sense amounts to a denial of the possibility of philosophy itself. At least, he maintains that there are no secure and reliable ideas upon which we can rest with a final mental satisfaction. It will be both clearer, however, and more amusing to quote Mr. Wells himself.

He says, 'Nothing endures, nothing is precise and certain (except the mind of a pedant). . . . Being indeed!—there is no being, but a universal becoming of individualities, and Plato turned his back on truth when he turned towards his museum of specific ideals.' Mr. Wells says, again, 'There is no abiding thing in what we know. We change from weaker to stronger lights, and each more powerful light pierces our hitherto

opaque foundations and reveals fresh and different opacities below.'
Now, when Mr. Wells says things like this, I speak with all respect when
I say that he does not observe an evident mental distinction. It *cannot* be
true that there is nothing abiding in what we know. For if that were so
we should not know it all and should not call it knowledge. Our mental
state may be very different from that of somebody else some thousands
of years back; but it cannot be entirely different, or else we should not
be conscious of a difference. Mr. Wells must surely realize the first and
simplest of the paradoxes that sit by the springs of truth. He must surely
see that the fact of two things being different implies that they are
similar. The hare and the tortoise may differ in the quality of swiftness,
but they must agree in the quality of motion. The swiftest hare cannot
be swifter than an isosceles triangle or the idea of pinkness. When we
say the hare moves faster, we say that the tortoise moves. And when we
say of a thing that it moves, we say, without need of other words, that
there are things that do not move. And even in the act of saying that
things change, we say that there is something unchangeable.

But certainly the best example of Mr. Wells's fallacy can be found
in the example which he himself chooses. It is quite true that we see a
dim light which, compared with a darker thing, is light, but which,
compared with a stronger light, is darkness. But the quality of light
remains the same thing, or else we should not call it a stronger light or
recognize it as such. If the character of light were not fixed in the mind,
we should be quite as likely to call a denser shadow a stronger light, or
vice versâ. If the character of light became even for an instant unfixed,
if it became even by a hair's-breadth doubtful, if, for example, there
crept into our idea of light some vague idea of blueness, then in that
flash we have become doubtful whether the new light has more light or
less. In brief, the progress may be as varying as a cloud, but the direction
must be as rigid as a French road. North and South are relative in the
sense that I am North of Bournemouth and South of Spitzbergen. But
if there be any doubt of the position of the North Pole, there is in equal
degree a doubt of whether I am South of Spitzbergen at all. The absolute
idea of light may be practically unattainable. We may not be able to
procure pure light. We may not be able to get to the North Pole. But
because the North Pole is unattainable, it does not follow that it is
indefinable. And it is only because the North Pole is not indefinable that
we can make a satisfactory map of Brighton and Worthing.

In other words, Plato turned his face to truth, but his back on Mr.
H. G. Wells, when he turned to his museum of specified ideals. It is

precisely here that Plato shows his sense. It is not true that everything changes; the things that change are all the manifest and material things. There is something that does not change; and that is precisely the abstract quality, the invisible idea. Mr. Wells says truly enough, that a thing which we have seen in one connection as dark we may see in another connection as light. But the thing common to both incidents is the mere idea of light—which we have not seen at all. Mr. Wells might grow taller and taller for unending æons till his head was higher than the loneliest star. I can imagine his writing a good novel about it. In that case he would see the trees first as tall things and then as short things; he would see the clouds first as high and then as low. But there would remain with him through the ages in that starry loneliness the idea of tallness; he would have in the awful spaces for companion and comfort the definite conception that he was growing taller and not (for instance) growing fatter.

And now it comes to my mind that Mr. H. G. Wells actually has written a very delightful romance about men growing as tall as trees; and that here, again, he seems to me to have been a victim of this vague relativism. *The Food of the Gods* is, like Mr. Bernard Shaw's play, in essence a study of the Superman idea. And it lies, I think, even through the veil of a half-pantomimic allegory, open to the same intellectual attack. We cannot be expected to have any regard for a great creature if he does not in any manner conform to our standards. For unless he passes our standard of greatness we cannot even call him great. Nietszche summed up all that is interesting in the Superman idea when he said, 'Man is a thing which has to be surpassed.' But the very word 'surpass' implies the existence of a standard common to us and the thing sur-passing us. If the Superman is more manly than men are, of course they will ultimately deify him, even if they happen to kill him first. But if he is simply more supermanly, they may be quite indifferent to him as they would be to another seemingly aimless monstrosity. He must submit to our test even in order to overawe us. Mere force or size even is a standard; but that alone will never make men think a man their superior. Giants, as in the wise old fairy-tales, are vermin. Supermen, if not good men, are vermin.

The Food of the Gods is the tale of *Jack the Giant-Killer* told from the point of view of the giant. This has not, I think, been done before in literature; but I have little doubt that the psychological substance of it existed in fact. I have little doubt that the giant whom Jack killed did regard himself as the Superman. It is likely enough that he considered

Jack a narrow and parochial person who wished to frustrate a great forward movement of the life-force. If (as not unfrequently was the case) he happened to have two heads, he would point out the elementary maxim which declares them to be better than one. He would enlarge on the subtle modernity of such an equipment, enabling a giant to look at a subject from two points of view, or to correct himself with promptitude. But Jack was the champion of the enduring human standards, of the principle of one man one head and one man one conscience, of the single head and the single heart and the single eye. Jack was quite unimpressed by the question of whether the giant was a particularly gigantic giant. All he wished to know was whether he was a good giant—that is, a giant who was any good to us. What were the giant's religious views; what his views on politics and the duties of the citizen? Was he fond of children—or fond of them only in a dark and sinister sense? To use a fine phrase for emotional sanity, was his heart in the right place? Jack had sometimes to cut him up with a sword in order to find out.

The old and correct story of Jack the Giant-Killer is simply the whole story of man; if it were understood we should need no Bibles or histories. But the modern world in particular does not seem to understand it at all. The modern world, like Mr. Wells, is on the side of the giants; the safest place, and therefore the meanest and the most prosaic. The modern world, when it praises its little Cæsars, talks of being strong and brave: but it does not seem to see the eternal paradox involved in the conjunction of these ideas. The strong cannot be brave. Only the weak can be brave; and yet again, in practice, only those who can be brave can be trusted, in time of doubt, to be strong. The only way in which a giant could really keep himself in training against the inevitable Jack would be by continually fighting other giants ten times as big as himself. That is by ceasing to be a giant and becoming a Jack. Thus that sympathy with the small or the defeated as such, with which we Liberals and Nationalists have been often reproached, is not a useless sentimentalism at all, as Mr. Wells and his friends fancy. It is the first law of practical courage. To be in the weakest camp is to be in the strongest school. Nor can I imagine anything that would do humanity more good than the advent of a race of Supermen, for them to fight little dragons. If the Superman is better than we, of course we need not fight him; but in that case, why not call him the Saint? But if he is merely stronger (whether physically, mentally, or morally stronger, I do not care a farthing), then he ought to have to reckon with us at least for all the strength we have. If we are weaker than he, that is no reason why we should be weaker than ourselves. If we are not tall enough to touch the giant's knees, that is no reason why we should become shorter by falling on our own. But that is at bottom the meaning of all modern hero-worship and celebration of the Strong Man, the Cæsar, the Superman. That he may be something more than man, *we* must be something less.

A MODERN UTOPIA

April 1905

---

35. Sydney Olivier, review in *Fabian News*

August 1905, xv, 38–9

Sydney Haldane Olivier, 1st Baron Olivier (1859–1943), Fabian colonial servant who was Governor of Jamaica from 1907 to 1913 and served in the Labour Government of 1924.

Utopian literature, the scheming of imaginary commonwealths in which life might be tolerable to all sensible, and even to all sensitive, citizens, is interesting to readers who have passed their Utopian age: not so much as a material for faith and a suggestion for program-drafting as in its indications of apprehension of human motive, its confessions of sympathetic heart's-desire. Every Utopist—even Mr. Shaw in his vague outcry for the Superman, under the nightmare of his indigestion of Nietzsche—carries us with him and engages our will in his cause in so far as he is, for the moment, a poet opening gates to our unconscious unrest. Mr. Wells' *A Modern Utopia* is on this account more important than his *Anticipations* or *Mankind in the Making*. It furnishes more of our common inclinations with aims clothed in forms that appear desirable; he offers himself—gives the body and blood of his own sentimentalities for us—more freely, combines the imagination and simple-minded romanticism through which he planned his earlier escapes from oppression into irresponsible fiction more intimately with his increasing grasp of the realities of human society and his encroaching conviction of responsibility in regard to them. It is a pleasant book; not magical with the music and visualization of *News from Nowhere*, but showing some of its most vital qualities.

Mr. Wells' social forecasts always remind us how dominant an oppression of civilized life is dirt, whether we regard it as a cause or a symbol. The cleanliness of *News from Nowhere* is the cleanliness of nature left as much as possible to herself; the cleanliness of *A Modern Utopia* is the cleanliness of minute and rigorous art and applied invention. One feels that this is paramount with Mr. Wells, to get the dirt out of our daily environment, the ugliness, untidiness, thriftlessness, dealt with by mere housewifely common sense. He cannot ignore the problems of dense population and city life, as did Morris. He does not despair of them. He imagines and shows us a civilized world in the first place clean and orderly, and shows it as, after all, a very simple achievement for sensible men and women. And one result is that we feel Mr. Wells' Utopia less Utopian than that of William Morris, for it deals with conditions in which, so far as we can reasonably forecast, it appears that modern societies in the mature nations must live; whereas we can only say that the life of *News from Nowhere* would suit us, if it were imaginably possible, very well, but that it does not seem to be so. Mr. Wells' clean world does seem possible; and he makes us feel that it would be really agreeable to live in. All he demands is the general production of his exceedingly modest ideal of the proletarian of the future, the man who has been drilled by the age of engineering and machinery into a certain amount of orderly common sense and the habit of adapting mechanical means to the serving of his own comfort and convenience.

A Modern Utopia is perhaps still rather too stiff reading for the great British middle-proletariate, whose education in ideals is the most important problem of modern progress. But Mr. Wells as an imaginative story-teller is steadily winning their ear; and they take improvement kindly if it comes in romantic form. We shall not quickly regain our confidence in their practical reason. Mr. Wells does not seem to expect great things of that in the future Republic. At best, he believes that if everyone were to be carefully educated 'the Dull' would be 'considerably in the minority' in the world; 'but it is quite possible that will not be the reader's opinion.' They certainly are waterlogging us now. But Mr. Wells apprehends, we fancy, some secrets of their possible growth, outside the economic stimuli altogether.

The demand that will, perhaps, strike readers as most exacting is that the citizens of the future should come so far to regard the amenities of human life as attainable rather by the efficient adaptation and control of machinery than by sentimental exercises as to consciously and deliberately acquiesce in the government of the state by a Platonic bureaucracy.

For this is Mr. Wells' expedient, a governing caste of 'Samurai,' a combination of Plato's idea of the philosophic guardians of his Republic with the actual and obvious fact that the administration of all civilized states is, and seems bound to be increasingly, conducted by such a specialized class. Mr. Wells faces this fact as he faces the facts of machinery. He does not propose to revert to the Thing and the Folkmote.

[Quotes ch. 9 'Typically, the *samurai* are engaged in administrative work' to 'follows the Rule'.]

No member of the Fabian Society will deem this an insane ideal. Let Mr. Wells conclude in his own poetry:—

[Quotes ch. 11 'Will is stronger' to 'must come'.]

36. R. Mayor, review in *Independent Review*

October 1905, vii, 235–40

Mayor (1869–1947) was a civil servant at the Board of Education from 1907 to 1926.

Human nature is always disposed to meet any suggestions for the world's improvement with two objections: first, that the thing proposed can not be done; second, that, if it could, it would be very dull. On one of these objections, or both of them, most constructors of Utopias come to grief. Either they explain by what ingenious regulations this evil was cured and that anomaly got rid of, until we find, at the end of the process, that all the spontaneity and interest of life has been got rid of too. This is the more usual and less pardonable alternative. Or else they convey us, as we are conveyed in *News from Nowhere*, into a fairyland where every one does what he likes, and everything goes right by nature. The people who might find themselves by happy chance in this fortunate country, would certainly be unreasonable if they were not content. But Morris, in his impatience of system and machinery, cut the links that might have connected his Utopia with the practical world; and thus he gives us no reason for believing, either that his commonwealth could ever have been evolved out of the present state of things, or even that it could be maintained in being.

Readers of Mr. Wells' earlier books will understand that his Utopia is not likely to suffer from any want of machinery. The world in the star beyond Sirius, into which his two travellers go down by the Lake of Lucendro, is, in its outward features, the same efficient scientific world which he has described before. It has the flying machines, universal tramways, dustless houses, and all the ingenious labour-saving appliances. In its political development, it has advanced a stage further. This Utopia is a World-state; inevitably so, since the elaborate organisation by which it maintains security and prosperity would be inconsistent with the survival of conflicting governments. It controls its citizens from childhood to old age, with a benevolent and pervasive supervision. There is a good deal that is interesting to say as to the manner in which this control is regulated, with a view to securing in all cases a minimum level of comfort and competency, while allowing those who can to rise above it. But, on the whole, the economic and social conditions of Utopia are passed over rather hurriedly. Its system of education, its care for public health, its dealings with monopolies, its method of regulating building and the growth of cities, its standard wage, its reservoir of work for the unemployed, its provision for infirmity and old age, are here sketched briefly, or only referred to in passing. They have been dealt with elsewhere, in *Anticipations* and in *Mankind in the Making*; and *A Modern Utopia* is intended, we imagine, not so much to repeat or alter those earlier books, as to supplement them on one important matter which was there omitted. We have to learn what sort of persons they are who inhabit this system, and, in particular, what sort of persons they are who control it and make it possible. References to a certain governing order appear early in the book and become more prominent as it goes on. And when Mr. Wells' mouthpiece meets his double in the Utopian metropolis, it is about these that he is most anxious to enquire. 'Tell me about these *Samurai*, who remind me of Plato's Guardians, who look like Knights Templars, who bear a name that recalls the swordsmen of Japan . . . For certainly this world turns upon them, as a door upon its hinges.'

The *Samurai* represent an ingenious device for securing efficient government, which is not quite like anything that has been suggested before. They are not a hereditary caste, nor an elected body, still less a plutocracy. They are members of an Order open to all the world, open, that is, to any one who fulfils certain conditions; and they hold the ruling positions in the State by weight of superior merit. The conditions of admission to the Order are designed to be a guarantee for character and intellect, and to exclude the unfit; while its monopoly of power will attract the capable. The qualifications for the Order, and the things which its members may and may not do, are described at some length. They cover a wide range, from the grotesque to the romantic. The Order is not communistic. Family life is allowed; and the members may hold property to such an extent as is necessary to secure privacy and personal freedom. But they may not live on wealth they have not earned; and all easy ways of getting rich suddenly are debarred to them. Most luxuries are forbidden; and there are strict sumptuary laws. Sometimes the requirements go into minute details, with hardly adequate results. 'Every month they must buy and read faithfully through at least one book that has been published during the last five years.' We seem to know these conscientious readers of new books at stated intervals; they come from somewhere nearer than Utopia. Mr. Wells, however, disregarding possible ridicule, continues his regulations; and presently we find him in a graver vein. Every year each member of the Order must travel by himself in some uninhabited part of the world, in deserts or snow mountains, sleeping in the open, and not speaking to any human being. As a cure for too much civilisation, this is well imagined. And, in the end, we find that Mr. Wells, steering a difficult course between the sublime and the ridiculous, contrives to build up a picture of a discipline which is rigorous without being intolerable, and a type of character that gets rid of many human weaknesses, without becoming inhuman.

It becomes evident, as we read, that Mr. Wells has been a student of Plato. He has drawn his materials indeed, as he frankly admits, from many of the imaginary commonwealths of the past—from the original *Utopia*, from the *New Atlantis*, from other less known writers and some modern ones. But he has drawn most of all from the *Republic*. The *Samurai* are, in fact, the Platonic 'guardians,' born again into an age of electricity and statistics. This debt to the past implies, it need not be said, no want of inventive power. To have transformed into keeping with the present age ideas which were conceived under such different conditions, while still retaining something of their essential quality, is an achievement equal to an original construction. No doubt a good deal has disappeared in the transformation. Plato's ideal figures have a statuesque dignity which it would be too much to expect to recover in the twentieth century. Few other writers have had that persistent sense of fitness which enables Plato to bring out just those details which heighten the effect of the picture, while avoiding all which would seem incongruous or absurd. Mr. Wells, in pursuit of actuality, struggles with details, not always successfully. His Utopia, though he protests against the charge, is occasionally fussy. Sometimes, too, we feel a want of proportion; but here it is fair to remember that Plato wrote as a philosopher at leisure, while Mr. Wells writes for the magazines and the reading public, under limitations of space and time. He seems hardly to have room to develop his ideas fully in a volume of this length. They might have had a better setting if he could have woven into this book the best part of the economic and social speculations of *Anticipations* and *Mankind in the Making*, adding, perhaps, something of the human quality of *The Wheels of Chance* and the romantic landscape of *The Time Machine*.

In one respect, Mr. Wells has made a step forward since he wrote *Anticipations*. He has become less rigidly practical, and more tolerant of genius and originality. But, even after this conversion, efficiency remains his passion, and a love of organisation his main weakness. It is natural that this should be so in the case of a writer who has shown himself, through a series of books, so constantly pre-occupied with the problem of poverty. To cure poverty, it seems reasonable to say you must prevent waste; and, to prevent waste, the most needful thing is organisation. This conclusion seems convincing; but certain things in history may raise the question whether it is safe to press it too far. Consider, for instance, the question of the World-state. From the point of view of reason, what could be more necessary? It is required, not only to stop the immense waste due to war, and the still more persistent waste due to armaments, but also because, as Mr. Wells urges, only a World-state could deal effectively with the social and industrial problems of the present age. Yet we recall the fact that most of the great ideas which the human race values had their origin in the petty States of Greece, or Palestine, or Italy, engaged almost constantly in purposeless and savage wars. There is no easy moral to be drawn from this; but it may suggest a doubt whether we can afford to part so easily with nationality. To take a smaller matter, that monstrous card-registry, containing the thumbmarks of the whole human species, and 'housed quite comfortably on one side of Northumberland Avenue,' has something of the effect of a nightmare. And, with regard to the *Samurai* themselves, is there not somewhat too much regulation? What, if we are to think it out practically, is to be the sanction for all these small commands and prohibitions? Exclusion from the Order, we understand, which means exclusion from all power and distinction. And then we ask: Exclusion by what tribunal, and on what evidence? And no very satisfactory answer suggests itself. There will be room here for enquiry on the part of the reformed science of Sociology, which is to study the psychology of associations. We should expect it to report that the attempt to enforce a code of rules, dealing with many intimate matters, on a large body of men would end, either in the pretence of keeping up a standard which is in practice ignored, or in an intolerable system of petty espionage.

Perhaps, however, on this last point criticism is somewhat unreasonable. Mr. Wells might reply that, though he means us to take him seriously, he does not mean us to take him too literally. The essence of the *Samurai* is, that they choose their way of life for themselves; and if the details of the Rule seem to conflict with this, they may be disregarded as merely picturesque accessories. And, on the whole, we should admit that, if the State gets its full rights in this Utopia, the individual has his rights recognised too. Indeed, the best quality in the book is the constant reasonableness with which it attempts to show that conflicting claims can be reconciled in practice. 'I feel,' says the Utopian traveller at the end of his journey, 'that I have joined together things that I had never joined before;' and this seems to us a true summary of what Mr. Wells has done here. He has brought together conceptions, apparently contradictory but really indispensable, which neither he nor anyone else had fitted together so ingeniously before. That he has succeeded so well, we attribute mainly to three things. First that he has, what is not very common in England at present, or perhaps anywhere at any time, a keen interest both in machinery and in human nature. Next there is his 'philosophy of the unique,' which, to whatever difficulties it may lie open in theory, does him good service in practice. It enables him to remember what even distinguished writers often forget: that statesmanship deals with human beings and not with abstract nouns. Lastly, there is his realistic imagination, at once solid and adventurous, by virtue of which he can present his ideal State visibly before us, and say to conflicting parties: 'Does not this give you at bottom the essence of what you are all wanting?' His audience will have their personal prejudices and hesitations; and he will not expect from us any sudden or enthusiastic assent to this question. But he may imagine us as admitting that Utopia seems a good deal more like a possible place to live in than one would have supposed beforehand.

37. T. H. Warren, unsigned review in *Spectator*

21 October 1905, xcv, 610–11

Sir Thomas Herbert Warren (1853–1930), poet and classicist, President of Magdalen College, Oxford from 1885 to 1928.

'In heaven there is laid up a pattern of such a city, and he who desires may behold this, and beholding, govern himself accordingly. But whether there really is, or ever will be, such an one is of no importance to him; for he will act according to the laws of that city and of no other.'* Such is the sublime passage with which the author of the first and most famous of all Utopias concludes the strictly definitive and operative part of his account of his ideal commonwealth. It is his *apologia*, and it is the *apologia* of all Utopias. They are in their nature ideal. Much they may contain that is unreal, unpractical, impracticable; but if they have not been and never can be realised, they have still their value, and they suggest laws and inner counsels in the light and spirit of which life may be lived even in the imperfect world in which the idealist finds himself to-day.

Such is pre-eminently the defence, if any were needed, of this interesting and original volume. It is not exactly a great book, though a very clever one. In some ways it seems as if it might have been better on

---

* Plato, *Republic*, Bk ix.

its own lines. It is certainly not an easy book to apprehend, but it is filled by a lofty and elevating spirit. We must be grateful to Mr. Wells for the effort and time which he has devoted to it, time and effort which he might readily have spent—and must often have been tempted to spend—on much easier and more lucrative writing and easier reading. In his very interesting prefatory note to the reader, and his equally interesting 'Philosophical Appendix,' both highly autobiographic, he hints something of its genesis, though not all. His 'art or trade,' he says, is that of an imaginative writer. How successful he has been in this every one knows. But he desires to be something more. He desires not merely to amuse or entertain, even in a semi-serious way, but to instruct and educate, to enlighten the thought and lift the ideals of himself and his fellows. He will write not merely for money or for fame, but for love and for truth's sake. He attempted this in *Anticipations* and in *Mankind in the Making*. He attempts it again here. And this is the most serious attempt of all. A very serious attempt it is, more so than might at first sight appear. The book, both in matter and in form, has been carefully studied and thought out.

A comparative history of Utopias would be a very interesting work to write. It would 'look before and after,' and throw much light alike on the history and the aspirations of mankind. It would not perhaps suit Mr. Wells to write it himself, but he has evidently gone some way in the preparation necessary, and in suggesting how it might be written. He has studied most, if not all, of the famous Utopias of the past, from Plato and Sir Thomas More and St. Augustine, through Bacon and Campanella, Harrington and Lord Erskine, to Cabet and William Morris and Bellamy. He has noted, too, the experiments that have actually been tried, such as Utah and Oneida Creek. He has dipped, nay, more than dipped, into political economy and many allied subjects. He is further a man of science, and at first of almost exclusively scientific training, who, following the imperious instinct of a rich and versatile and sincere nature, has made himself a man of letters and a philosopher. He is no mere 'idle singer of an empty day'; no trifling novelist with a little more than the usual imagination and scientific information; not even a Jules Verne, delightful and educating as Jules Verne was, telling 'fairy-tales of science' to amuse children, old and young, suggesting the marvellous and delightful possibilities which its Aladdin lamps and magic carpets have placed in our hands. His purpose is more deep and severe than this. The result is that the book is by no means an easy one, and may daunt many of his ordinary readers. But it is a book well worth reading, and reading carefully, if only for the spirit which it engenders.

The difficulty of all Utopias is at once to give the outer picture with sufficient naturalness and concreteness, and to convey the apprehension of the inner spirit which is to be the secret of this outer life. Mr. Wells's method of attacking this difficulty is highly ingenious. He imagines a new planet, the exact counterpart of our own, excepting that, by a certain alteration in what we call and think of as the chance, or the alterable elements, in the course of human history, the race has developed quite differently, has acquired far greater command than even our own in its most modern hour, of material science, has escaped from many of the grinding drudgeries and limitations of our physical condition, and reached, too, a higher social and moral plane. It is—and this is of its essence—a world still in progress. 'Mankind' is still 'in the making' in Utopia, but man's present condition there is far in advance of ours, and, moreover, discovers a still further promise and potency. Into this world two tourists, after a good lunch, enjoyed on the top of a Swiss pass just before they descend again, find themselves, whether in 'the body or out of the body,' whether in a waking or sleeping dream, as Plato would say, suddenly projected. They retain their own individuality—that is a large part of the interest—and it is here that Mr. Wells's skill as a novelist comes in. They go through a variety of experiences, a good deal of time being spent in a Utopian Lucerne; and finally they come back, if they ever really went away, to a Utopian London, where the iridescent bubble of their vision is rudely broken in Trafalgar Square, and the story ends. The method as handled by Mr. Wells has one great merit,— it produces illusion, that effect so hard to achieve. We are transported out of this world into its twin star in the most natural and easy way. We feel the new to be unlike the old, yet not so unlike but that the old might have grown, might yet grow, to be somewhat thus. We are not troubled with the slow processes of development, and ever so many factors which require elimination to give the hypothesis a chance are, *ipso facto*, quietly eliminated. Yet Utopia is not so strange that an intelligent Englishman of to-day could not live there, and even by degrees feel himself almost at home.

Science, it need hardly be said, plays a very prominent part in Mr. Wells's Utopia. Plato, he says truly enough, thought little of machinery, though it must be remembered that Hephaestus and Daedalus were Greek ideals as well as Zeus and Solon, and that to Homer, at any rate, the conception of automaton tables and ships self-propelled and self-steering was present. But even Bacon developed the idea of mechanical appliances very little. Yet, as Mr. Wells excellently points out, it is the gradual application of science which has relieved mankind of slavery, professional and unprofessional; and even now, he says, 'Science stands a too competent servant behind her wrangling, underbred masters, holding out resources, devices, and remedies they are too stupid to use.' And on its material side a modern Utopia must needs present these gifts as taken, and show a world that is really abolishing the need of labour, abolishing the 'last base reason for any one's servitude or inferiority.'

This is one of Mr. Wells's main themes. Another, as those who know his works will expect to hear, is the position of women and the question of 'eugenics,' or the possibility of improving the race by the methods of the horse-breeder and the pigeon-fancier. He introduces it with a deft Platonic indirectness by means of his character—a most ingenious creation, by the way—the sentimental 'botanist.' Here he is partly Platonic, but still more Darwinian, preferring the natural selection by mutual affection to 'compulsory pairing' by the State, and in some ways, as elsewhere, comes near to the hedging audacity shown by Professor Jowett in dealing with this question, in that, while recognising the greatest possible theoretical freedom, he proposes, or anticipates, that in practice this license will be limited by regulations in detail. His central suggestion is the rewarding of motherhood by State endowment, and the consequent reduction of infantile disease and mortality. In the same way, in dealing with the immemorial question of private property it is not in any sweeping method of communism or abolition that he finds a panacea. He shows Utopia proceeding—by increased limitation and taxation, by extension and multiplication of State rights, by frequent revision of endowments, and other very prosaic and humdrum methods —to rob property, not of all its pleasures, but of most of its terrors. One feature he avowedly borrows from Plato. His 'Republic' turned on the institution of the Guardians; in other words, the rule of the wise. Mr. Wells's State turns, like, and as certainly as, a door on its hinges, on the institution of the 'Samurai,' the superior race. They are, as Matthew Arnold might have said—and Mr. Wells will evidently not resent the comparison—though their name is borrowed from the fighting nobles of Japan, a race of President Roosevelts living the strenuous life, vowing themselves to the public service, and bound by a 'Rule' with a capital 'R.' *More Platonico*, there is much about their education and selection and the minutiae of their discipline: how they must read a new book once a month, and bathe in cold water, keep in perfect health and hard condition, and also talk at the club to any other Samurai, who want to talk, for an hour three days a week, and once a year for seven days go out into the wilds and, like Tennyson at Boscastle, alone with God, be 'alone with Nature, necessity, and their own thoughts.' Like Plato's Guardians, they are forbidden to act, sing, or recite, though they may 'lecture authoritatively' (as they evidently do) or debate. Much of this is picturesque and suggestive reading, and so, of course, is a great deal of the book. Specially graphic—pathetic too—is the meeting of the hero with his Utopian 'double.' For we all have doubles in Utopia, ourselves, as we might have been in a more perfect world.

It is not easy within the limits of an article like this to give an adequate idea of a book of large scope, of much originality, above all, with a very subtle and elusive, yet very real, individuality of its own. While we recognise the difficulties of presenting a Utopia at all, adequate to the complexity of the modern world, we still think the old-fashioned simpler method of Plato or More was better. Mr. Wells's book seems hardly likely to rank as, or to remain, a classic Utopia. But if the reader will take him in his own way, and read him with patience, he will find more and more meaning in what is a very notable and generous essay on topics wide, deep, and difficult, yet of the most simple and natural interest to us all. We hope that this will not be, as Mr. Wells warns us it may, his last excursion of the kind from fiction to philosophy, but that he will still continue to give us his thoughts, and show us how, in his own eloquent language, we may attempt, 'not to rob life of incentives, but to change their nature, to make life not less energetic, but less panic-stricken and violent and base, to shift the incidence of the struggle for existence from our lower to our higher emotions, and so to anticipate and neutralise the motives of the cowardly and bestial, that the ambitious and energetic imagination which is man's finest quality may become the incentive and determining factor in survival.'

KIPPS

October 1905

---

38. C. F. G. Masterman, review in *Daily News*

25 October 1905, 4

Charles Frederick Gurney Masterman (1873–1927), writer and Liberal politician. Author of *The Condition of England* (1909) and leader of the 'philosophical Liberals', Masterman became a friend of Wells and acknowledged a considerable intellectual debt to him. He was a Member of Parliament (1906–14) and held a succession of Government posts culminating in the Chancellorship of the Duchy of Lancaster (1914–15).

I have read—and I suppose all sensible men have read—all Mr. Wells's novels and social prophecies; and I should unhesitatingly affirm *Kipps* to be the best story he has yet given us. The style is firmer, the control of the material more complete, the sincerity and purpose more deliberate and defined, than in all his past studies of a similar atmosphere. There are indeed obvious challenges to criticism. I am not happy when Mr. Wells suddenly splashes into the narrative, to address the gentle reader in protest and exhortation; and I think however much the story may gain in vivacity by such intrusions, it loses as a work of art. Purpose and bitterness are everywhere apparent, with a revolt that is sometimes ironical and sometimes passionate against all that silly muddle of life which has turned out Art Kipps, draper's assistant, as the ultimate product of a civilization. At present Mr. Wells is too ardent a soldier in the warfare against the mean ideas, starved existence, and futility of the life now flourishing in English watering places and the suburbs of the cities to be able to assume that detached and serene attitude which the greatest fiction demands.

But here is sincerity; and for the manifestation of such a virtue—for lack of which English literature at the present seems sick unto death—all lesser deficiencies can be forgiven. I know of no recent novel which so completely convinces the reader of the transparent truthfulness of the author. One who has escaped, and with but difficulty, from the swarm —with 'the vague distinctive smell of Manchester goods' still biting the nostrils, and memory of (in the words of a character in this volume) that 'blessed drainpipe' which 'we've got to crawl along till we die'—will testify a personal experience of a life as fantastic, monstrous, and inane as any life conceivable in the Martian continents or beneath the mountains of the Moon.

'*Kipps* may describe a draper's assistant', said a well-known critic to me when the book was appearing in serial form; 'but drapery assistants make me rather tired.' To those who appreciate the work of the novel in portrayal and criticism of life—in (at its highest) a portrayal which is itself a criticism—the interest and value alike will be judged by the one test of sincerity: and the draper's assistant, interpreted against a back-ground of real experience, will become a figure of ultimate significance.

Those familiar with *Mankind in the Making*, and the violence of its attack upon so much in modern progress which is tolerated or applauded, will find *Kipps* a kind of materialisation in fiction of that social impeach-ment. The translation through an oppressive atmosphere of sham and 'make-believe' of one of the children of the lower middle class into the shallow, satisfied, awkward product of the city civilization is the subject of the narrative. The process commences at the private school, which still, despite all onslaughts from Matthew Arnold and Government Education Bills, flourishes mightily in the land. The child, with his healthy instincts from his home in the little Kentish village, is deported to the select academy where 'pith' (in the words of the tramp in the *Wonderful Visit*) is clumsily substituted for the 'nice juicy brains', and the developing mind steered into the shabby ways of conventional life. 'At times', says Mr. Wells, of 'Dr. Woodrow, F.S.Sc.,' the proprietor of this evil place, 'at times his face was utterly inane; at times it had an expression of stagnant amazement, as if he saw before his eyes with pitiless clearness the dishonour and mischief of his being'.

The process but half completed by the select academy is consum-mated in the wholesale emporium. The vision of Kipps sacrificed to the 'Moloch of Retail Trade' is a vision of a kind of cosmic desolation, the river of human life midway in its courses draining into a kind of muddy marshland far from the wind and salt scents of the sea. At the summit is the owner, Mr. Shalford. 'His political creed linked Reform, which meant nothing, with Peace and Economy, which meant a sweated expenditure, and his conception of a satisfactory municipal life was to "keep down the rates".' At the base are the young men and women caught in an enchanted land.

Most of Mr. Wells's novels depict the coming of miracle into the life of ordinary man; with the effect upon different classes when Society breaks up or their rules of existence fail them, and for the first time in their lives they are called upon to face real things alone. This book tells of the coming of miracle into the life of a draper's assistant. An entirely unexpected legacy leaves him in possession of a house and twelve hundred a year. He determines to rise to the greatness of his new position. He essays culture—the culture of Folkestone—and labours at the *Encyclopedia Britannica* (tenth edition) and *Sesame and Lilies*. He seeks reform of pronunciation, and makes uneasy efforts at 'Calling', 'dinner parties' and 'Anagram Teas'. He finds himself in his new wealth embedded in a society with more comfort, leisure, and opportunities of enjoyment than the crowd that crawled through the emporiums of trade, but as feeble and futile, more scared of public opinion and the conventions, more afraid of doing the things it desires, more entirely divorced from any life that is gentle and rational and free.

All the mordant power of Mr. Wells's revolt against the mess which men and women are making of their world, against the failure of a life which has attained comfort but no inner serenity or passion or large and intelligible purpose of being is woven into his picture of the struggles of Kipps to attain a footing in these regions of social advancement. He is compelled to do the things he hates rather than the things he desires. He is driven to construct a gaunt and hideous villa, to live up to his station, instead of the little home of his dreams. Everywhere he is hedged in, before and behind, by the spiked and barren branches of aimless, conventional, respectable things: with life and its strong reality, Love and Sorrow and Death, everywhere avoided. It is an atmosphere 'of neglected great issues, of insistent, triumphant little things': where the victim, 'divorced from all his deities and grazing in the meadows under the Argus eyes of the social system', feels raining upon him the 'innumerable mean judgments' of a 'meanly conceived world'.

Kipps escapes, though hardly, and scarcely conscious of his good fortune. He attempts flight at the 'upper' end, migrating to London and a 'Grand Hotel', where he becomes conscious that all the inhabitants and servants are contemplating him and despising him, and an accident with the ice pudding at dinner converts him to 'Socialism'. He meets a bicycle maker of advanced opinions, and a voluble 'Socialist' (unhappily named 'Masterman'), who discourses concerning 'the beginning of the sickness of the world' and exhorts him to 'wait for the lean years'—a figure at once crumpled, windy, and pitiful. This way failing, he crawls out on the under side, repudiating the 'cultured' lady to whom he has become betrothed, in order to marry Ann, now a servant, once the object of his childhood's affections. A fortunate loss of his fortune enables him to sink back into the universe for which alone he has been prepared; and, as husband and father, behind the little bookshop, wondering still at the meaning of it all, thinking, in rare moments of solitude, 'jest what a Rum Go everything is', this 'Simple Soul' drifts beyond the horizon of the reader.

Kipps never encounters reality. The world of 'make-believe' envelops him like a garment. The 'stupid little tragedies of these clipped and limited lives' appear symbolised in the Crystal Palace Labyrinthodon beneath whose grotesque figure Kipps and Ann make love. In such a lumpish, clumsy monster Mr. Wells finds gathered up the brooding 'antisoul' of Stupidity and Fear from the shadow of which Kipps can never escape: which broods to-day over the conquering English race. The vision stands beside that in which Rossetti hailed the blind bull god of Nineveh as the Deity of Imperial London.

Meantime (in an ultimate satire upon life's queer ways) the draper's assistants under the gas light discuss the folly of giving votes to the Indians, with their 'tricky, dishonest minds'; large clergymen deliver 'manly' sermons upon 'the duty of doing whatever the hand finds to do': and patriots pray for the hastening of the time when the whole four hundred millions under the sway of British rule shall be elevated to the condition of Arthur Kipps.

39. Henry James's view

19 November 1905

Extract from letter to Wells, in *The Letters of Henry James* (1920), ed. Percy Lubbock, ii, pp. 41–2.

James and Wells were neighbours on the Kent coast and had been on friendly terms since 1898. This letter records the peak of James's approval of Wells as an artist.

And now, coming to Kipps, what am I to say about Kipps but that I am ready, that I am compelled, utterly to *drivel* about him? He is not so much a masterpiece as a mere born gem—you having, I know not how, taken a header straight down into mysterious depths of observation and knowledge, I know not which and where, and come up again with this rounded pearl of the diver. But of course you know yourself how immitigably the thing is done—it is of such a brilliancy of *true* truth. I really think that you have done, at this time of day, two particular things for the first time of their doing among us. (1) You have written the first closely and intimately, the first intelligently and consistently ironic or satiric novel. In everything else there has always been the sentimental or conventional interference, the interference of which Thackeray is full. (2) You have for the very first time treated the English 'lower middle' class, etc., without the picturesque, the grotesque, the fantastic and romantic interference, of which Dickens, e.g., is so misleadingly, of which even George Eliot is so deviatingly, full. You have handled its vulgarity in so scientific and historic a spirit, and seen the whole thing all in its *own* strong light. And then the book has, throughout, such extraordinary life; everyone in it, without exception, and every piece and part of it, is so vivid and sharp and *raw*. Kipps himself is a diamond of the first water, from start to finish, exquisite and radiant; Coote is consummate, Chitterlow magnificent (the whole first evening with Chitterlow perhaps the most brilliant thing in the book—unless that glory be reserved for the way the entire matter of the *shop* is done, including the admirable image of the boss.) It all in fine, from cover to

126

cover, does you the greatest honour, and if we had any other than skin-deep criticism (very stupid, too, at [th]at,) it would have immense recognition.

40. William Morton Payne, review in *Dial*

1 January 1906, xl, 17–18

William Morton Payne (1858–1919), critic and associate editor of the *Dial* (1892–1915).

The appalling vulgarity of English lower-class society, its absolute aloofness from everything that gives a spiritual meaning to life, its utter imperviousness to ideas of any kind, are the impressions that chiefly remain after reading *Kipps*. Mr. Wells describes the hero of this realistic narrative as 'a simple soul', but the description is inadequate, for he is represented as an *esprit borné* beyond our powers of credulity, if we are to regard him as being in any way of a normal type. For experience will knock even the meanest of normal natures into some sort of conformity with a new environment, but Kipps, born in poverty, and unexpectedly raised to affluence, shows no adaptability whatever, and proves incapable of sloughing off even the externals of the habit that has been fashioned for him by his instincts and his surroundings. Persistence of essential character under changed conditions is undoubtedly one of the deepest lessons of psychology, but average human nature is capable of a good deal of transformation to superficial seeming. Kipps, the draper's assistant, however, when he becomes Kipps the opulent, courted by society, remains a shop-boy no less in manner than in soul, and this despite his most resolute determination to acquire the ways of the class into which he has been suddenly elevated. This serves the author's purpose of humorous exaggeration, but it is not good science, and science is supposed to be Mr. Wells's trump suit. Nevertheless, the story of Kipps and his social mishaps is fascinating because of its merciless analysis of the irredeemably vulgar type of mind, because of its truthfulness of sordid detail, and because of its satirical sidelights upon the fads and follies of the age. We cannot easily forget, for example, such a characterization as that of one of the minor figures, the young man 'who had been reading Nietzsche, and thought that in all probability he was the Non-Moral Overman referred to by that writer.' We are quite prepared, after this, to expect the eventual crash in the finances of Kipps, who has rashly placed his property under the management of the young man thus neatly described. The book offers many such bits of entertainment as this, besides displaying an almost Dickens-like gift for the portrayal of eccentric traits and types of character.

41. William Dean Howells, review in *North American Review*

31 October 1906, clxxxiii, 795–8

William Dean Howells (1837–1920), novelist and critic. Howells, James's friend and the leader of the Realist movement in American fiction, had met Wells in 1904.

The mind of Mr. Wells is so manifold, and his work in such very widely different sorts, that it is not easy to know where to have him at his best; where to have him at his worst is no part of the inquiry which my pleasure in his latest fiction has disposed me to make very friendly. In fact, nearly everything of Mr. Wells's which I have read disposes me to a friendly inquiry. His fantastic romances have all an air of good faith; the illusion is so artfully respected that you are glad to be in it; the people are so much like your every-day acquaintance that you feel the impossibilities in which they figure to be entirely probable; if things did not happen as he says, that seems to be a fault in the frame of things, and no mistake on his part. His vaticinations as to our social future are so wisely as well as justly hopeful (I am speaking humanly, not Americanly, for he has his doubts, apparently, of the American future) that they win the heart while they convince the reason; and, when he drops his plummet into the abysm of the unknown, and draws it up to find some proof of the practicability of forecasting the future on the lead, you look affectionately over his shoulder, eager to believe that he has got it. When it comes to his forays in the realm of realism, you are, if possible, still more cordially with him.

There are few novels of the last three or four years, which have so abandonedly abounded in novels, half or one-tenth as good as *Love and Mr. Lewisham*, and I will frankly own that *Kipps* is not so good, though I found it, too, better than the multitudinous wash of recent fiction. Like the elder and the better novel, it deals with the simpler life, curiously streaked with the æsthetic life, which would like to be simple if it knew how. But, whereas Lewisham was eager to get on, education-ally, and was glad to be rid, but not ignobly glad to be rid, of the past in the form of his first love, Kipps quite as gladly reverts to his earliest days, even to the days before he became a dry-goods clerk, and turns with relief from the æsthetically and socially ambitious girl (she is never more than a polite Bohemian) whom he has unexpectedly won, to marry the little maid whom he loved when a boy, and finds that he still loves when she has grown up a little serving-maid. A good deal more of a plot than I like is needed to bring this about, or rather employed to bring it about. Kipps has to inherit a fortune from his grandfather, who had ignored him till the author's necessity, real or fancied, constrained him to leave Kipps his money; and the knowledge of his good luck has to come to Kipps by one of the most surprising chances, such a chance as art should be charier of than life is. Then he has to make friends on the borders of that great world which he ultimately finds he is not fit for, and these have to bring him in relations with the young lady whom he had idolized afar, but who, when she comes to idolize him, wishes to form him over in the image of that world, so much as she herself knows it, and to orient him anew in regard to his aspirates, and so wearies and wounds him with her instruction that his heart turns from her. It is very prettily imagined that she gets more in love with Kipps as he gets more out of love with her, and the whole situation is very humorously conceived. The courage with which Mr. Wells lets his hero be himself is most uncommon; less daring would not have been equal to turning him aside from the social longings which come to

Kipps with his fine clothes and his limitless money. At times the humor mounts till, in the chapter of the Anagram Tea, it reaches its highest; but it is never unkindly, and it touches pathos in the passage of Kipps's ineffectual stay in a great London hotel with all its incidents of mortifying failure in the endeavor to be a man even of the hotel world.

What is very admirable in the author is that he knows how to hold his hand, except at one supreme moment, where I foresee that I am going to lose my patience with him, when I come to it. He does not satirize the girl who has too interestedly accepted the simple soul, and he does not satirize her mother or her brother, or her family friend, the courtly Coote; he lets them satirize themselves; and, upon the whole, though he does conceal the girl's interestedness, he lets you feel a little sorry for her when Kipps quite ruthlessly, but not malevolently, jilts her. Some more plot comes in, I am sorry to say, when it is desirable to confront Kipps and his earliest love with themselves, and with the fact that they are not equal to their sudden riches. The brother of the jilted girl has to lose Kipps's money in a speculation, and they have to come down to very small things, and work slowly up from the fear, for there is never quite the danger, of poverty. They are entirely equal to that; but, in behalf of the weak-minded reader who wants his endings very good indeed, and his butter in a lordly dish, more plot is used to bring the Kippses back to a reasoned and prudent affluence. A rather improbable young playwright has induced Kipps to buy a share in the play which he cannot get produced, and then can, and begins to earn untold gold with it, and faithfully pays over to Kipps his princely share. But he is a very amusing playwright, if not a very probable one, and it is not he whom I am to find fault with in the inquiry which I promised, or expected, to make so wholly friendly.

It is the author whom I am to find fault with, and yet not the author either so much as that bad English school of fictional art, whose teachings he ought to have forgotten. When it comes to the lowest period of the Kippses' spiritual squalor, when their sufferings are too much for their principles, and the author conceives that you are perhaps thinking he is not aware how much they are suffering, but is hardheartedly having fun with their misery, he comes forward and openly tells you that he is not, but is really and truly sorry for them. No greater break was ever made by Thackeray, of whom Mr. Wells must have learned the bad business of coming forward in person, and talking directly to the reader. It is the greater pity, because the art of the book though at some times less than fine, at others is for the most part so very good, and needed so very little this piece of extraordinary self-sacrifice on the part of the artist.

42. Arnold Bennett on Wells as reformer

30 September 1905

Extract from letter to Wells, in *Arnold Bennett and H. G. Wells* (1960), ed. Harris Wilson, pp. 124–5.

Arnold Bennett (1867–1931) was one of Wells's most loyal friends. He had written an effusive survey of Wells's career for the *Cosmopolitan Magazine* (1902: see Introduction). Here he is responding to Wells's provocative remark that 'You are not a poet, you are not a genius' (letter of 25 September 1905) with a letter full of insight and rivalry.

You aren't an artist, except insofar as you disdainfully make use of art for your reforming ends; you are simply a reformer—with the classic qualities of the reformer. Hence your amazing judgments on Balzac, Milton, etc. Like all great reformers you are inhuman, and scornful of everything that doesn't interest you. Hence the complaint of the anti-Wellsites that in your 'scientific' novels, there is no individual interest, that the characters don't exist individually. A not unjust complaint. The pity is that these persons cannot perceive the 'concerted' interest of your 'scientific' novels. You are not really interested in individual humanity. And when you write a 'non-scientific' novel, you always recur to a variation of the same type of hero, and you always will, because your curiosity about individualities won't lead you further. You are concerned in big crowd-movements. Art, really, you hate. It means to you what 'arty' means to me. You live in a nice house, but you know perfectly well you wouldn't care what sort of a house you lived in. When you say that a great pianist is not a marvellous person, you give the show away. For you he is not. The astounding human interest of a dramatic triumph is for you a 'silly uproar.' In these two instances you show clearly, as regards art and as regards life, where your interests stop. You won't have anything to do with 'surface values' at all. You don't merely put them in a minor place; you reject them. A couple of pages devoted to surface values will irritate you. You will never see it, but in rejecting surface values you are wrong. As a fact they are just as important as other values. But reformers can't perceive this. They are capable of classing chefs, pianists and *trains de luxe* all together and saying: 'Go to, I am a serious person.' You are, you know. The same spirit animates you as animated George Macdonald's grandmother, who objected to the violin as a profane instrument. And the mischief is that, though you will undoubtedly do a vast amount of good in the world, you will get worse and worse, more and more specialised, more and more scornful. All this is not an explanation of you; but an explanation of me. It 'connotes' the difference between our minds. I proposed writing to you to offer Mrs. Wells and you the advantage of my presence for a night or so on my way to England early in December. If this suits, I can then respectfully listen to your defence. . . .

IN THE DAYS OF THE COMET

September 1906

---

43. Unsigned review, *Outlook*

15 September 1906, xviii, 351–2

This and the following items reveal some of the responses to Wells's emergence as a committed and 'sociological' novelist. At the same time, the appearance of the adjective 'Wellsian' marks a new stage in his literary eminence.

The place to be claimed for Mr. Wells in contemporary letters has never yet been determined. A high position of some state and ceremony has been definitely conceded to him, but its exact character has not been settled. We all know him as a writer of sparkling humour, as a caustic wit, as one brimming with invention, and simultaneously instinct with a powerful imagination. And finally we know him as an expert, almost a fanatical, sociologist and reformer. The problem before him and before us is the reconciliation of these sides—the composition, to vary the figure, of all these facets into a single and integral jewel. Many a satirist has stepped forth to whip hypocrisy, but it is not usual to travel to that goal along a romantic road. Mr. Kipling may be taken as an illustrious example of the desertion of art for a mission. He has 'found religion,' as the phrase goes, and roves no longer carelessly of moonlit nights and summer days. Once he was a vagrant; and now he has a pulpit. So, too, with Mr. Wells. The evolution has been subtle in either case, but subtler probably in the case of Mr. Wells. His first ventures were sheerly fictional. He took up the chips of his scientific workshop, and made use of them because he lived in the workshop and they were nearest to his hand. He manipulated his material with a fine sense of its largeness, its possibilities and its romance. There were critics who could see in *The Time Machine* and *The War of the Worlds* nothing but an ingenious invention and a great brain. The fact was that for the first time in the history of the novel scientific truths and theories were treated with imagination. It was not the science that made the value of Mr. Wells's earlier work. That was but an accident. It was the imagination and it was the artistry. It is impossible to read, say, *The Invisible Man* or *The First Men in the Moon*, without seeing that the author took an exquisite satisfaction in the composition of those books as tales. He is surrounded by scientific fact and fancy, and he has not yet reached the stage of being barricaded in by it. It is otherwise when we come to such a book as *The Food of the Gods* or *In the Days of the Comet*. In them Mr. Wells surrenders to his perfervid zeal. If he is not there a propagandist at work, he is a propagandist on his holiday. He is amusing himself, but it is not whole-hearted amusement.

The course of his career was arrested and deflected by his important sociological studies which resulted in *Anticipations, Mankind in the Making* and *A Modern Utopia*. Henceforward there would always be a temptation to model his fiction on the last-named work, which in a way is comparable with the present book. In his last philosophic treatise Mr. Wells bade farewell to sociology and announced his intention of returning to his first love. Is it, perhaps, too late? At least it is certain that all his work in the future must be coloured by his missionary efforts. The hero of this book, Leadford, is a proselyte, and we leave him proselytising. The world has suffered a great change; it has been exalted. And the issue of that exaltation is that men are living nobler, better and more wholesome lives. The secret is not revealed to us, nor do we get a full picture of the reformation. But indications in plenty show us vices deciduous in a new world. The comet is the author of this change, the comet which we find impending in heaven in the first chapter through Parload's glasses, and which tantalises us for nearly two hundred pages by its non-arrival. The catastrophe broods over us so long as that, which is Mr. Wells's old manner, and which imparts to the story an amazing thrill of expectation which is the essence of artistry. We can realise that instantaneous revolution in the fumes of the green vapour.

[Quotes Bk II, ch. 2 'For the whole world' to 'slowly clears again'.]

It is in passages such as this that we have Mr. Wells at his best. His vivid insight, his strong grip of fact, and his indomitable confidence—all unite in seizing one's imagination by the throat. We can conceive how he discovered the essence of his theme just there: the rejuvenation of the world in an instant as by a divine interposition. He has always shown a yearning towards miraculous science, and here is an orderly scientific exposition and rationalisation of the most orthodox aspirations of good and simple faith. There is nothing miraculous in science, he would say, for all is miraculous. The strength of his position is that he entices you into crediting his assumption, which for you thus lights up the world and the story about you.

One is convinced that at the outset this story was designed to be more of a story, to furnish more entertainment; but Mr. Wells apparently gets enmeshed in the web of his own invention. He soars so high that he loses the power of descent. The love affair of Willie and Nettie, which we started to follow with the zest with which we followed after Mr. Lewisham, becomes of less importance; it dissolves; it comes bump against the comet and disappears in green vapour. When the meteor struck Mother Earth Willie was madly careering after Nettie and her lover with a loaded revolver. On that transfigured morrow they met on amiable terms, discussed affairs very calmly and wisely, and showed no distress or emotion. Verrall will marry the girl now, and Willie will seek new pastures. Peace has descended on earth, and goodwill reigns under the stars. In the shelter of that benignancy we leave Willie to bury his mother and meet his fate in an unknown Anna. We must confess that the vagueness of the conclusion is disappointing. It appears that we have lost Nettie from our pages, and gone back to theory. With Nettie's appearance enters the tale, but when she goes we resume sociology with a brilliant mentor. Let us see how he writes in this mood, satiric pen in hand:—

[Quotes Bk I, ch. 1 'Let me tell you' to 'some very complicated problem'.]

His satiric comments and criticisms are scatterbrained throughout the book, and are essentially Wellsian. Here is one on caricature—the caricature which has disappeared from the reformed world:—

[Quotes Bk II, ch. 3 'They presented' to 'a shocking bad hat'.]

The fine portrait of his mother which Leadford draws is indicated in a few brilliant strokes, including the religious formulas which 'had no more relevance to the realities and needs of everyday contemporary life than if they were clean linen that had been put away with lavender in a drawer.' And those who know Mr. Wells's descriptive work will not need to be told of the magnificent way in which he handles such a theme as the Black Country by night, with the final crescive horror of the trains, 'articulated black serpents breathing fire.' If we are to lose our teller of tales, we rejoice at least in so brilliant a book as this. It is rich with atmosphere and strength. The philosopher and the satirist overlay the artist; but one remembers that, with a perfect equipment for art, Mr. Wells has always displayed a certain dissatisfaction with mere art. Yet art which clothes a book of purposely disjected earnestness like this is of great service to humanity.

44. Unsigned review, *Saturday Review*

22 September 1906, cii, 365

Mr. Wells' new novel, if this is the proper term for *In the Days of the Comet*, shows that he has not yet lost the momentum which he acquired while writing *Anticipations, Mankind in the Making* and *A Modern Utopia*. In the latter work he promised a return to his early and proper vocation of the writing of scientific romance or romantic science; at any rate that he would refrain in future from writing those popular essays of his with their clever criticism of the defects of our social, industrial and political arrangements, and those equally clever rearrangements prophetic of the socialist millennium. He has hardly kept his promise, though in the interval between *A Modern Utopia* and the present work he gave us the notable *Kipps* which contained nothing of the abnormal scientific but, what was infinitely better, a most human and life-like character in the environment of everyday life. We wish we could have had a successor of *Kipps*, which was a real creative product of head and heart, whereas *In the Days of the Comet* is at best only a clever kind of polemic, and a compilation of a good deal of material which Mr. Wells has used before in magazine articles. It would be a literary misfortune if Mr. Wells' imagination has given out in the production of such fantasies as *The Time Machine* and the rest of the series of brilliant romances. We should be delighted with a worthy successor to *Kipps* or *Love and Mr. Lewisham*; but *In the Days of the Comet* is a hybrid which we hope will have the destiny of hybrids; be sterile and produce no offspring. It is no use Mr. Wells trying to dramatise *Anticipations*, or to fuse the elements of this book into an artistic product. The novel with a socialist moral is a failure in Mr. Wells' hands, and where he fails it does not seem likely that anybody else will be more successful. A time may come, whether introduced by a comet's marvellous action on human nature or otherwise, when readers will be interested in the character and fortunes of a heroine who proposes to her two lovers a ménage à trois, but it is not yet. Mr. Wells would of course not have perpetrated so inartistic a bêtise if he had been writing simply a novel. He would have felt the impossibility of it as men and women are constituted here and now. But Mr. Wells is 'anticipating'; he is inventing paradoxes, as startling as may be to our conventional opinions and conduct. Possibly Mr. Wells may regard this as a daring but rational suggestion of what love-making in an ideal state of society would imply.

Whether he is in earnest we do not know; whether he really supposes there is a still unrevealed feminine psychology which would make such a proposition by a woman a possible or probable occurrence in a society untrammelled by a traditional code of morality. What he does is to make the disappointed lover from whom the lady is unwilling to part, she being happy with neither when t'other dear charmer's away, reject her proposition more in sorrow than in anger, yet with a tone of physical dislike and moral disapproval. So that it comes to this, that Mr Wells' 'audacious thinking' would not do even for a comet-transformed world; and what he has really achieved is that he has insulted his own heroine. But really he has not made up his mind what the love-making of the future is to be; he waters down the lady's original proposition into the sort of thing which looks like what is stupidly called a platonic relationship; but which leaves the reader with the impression that possibly the lady may not have altogether failed in her proposals after all. On the whole we are inclined to think Mr. Wells is giving us a satire on women, possibly after reading Mrs. Laura Marholm's *Psychology of Woman* the conclusion of which seems to be that nothing can be concluded from the dispositions, and whims and vagaries of the feminine character. It is not a novel subject for satire, nor a very original demonstration; but this strikes one as being the result of Mr. Wells' creative fancy dwelling on the coming new time when the scales have fallen from our eyes as to the relations of the sexes. As we are still living in pre-comet days, we can imagine the unsophisticated novel-reader being greatly indignant at Mr. Wells' dealings with his heroine. But when a novelist leaves his proper rôle of a describer of human nature as it is, and manufactures characters with a nature invented for artificial conditions, they cease to be characters and become theses or disquisitions.

This is what all the personages of *In the Days of the Comet* are. They are puppets with quotations from *Mankind in the Making* and *A Modern Utopia*. They are not types of character or of classes; they are not of value for their own sake; they are intended to personify opinions, views, practices, institutions and customs from the point of view of a satirist; and Mr. Wells' book is in short a satire on everybody and everything. It is an allegorical satire or a satirical allegory: whichever we may choose to call it. Mr. Wells goes at his work with plenty of gusto, and he derides and sneers at private property, theology, the press, trade and industry with the same vigour that he satirises the architecture of our houses, and the squalid kitchen and table and general meanness of surroundings in which the greater part of people pass their lives. But it is a thrice-told tale; and no writer has made us more familiar with it than Mr. Wells. If it is to be retold the novel is not the place for doing it; and especially it appears that this book proves the novel is not the medium for advocating a set of opinions about it. A novel with a purpose is not necessarily a failure; there are well-known instances to the contrary. But it would be as hopeless an artistic attempt to write a novel on free trade or tariff reform as to write one on socialism; which is what Mr. Wells has attempted in writing *In the Days of the Comet*. The real hero of the story is the comet, it is the only real personage, as one may say, in the book, and it is dramatic, impressive, surprising and dignified until it brings about the catastrophe from which is re-created the new world of Mr. Wells' dream. Then its effects become mixed. Its fumes apparently corroded Mr. Wells' pen; for he writes with rancour and violence and bad taste on current politics; and sketches living politicians in vulgar and coarse caricature. Readers who may be rather bored with the impossible cabinet councils of politicians whom Mr. Wells has converted into socialists bent on accomplishing his socialist ideas of the new world will find a sort of comic relief in these sketches. His curiosity may be stimulated to discover for whom they are meant, though if he traces the lineaments he will exclaim at the want of skill which Mr. Wells shows in personal portraiture. Two of these portraits, Lord Rosebery and Lord Goschen, are so rough and inartistic that the very tyro in newspaper personal sketching might have done them.

Against these lapses may be set some of the best writing in the book; the tableaux of the scenes throughout the world when the comet, long brooding over man, at last fulfils its mission and the old order vanishes. The ingenuity is admirable with which Mr. Wells avoids any scientific solecism as to the effects of a cometary collision with the earth, and at the same time seizes a scientific suggestion founded on spectroscopy for bringing his mechanism within a certain range of probability. That the comet should go further and bring about the change to socialism, introduces other considerations which we have already sufficiently dealt with. But we may remark on the really fine thought which Mr. Wells infuses through the whole of his traffic with the comet; that all great external changes must come through a change in the intellectual and moral views of men about themselves, their fellow-men and the obligations they are under to each other. Yet Mr. Wells is so excessively satirical that we might almost doubt whether he has not in fact written a satire against socialism itself. May we not understand him to hint that it would require at least the intervention of a comet to make men appreciably different from what they are; and that, as comets are rather shy of visiting the earth, nothing very remarkable is likely to happen for an indefinitely long time?

45. L. Haden Guest, review in *Fabian News*

January 1907, xvii, 13–14

Leslie, 1st Baron Haden Guest (1877–1960), Labour M.P. from 1923 to 1927 and from 1937 to 1950.

This review, which illustrates the excitement Wells aroused among the younger Fabians, was written at the height of the battle in the Society caused by Wells's challenge to the leadership of Shaw and the Webbs.

This book is not only as interesting as Mr. Wells's books always are, it is, in addition, very beautiful. And its interest is a new interest, much more straightforwardly human and very little mechanical. Most readers will for this very reason probably miss something; the keen analysis of *Anticipations* and the suggestive details of *A Modern Utopia* are alike absent. But what is missed is more than made up for by certain new elements which appear in Mr. Wells's writings for the first time. To begin with, the scene is laid largely in the industrial regions of England, a detail in itself of some significance, and in this Industrial England Mr. Wells seems to have been converted to a real living faith in Democracy and in fellowship. At least the world 'after the change' caused by the comet striking the earth, would appear to be founded on Democracy and fellowship. And one finds phrases indicating that a world sordid in one corner is sordid throughout.

The omissions are as interesting as the insertions. There is no talk here, as in *Anticipations*, of efficient engineer persons and trust managers brushing on one side the flag-waving and bumbledom of Democracy. There is even no suggestion of a 'Samurai' class. But there is talk of 'our commune or group,' an organization which appears to be the administrative machine of 'after the change.' The beauty of the book, however, is what most readers will like it for, a beauty that is made up of ugly things and consists in setting them in new relations. Ugly things are so terribly insistent and ungetoverable, so that to put them into a relationship with great things where their ugliness is manifest and yet a beauty beyond them obvious is to do one of the greatest of services. To do this in fact is to destroy the possibility of their continuance. When we see Dr. Gebbite's sitting-room or Parload's bedroom set against a background of planetary happenings we are at once emancipated from them, they can no longer limit us.

Possibly there is moral dynamite, but assuredly there is a moral catalytic ferment. And the 'Comet' introduces ideas and relationships that must inevitably disorganize our present relationships to life and set about creating others. When men read of 'Clayton' pictured and described as it here is, then the end of Clayton's sway has come. Not the most pig-headed local town councillor can read and be unchanged. He may object, pooh-pooh, or be grievously shocked at sex-relations he does not understand, but he can't be the same, and he must inevitably set about changing Clayton in the new direction his ideas have taken. Probably if the matter became one of debate and Wells's name were mentioned by, for instance, the newly elected Socialist member, the pig-headed one would get up and protest at the introduction of the names of visionary Socialists and observe that of course he'd always believed in—doing whatever might be the subject of debate—provided of course it could be done on a business basis.

Books like the *Comet* are perhaps more than catalytic, they are incendiary. They light 'Beltane fires' as the new world 'after the change' lighted, which will not be put out until all dross is burned away. In the meantime, and before the fire is too hot for comfort, they serve to light up what is otherwise hopeless darkness. Socialists always seem to be lighting these fires. Bernard Shaw I confidently believe has destroyed Hackney by writing *Candida*, Wells has destroyed 'Seven Dials' with 'The Star,' Folkestone and its like with *Kipps*, and now the Clayton world with the *Comet*. Thus our business is plain. It is to hurl *Comets* into every constituency, let the ferment work and the light blaze up and then step in to explain its economic significance and the obvious practical steps in local administration that lie before all men of good intent.

46. T. de Wyzewa on 'socialist' fiction

15 November 1907

Extract from 'Le Roman Anglais en 1907', *Revue des Deux Mondes*, xlii, 443–6.

Teodor de Wyzewa (1862–1917), musicologist and critic, was a staff writer on the *Revue des Deux Mondes* and had earlier written a ten-page review of *Love and Mr. Lewisham* (15 August 1900, clx, 936–46).

Mr. George Wells has never withheld this precious gift [of sympathy] even in the strangest adventures which have sprung from his fertile and delightful talent. Whether his subject was the frightful invasion of England by the inhabitants of Mars, or simply the mediocre love-affair of an assistant master and a shorthand-typist in the London suburbs, he has always made us feel his own profound engagement with his inventions: and so there is no improbability which he has not succeeded in making us accept. When in a few years' time it can be judged as a whole, his work will be seen to embody a surprising abundance of life; beneath the more or less 'scientific' bent of the subjects of his novels, there will be found a large group of typical figures, each with its proper physiognomy, and each observed and represented with a psychological novelist's skill. Unfortunately, in the last few years an accident has befallen Mr. Wells which threatens to harm the literary quality of his present and future output. In his latest novel, he imagines that a comet grazing the earth has transformed it to the extent of making it a veritable paradise; and the hero of the novel, in the 'memoirs' that he is supposed to write for us, constantly divides the history of the world into two epochs: 'before' and 'after' the comet. Indeed, it would be tempting to divide the fiction of Mr. Wells into two epochs as well: 'before' and 'after' the author's conversion to socialism.

Mr. Wells was born to a perception of the incurable weakness of human reason, the emptiness of the so-called 'conquests' of science, and the depths of animality which are hidden by the wholly external development of civilisation. He was able to express these things in a highly original vein of irony. One does not forget the admirable mixture of actual observation and fantastic invention in *The Island of Doctor Moreau*, *The War of the Worlds*, *The Time Machine* and *The Food of the Gods*, stories which, insofar as they showed the miserable pettiness and fundamental ignominy of our lives, presented variations upon a philosophical doctrine which might have come straight from Montaigne or Pascal's *Pensées*. And Mr. Wells drew his inspiration from a similar doctrine when, in other novels, he described the triumph of folly and injustice in the society of the future, the exploitation of science for the enslavement of the poor by the rich, and the imminent supplanting of all spiritual and moral beauty by an evil and selfish 'intellectualism.' Even in his novel of sentimental analysis, *Love and Mr. Lewisham*, he could not help contrasting the vain strivings of thought with the delicious and salutary sweetness of an artless love-affair. As some are made to extol their own period, Mr. Wells was evidently made by nature to disparage it; or rather, he was made to disparage that human pride which has existed at all times, but which was never affirmed so noisily as in the present realm of the automobile and the gramophone.

Against this pride Dickens struggled; and the fact is that everything seemed to promise to Mr. Wells a comparable role in English literature to that of the author of the *Christmas Books*: the role of a genuinely 'national' novelist, enjoying simultaneously the esteem of the educated public and the tender affection of the people. But Dickens had religious belief as his support, while Wells lacked this good fortune—on the one hand too full of the hypotheses of Huxley and Haeckel to be able to accept the Christian faith, yet on the other hand too sensible to follow these scholars beyond their negations to the dogmas of the 'scientific' idolatry which they claimed to set up. And so, being fundamentally in need of a spiritual belief, circumstances led him to seek it in the socialist Utopias which at least satisfied the generous promptings of his heart. Not long ago he was repeatedly describing for us the nightmare of a social organisation extinguishing all liberty and beauty from the world in the name of collective equality: but he then began himself to dream of such an equality, and expounded his new dream at first in purely theoretical works, full of ingenious insights and amusing paradoxes. But then, fatally recaptured by his storytelling demon, he wanted to resume the sequence of his novels, but to use them in future for the propagation and defence of the socialist idea. Thus there began a second period in his work, in the same way that he predicts that a second era for the whole globe will issue from its happy collision with a comet.

But even among his most assiduous admirers I do not think that anyone could consider this second era of his career as a novelist as a happy one. It is not only that the ardour of his convictions prevents him at present from taking as much interest as he should in the fictional inventions which serve as the support and framework of his thesis, and that the sociologist is always visible beneath the novelist. One feels that the socialist and 'modernist' ideal he preaches has a much firmer hold on his head than on his heart, and that he is obliged to make a continuous effort to imbue himself with the seriousness and truth of his affirmations. In particular, his latest novel, *In the Days of the Comet,* will be a sad disappointment to all those whom he formerly enchanted with *The War of the Worlds* and the delightful tale of *Love and Mr. Lewisham.*

They will find a love intrigue in it, the adventures of a young clerk who learns of the elopement of his fiancée with a rich *milord*, rushes off in pursuit of the abductor, catches up with him and is already raising his hand to kill him, when the sudden impact of the comet transforms the earth into a paradise. The clerk is immediately transformed into a perfect communist, ready to yield his loved one to his former rival, who is now his brother. Around this intrigue, Mr. Wells presents a number of further episodes, intended to show up the enormous difference in manners, feelings, and human life as a whole, *before* and *after* the timely comet. During the 'pre-cometal' period, for example, we are made to be present at a strike, at a theological discussion followed by a theft, and even at the beginning of an Anglo-German war. Then during the later period we are shown an extraordinary gathering of Cabinet ministers, at which these gentlemen—abruptly converted to socialism, thanks to the comet—take advantage of the accidental presence of the young clerk to confess their ambitions, their crimes, and the scandalous folly of their policies. There is no lack of facts, to be sure, in this new story; but the author recounts them so hurriedly, with such an air of attaching no importance to them, that we perceive them as if in a mist; they never succeed in moving us or pleasing us. Up to the moment of the arrival of the comet, heralded at every turn from the opening of the book, we await this intervention and get impatient at being held in suspense; and when at last it does arrive, we are astonished at the poverty of those of its consequences which are revealed to us. Waking up from a swoon caused by the impact, the hero records that everything around him is more beautiful and seems more living; then he chats fraternally (on terms of equality) with a stranger whom he sees lying nearby, and who turns out to be the Prime Minister; after which come the ministerial meeting I have mentioned, the reconciliation with the abductor, the death of an old lady, and, to end up with, a summary picture of the improvements introduced into public and private life by the people of tomorrow. And it is upon this picture that Mr. Wells rests his affirmation that, when his socialist ideal is realised, man will no longer have any metaphysical curiosity or need for religion, and will experience a truly celestial joy! Not to mention that he completely neglects to tell us how we can hasten the collision of our globe with the comet—which, in his novel, seems to be the sole and necessary condition of the advent of his socialism among us!

TONO-BUNGAY

February 1909

47. Hubert Bland, review in *Daily Chronicle*

9 February 1909, 3

Hubert Bland (1855–1914), journalist and founder-member of the
Fabian Society.

George Ponderevo, who writes his own story, tells us on the first page
of it that it is to be 'something in the nature of a novel.' Well, it is
something in the nature of a novel. It is not very much in the nature of a
modern novel but it is, perhaps, about as much like a novel as *Tristram
Shandy* is like a novel. 'I suppose' George goes on with his explanation
'what I'm really trying to render is nothing more nor less than Life—as
one man has found it. I want to tell *myself*, and my impressions of the
thing as a whole.' Now, of course, it is impossible to render nothing
less than Life in a novel, in a work of art that is. The utmost that can be
done is to render a little bit of life, and the attempt to do more than that
is pretty sure to result in something rather incoherent, not to say rather
chaotic. In point of fact, *Tono-Bungay* suffers, suffers badly, from this
attempt of its author's to say too much, to deliver his soul too fully—
from his determination to reject as little as possible. It suffers more even
than *Kipps* suffered. Mr. Wells's habit of letting his pen wander at large
is growing upon him. Presently the artist who gave us *Love and Mr.
Lewisham* will be no more. We shall have only a greatly inferior Sterne.

Tono-Bungay is a story and a series of essays bound up in one volume,
and I feel quite sure that nine readers in ten will wish that the story and
the essays had been bound up in separate volumes. It is irritating just
when one has become interested in a story to have to drop it, and read
an essay, and it is almost as irritating to find the essay cut short with three

or four dots thus . . . and to be brought back to the story again. One wishes that Mr. Wells had subjected himself to rather more of that 'discipline to refrain and omit' of which he speaks in the first chapter.

[Summarizes plot and main characters.]

It is difficult to avoid a suspicion that a good deal of this book was written while Mr. Wells was writing his *War in the Air*, or, at any rate, while he was mugging up the matter for his *War in the Air*. There are long, long passages treating of aerial navigation and the construction of flying machines, passages in which it is impossible for the uninformed mind to be even slightly interested, passages replete with 'foaming recondite technicalities,' to use Mr. Wells's own phrase. Then there is a wholly irrelevant account of a voyage to the coast of Africa in search of some wonderful stuff called quap, an episode that hinders rather than helps the progression of the story and does nothing whatever towards the development of any of the characters, an episode that had much better have been given as a short story. The fact is it is impossible for a writer even of Mr. Wells's fertile imagination and literary fluency to write a book of 500 pages and to keep to the point, or to anywhere near the point. But to do Mr. Wells justice, he did not set out with a view to keeping to the point; on the contrary, he rather boasts and glories in not keeping to the point. He zigzags.

48. Unsigned review, *Daily Telegraph*

10 February 1909, 15

It has been said, with some truth, that, while the impetuous and unbalanced young novelist puts all his knowledge and observation into his first novel, and finds himself left stranded at the outset of his career, the wise and deliberate artist bides his time, and produces in the full flood of his maturity the rich and broad-minded masterpiece which sums up his attitude to life. It was certainly so, to go back no further than the Victorian era, with Thackeray and Dickens. *Vanity Fair* and *David Copperfield*, epitomising, each in the light of its author's own temperament, the wisdom whispered to him by the years which bring the philosophic mind, were both of them the fruit of practice in art and maturity in judgment. And we think that we shall be within the limit of reasonable prophecy if we suggest that *Tono-Bungay* will prove to be Mr. H. G. Wells's *David Copperfield*—the full-fledged, four-square epitome of all that modern life and character have to tell him. It emerges, like the full flower of performance, from among any number of buds of promise, and it displays a breadth of view and an intensity of purpose unrivalled by any of its predecessors. Unless we are greatly mistaken, *Tono-Bungay* is one of the most significant novels of modern times, one of the sincerest and most unflinching analyses of the dangers and perils of our contemporary life that any writer has had the courage to submit to his own generation. Mr. Wells has certainly done nothing to approach this book, both for courage and for conviction. It may not be pleasant reading, but it is surely no less than the duty of every thinking citizen to read it, and to give it respectful consideration.

'Tono-Bungay' is a patent medicine, harmless but vain, invented by a provincial chemist, and upon its shoulders the inventor rises to universal repute and incalculable fortunes. And 'Tono-Bungay' is taken by Mr. Wells as a symbol of all the ugly reality of modern commerce— the greedy trade, the base profit-seeking, the bold, shameless advertisement of the age—the 'push' and 'boom' by which a gross imposture can be foisted upon the public. In the story of 'Tono-Bungay', moreover— in the history of the rise and fall of this invertebrate humbug—the fortunes of almost every side of modern society are gradually involved. The narrator of the tale, George Ponderevo, is the son of a decent, black-habited housekeeper in an old English family. His boyhood is spent in the servants' quarters of this dignified, if somewhat effete, establishment; and he only loses his position there through the Socialistic tendencies which no reader will be surprised to find in a hero of one of Mr. H. G. Wells's novels. From Bladesover, after certain discouraging experiences in the household of a violently Evangelical baker-uncle, the young Ponderevo is taken to be apprenticed to the inventor of 'Tono-Bungay,' the great creation of this story, which bears the name of his own ingenious fraud. Edward Ponderevo—'Uncle Ted'—is of the same class as Chaffery in *Love and Mr. Lewisham*—a class which Mr. Wells portrays with something of the analytic skill animating Browning's 'Sludge.' He is an absolute impostor, of very narrow wits, but of inveterate opportunism, who so thoroughly deceives himself into crediting his own lies that the reader (who is naturally behind the scenes) finds his sympathy compelled to take the impostor's side against the very world he wrongs. Specious, slippery, enthusiastic, born with the quick mastery over circumstances which helps every village Napoleon to control his own fate up to a certain fatal point, Ponderevo is a master-piece of whim, the very conception of which would have been impos-sible to the novelist of fifty years ago. He is entirely a product of later-day competition, of the Americanisation (perhaps) of English business morality. His fall, of course, is inevitable. The reader begins to perceive it while it is already afar off; but, when it comes, the pathos of it drowns out all the half-conscious humours of the situation. His true epitaph is pronounced by his devoted, if continually contemptuous, wife: '. . . "It wasn't fair, George; it wasn't fair. Life and Death—great serious things —why couldn't they leave him alone, and his lies and ways? If we could see the lightness of it . . . Why couldn't they leave him alone?" . . .' It is very true. Ponderevo, wildly irresponsible, a pierrot of the counting-house, a Napoleon among the dispensing bottles, was not one to be brought face to face with austere problems of justice and morality. His life is one vast panorama of human waste, and that is, indeed, the theme of the entire story.

For Waste—dire, irremediable human Waste—this is the black angel which spreads its wings over the whole record of *Tono-Bungay*. Mr. Wells's sincerity compels respect, even where his depression becomes almost intolerable, and the grey pessimism of his outlook is not to be resisted. With all the old definite pathology of *Love and Mr. Lewisham*, he pricks the bubble of Modern Love, leaving little remaining beyond crude physical attraction and equally crude, recurrent repulsion. His women waste his men (and themselves) in a vain conflict of the emotions: his stage is as full of the dead bodies of hopes and yearnings as the final platform of *Hamlet*. The sermon which Mr. Wells preaches (and, even in a novel, he is never long out of the pulpit) is the dreary lesson of futility. We 'make our lives,' he says, 'one vast dismal spectacle of witless waste.' Something, perhaps, emerges from the fog at intervals, some shaft of light amid the cloud-wrack. . . . 'Sometimes I call it Science, sometimes I call it Truth.' . . . but all in a moment the clouds have closed again, and there is no answer, nor any to regard. 'We are all things that make and pass, striving upon a hidden mission, out to the open sea'; and for the most part, what we make for ourselves is either a fraud or a failure. It is a dark reflection, darkly imagined; but it is Mr.

Wells's contribution to philosophy. And in *Tono-Bungay* it is embodied in actual life, with all the intense conviction of a masterpiece.

49. Beatrice Webb, diary entry

24 February 1909

Extract from unpublished MS. diary, Passfield Papers.

Wells had resigned from the Fabian Society in September 1908, and what had begun as a political battle with the Executive continued as a personal quarrel with the Webbs. This extract from Beatrice Webb's diary is immediately preceded by her reaction to a grudging letter from him (22 February 1909) on the publication of her *Minority Report of the Poor Law Commission*.

His two last books—*War in the Air* and *Tono-Bungay* are amazingly clever bits of work. I have the bad taste to prefer the former. Both illustrate the same theme—the mean chaos of human affairs. But *War in the Air* is avowedly a sort of allegory—or a parody—In form, an extravaganza, it is, in substance, a realistic description of the lowest and poorest side of social life. *Tono-Bungay*, on the other hand, sets out to be a straightforward description of society as it exists today—a sober estimate of the business world. But it turned out to be a veritable caricature—and a bitter one. Moreover, it bores me, because its detail is made up, not of real knowledge of the world he describes, but of stray bits he has heard from this or that person. There are quite a lot of things he has picked up from me—anecdotes about business men that I have told him are woven into his text, just all wrong—conveying an absurd impression of meaningless chaos. But he is a useful missionary to whole crowds of persons whom we could never get at. It will be sad if he turns completely sour: if after all, it turns out to be a misfortune to the cause we both believe in that we should have known one another.

50. Charles L. Graves, unsigned review in *Spectator*

27 February 1909, cii, 346

C. L. Graves (1856–1944), assistant editor of the *Spectator* from 1899 to 1917.

In this strange go-as-you-please narrative, which, spite of its irregular and discursive method, is the most serious attempt at a novel which he has hitherto undertaken, Mr. Wells has given us a strong, sincere, but in the main repellent work. It is a difficult book to review because of its wide range and varied suggestiveness, and, above all, because of the entire absence of that self-effacement deliberately practised by some of the greatest artists in fiction. It is true that at the outset the author, in the person of the narrator, disclaims all pretensions to artistic presentation. It is true, again, that the story is cast throughout in the form of an imaginary autobiography. But the narrative is freely interspersed with digressions, reflections, monologues, and essays, which so closely accord with the views expressed by Mr. Wells in his other works that it is difficult to avoid identifying the views of the author with those of the narrator. Again, some of the touches in the narrative are so curiously circumstantial as to convey a strong impression that we are reading, not of imagined, but of actual experiences. The blending of *Wahrheit und Dichtung* in fiction can never be wholly eliminated; but when it takes the form of confessions of a most intimate character, in which the narrator turns himself inside out with ruthless conscientiousness, the result is often disconcerting, and even painful. The author has not preserved a judicial detachment from his characters; on the contrary, by associating all these reflective comments with the narrator, and attributing to him a number of opinions and interests which he has himself espoused, he has to that extent chosen to challenge rather than conciliate the reader. It would have been quite possible, so far as we can see, to have kept his personality entirely apart; but Mr. Wells has chosen otherwise, and the skill with which he has reproduced the mingled complacency and humiliation of George Ponderevo's confessions only serves to prejudice one against the Wellsian philosophy of life.

As for the story, it is the life-history of George Ponderevo, the son of the housekeeper in a great Kentish mansion, organised and administered on feudal principles. Mrs. Ponderevo, who has been deserted by a worthless husband, is a hard, honest woman, obsequiously attached to her mistress, Lady Drew. George lives or spends his holidays at the great house in more or less inarticulate revolt against the system, until he incurs a sentence of banishment for thrashing a young nobleman, but not before he has made precocious love to an even more precocious young lady of rank.—This whole episode, we may remark, strikes us as extremely improbable, and wholly untypical of the treatment that would have been meted out in real life to such conduct on the part of a servant's son.—George is then apprenticed to his uncle Edward, a chemist in a small neighbouring town, and lives with him until his speculations involve him in a bankruptcy which swallows up George's patrimony. The boy is taken on by his uncle's successor, works his way up the ladder of learning, matriculates at London University, wins a scholarship, and is already resolved to specialise in science, when his uncle, who has successfully launched a quack remedy on the market, offers him a salary and a share in the business. George is fully aware that his uncle is a charlatan and the drug a fraud, but he is anxious to marry, and closes with the offer. For seven years he is bound up with the fortunes of 'Tono-Bungay' and its various offshoots, tastes the illicit sweets of company-promoting, shares the successes and is involved in the collapse of his uncle's unscrupulous enterprise. Meantime he has wearied of, deceived, deserted, and been divorced by his blameless but insipid wife; he has achieved distinction as a man of science and aerial navigator, conducted an expedition to West Africa in search of a mysterious radio-active substance, and murdered a negro. He has long broken off the liaison with the 'magnificently eupeptic' typewriting girl which led to his divorce, and resumed amorous relations with Lady Beatrice, the precocious girl mentioned above, who has developed into an aristocratic courtesan of the most advanced and aggressive type. He offers her marriage, but she repeatedly refuses, realising her antipathy to domestic life, and they drift apart, George henceforth devoting his energies to the construction of destroyers.

Though by no means impartial in his analysis of the slow decay of the old social system, Mr. Wells bears adequate, if reluctant, testimony to its tenacity and permanence, and frankly admits that, with all its limitations, it is preferable to the new plutocratic régime which threatens to take its place. (Curiously enough, however, he chooses the name Lichtenstein, borne by one of the most exclusive Austrian noble houses, to typify the Semitic invasion!) On the other hand, though from boyhood instinctively inclined to rebel against authority, the narrator-hero is at best half-hearted in his antinomianism. He is not a valiant or, to borrow Mr. Wells's own phrase, a magnificently eupeptic sinner. He is painfully self-conscious, always on the defensive with his social superiors, anxious to impress them by his speech or his actions. He is unable to defy convention with equanimity, and casts the responsibility for his lapses on Nature, or the social system, or his neighbour. Driven by mere passion into an ill-assorted marriage, he extricates himself ignobly. Love with him is not a liberal education, but an appetite: there is no touch of spirituality in his *grande passion* for Lady Beatrice, who, for the rest, is quite a melodramatic and phantasmal figure. Far better than this dreary or lurid harping on the sex problem are the passages in which Mr. Wells is stirred to eloquence by the contemplation of the grandeur or squalor of London, by the magic of its ancient river. The romantic side of the mad game of modern commercial and journalistic adventure; the dodges of forcing worthless wares on a gullible public and getting rich quick,—all this is described with the utmost verve and a strange mixture of contempt and tolerance. Without justifying these methods, Mr. Wells conveys the impression that they may prove a valuable school for sharpening one's wits. As for his general outlook, nothing could be more pessimistic. We are on the eve of tremendous discoveries in the direction of applied science; but, as a set-off, the race is degenerating, and the individuals who 'come through'—like the narrator—do so by virtue of vehement self-assertion, by stifling the voice of conscience, by a callous disregard of human life and family ties. Yet this inhumanity is tempered with moments of misgiving and spasms of remorse. Viewed, therefore, as a novel with a purpose, *Tono-Bungay*, with its reluctant tributes to orthodoxy and the training of the old school, cannot be regarded as an effectual protest against the existing order. It is disfigured in places by a perverted sincerity which disregards the Tacitean precept, *abscondi debent flagitia*, but it is at least never dull, and it introduces us to one character, Susan Ponderevo, the wife of the quack medicine-man, whose undistinguished but delightful humour renders her almost as captivating a personage as the immortal Mr. Hoopdriver.

51. Arnold Bennett, review in *New Age*

4 March 1909, n.s. iv, 384–5

This review appeared in Bennett's regular column, 'Books and Persons', under the pseudonym 'Jacob Tonson'. It was reprinted in *Books and Persons* (1917), 109–16.

Wells! I have heard that significant monosyllable pronounced in various European countries, and with various bizarre accents. And always there was admiration, passionate or astonished, in the tone. But the occasion of its utterance which remains historic in my mind was in England. I was indeed in Frank Richardson's Bayswater. 'Wells?' exclaimed a smart, positive, little woman—one of those creatures that have settled every question once and for all beyond re-opening— 'Wells? No! I draw the line at Wells. He stirs up the dregs. I don't mind the froth, but dregs I—will—not—have!' And silence reigned as we stared at the reputation of Wells lying dead on the carpet. When, with the thrill of emotion that a great work communicates, I finished reading *Tono-Bungay*, I thought of the smart little woman in the Bayswater drawing-room. I was filled with a holy joy because Wells had stirred up the dregs again, and more violently than ever. I rapturously reflected, 'How angry this will make them!' 'Them' being the whole innumerable tribe of persons, inane or chumpish (this adjective I give to the world), who don't mind froth, but won't have dregs. Human nature—you get it pretty complete in *Tono-Bungay*, the entire tableau! If you don't like the spectacle of man whole, if you are afraid of humanity, if humanity isn't good enough for you, then you had better look out for squalls in the perusal of *Tono-Bungay*. For me, human nature is good enough. I love to bathe deep in it. And of *Tono-Bungay* I will say, with solemn heartiness, 'By God! This is a book!'

You will have heard that it is the history of a patent medicine—the nostrum of the title. But the rise and fall of Tono-Bungay and its inventor make only a small part of the book. It is rather the history of the collision of the soul of George Ponderevo (narrator, and nephew of the medicine-man) with his epoch. It is the arraignment of a whole epoch at the bar of the conscience of a man who is intellectually honest and powerfully intellectual. George Ponderevo transgresses most of the current codes, but he also shatters them. The entire system of sanctions tumbles down with a clatter like the fall of a corrugated iron church. I do not know what is left standing, unless it be George Ponderevo. I would not call him a lovable, but he is an admirable, man. He is too ruthless, rude, and bitter to be anything but solitary. His harshness is his fault, his one real fault; and his harshness also marks the point where his attitude towards his environment becomes unscientific. The savagery of his description of the family of Frapp, the little Nonconformist baker, and of the tea-drinkers in the housekeeper's room at Bladesoever, somewhat impairs even the astounding force of this, George's first and only novel—not because he exaggerates the offensiveness of the phenomena, but because he unscientifically fails to perceive that these people are just as deserving of compassion as he is himself. He seems to think that, in their deafness to the call of the noble in life, these people are guilty of a crime; whereas they are only guilty of a misfortune. The one other slip that George Ponderevo has made is a slight yielding to the temptation of caricature, out of place in a realistic book. Thus he names a halfpenny paper, 'The Daily Decorator,' and a journalistic peer, 'Lord Boom.' Yet the few lines in which he hints at the tactics and the psychology of his Lord Boom are masterly. So much for the narrator, whose 'I' writes the book. I assume that Wells purposely left these matters uncorrected, as being essential to the completeness of George's self-revelation.

I do not think that any novelist ever more audaciously tried, or failed with more honour, to render in the limits of one book the enormous and confusing complexity of a nation's racial existence. The measure of success attained is marvellous. Complete success was, of course, impossible. And, in the terrific rout, Ponderevo never touches a problem save to grip it firmly. He leaves nothing alone, and everything is handled—handled! His fine detachment, and his sublime common sense, never desert him in the hour when he judges. Naturally his chief weapon in the collision is just common sense; it is at the impact of mere common sense that the current system crumbles. It is simply unanswerable common sense which will infuriate those who do not like the book. When common sense rises to the lyric, as it does in the latter half of the tale, you have something formidable. Here Wells has united the daily verifiable actualism of novels like *Love and Mr. Lewisham* and *Kipps*, with the large manner of the paramount synthetic scenes in (what general usage compels me to term) his 'scientific romances.' In the scientific romance he achieved, by means of parables (I employ the word roughly) a criticism of tendencies and institutions which is on the plane of epic poetry. For example, the criticism of specialisation in *The First Men in the Moon*; the mighty ridicule of the institution of sovereignty in *When the Sleeper Wakes*, and the exquisite blighting of human narrow-mindedness in 'The Country of the Blind'—this last one of the radiant gems of contemporary literature, and printed in *The Strand Magazine*! In *Tono-Bungay* he has achieved the same feat, magnified by ten—or a hundred, without the aid of symbolic artifice. I have used the word 'epic,' and I insist on it. There are passages toward the close of the book which may fitly be compared with the lyrical freedoms of no matter what epic, and which display an unsurpassable dexterity of hand. Such is the scene in which George deflects his flying-machine so as to avoid Beatrice and her horse by sweeping over them. A new thrill, there, in the sexual vibrations! One thinks of it afterwards. And yet such flashes are lost when one contemplates the steady shining of the whole. *Tono-Bungay*, to my mind, marks the junction of the two paths which the variety of Wells's gift has enabled him to follow simultaneously. And at the same time, it is his most distinguished and most powerful book.

ANN VERONICA

October 1909

52. R. A. Scott-James, review in *Daily News*

4 October 1909, 3

Rolfe Arnold Scott-James (1878–1959), critic and journalist.

'Thank God for Mr. Wells,' is the ejaculation which has been uttered by some of his wisest readers; 'thank God for Mr. Wells, who is a rock of sanity in this sea of madness.' When I had read about half of this book I was inclined to endorse this pious sentiment. Here is a living writer who has shown a singular faculty for envisaging the vast complex of modern society, sorting out the human compartments, generalising, making rules, but, above all, a man whom rules are not big enough to hold— one who makes rules and defies them, because nature, and especially human nature, does so too.

But as I approached the end of this book a fear began to creep unpleasantly over me. Mr. Wells was weakening; he has succumbed. The tendency of the human mind to create conventional habits has become too strong for him. Having spent the best part of his life combatting this tendency, having been one of those who started the intellectual fashion of combatting it, he has only succeeded, like the other demigods who are dominating modern thought, in substituting for the old traditional morality a new morality which is merely its opposite. In effect he is content to negate the old morality as something out of date, effete, harmful, tiresome; he puts in its place a negative which masquerades as the supreme assertion of individuality.

Mr. Wells has not leapt to this conclusion all at once, or willingly. Again and again in this new book of his he seemed about to come to quite a different conclusion, to be on the verge of some supreme assertion which would suggest a way of escape for the more sincere theorists of to-day. For a moment he hovered on the brink of such an assertion, but after all no vision came to him; thoughts which he did not wish to repudiate held him back, and in the end he seems to have thrown in his lot with the new fashion and to have bound himself over to the latest convention. I wonder if he has reflected upon the influence exercised by his books upon enormous circles of readers.

No apology is needed for treating this work as an exposition of the author's views about modern society. It is in form a novel; and it has much excellence as a novel. The plot is more firmly welded together than has been the case in some of his books. In the early pages there are a few faults which spring from a grotesque exaggeration of satire, a treatment not quite light enough, not so genial as the treatment to which he has accustomed us. In the middle of the book there are allusions to some members of the Fabian Society under their real names, personal allusions which ought not to have been dragged into the charmed atmosphere of fiction. Nevertheless it is an excellent novel. The characters gradually grow into vital personalities. The heroine from whom the book takes its name begins as an impetuous, capricious girl, with a sense of humour, and ideals which she does not understand. She becomes a woman, experienced, self-reliant, reflective, capable of discipline, yet with a capacity of concentrated passion which she is willing to regard as the true channel of her destiny. At least two of the men are individual creations: Mr. Ramage, a middle-aged man of the world with hardened views, cynical, erotic, and ruthless, yet not ill-disposed so far as he is not thwarted; and Capes, a curious combination of the scientist and the idealist, a quiet, thoughtful, persuasive man, who allows instinct to play its part in life, and in the end is willing to stake all on an adventure, an adventure upon which Mr. Wells expends a fine rhapsody worthy of a more truly romantic ending.

As a novel it is a brilliant and an interesting one. But, as everyone knows, Mr. Wells uses the novel as a medium for expressing his views, and therefore we cannot fail to be concerned with those views. And in the first place it must be said that he has stated his problem, the problem of the young woman of to-day, in the most masterly fashion. He presents to us as a fine type Ann Veronica, the young woman of strong character and ideals, who lives in a conventional semi-suburban home. Her situation is that which confronts thousands of young women. What has life got to offer her? The choice seems to lie between a limited life in a home where she is bound to conform to the life-denying ideas

of the generation to which her parents belong and to the foolish conventions of her suburb; and an equally limited existence as the wife of the
first man whom circumstances, not of her choosing, offer as a husband.
No, there is a third course, the course she adopts; she throws herself
upon the world of London, hoping there to earn her own living; and
she finds that she has no industrial value, that there is no opening for her.

And so Mr. Wells shows us this girl seeking to find something in
life, she knows not what, and perpetually frustrated. She comes forth
from her home like a 'female ant from its nest.' She longs vaguely for
'the world of romance, the world of fascinating, beautiful things,' at
the same time exclaiming, 'I wish I had some idea what I was really up
to.' Alone in London she finds no outlet for her ambition. She is pursued
by one unscrupulous man. She is crudely told by another that 'home is a
place to hang on to.' She finds herself in love with another beyond her
reach. She finds herself somehow or other 'up against the whole order
of things—the whole blessed order of things.' In her vague rebellion she
naturally joins the Suffragette movement, and even there cannot help
observing that 'so many of the people "in the van" were plain people,
or faded people, or tired-looking people.' It was not without significance that there was a 'perplexing contrast between the advanced
thought and the advanced thinker.' A short course of agitation, and of
self-martyrdom in prison, makes her reflect on her world of 'egotistical
children and broken-in people.' 'What have I been all this time?' 'Just
stark egotism, crude assertion of Ann Veronica, without a modest rag
of religion or discipline or respect for authority to cover me!'

Did Mr. Wells mean anything when he put these words into Ann
Veronica's mouth? Why did he make her go back and try and endure
her home? Whatever he may have meant it comes to nothing. He sends
her into the arms of a man who defies convention for her and for him
in order to be united with her, and in the sublimity of a union made in
Heaven the book closes, the solution is found!

This is quite the modern intellectual solution, the wonderfully simple
solution, for all the ills to which man is heir. However, it is rather
difficult of universal application. Even if, ideally, it were the true solution,
it must be pointed out that in practice passion has a curious way of
representing itself as ordained by destiny, and a curious way of vanish-
ing when it is put to the test of time and of the commonplaces.

But quite apart from that question, I maintain that Mr. Wells's
psychology is wrong in its foundation. He is right in his protest against
the modern world, against its lack of opportunities for development,

its crushing, stifling effect. But it is not merely the unmarried or the unhappily married women who feel this; it is a feeling common to all the men and women alike of this age who have attained a measure of self-consciousness. It is not frustrated sex impulses which are responsible for the evil; they are merely a symptom; you will not put things right by promoting some mighty sex-passions. It is something deeper than that which is at fault; and a profounder remedy must be sought. But this review of a book is not the place in which to embark on a counter theory.

53. John O'London, review in *T.P.'s Weekly*

22 October 1909, xiv, 537–8

John O'London [Wilfred Whitten] (d. 1942), journalist and editor of *John O'London's Weekly* from 1919 to 1936, explains why *Ann Veronica* is a 'dangerous novel'.

'She wanted to live.' At this sentence on page 10 of *Ann Veronica* many a dainty thumb will tighten on the volume. For it is seen that Mr. Wells is about to bring his rare powers of dramatic synthesis to a theme no less piquant and personal than the modern daughter's revolt against the alleged dullness of the home, the suburb, and the wedding-ring. *Ann Veronica* leaps with the times. It will thrill many an English girl who, educated and aglow, looks out from her father's ordered and defensive home on the spectacle of modern life, with its immense new currents of thought and its surpassing horizons, be they mirage or reality. Most things are questioned nowadays, and here is a sympathetic portrait of a young educated English girl who not only questions 'the wise world' on themes of vital importance, but insists on dictating its answers.

'She wanted to live.' There is a betraying truth in every tricky phrase, and this is such a phrase. The girl who passionately exclaims that she wants to live implies that the life she is living is not worthy to be called life. I am not investigating her precise thought, but am tracing, as well as I can, the quality of the phrase which her unsatisfactory thought has created. Still less am I turning a chill or sneering glance on her situation. Heaven forbid! The desire to live—that is to say, to live intelligently, rejoicingly, and abundantly—is altogether good, but its realisation is not, has never been, and never can be half so dependent on environment, society, and personal liberty as is now so commonly and loosely supposed. When Ann Veronica looks at the villas and snug avenues of Morningside Park, and, seeming 'to be making some sort of inventory,' exclaims. 'Ye gods! *what* a place!' we at once catch her whole meaning and outlook. But shall we endorse it? Are her words the eloquence of a rich nature cribb'd and cabin'd, or do they reveal the essential poverty of her mind—an inability, at any rate, to see where her treasure lies? Thus Mr. Wells pictures Ann Veronica:

[Quotes ch. 1 'She wanted to live' to 'in undertones'.]

We shall all recognise the great amount of truth and typical value in this picture. The problem is fairly stated.

Decidedly, then, *Ann Veronica* will be read and talked about this winter by the British daughter. All I can say is that I hope the British daughter will keep her head. That Mr. Wells's story may do considerable mischief is too clear. On the other hand, I think that no girl who is possessed of the priceless qualities which one may briefly call balance and spirituality will be deceived by Ann Veronica's peculiar gospel of self-fulfilment. She will be interested, and that in feverish ways; but when she has laid down the book and surveyed this strange hegira of revolt and adventure she will whisper to herself, out of a mood of tense reflection and self-reference, 'To the old paths, my soul!' She will decide that whatever denial of life the present mixed standards and conditions of society may involve to herself, she will be happier in taking her share of the travail and frustration than in choosing as her guide and madonna a young woman who severs her home ties without tears or remorse to plunge into the welter of London life and find her happiness in a union with a man who, whatever the spell of his intellect and masculinity may be, is already married, and is besides an adulterer of the worst type. Such, I imagine, will be the conclusion of the level-headed and self-communing British daughter who reads Mr. Wells's story, and she will come to it the more easily because, in rejecting Ann Veronica's way, she need not despise Ann Veronica. The truth is that

Mr. Wells's heroine is not sufficiently real and human to be criticised. In so far as she is human she is splendidly courageous and intelligent. But actually she is rather a type than an individual; rather an embodiment of ideas than a person. It is still more true to say that she is both by turns, but whenever one begins to consider the deeper issues of her story she shows as an idea in petticoats. And in its briefest form the idea is found in these words, 'She wanted to live.'

Self-fulfilment at any price is Ann Veronica's motto. It is a rule of life, or an absence of rule, full of a wild attraction. Mr. Wells, as the disposer of Ann Veronica's fate, can bring her through, but in real life the girl who thus threw the reins on the neck of Destiny would be courting irretrievable disaster. She may know this, and yet in these days of liberation and shifting standards she may be startled into something like passionate admiration of Ann Veronica's courage and unfaltering self-sufficiency. It is nothing to her that Capes, the biologist, has a wife to whom he has already been unfaithful. And when these two have eloped to Switzerland, and are able to look at themselves, not all Capes's candour can shake her ratification of their position.

[Quotes ch. 16 'We just hit against' to 'thoughtful eyes upon him'.]

Here, then, you have a modern British daughter defying the old morality, and saying it is glorious to do so. To quote the Decalogue against her is clearly useless. To condemn her at all will seem to many a young reader like depreciating love, courage, and emancipation. This is why *Ann Veronica* seems to me to be a dangerous novel.

It is best to question Ann Veronica without the aid of the Decalogue or that old morality which she so learnedly rejects. For if Mr. Wells has not wholly mistaken his audience there must be British daughters who are nearly as ready as Ann Veronica to dismiss the experience of mankind as effete. They may quote one of her bursts of impassioned snip-snap in which she tells the married Capes, 'You are just necessary to life for me. I've never met anyone like you. To have you is all-important. Nothing else weighs against it. Morals only begin when that is settled. . . . I shan't care a rap if one can never marry. I'm not a bit afraid of anything—scandal, difficulty, and struggle. . . . I rather want them. I do want them.' In this and similar speeches there is no doubt a sort of spendid defiance. The ear loves the sound of any trumpet, and the heart-strings will respond always to the vibrations of self-reliance and abandonment: it is their nature to do so. But Ann Veronica's love for Capes, her rage for self-fulfilment in a union with the married biologist, is seen to be a savage and devouring selfishness originating in an untutored greed of life, intellectual in character, but essentially hard, cheap, and unspiritual. For, with all her allurements, Ann Veronica is denied spirituality, that fine flower, say rather that scent, of the hidden garden of the soul which is the greatest thing under heaven, and must remain the breath and test of all successive faiths, all widening knowledge, and all truly emancipated women. The girl of the suburbs who keeps a dissected frog in her bedroom, but never the dove of peace in her heart, rightly says that she is 'hard stuff.' The truth is that she belongs to that growing mob of clever supermannikins who mistake their own intellectual spasms for the world's progress. It may be granted in her favour that she is wise enough to rise above the Miss Minivers of the Movements, so effectively satirised by Mr. Wells, whose bosoms palpitate with 'causes' and 'coming waves' while their lips utter foolishness the day long. She has also the wit to think out in prison the folly of the militant Suffragette and to discover that many things which conflict with the hopes of man must be accepted by the wise, because for the time being they *are so*.

Had Mr. Wells's prudence been as small as Ann Veronica's he would surely have left the lovers to fight the world on the basis of their irregular union. But no. Four-and-a-half years have passed, and we discover Capes and Ann Veronica—legally married. The world has been placated in the persons of Ann Veronica's father and aunt, a child is expected, and the majestic everyday world is asserting its customs and routine once more. One keenly understands Ann Veronica's sense of bewilderment and disillusion. In her husband's arms she pours out her broken thoughts and new discernments.

I've loved love and you, and the glory of you; and the great time is over, and I have to go carefully and bear children . . . and when I have done with that I shall be an old woman. The petals have fallen—the red petals we loved so. We're hedged about with discretions—and all this furniture—and successes.

So Ann Veronica has run her race. She has fled from discretions and furniture and successes to plunge through mud and danger to a haven of successes, furniture, and discretions. No wonder her petals are falling. The petals are falling from the whole theme. The things that 'are so' begin to be revealed. For so much we may be grateful, and the pity is that a story which touches modern life at so many points is not oriented properly. It stands as an alluring picture of revolt against those barriers of life which are really conterminous with its deepest facts. It invites the British daughter to run amuck through life in the name of self-fulfilment.

Mr. Wells's novel, of course, separates itself from that large and increasing mass of 'sexual' fiction which is steadily introducing a hot and baneful tetter into the blood of the nation, but it shares the responsibility of a futile meddling with the marriage tie, and a tendency to glorify the woman who has had sexual adventures. I hope that Mr. Wells is not going to join that large school of writers who conceive that life has no value unless things 'happen.' No doubt they reflect a tendency to which we are increasingly subject. The world is moving so fast, new ideas and horizons are opening so quickly, that young people are dazzled by life as a spectacle, and as an aggregate of brilliant contacts and opportunities. They want 'to live.' They become, like Ann Veronica, greedy of life, and commiserate the suburb and the country town as 'a world in which days without meaning, days in which "we don't want things to happen" follow days without meaning.' But the culture which exclaims 'Ye gods! *what* a place!' is worth very little, and the girl who exclaims to a man 'You can think all round me' has little dignity or interior wealth. All sorts of new things are true, but all sorts of true things are old. The test of culture is still the ability to make our own satisfactions. The legal husband, wife, and child are still the units of society. The best woman is still the good woman, who maintains her culture by imparting it to her children, who interpolates her mother wit in a world of pioneering and argument, and who, as far as may be, makes her own home a microcosm of Utopia. It may be all very difficult, and may require some self-limitation in exchange for some self-fulfilment. Such a woman will suffer, as all men and women suffer, but she will be lovely and lovable in her life, and in her coffin more beautiful than she whose beauty launched a thousand ships and burned the topless towers of Ilium.

54. Unsigned review, *Nation*

23 October 1909, vi, 167–70

The story is simple enough. Ann Veronica, living in the suburbs with a suburban father, breaks away from his suburban dominance: determines to 'live her own life.' She speedily discovers the impossibility of a pretty girl with no wage-earning capacities 'living her own life.' She borrows money from a man who, in return, demands a customary and expected reward. She engages herself to a sentimental humbug and breaks off the engagement without compunction. She essays various outlets for unsatisfied and stifled woman's desires: mingling with the pitiful company of the ineffective 'moderns,' who discuss, egotistically and with tragic futility, various methods of unattainable reform. She plunges into the 'Suffragette' agitation, goes wearily to prison, emerges disgusted and disillusioned. Finally, in passionate and reckless love for her teacher in biology (a married man), she snatches at one crowded hour of glorious life: heedless of honor and the moralities, confident in the attainment of some transfiguration beyond them all. The end of the book is, in reality, the journey of Capes and Ann Veronica to the mountains and their sojourn there. The rest is the conventional conclusion which Mr. Wells, good artist as he is, might well have spared us. The phantom Mrs. Capes has disappeared: Ann Veronica becomes decently married to her lover: father and aunt accept reconciliation and dinner with affable forgiveness: Capes makes a huge financial success as a writer of plays. The author must have mocked at himself as he added this fairy tale ending to a work that is otherwise a study of reality. It may have been necessary for the quieting of the public conscience: but it lacks the sombre sincerity of Mr. Lewisham's gaze from his dingy lodging into the London darkness with some vague, faint hope that, through the child who has been born, his life will be linked with a less intolerable future: or the passage of George Ponderevo on his destroyer past a world symbolic of waste and confusion down to the large breath and salt airs of the open sea.

It is less a story than a study: a study of the unrest and dissatisfaction which has entered into the soul of the modern city-bred girl, who from the beginning has been relieved from the need for wage earning, and finds herself condemned to waiting for the suburban husband who will condescend one day to ask her to be his wife. In part, Mr. Wells is dealing with present peculiar conditions, the revolt which comes from idleness, and artificial occupations, and the circumscribing tumuli of dead moralities, dead conventions, dead religions. In part the study is more universal: of the stimulus and great desires of adolescence, with the world suddenly opened to the mind first attaining self-consciousness, oppressed partly by vague unattainable longing, partly by revolt against the 'shabby second best,' which is the utmost most can make of life. Ann Veronica finds herself called to a crusade—to a dozen crusades. Here are things so obviously out of joint: here are evils eagerly demanding remedy. A little propagandism, a little preaching of reasonableness, a little general kindly feeling, and the world can be made beautiful and dramatic again. Only towards the end does she realise that she is campaigning—with no adequate weapons but egoism and some vanity and a wavering resolution—against the inheritance of a hundred centuries, and all the solid amalgam of good and evil of a world which is very old. Her meditations in prison amongst the 'Suffragettes' bring her sharply against the blind jagged edges of reality. Religious faith is gone. 'I suppose I believe in God. . . Never really thought about Him—people don't.' 'Violence won't do it' (again). 'Begin violence and the woman goes under.' 'Life is difficult,' she cries; 'when you loosen the tangle in one place you tie a knot in another.' She has descended suddenly into regions she had never appreciated—the underside of civilisation, the kingdom of force, against which even the refinements and securities of suburbandom maintain their continuance but hardly. 'This is the real texture of life,' she cries. 'This is what we secure people forget. We think the whole thing is straight and noble at bottom: and it isn't. . . . One doesn't realise that even the sort of civilisation one had at Morningside Park is held together with difficulty.' 'Life is many-sided and complex and puzzling. I thought one had only to take it by the throat.' 'It hasn't *got* a throat.'

That absence of throat to grapple with in life is the crowning discovery. Having lost all through its apprehension, Ann Veronica can gain all through the acceptance of one transfiguring passion in which the world (without a throat) becomes remote and negligible. Capes has come 'damaged goods': with a wife that refuses to release him, 'of a very serene and proud and dignified temperament.' 'I worshipped her and subdued myself.' He has come through the divorce courts as co-respondent in a 'shabby, stupid, furtive business.' He and Ann had met dissecting dog-fish in the atmosphere of the laboratory amid the smell of decay and cheap methylated spirit. They escape to moonlight on the mountains: through great waste spaces of snow and star-lit sky, in which for one moment the 'earth life' of the 'earth bowed' confusion below vanishes in an ecstacy of intoxication. And the place of return is still the region of dissecting dog-fish and the smell of decay and cheap methylated spirit: in which the 'wrappered' conventional existence, the set grey life and apathetic end, seem only less unendurable than the feeble efforts of all who essay escape except into the Kingdom of Passion—where man and woman, indifferent to all pasts and futures, are plucking the red petals which they know must fall.

Mr. Wells devotes all his extraordinary ironic power to destructive, savage criticism of the modern emancipators. Their dinginess, their utter futility, their intoxication with words, their egotisms and vanities, fill him with bitterness and disgust. Perhaps his revolt is, in part, the resentfulness of one who once resided in that fantastic world, and is angry at the time wasted there. Fabians attempting to transform modern civilisation with surreptitious intrigues, 'Suffragettes' whose 'martyr-doms' in prison consist in howling before the midday meal, and imitating 'the noises made by the carnivora at the Zoological Gardens at feeding time,' little literary coteries who discuss the sincerity of Tolstoy or the significance of Chesterton, or whether Bernard Shaw should be elected to Parliament—all this appears to him less as a revolt than as a disease, compounded of unrest and ineffective vanity. He sees the huge, clumsy world, blundering along with its Atlantean load, in some strange progress towards an uncertain goal. He sees all the apparatus of sedentary life, the small cunnings and hysterias of those who have never faced death or been challenged by Hunger and Cold, producing not even a scratch upon the surface of this Cosmic Colossus. Life and Death, huge stark forces of Lust and Avarice and Hatreds and Affections, judge and condemn all these 'sloppy' and gushing and furtive move-ments towards change. And when Ann Veronica borrows forty pounds from a man who had appeared a genial suburban gentleman of unim-peachable reputation, she finds that the wolf and tiger instincts have only dressed themselves up in thin clothing—that 'primitive man will feed and must take his pasturage.' Ann Veronica is out for sincerity, while others are wrapped in deception. She is breaking her teeth biting at her chains in prison, while her comrades are content with making noises like the carnivorous animals. 'Your queer code of Honor'—she can say to Capes at the end—'Honor! Once you begin with love you have to see it through.' It is this demand for bedrock fact—for some hard ground beneath all the slush and make-belief of contemporary illusion—which drove George Ponderevo into the study of machines, aviation, something solid and real—which drove Ann Veronica into open repudiation of it all.

[Quotes ch. 7 'Morningside Park had been passive' to 'its own assertions'.]

It is the revolt of the stomach against a diet of *Justice*, the *Vegetarian*, *Friends of Egypt*, *Votes for Women*, and other similar periodicals. Ann Veronica escapes for a moment—to the mountains. The hero of *Tono-Bungay* finds less satisfying experience in the sense, haunting and persistent, of a search never attained: all life the secret—revealed as but for a moment in a sudden sunset, in music, in a passionate love episode, in moments of half-apprehension—eluding and baffling those who would solve the mystery. At the end one may still, like Ulysses, resolve to 'sail beyond the sunset' or blow dauntlessly 'Childe Roland to the dark tower came.' Meantime the Mountains cannot be occupied for ever: and back again, half-stifled in the crowd, its visitants must set themselves to the wrappered life with but little guidance from sun or star.

'Some day, perhaps,' says Ann Veronica's lover, 'some day the old won't coddle and hamper the young, and the young won't need to fly in the faces of the old. They'll give facts as facts, and understand. Oh! to face facts! Gods! What a world it might be if people faced facts. Understanding. There is no other salvation.' All Mr. Wells's later work has been an attempt to face facts. He has brought an enthusiasm for reality, born of his scientific training, into union with an enthusiasm for humanity, born out of disgust at the disorder of life, and pity at its sufferings. *Ann Veronica* is his latest attempt to face facts. It is lacking in the intimacy and kindliness and humor of *Kipps*. It has little of the broad, sombre, epical effect of *Tono-Bungay*. It is written in irony and in bitterness. But it is extraordinarily honest, and in consequence extraordinarily readable. Here is a man who is applying the dissector's scalpel to the society of modern England. The ordinary investigator will deliberately omit the tearing open of certain parts; you must leave the heart intact, or make no search for this nerve ganglion, or confine yourself to slices cut off the surface of the skin. Mr. Wells will have none of it. He will tear the whole organism into tatters, till the skeleton and all the organs stand revealed—'far too naked to be 'shamed.' He is not content with attacking illusion: he will dissect also the revolt against illusion itself, and the revolt against the revolt against illusion: until no wrappings and curtains and figments and phrases remain. He may not—by such method—achieve the naked Truth. But at least he is sincere in his effort towards that perilous attainment.

55(a). 'A Poisonous Book', unsigned review in *Spectator*

20 November 1909, ciii, 846–7

The author is John St Loe Strachey, editor of the *Spectator* and a supporter of the National Social Purity Crusade. Beatrice Webb suggested in her diary (27 December 1909) that Strachey's motive was to make a veiled attack on Wells's private life—a suspicion which illustrates the atmosphere of scandal which surrounded Wells, but appears to be quite unfounded. Wells wrote in *Experiment in Autobiography* that 'Strachey's hostility, if a little clumsy and heavy, was perfectly honest. . . . I was indignant and expostulatory at the time, but on the whole I really had very little to complain of' (ii, p. 471).

It has long been the rule of the *Spectator* to avoid giving the advertisement of scandal to any book, and especially to any novel, which appears to us to be in its essence depraved, and therefore likely to do injury to those who read it. When, however, the poison is contained in a work by some popular and well-known author, little or no additional harm can be caused by the extra publicity of a review. Such an exception is to be found in Mr. H. G. Wells's new novel, *Ann Veronica*. We have headed this article 'A Poisonous Book,' and that is the epithet which we desire deliberately to apply to it. It is a book capable of poisoning the minds of those who read it. Our readers will, we feel sure, acquit us of being unreasonably and exaggeratedly Puritanical in our attitude. We do not desire to set up any too exacting moral standard, or to condemn a book altogether because it may take a much freer view of the relations of the sexes than we ourselves hold to be consistent with the public welfare. We do not wish to boycott or denounce any and every book which does not accept the ethical standard of Christianity. Again, we should not dream of denouncing a book as likely to poison the minds of men and women merely because it was coarse in language, or dealt plainly, or even brutally, with the facts of human life. Between such books and a book like *Ann Veronica* there is a gulf deep and wide. *Ann Veronica* has not a coarse word in it, nor are the 'suggestive' passages open to any very severe criticism. The loathing and indignation which the book inspires in us are due to the effect it is likely to have in undermining that sense of continence and self-control in the individual which is essential to a sound and healthy State. The book is based on the negation of woman's purity and of man's good faith in the relations of sex. It teaches, in effect, that there is no such thing as woman's honour, or if there is, it is only to be a bulwark against a weak temptation. When the temptation is strong enough, not only is the tempted person justified in yielding, but such yielding becomes not merely inevitable but something to be welcomed and glorified. If an animal yearning or lust is only sufficiently absorbing, it is to be obeyed. Self-sacrifice is a dream and self-restraint a delusion. Such things have no place in the muddy world of Mr. Wells's imaginings. His is a community of scuffling stoats and ferrets, unenlightened by a ray of duty or abnegation.

We do not wish to make appeal solely to the principles of Christian morality or to the sanctions of religion, though to our mind that appeal is the strongest and greatest of all. What we want to do on the present occasion is to ask even those whose ears are deaf to such an appeal whether they think that it is possible to build up a self-sustained and a permanent State upon the basis which underlies not only Mr. Wells's latest novel, but so considerable a section of the thinking and writing which are described as modern.—Mr. Wells, for example, terms his book a 'modern love story.'—Unless the citizens of a State put before themselves the principles of duty, self-sacrifice, self-control, and continence, not merely in the matter of national defence, national preservation, and national well-being, but also of the sex relationship, the life of the State must be short and precarious. Unless the institution of the family is firmly founded and assured, the State will not continue. We are far from saying that the duty of self-control and continence in the interests of the family is not as imperative upon the man as upon the woman, but at the same time one must note the universal instinct of mankind in placing the duty of self-restraint in this issue in a special degree upon the woman,—just as the duty of giving his life for the State is imposed in a special degree upon the man. It is not for nothing that the world has learned to think of a woman's honour as involving a peculiar self-sacrifice. The general voice of mankind is right when, if it speaks of a woman's dishonour, it means thereby a sacrifice of her purity in mind and body.

It must not be supposed that we wish to insist upon a different standard for the woman than for the man. If we have appeared to dwell more on the woman's obligation, it is because the book in question is primarily a woman's book, and tells the story of a woman's voluntary fall from honour and self-respect. Yet at the same time, though not in anything approaching the same detail—indeed, only incidentally—Mr. Wells has depicted the faithlessness of a man to his marriage vows. Such faithlessness is treated as something to be just as easily and as lightly disregarded as a woman's loss of virtue. He who passes as the hero of the book is an erotic science lecturer. When he accepts the advances of one of the girl members of his class, he makes it quite clear to her that he has broken his own marriage vows in circumstances of bestial depravity. He does not even plead the force of a great passion for his double adultery, but merely opportunity. He had the chance of debauching the wife of his intimate friend and of being unfaithful to his own wife, and he points out how very natural it was of him to seize that chance.

Very possibly a certain number of the readers of this review will declare that even if the book is not one to be recommended to the young person, we have used the language of exaggeration in our strictures upon it. We shall be told that there is a great deal of charm, and even of goodness, in Ann Veronica, that to understand all is to pardon all, and that 'to step aside is human.' No doubt it is. We should be the last to condemn in harsh or vindictive terms the Ann Veronicas of real life. But while it is human to err and Christlike to pity and forgive, the great duties and prohibitions of life remain, and woe to those who cover them with the slime of their faint-scented sophistries. Boswell tells us of a conversation in which he defended with sophistical excuses a woman who had betrayed her husband. Dr. Johnson cut him short with his immortal—'My dear Sir, never accustom your mind to mingle virtue and vice. The woman's a ——, and there's an end on't.' Mark that he did not say, and of course did not mean, that the woman was necessarily bad all through, that she was to be condemned unmercifully, that she had no excuses for her action, or that her sin was unforgivable. He knew human life far too well, saw it too steadily and saw it too much as a whole, to take up so pedantic or cloistered a notion of the relations of the sexes. He was determined, however, not to allow a piece of dangerous and demoralising sophistry to pass unmasked, and this, humbly following his example, is what we desire to do in the case of the poisonous and pernicious teaching of *Ann Veronica*.

55(b). H. G. Wells, a rejoinder

4 December 1909

Letter to the editor, *Spectator*, ciii, 945.

This was followed by a long editorial reply, which concluded that Wells's defence amounted to this: ' "Don't you realise that in writing an exciting and sympathetic description of how a girl bolts with a married man I am helping to solve the decline in the birth-rate?" Perhaps, after all, silence would have been the best answer to so impudent a plea.'

Sir,—My attention has been called to your strenuous review of my last book, *Ann Veronica*, under the heading 'A Poisonous Book.' I have considered that review very carefully, and after a first phase of natural resentment, I am disposed to acquit the writer of anything but an entirely honest and intolerant difference of opinion. I would like with your permission to offer a few remarks upon that difference, because I think very wide issues are involved in your suggestion that my book should be burnt, so to speak, by the common hangman and myself trampled underfoot.

My book was written primarily to express the resentment and distress which many women feel nowadays at their unavoidable practical dependence upon some individual man not of their deliberate choice, and in full sympathy with the natural but perhaps anarchistic and anti-social idea that it is intolerable for a woman to have sexual relations with a man with whom she is not in love, and natural and desirable and admirable for her to want them, and still more so to want children by a man of her own selection. Now these may be very shocking ideas indeed, but it is not the first time they have crept into literature, and I submit that a case can be made out for tolerating their discussion. The case lies in the fact that the opposite arrangement by which a woman is subdued, first to her father, and then to a husband of his choice, is not in our present phase of civilisation working satisfactorily. I do not, of course, expect you to attach any great value to the distress, inconvenience, and even misery that this inflicts upon many women, over-educated to a painful delicacy of perception; but I know your keen and vigorous patriotism, and it seems to me that you overlook the fact that in practice the arrangement you manifestly approve is not giving the modern State enough children, or fine enough children, for its needs. Your ideals have had the fullest play in the United States of America among the once prolific population of English and Dutch descent. There, if anywhere, the Christian ideal of marriage and woman's purity, as you conceive it, has prevailed exclusively. So late as 1906, the Gorki incident in New York called attention to the continuing vigour of these conceptions. And yet that colonial strain has dwindled to a mere fraction of the population of the States, and still dwindles. In France, again, the man-ruled family has become insufficiently prolific for the public need. People of your persuasion have denounced 'race suicide' with a quite remarkable eloquence, but it has produced no appreciable effect upon the decline. Now I explain this decline, rightly or wrongly, by the fact that the man in a man-ruled family, which is competing for existence against other families, has not only no great national passion for offspring, but has also under our present conditions every practical inducement to limit their number; that there is an enormous pressure as well as an enormous temptation for the wife to shirk what you, I think, would agree with me in regarding as her chief public duty; and so I believe that the development of civilisation demands a revision of the constitution of the family and of our conventions of the relations of men and women, which will give the natural instincts of womanhood freer play. I have come to this belief after years of thought and hesitation, and I mean to give it expression. The Family *does not work* as it used to do, and we do not know why, and we have to look into it. With the best will in the world to damage my book, your reviewer could not find anything to call pornographic in it, and so I enter my plea for an arrest of judgment and liberty of discussion in this vitally important field.—I am, Sir, &c., H. G. WELLS

56. Unsigned review, *The Times Literary Supplement*

21 April 1910, 144

If we may regard Mr. H. G. Wells's new book, *The History of Mr. Polly*, as an interlude, a piece of work airily thrown off for the amusement and recreation of the author, it is enough to say that it is a highly spirited and delightful tale, in Mr. Wells's most sympathetic vein, full of the familiar charm of his careless felicity and rapidity and ease. Here, as so often before, the story streams forward with a gay relish which appears to be solely concerned with the matter in hand and to have not a thought for construction or 'style'; here, as before, we realize by the time we have reached the end how much just and delicate art has in fact controlled it from the beginning; here, moreover, the story rounds itself neatly off at the right moment, without drifting into the anti-climax which some of its predecessors have not avoided. This tribute could be left to stand unqualified but for the suspicion that we may perhaps be meant to take Mr. Polly more seriously, as a new and deliberate creation. If that is so, and Mr. Polly is to be thrown into relation with Hoopdriver and Mr. Lewisham and Kipps, then it is altogether another affair. We then have to object that good as it is, Mr. Wells has done it all before. The humorous original sensitive soul battling with ignorance, obscurely aware of beauty and brilliance, but aware of them as knowledge which it has not learnt and does not know how to acquire—Mr. Wells long ago proved that he is a consummate master of this type; and it is a dangerous sign that he should begin at this time of day to prove it again. Mr. Polly is differentiated in various ways from Kipps, but essentially he is the same. Even the accessories are borrowed right and left by the author from himself. We have the linen-draper's shop, the unexpected legacy—even the bicycle that wobbles inexpertly in pursuit of romance. This is all very painful to us whom Mr. Wells has taught, by his last three or four books, to expect that he will go on breaking new ground. Let us, however, cling to the idea that this new story is merely an 'occasional' piece; in which case to throw the full weight of criticism on it is disproportionate and unnecessary. The book anyhow contains some admirable scenes and a well-sustained climax. Mr. Wells's art of construction is always interesting, with its quite deceptive appearance of recklessness. This appearance is due to his disdain for mere plot-carpentry. He never relies for artistic effect upon a coherent sequence of incident; the plot, as a plot, will start in one direction, branch off suddenly in another, pick up fresh characters, bring them swiftly to the front, and abandon them again as suddenly. He has two ways, two more subtle ways, of achieving completeness. One is to lay bare a section, by broad sweeping strokes, of the super-imposed layers of social differences—as though by the shaving off of the front of a house—the method of *Tono-Bungay* and the first part of *In the Days of the Comet*. The other is to take a single figure and to work out its development as a whole, allowing the illustrative events to happen just as arbitrarily and incoherently as they do in life—and this is the method of *The History of Mr. Polly*. Not indeed that the methods exclude each other; for Mr. Polly, though pictured for his own sake, has always an inherent reference to the strange wasteful organisation which lavishly produces him and yet seems to provide no place for him. He wedges himself into it only to be ruthlessly squeezed out; and though he finds his place at last, it is by virtue of his own small spark of originality, which nothing quite succeeds in quenching. The bright side of Mr. Wells's drama is the challenge to originality offered by the very stupidity of life; the dark side is the huge and pitiless waste which it involves. Real drama, and beautifully worked out—but he has done it before.

57. Unsigned notice, *North American Review*

July 1910, cxcii, 136–7

If *Mr. Polly* is offered as a pendant to *Ann Veronica* he is not good enough for the place. That rebellious daughter had at least a robust vitality and, as one critic mentioned, she meant well. But he is dyspeptic, low-spirited and means nothing at all. The sad case of the small tradesman crowded into bankruptcy by the department stores lies at Mr. Wells's heart for good and sufficient reasons, doubtless, but it has not yet been written. Mr. Polly would have failed, more or less, anywhere, at any time, except perhaps on a Pacific island before the white man came. There seems small profit in being sorry for him over 318 pages. The tragedy of mean people of the stuff that classical comedy is cut from can indeed be written, but only by a man big enough to laugh at their meanness and pierce below it to squeeze his little piece of human nature (as a great critic once put it) until it grimaces or bleeds. Not the surface and sentiment, but essential humanity and cosmical irony, is wanted to write the history of our own times. *Tono-Bungay* had the virtue of setting down a period whole and complete as a picture of Degas or a novel of de Goncourt's, and it had the greater virtue of vibrating for a moment to the great current of contemporary life. But *Mr. Polly*, when he has done whimpering, is become impossible and—which is worse—incredible.

58. H. L. Mencken, review in *Smart Set*

July 1910, 153–5

Henry Louis Mencken (1880–1956), journalist and critic, editor of the *American Mercury* from 1924 to 1933. Mencken's brash approach did much to efface the genteel academicism of American criticism; he felt a natural affinity for Wells, whose books he recommended regularly until he lost patience with the 'messianic' tinge of the later discussion novels. He was virtually the only reviewer to recognize the achievement of *Mr. Polly*.

It seems to be pretty generally agreed by the critics, at least in the United States, that H. G. Wells has stepped into the long vacant boots of Charles Dickens, and for that notion, it must be confessed, there is no little excuse.

Wells, in truth, and to change the figure, has rediscovered and staked out for himself the English lower middle class that Dickens knew so intimately and loved with such shameless sentimentality—that hunkerous, uncleanly, tea swilling *garde du corps* of all the more disgusting virtues, traditions, superstitions and epidemic diseases of the Anglican people. The other novelists across the water strike either above it or below it—above it at the magnificent and, as it were, almost supernatural indecency of the aristocracy, or at the moral anarchy of the self-conscious class of social climbers; or below it at the ingenuous swinishness of the herd. Thus we have on the one hand a copious outpouring of novels of the 'Dodo' school (even *Esther Waters* and *What Maisie Knew* belong to it), with their melancholy presentations of perfumed polygamy; and on the other hand a steady supply of novels of the Hardy-Phillpotts-Morrison school, with their tedious prying into the amours and political ambitions, the theology and gnosiology of Wesleyan farmhands, seduced milkmaids, Whitechapel paupers and other such vermin. Now and then, of course, a writer may be found who belongs to both schools, or who flits irresolutely from one to the other—George Moore, for example; but it is seldom that any halt is made between the two. In other words, little attention is given in the current English fiction to the average Englishman. You will find plenty of degenerate dukes there, and plenty of Parliament men conducting low intrigues with clergymen's wives, and plenty of felonious parlor maids and derelicts of the Embankment; but you will seldom find an honest English haberdasher, lawfully married to one wife, and a true believer in hell, monogamy, Beecham's pills and the British constitution. I know not why, and do not guess, but so it is.

It is to this common and intensely human man, to this private soldier in the ranks of Christian civilization, that Mr. Wells turns in his new novel, *Mr. Polly*. Dickens would have loved Mr. Polly—loved him for his helplessness, his doggish joys, his calflike sorrows, his incurable nationalism—but it quickly appears that Mr. Wells loves him no more than a bacteriologist loves the rabbit whose spine he draws out through the gullet; and so we arrive at the notion that, despite a good deal of likeness, there are many points of difference between Dickens and Wells. They are, in truth, as far apart as the poles, for Dickens was a sentimentalist and Wells is a scientist, and between sentiment and science there is even less in common than between kissing a pretty girl and kissing her mamma. Dickens regarded his characters as a young mother regards her baby; Wells looks at his as a porkpacker looks at a hog. Dickens believed that the way to judge a man was to test his willingness to give money to the orphans; Wells believes that it is safer and more accurate to find out the percentage of hydrochloric acid in his gastric juices.

As a matter of fact, the history of Mr. Polly, as Wells presents him to us, is a history of Mr. Polly's stomach. We are told, on the very first page of the book, that the low spirits in which we find him are due to the fact that his wife is an atrocious cook. 'He suffered from indigestion ... nearly every afternoon ... but as he lacked introspection he projected the associated discomfort upon the world. Every afternoon he discovered afresh that life as a whole, and every aspect of life that presented itself, was "beastly." ' It is the business of the first half of the book to trace the origin of Mr. Polly's indigestion—in coarse, ill cooked food; in badly ventilated sleeping quarters; in lack of exercise; in the dull, sedentary life of a haberdasher in a small town, with a sluttish, unimaginative wife and no means of escape from her—and to show its lamentable consequences. Mr. Polly goes constantly from bad to worse, from mere discomfort to pessimism and despair. His day's work becomes intolerably painful; he is eternally irritated; he quarrels with his neighbors; he begins to lose money in his shop. Finally he decides to put an end to his woes by burning down that shop and cutting his throat.

The first of these desperate acts is accomplished with brilliant success, but Mr. Polly loses courage when he comes to the second. Thus he finds himself still alive and still very uncomfortable, but with a hundred pounds of insurance in his wallet instead of a wad of bills payable. What to do? Set up another shop? The thought of it sickens! Take to the woods? Well, why not? It is a short step from the idea to the act. Mr. Polly separates that insurance money into two parts, puts one where his wife will find it—and fares forth into the open country. He is a free man again, an opulent bachelor, the most enviable of creatures.

Thereafter the story describes the gradual salvation of Mr. Polly's stomach, and through it, of Mr. Polly's immortal soul. He happens one day, quite by chance, into a quaint sixteenth century hostelry on a river bank—the Potwell Inn, to wit—and the motherly old soul who owns it sets a plate of honest roast beef before him. Mr. Polly eats and is thrilled.

Eight years afterwards he is still there—still eating the nourishing, digestible victuals of that saintly and accomplished cook, and moving ever upward and onward in the scale of brute creation. He becomes a sound man, a brave man, an efficient man, a happy man. As we part from him, he is sitting on the river bank in the cool of a golden summer evening, tranquilly smoking his pipe and meditating upon the great problems of existence. 'Whenever there's signs of a good sunset,' says Mr. Polly, 'and I'm not too busy, I'll come and sit out here.' Enviable man! True philosopher! He has found the secret of life at last!

Mr. Polly is written with all of Mr. Wells's customary facility and humor. The sheer fluency of the writing, in truth, is one of the book's faults. One feels that more careful polishing would have improved it— that it should have remained in the author's desk a year or so before going to the printer. Another fault lies in the fact that Mr. Wells is sometimes just a bit too scientific. Intent upon exploring Mr. Polly as a biological specimen, he seems to forget, now and then, that Mr. Polly is also a human being. In other words, a dash of Dickensian sentimentality would often add something to the flavor of Wells. But I have no hesitation whatever in saying that Wells, as he is, entertains me far more agreeably than Dickens. I know very well that the author of *David Copperfield* was a greater artist than the author of *Mr. Polly*, just as I know that the Archbishop of Canterbury is a more virtuous man than my good friend, Fred the Bartender; but all the same, I prefer Wells and Fred to Dickens and the Archbishop. In such matters one must allow a lot to individual taste and prejudice.

THE NEW MACHIAVELLI

January 1911

---

59. Beatrice Webb, diary entry

5 November 1910

Extracts from unpublished MS. diary, Passfield Papers (5 November 1910).

Wells took his political and personal revenge on the Webbs by caricaturing them as Oscar and Altiora Bailey in *The New Machiavelli*. This is Beatrice's dignified and remarkably objective response.

H. G. Wells's *New Machiavelli* is now all published in the *English Review*. We have read the caricatures of ourselves, the Trevelyan brothers[*] and other old acquaintances of H.G.'s with much interest and amusement. The Portraits are really very clever in a malicious way. What interests us most, however, is the extraordinary revelation of H.G.'s life and character—idealized of course but written with a certain powerful sincerity. Some of the descriptions of Society and of the political world—some of the criticisms of the existing order are extraordinarily vivid—and the book as a whole to a large extent compels agreement with its descriptive side. But it lays bare the tragedy of H.G.'s life—his aptitude for 'fine thinking' and even 'good feeling' and yet his total incapacity for decent conduct. He says in so many words that directly you leave your study you inevitably become a cad and are indeed mean and dishonourable and probably cruel. As an attempt at representing a political philosophy the book utterly fails—swaying between a dreamy and inconsistent Utopianism and a complete and

---

[*] Sir Charles Trevelyan (1870–1958) and G. M. Trevelyan (1876–1962) are portrayed as Willie and Edward Crampton in *The New Machiavelli*.

dreary cynicism as to the possibility of any other motive but self interest tempered by class bias. All parties are in turn rejected and no measures are indicated but a vague proposal to endow motherhood! 'Love and fine thinking' which Remington advances as his motto is in the end effectively countered by the drunken little Don's demonstration that all political parties are based on 'Hate and coarse thinking.' And H.G. leaves you guessing that in his heart he agrees, with this summing up of the whole business. You are left wondering also whether having betrayed Margaret he will not presently cut off Isabel. Why not?

One small matter interested us. In his description of his acquaintance-ship with the 'Oscar Baileys' he shows that he never really liked us—at any rate after the first blush of the intimacy. What annoyed him was our puritan view of life and our insistence on the fulfilment of obliga-tions. There is even a passage in which he distinctly says that he was irritated at our blindness to the fact that he was leading a sexually irregular life; that we *would* assume him to be a conventionally respec-table man! Of course that is absolutely true. . . . For a little while I think we influenced him—at any rate, in thought—and the Samurai of the *Modern Utopia* was the literary expression of this phase. But he passed back again to the theory and practice of sexual dissipation and vehemently objected and disliked what he knew would be our judgment of it.

60. R. A. Scott-James, review in *Daily News*

17 January 1911, 4

Arnold Bennett wrote of this review that 'Mr. Scott-James, in the *Daily News*, ought to know better than to go running about after autobiography in fiction. . . . When I was discussing this topic the other day a novelist not inferior to Mr. Wells suddenly exclaimed: "I say! supposing we *did* write autobiography!" ' (*New Age*, 2 February 1911, viii, 325).

No book of recent times has afforded so much gossip, excitement, scandal, and heart-burning as the serial which has been running in the *English Review* and is today published in book form. Mr. Wells announces that the persons in the novel are composite characters and are not to be taken as likenesses of real persons. No doubt there are scenes which he has imagined, conversations he has invented, incidents which he has transposed. But the fact remains that in many essentials this story is photographic. Though Mr. Wells was never, like Remington, at Cambridge or in Parliament, he came under the same educational, social, and political influences which determined the character and career of Remington. Remington's friends, who are here exposed in all the intimacy of private life to the public gaze, were once the friends of Mr. Wells. No one who has any acquaintance with public personages in London can fail to identify those apostles of social organization, Mr. Bailey and his wife Altiora. Equally transparent are the young Liberals, Edward and Willie Crampton. If Mr. Wells has ridiculed and caricatured these persons he has seen to it that he has never distorted them out of recognition. The realism with which he describes these and a score of popularly 'esteemed' public men is applied also to their womenkind; Isabel is not spared; nor is Margaret, Remington's wife.

Here, then, we have what is at the same time Remington's Apologia for his admitted faults, and his revenge upon the society which decided to discredit him. He presents himself as an 'unarmed, discredited man,' whose power with the pen cannot be checked or curbed; a man 'half out of life already' because of the 'red blaze that came out of my unguarded nature, and closed my career for ever'; a man who 'cries out of his heart to the unseen fellowship about him,' and to those who 'have heard already some crude inaccurate version of our story and why I did not take office, and have formed your partial judgment on me.' Remington's reply to the man who urges him to hush up the scandal may seem to give a colour of disinterestedness to the whole story.

[Quotes Bk IV, ch. 3 'It's our duty' to 'such a score!']

It is clear that Mr. Wells intends something more than to explain the state of mind which led a distinguished politician and moralist, a married middle-aged man, to victimise—that is the 'worldly' way of looking at it—a beautiful young girl who had fallen in love with his genius. Here we have the life-story and the character of Remington portrayed at full length—Remington an individual product of the social conditions which Mr. Wells has the critical genius to analyse—Remington in relation to the vast national processes which have been changing England from the 'muddle' of the Victorians to the muddle of today; a Remington clever enough to see our representative institutions stripped of their hollowness and their cant, quick to pierce through the shell of Liberalism, not, indeed, to the kernel, but to such part of it as seems insincere; quick to see a profound psychological meaning in the Suffragette movement, and to distinguish between the outer bearing of public men and the individuality which lies behind—the 'hinterland.' Never before has he given us a more brilliant analysis of England in macrocosm and microcosm than this which is welded into the life-story of Remington. His hero is not one of Mrs. Humphry Ward's puppets set up to be great politicians. Remington as a thinker *is* almost a great man; he *is* a profound analyst of society on its human side; he *is* a gifted critic of public institutions; even his absurd perversity in trying to invent a constructive, motherhood-endowing Toryism is the perversity of a versatile and clever man whose action is precipitated by bitterness or pique.

This envisaging of England in her social, political, and intellectual life, this acutely and diabolically observed crowd of *real* persons, this minute psychology, this exact history, this elaborate philosophy, all is subservient to the purpose of explaining how it was that Remington was drawn into the net of sex, and Isabel was enabled to 'darn his socks.' *Parturiunt montes.* Thus it may be that Remington will make himself immortal in literature, the twentieth-century Benvenuto Cellini swaggering, in a self-conscious, twentieth-century way, through the tale of his glorious peccadilloes. Or should it be a Jonathan Wild, memorable as the hero of a hundred magnificent felonies with which a Fielding or a Wells could endow his sturdy outlaw? But Remington writes in bitterness; his pen is steeped in the gall of Swift; he feels rancour against Altiora, against the Cramptons, against all the 'Pinky-Dinkies' who prescribe morals for a genius erratic in his desires. His satire is so brilliant that there must be many who will feel that it has 'gone home'; at the same time it is so faithless to old friendship, so indecent in exposing intimacies concerning those who have never deserved to suffer by such exposure, throwing so much responsibility on Margaret and Isabel whilst he, in middle life, is the simple, splendid, unwarned child, that he clearly is betraying himself into the hands of his enemies.

I cannot here discuss the successive mental stages by which Remington emerges. They have already been set forth each with a separate volume to itself,★ and each of them, as here surveyed, would require a separate column of criticism. What he is looking for again and again in the sets of persons arrayed before us is what he calls the 'self-behind-the-frontage.' 'In the ostensible self who glowed under the approbation of Altiora Bailey, and was envied and discussed, praised and depreciated, in the House and in smoking room gossip, you really have as much of a man as usually figures in a novel or an obituary notice.' His ideal is the individual who lives and acts in the full light of that 'self-behind-the-frontage'—the 'hinterlander'; his literary *method* in this book is to expose the emptiness of the shop window, to cast his satire upon the poor show. This, in another way, Mr. Galsworthy has done. But Mr. Galsworthy's background is illuminated by a purposeful ideal; Mr. Wells's background is shifty, uncertain, ill-realised; being undetermined, that space which the ideal should have filled is left to chance, to accidental impulse rather than to will, to human frailty rather than to human strength. Hence it is that he trumpets the claims of sex on its weakest side; now applauds the conduct of Remington, now apologises for it; now is elaborate in explaining that the mere sensual part of him would assert itself, now that sex never appealed to him without an admixture of the ideal; now he cries out for discussion and public enlightenment on this subject, now he acknowledges that Remington, who had discussed it for years, acted on impulse in the dark. Discussion is necessary enough, but not discussion impregnated with meanness, spite, and prejudice.

★ I.e. not separate volumes, but the four 'Books' into which the novel is divided.

This book bristles with brilliant and even profound social philosophy, and it assails the nostrils with its meanness and its atmosphere of petty scandal. The fine and the paltry, the magnificently courageous and the insignificantly small, unite to make a book which will possibly become a notorious classic.

61. Unsigned review, *The Times Literary Supplement*

19 January 1911, 22

An early analysis of the technique of the Wellsian discussion novel.

This book is without doubt the most important (which is not to say either the most perfect or the most entertaining) piece of work that Mr. H. G. Wells has yet given us. It is on a larger scale than any other book of his, it covers a very wide extent of ground that he has never touched before, and its main idea is a more comprehensive one than any he has hitherto treated. It is, moreover, of great interest technically as the most finished example of the form which the novel has gradually arrived at in his hands. That it is a form, with a consistent unity of its own, is due less perhaps, to conscious art than to the nature of the mind which is poured out in it, a mind which has to an extraordinary degree the power of self-expression. From this point of view it does not matter whether its quality is fine or blunt, sensitive or crude; it can give itself in its completeness, which, like any other completeness, is achieved logical form. The ground-plan of *The New Machiavelli* is simply the whole of a single mind. It is plain that a markedly subtle or prehensile mind could adopt no such plan as this, for it would have filled all reasonable space before it had dealt to its satisfaction with one detail of its complexity. The mind of this book is not thus hampered by itself. It is a mind on very simple and direct lines, summary, impatient, self-confident, a little unsympathetic, at times decidedly unjust, creative and freely experimental rather than philosophical or perceptive. On the other hand (for the purposes of such a book the one all-important consideration), it is utterly and untiringly candid, fired by a really impressive passion for the complete exposure of itself. So much for the outline of the book. Its guiding principle is plain and radical. It is the clash between order and disorder, between the element in man that desires to construct and co-operate and prepare for a rational future, and the equally original element in him that refuses to fall in with any such idea, that demands a private and individual expression of itself which, at all events here and now, seems directly antagonistic to the other, seems to unmake as fast as the other can construct.

The principle could obviously be embodied in a thousand ways. Mr. Wells takes perhaps the most straightforward in making his book the autobiography of a man who, with no inherited privileges, builds up a conspicuous place for himself in political life, till a moment comes when his private life thrusts itself intractably forward and involves the other in its catastrophe. And here we reach Mr. Wells's art and recognize how steadily it has developed itself through his successive books. His arrangement of his seething mass of material is up to a certain point (we will suggest in a moment where it falls short) altogether masterly. He has to deal with a series of scenes and phases which crowd upon each other, from Remington's childhood in a London suburb, through school and college, married life and political life, till the whole story drops suddenly from its climax to failure and exile; and through all these phases, with their throng of characteristic episodes and figures, he has to hold and trace his two threads, the double history of his hero's desire to build a new state, and his failure to adjust to this constructive ambition the passions of his inner life. Mr. Wells has evolved for himself his method of dealing with his subject, not as a continuous narrative, but by what we may call successive pools of description, each chapter forming a generalized account, as self-contained as may be, of a particular stage in the man's life and thought, worked up by rapid summaries, illustrated by quickly-outlined portraits, and fined down in the end to significant incidents and conversations. Some of these pictures are much less good than others; but the prodigality, the broad free lines, the bubbling life of the best of them are what we now expect from Mr. Wells, and need not be enlarged upon here.

Our criticism of his handling of his material lies in a different direction. It will easily be supposed that the flood of speculation and suggestion about the ends of being, which finds its way into all Mr. Wells's work, whatever the literary form, has risen higher than ever in a book where it is of course directly appropriate to the matter in hand. It is part of the scheme of the book that Remington should have a great deal to say on life in general, and it is not necessary to criticize his speculations beyond noting the fact that they are dramatically apposite to his tale and to himself. Our objection is that Mr. Wells has not fully achieved the fusion of Remington's views of life with his telling of his story. His criticism of the social structure drifts at times so far away from his own affairs that we are liable to lose the sense of its dramatic place in the book and to hear Mr. Wells's voice above Remington's. This is a serious fault, and a reader who did not happen to be interested in the views themselves might easily find a good many pages unpictorial and tedious. As for the other thread in the story, the history of Remington's private adventures and love affairs, we cannot possibly do justice to it here. Its treatment is in some ways too novel to be criticized without lengthy detail. We can only say that the spirit of it, in its passionate search for reality, its intense desire to do justice to all the elements of the case, its almost hard and quite unsentimental impartiality, is at once absolutely original and perfectly artistic. Of the two women in the story, Margaret, the betrayed and deserted wife, is possibly the most finely touched portrait that Mr. Wells has drawn. The way in which he has given due weight both to her charm and her ineffectiveness, her charm (for the reader) just predominating and no more, is a triumph over immense difficulties of presentment. With her in mind we can say that a vital problem is here fairly stated, which is the highest tribute that could be made to this remarkable book.

62. Francis Hackett, review in *Chicago Evening Post*

20 January 1911

Francis Hackett (1883–1962), author and reviewer on the *Chicago Evening Post* and *New Republic*. This review was reprinted in *Horizons* (1918), 109-17.

In *Tono-Bungay* H. G. Wells criticised the tragic farce of modern business with a cleverness incomparable. Where other men had scratched the surface, Mr. Wells ripped down with a clean surgical blade. The vulgarity of plutocrats, the fatuity of competition, the idiocy of modern Jew aggressiveness—these he attacked in a satire as sound as it was hard. Remarkable, too, was his version of modern love, from the standpoint of adventure and service. And apart from all its ideas *Tono-Bungay* was a vivid, nervous, quick-moving, multicolored picture of the modern city and the modern man.

Again, in *The New Machiavelli*, Mr. Wells gives us London and confused contemporary life. But there is hardly a word of business, except of the nouveaux riches in Staffordshire. The new Machiavelli is an Englishman of 42, whose political career has just been ended by divorce: the story gives that career autobiographically, in all its white passion of statecraft, and its 'white passions struggling against the red.'

The New Machiavelli is no more like the ordinary novel than a cup of blood is like a cup of milk. Into every line of the story Mr. Wells has put his wits, his imagination, his experience and his personality. Not only has he made his hero his own age exactly, not only has he made him the living exemplar of his own publicist ideas; he has even utilized such known experiences as his visit to Chicago (which place he flips away as an 'amazing lapse from civilization').

How far Mr. Wells has gone in utilizing his personal experiences is his own affair. But that he has utilized both his known and his unknown experiences is quite clear; and one's most vital criticism of *The New Machiavelli* is that he has been 'true to himself' in a literal sense at the expense of a wiser and more sophisticated truth. For in this amazing transcript of Mr. Wells's heart and mind, this amazing, headlong confession, there is precipitation of much which is irrelevant, fatuous and egotistic. In an autobiography such things suggest the living man. In a novel (which is intrinsically conventional) they suggest an author bursting with his own ego, and bursting not like a gas that turns into flame, but like a gas escaping in a room; and making a very unpleasant odor.

This is a dangerous thing to do, if one is born preacher oneself, and Mr. Wells is born preacher. One harangue succeeds another in *The New Machiavelli* (fine harangues in most cases) and in his own person H. G. Wells is continually speaking, continually inviting attention to his person. It destroys one's faith in the actuality of *The New Machiavelli*. It makes him a mask for God knows what personal purposes, and certainly not for the best purposes of art.

Yet as soon as one forgets the obtrusive, restlessly self-centred Mr. Wells, one does get the virus of his extraordinary excitement about life. Of this excitement, this hectic interest in affairs, hectic ambition, hectic curiosity, hectic desire to know and to be, to have others know and have others be, *The New Machiavelli* is the contagium. I say hectic because I think Mr. Wells is in many ways unsafe and insane. Produced in a metropolis and fed up on all sorts of urban notions, theories and ideas, he mistakes nightmares for visions and witty theorizing for important cerebration. Seeing more in a flash of lightning brain than one out of ten thousand, he still is subject to illucid intervals; and these intervals occur, as they are apt to occur with clever people, in dealing with people less clever. Mr. Wells's rapid little brain keeps rapping out criticisms that are astonishingly acute and astonishingly inhuman.

In psychology Richard Remington, the new Machiavelli, is very similar to the Mr. Wells of *First and Last Things*. He is an idealist who dreams of 'a world of men better ordered, happier, finer, secure, . . . the ending of muddle and diseases and dirt and misery; the ending of confusions that waste human possibilities.' His catch phrase is 'Love and Fine Thinking.' But although a social idealist loyal to ideas, Remington is no saint. The symbol of his state-making dream; Machiavelli is also the symbol of 'his animal humor, his queer indecent side,' his meanness, his selfishness, and his squalor.

Few careers could be more interesting than that of Remington, once he starts to mount politically, and Mr. Wells is unfailingly clear in showing the man's evolution: First he is intellectual, a young liberal, socialistically inclined. He is pushed by the Baileys, two self-appointed guardians of reform's Thermopylean Pass. Altiora Bailey is described by Mr. Wells with some sharpness. 'Altiora thought trees hopelessly irregular and sea cliffs a great mistake.' Bailey is characterized with a pointed and almost personal malignance: 'A nasty, oily, efficient little machine.' Despite odious characteristics, however, these are profitable allies of Remington's, and he stays by them, breathing hard in their 'tremendously scientific air' until long after Altiora has promoted his marriage.

Courtship is not romantic in Mr. Wells. The sex side of Remington is very frankly represented long before, perhaps more frankly than the sex side of any man in English fiction. From his first precocious glance, down through his 'stark fact' period at Cambridge, and his celibate experience in London, there is nothing glossed over or concealed. Something may be misunderstood. If so, the misconception, the lack of beauty, is inherent in Mr. Wells. But what candor can give, he gives. And that is admirable. It is admirable not because it is beautifully done, but because it is done so honestly. Where all, even the best, have been evasive, it is magnificent that one should be true and explicit. The Anthony Comstocks may lie about it. They may say that Mr. Wells is salacious, indecent, indelicate and so on. As a matter of fact, Mr. Wells is coldly if eagerly clever. He is much less salacious than many medical textbooks. He tells part of the truth as it is known by adults; that is all. And only dirty-minded people like Anthony Comstock will object to it.

Being an English middle-class boy, Remington is brought up under the assumption that ignorance fosters idealism. The result is, as usual, inglorious. 'I had had my experiences and secrets and adventures,' he says, 'among that fringe of ill-mated or erratic or discredited women the London world possesses. The thing had long ago ceased to be a matter of magic or mystery, and had become a question of appetites and excitement, and among other things the excitement of not being found out.' That sex should have become 'a question of appetites and excitement' is an indication of what ignorance leads to, in a Remington. And no lovable woman saved Remington. 'I had never yet even peeped at the sweetest, profoundest thing in the world, the heart and meaning of a girl, or dreamt with any quality of reality of a wife or any such thing as a friend among womanhood.'

Margaret, a tepid character, is unfortunate to marry Remington. She is a good woman, depicted without prejudice; cultivated, moral and conventional. She would willingly die for her husband, but she must make an issue of his saying 'damn.' The estrangement is fated. From the start 'trifling things began to matter enormously, that she had a weak and easily fatigued back for example, or that when she knitted her brows and stammered a little in talking, it really didn't mean that an exquisite significance was struggling for utterance.' What Remington could not turn to delight made him bitter. He could not indulge without loving, and he did not love.

When a man who needs so much as Remington marries a woman so patently and pitifully inadequate as Margaret, what is he to do? Remington goes on as a 'careerist,' more and more occupied with political ideals, and now shifting, for Machiavellian reasons, from the Liberal to the Conservative machine. His ideas of party are amazingly vivid and significant. They exhibit at once the fluidity and the accessibility of his character. They do not for a moment sound like an executive's ideas, and they are full of wind, full of Zeitgeist. But they serve both Remington and Mr. Wells in the exposition of statecraft: they give excuse for as brilliant a chapter on the party system as one could hope to find anywhere.

One's fundamental criticism, however, is that Remington, esteeming himself tough-minded, is, as a fact, utterly and unhealthily critical of human nature, impatient of limitations in others, and in himself, that are 'limitations' only from the standpoint of a 'nasty, oily, efficient little machine.' It is this prejudgment of human nature, this impatience of 'chaotic indiscipline, ill-adjusted efforts, spasmodic aims,' that makes Wells so querulous and so childish. He is too hard on himself, on this score, and much too hard on others. Were he strong enough, were we strong enough, to achieve his ideal, all would be well; the ideal is logical, spick-and-span. But not being strong enough as yet, nagging each other does no good. And one gets so tired of Mr. Wells's intrinsically stupid nagging, especially as the muddlement, the disorder, the indiscipline, the ill-adjustment, the spasmodic behavior, of his own hero are more and more confessed.

But while Remington's career preoccupies him, so long as no woman attracts him, he is in a peculiarly susceptible position when he meets Isabel Rivers. She is a person of the clearest charm, a delightful, lovable and admirable woman: and so much too good for Remington that one does not believe he would in reality run away with her. For that is Wells's solution, his answer given without moral defense. He sends Isabel and Remington off together, the choosers of an evil. Whether the lesser or the greater, he does not dare to say.

After all the moil, all the contradiction, all the confusion, all the neurosis of Remington's life till he meets Isabel, it is a great relief to experience their big and heartfelt harmonies. The passages between them are beautiful, and wonderfully actual. The woman loves without stint, is clear-headed, unafraid and passionate. It is only when Remington tells his wife about it, tells her he 'knew it was stupid, but thought it was a thing that wouldn't change, wouldn't be anything but itself, wouldn't unfold consequences,' that one is utterly disgusted. In the same tone is the whine that 'this business has brought me more bitterness and sorrow than I had ever expected to bear.' In the same tone is the feeble protestation that there is 'a sort of wild rightness about any love that is fraught with beauty.' Would a man capable of such doubts, such maunderings about expediency, such reproaches and hand-wringing, be capable also of the final drastic step? One feels dubious. Remington wears fine feathers, but it is hard to believe they are his own. And when he hands Isabel over to a good, conventional man who wants to marry her, without one reflection as to what such prostitution means, the action consists much more with going back to his wife than with his final flaming resolution to take exile and love.

With so much to urge against the philosophy of this remarkable novel, it may seem captious to go further and criticise its construction. But indeed it is badly put together and badly managed. Mr. Wells is a real stylist, a master of actuality, and the vignettes of London in *The New Machiavelli* are unmatched in contemporary fiction. Yet there is an excess of cleverness and a tiresome triteness of epithet. Over and over again Mr. Wells uses such words as 'vast,' 'splendid,' 'enormous,' 'stupendous,' 'passionate,' 'irresistible,' 'extraordinary,' 'immense.' These words are not exactly leprous, and several of them are applicable to the book itself; but in Mr. Wells they are extravagantly and flippantly used. And they give an effect of puerile sensationalism which a radical cannot afford.

But the bad construction is not a matter of heaped up epithets and ejaculatory statement. It is a matter of impeded and disconcerted narrative. The narrative is forever being halted for the sake of a sermon. No reminiscence seems to be complete without a debate, and no description without a moral. When one thinks of a masterly story like *Jean-Christophe*, this seems flimsy and ill conceived. It is held together by pins, strings, needles, tags, clips, everything but the conventional buttons and threads. 'I'll tell you a little later,' 'It is very hard to tell,' 'I must go back a little way'—how distracting and inefficient.

It is this parvenu in Mr. Wells that leads him to take nothing for granted, that leads him to put the universe on trial. And, incidentally, it is this parvenu in him which makes him attempt to win distinction by shunning familiar names for most of his characters, and call them Blupp, Willersley, Mottisham, Clynes, Esmeer, Bunting Harblow, Cladingbowl, Tumpany, Bulch, Pipes, Toomer, Waulsort, Rumbold, Minns, Tohrns, Kindling, Crupp, Flack, Wrassleton, Forthundred, Paddockshurst, Plutus, Fester, Panmure and Quackett. I resent all these odd names especially Quackett.

More serious is his effort to clear out weeds by slashing thistles with a vicious cane. More serious is his willingness to believe of the poor that 'mean fears enslave them, and satisfactions decoy them.' Such half truths are disheartening from Mr. Wells.

Perhaps the megalomania of Remington, of which these are symptoms, is deliberate. If so, I have read the book in the wrong spirit. And at any rate the book is a stimulant not to be refused. It is easy to understand people being apathetic to Mr. Wells. But while absence of desire sometimes indicates refinement, it more often indicates anæmia; and Mr. Wells challenges the anæmic. He is not a scrupulous artist. He writes in a riot of the blood. He undervalues the poised and the equable. His mind at present is restless, perplexed, feverish and unprincipled. And he favors change for its own sake, captiously. It is easy to repudiate many things in Mr. Wells. But he is better to assimilate than to reject. To assimilate him is to assimilate him as a man in whom there is much that is provocative (as where he criticizes Liberals), much that is suggestive (as where he criticizes the old ideals of education), much that is fine. He has the yeast of life in him, the microbe of adventure. And to exclude him is to cut off an influence which, if not wholly reasoned or successfully sublimated, still has vitality irresistible and staunch sincerities.

63. Unsigned review, *Nation*

21 January 1911, viii, 690–2

This review opens with what is perhaps the earliest comparison of
Wells and Bennett as novelists.

It is difficult to read *The New Machiavelli* without noting the persistent
contrast between the literary temperament and method of Mr. Wells
and that of Mr. Arnold Bennett. Mr. Bennett is, beyond all doubt, the
foremost of our contemporary exponents of the great art of represen-
tation. To him life passes as a show, to which he, as a spectator, is
determined to apply his utmost powers of memory, observation,
choice, and comparison. This effort has given us two of the most
perfect pictures of a selected English society and its environment that
our literature contains. Neither Mr. Wells's character nor his design as a
writer allows him to write such a book as *Clayhanger*. Since he quitted
the sphere of prophetic fantasy as to the material texture of the world,
he has insisted on mingling, not always, or perhaps at all, in a god-like
way, with the game of life, and delivering his full message of self-
expression. The latest mode of this deliverance is indeed peculiar to
himself. It is not a frank autobiography like Rousseau's, presented as if
it were the truth about every man if only he chose to tell it. It is not,
though Mr. Wells seems to say so, founded on the scandalous model of
Machiavelli's correspondence with Vettori, save in so far as Mr. Wells's
hero, Richard Remington, chooses, like Machiavelli in an episode
between a great political and a greater literary career, to discuss his
passing amours. Mr. Wells takes a line of his own, which cuts between
the personal and the impersonal method. Occasionally he takes a slice
out of a body of clearly personal opinions, such as a somewhat undefined
'Endowment of Motherhood' or the government of the State by a class
of uplifted Samurai, who, at critical moments, seem to sink into the
common ruck of infirm wills and narrowly individual passions and
experiences. Again, in the mere furniture of his story, he mixes the
imaginative and the actual, so that in one moment we have a couple of

distinguished people with their names attached and at another their obvious pseudonyms of 'Oscar and Altiora Bailey,' while we choose between a named 'Mr. Campbell Bannerman' and a highly flattered and easily recognisable portrait of Mr. Balfour as 'Mr. Evesham.' We have no doubt at all what we should have liked Mr. Wells to do. We should have liked to see him carry the art of imaginative writing into its proper sphere, and to keep it there. In his opening chapter he states with much eloquence the theme of *The New Machiavelli*. That theme may be stated in rather different terms. It may be a moralisation of the old trouble of the instability of the political man; of the truth that he who is on fire for 'social service'—who has dreamt what Mr. Wells calls the 'statemaking dream' of order and progress—is specially liable to become a victim of dire confusion, of tormenting distractions, in his private life. It may be that Mr. Wells wishes to say that much is amiss with the state of Denmark, that its sexual ideals and customs are wrong, that it was wrong in not using Richard and Isabel for all that they were intellectually worth in spite of their several admitted sins against Margaret, his wife, and Shoesmith, her affianced husband. Sometimes it seems to us that Mr. Wells wants us to see his hero ''fess,' and sometimes that he thinks he was right to explode. But all this exposition, moralisation, personal satire, intimate psychology, indignant or excusing rhetoric, would have gone nearer to its mark if the author had stepped more completely out of his work, and had filled his stage only with thoroughly realised types of men and women of our day, instead of with a medley of actual and fictitious personages. We do not want a malicious photograph even of the National Liberal Club. What we do want is an artistic vision of the world of clubs and politics.

On one point, indeed, there can be no doubt. *The New Machiavelli*, inferior to *Tono-Bungay*, and much superior to *Ann Veronica*, is the most vivid and powerful picture of social and moral discontents that Mr. Wells has drawn. In a sense it has no characters. Isabel is nothing, the motley host of Remington's friends are nothing; only his father, the irascible, ineffectual man, smashing up his ill-grown vegetables with a hoe, and Margaret, the sad apparition of his beautiful, ineffectual wife, are real. But for a sketch of a profoundly uneasy society, conscious of its muddles and unable to see a way out, *The New Machiavelli* would be hard to beat. It is written with a passion that seems always at high tension, always driven on by a sense of personal grievance and defeat. Thus, for example, does Remington the elder, the half-baked product of 'Science and Art Departments' and small middle-class schools, curse the life of the suburb and the little villa:—

[Quotes Bk I, ch. 2 'Property's the curse of life' to 'blithering rubbish'.]

And thus does the younger Remington impeach the whole texture of English life when the pattern of his own has broken out in the most flagrant disharmony with it:—

[Quotes Bk IV, ch. 3 'I went through my life' to 'mumbled at'.]

To such a mood the story of Richard Remington's life is attuned, so that the general note is one of undeviating, if half-articulate, protest. 'Why the devil did I start gardening?' says the father. 'Why the devil did I start living?' in effect says the son. Must an orderly brain, with visions of 'scientific boys' schools,' 'a new college system' cutting 'the umbilicus' of the classics, 're-organised internal transit,' endowed mothers, flying machines, and a new War Office, be vexed by our party system—made up of a Liberal party of 'many small men against the fewer prescribing men' of a Tory party based on the 'big established classes,' of a Socialist party, whose actual members may not as yet have learned their 'table manners?' Must a hot-blooded, imaginative man, prompt to stray, be made to suffer all things, so far as his political career is concerned, because he has failed in some? Is it he who has sinned or Society before him?

So far as Mr. Wells, turning over and over all these problems of conduct and experience, has aimed at presenting a political reformer of fixed quality and dimensions, he seems to us to have failed. Remington's venture into neo-Imperialism, with a great Conservative backing for the 'endowment of motherhood,' gives us no tangible idea of a renovated community. Remington proposes to get at 'the schools, the services, the universities, the Church.' He wishes to 'strengthen the public consciousness, develop social organisation, and a sense of the State.' And Mr. Evesham-Balfour is to help him. This is indeed to verify Remington's description of himself as 'putting things in a windy way.' But if Mr. Wells-Remington's politics lack precision, no such failure belongs to the passionate presentment of a moral life, of a personality and temperament, not merely as problems to be studied and solved, but as a human being to be judged and dealt with. The lines of this presentment are broad and commanding. They are disfigured by very literal, though not salacious, detail, which many readers will dislike; by conclusions, or half-conclusions, which they may dread or vehemently disapprove. It is, at least, a question-begging method to set out a man like Remington, who as he says of himself takes beauty 'as a wild beast gets its salt, as a constituent of the meal,' and ask that one so wild of nature should develop his physical and emotional needs as he will, and yet demand a continued and powerful part in the self-subordinating work of social construction. Which is it to be—fiery untamed steed, or yoke-fellow with 'Mr. Evesham' and company? It cannot be both. Remington cannot himself excuse his betrayal of Margaret, his seduction of Isabel, or Isabel's seduction of him. Then why should he bemoan society's refusal to recognise it? But though we follow the psychology of Remington with many perplexities, it would be absurd to deny to him what his creator attributes to another character in a phrase more memorable than usual—a 'raw and bleeding faith in the deep things of life.' The literature of self-revelation, so long as it is honest, has its place in an age so full of empirical stuff as our own. Mr. Wells's artistry is seldom great. His political ideas are so vague as to give the suggested parallel of Remington with the author of *The Prince*—one of the most precise books ever written—a faint color of absurdity. But his intensity of mood is a truly remarkable quality. There is hardly a page of *The New Machiavelli* in which his impressionist sketches of modern people and institutions—schools, colleges, suburbs, clubs, economic and political groups, societies, and households, elections, dinners, social gossip and speculation—are untouched by this inquisitive, sceptical, not profound, but fiery and impatient spirit. He has chosen to make sexual rebellion his theme, some critics will say his standard. It is a choice of gravity; it is also a trodden and a stricken field of literature.

64. Henry James to Wells

3 March 1911

Extract from letter to Wells, in *The Letters of Henry James*, ii, pp. 187–9.

Wells replied on 25 April 1911: 'You put your sense of the turbid confusion, the strain and violence of my book so beautifully that almost they seem merits. But oh! some day when I'm settled-er if ever, I will do better. I agree about the 'first-person'. The only artistic 'first-person' is the onlooker speculative 'first person', and God helping me, this shall be the last of my gushing Hari-Karis' (*Henry James and H. G. Wells*, p. 130).

I have read you then, I need scarcely tell you, with an intensified sense of that life and force and temperament, that fulness of endowment and easy impudence of genius, which make you so extraordinary and which have long claimed my unstinted admiration; you being for me so much the most interesting and masterful prose-painter of your English generation (or indeed of your generation unqualified,) that I see you hang there over the subject scene practically all alone; a far-flaring even though turbid and smoky lamp, projecting the most vivid and splendid golden splotches, *creating* them about the field—shining scattered innumerable morsels of a huge smashed mirror. I seem to feel that there can be no better proof of your great gift—*The N.M.* makes me most particularly feel it—than that you bedevil and coerce to the extent you do such a reader and victim as I am; I mean one so engaged on the side of ways and attempts to which yours are extremely alien and for whom the great interest of the art we practice involves a lot of considerations and preoccupations over which you more and more ride roughshod and triumphant—when you don't, that is, with a strange and brilliant impunity of your own, leave them to one side altogether (which *is* indeed what you now apparently incline most to do.) Your big feeling for life, your capacity for chewing up the thickness of the world in such enormous mouthfuls, while you fairly slobber, so to speak, with the multitudinous taste—this constitutes for me a rare and wonderful and admirable exhibition, on your part, in itself, so that one should doubtless frankly ask one's self what the devil, in the way of effect and evocation and general demonic activity, one wants more. Well, I am willing for today to let it stand at that; the whole of the earlier part of the book, or the first half, is so alive and kicking and sprawling!—so vivid and rich and strong—above all so *amusing* (in the high sense of the word;) and I make my remonstrance—for I do remonstrate—bear upon the bad service you have done your cause by riding so hard again that accurst autobiographic form which puts a premium on the loose, the improvised, the cheap and the easy. Save in the fantastic and the romantic (Copperfield, Jane Eyre, that charming thing of Stevenson's with the bad title—'Kidnapped'?) it has no authority, no persuasive or convincing force—its grasp of reality and truth isn't strong and disinterested. R. Crusoe, e.g., isn't a novel at all. There is, to my vision, no authentic, and no really interesting and no *beautiful*, report of things on the novelist's, the painter's part unless a particular detachment has operated, unless the great stewpot or crucible of the imagination, of the observant and recording and interpreting mind in short, has intervened and played its part—and this detachment, this chemical transmutation for the aesthetic, the representational, end is terribly wanting in autobiography brought, as the horrible phrase is, up to date. That's my main 'criticism' on *The N.M.*—and on the whole ground there would be a hundred things more to say.

65. Margaret Sherwood, review in *Atlantic Monthly*

October 1911, cviii, 563-4

Margaret Pollock Sherwood (1864-1955) was professor of English at Wellesley College from 1912 to 1931.

The New Machiavelli deals with the life of an English statesman engaged in great political affairs, and it presents, to quote the author, 'the subtle, protesting, perplexing play of instinctive passion and desire against too abstract a dream of statesmanship.' The story of the hero is carried from earliest boyhood through his years of education and his political activity, through his change from radical to conservative conviction, to the time when, at the age of forty-two, he ruins his career by deserting his wife and going to Italy with a woman who has wakened a deeper love in him.

In spite of its well-nigh five hundred pages, the book lacks body; the political part hardly carries conviction, perhaps partly because there is not enough close detail; there is about it something of the airy unreality of Mr.Wells's earlier style. The development of the hero is blurred and uncertain in its progress and its outline; it is as if the writer not only did not have in mind an interpretation of his material, but were not even searching for it. It may be legitimate, it may even be desirable at times, for the scientist to present facts with no clear idea of their significance; not so the novelist; and the pseudo-scientific method, which we find in many a novel, in the presentation of an array of closely observed, but meaningless facts, has grown well-nigh unendurable. Art cannot do without informing ideas, and in it the non-assorted, miscellaneous stuff of life has no place. 'The relation of the great constructive spirit in politics to individual character and weakness' is a most interesting theme, but neither through the action nor by comment does the author make his interpretation clear. The meaning evades you; the facts are not marshaled so that you must understand. You share the bewilderment in the hero's mind, and are as completely involved in it as he, without getting the artistic significance. For all that he says about himself the hero never grows clear, and, in watching him, you feel as you would if a portrait-painter should crowd his canvas with details of costume and of feature, but should draw no person.

The wild invention of Mr. Wells's early tales made no demand for the presentation of character in action; the careless epic manner of *Tono-Bungay* was reinforced by humorous comment, so that the reader got a fairly clear idea of the hero's way of stumbling on with some sense of a goal. Here, with more exacting material, the lack of dramatic gift on the part of Mr. Wells becomes clear; cause and effect are not made apparent. It is not that one would quarrel with the theme: the theme as stated is a good one; or with the outcome, which is quite humanly possible. It is the inconclusiveness that leaves one unsatisfied; the story might have been written by Kipling's Tomlinson, so uncertain is it in its treatment of the great problems involved.

One misses here Mr. Wells's usual humour, but some compensation is to be found in pages here and there of sound wisdom, set forth in expository fashion, and betraying the active thinker.

MARRIAGE

September 1912

66. Rebecca West, review in *Freewoman*

19 September 1912, ii, 346–8

Rebecca West [Cicely Fairfield] (b. 1892), critic and novelist, became a close friend of Wells after writing this review. She discussed many of his subsequent books in the *New Freewoman*, *Clarion* and *New Republic*.

Mr. Wells' mannerisms are more infuriating than ever in *Marriage*. One knows at once that Marjorie is speaking in a crisis of wedded chastity when she says at regular intervals, 'Oh, my dear!... Oh, my dear!' or at moments of ecstasy, 'Oh, my *dear! My dear!*' For Mr. Wells' heroines who are loving under legal difficulties say 'My man!' or 'Master!' Of course, he is the Old Maid among novelists; even the sex obsession that lay clotted on *Ann Veronica* and *The New Machiavelli* like cold white sauce was merely Old Maids' mania, the reaction towards the flesh of a mind too long absorbed in airships and colloids. The Cranford-like charm of his slow, spinsterish gossip made *Kipps* the delightful book it was; but it palls when, page after page, and chapter after chapter, one is told how to furnish a house....

And then there is Mr. Wells' habit of spluttering at his enemies. He splutters less in *Marriage* than in *The New Machiavelli*, but in the hospital atmosphere of the latter, where a soul-sick man drugged himself with the ether of sex, it seemed less offensive than in this purer, brighter air. Altiora Bailey reappears as Aunt Plessington, and makes a speech that would be perfect but for its omission of the phrase, 'the morass of destitution.' There is a devilishly realistic picture of the English humorist whose parodies have drawn tears from the sentient part of the nation for the last twenty years. It is great fun, but at times it is ill-mannered. It offends one beyond measure in the last impressive pages of the book. Trafford has withdrawn from busy, sterile London, where he sold his scientific genius to buy pretty things for his wife, and now knows himself to be a commercial prostitute, and has sought the clean snows of Labrador. There, he thinks, he can clear his mind of the lies of civilisation and begin to seek God. Sickness strips him of all fear and deceit, so that he communes with God. Wonderingly he finds out what Life is.

[Quotes Bk III, ch. 4 'Something trying to exist' to 'pictures on a bone'.]

In the midst of this ecstatic perception of Life he stops to define Mr. Pethick Lawrence. 'A Gawdsaker? . . . Oh, haven't you heard that before? He's the person who gets excited by any deliberate discussion and gets up wringing his hands and screaming, "For Gawd's sake, let's *do* something *now!*" I think they used it first for Pethick Lawrence, the man who did so much to run the old militant Suffragettes, and burke the proper discussion of woman's future.' It is good, but not worth while interrupting a triumphant meditation over the disordered earth. It is really a matter of good manners.

This Trafford had fallen a victim to a parasitic woman; he had laid his very soul on the altar of Our Lady of Loot. An aeroplane accident dropped him on to the lawn of a Kentish vicarage, in which was staying Marjorie Pope, a beautiful girl of twenty. At that age, when the fine body should have been protected by a vitality that bared its teeth at weakness and ugliness in fierce fastidiousness, she was seriously thinking of marrying Will Magnet, the humorist, 'a fairish man of forty, pale, with a large protuberant, observant grey eye—I speak particularly of the left—and a face of quiet animation warily alert for the wit's opportunity.' But she was willing to do it, her life being governed by gluttony and laziness. . . .

[Quotes Bk I, ch. 2 'After Oxbridge' to 'an importance'.]

For the sake of sideboards and prestige she was willing to give herself to a fool, and transmit folly to her children. . . . And the really fine and encouraging thing about the book is that Mr. Wells sees that Marjorie is a thorough scoundrel. The horror of it is that, confused by her clear eyes and copper hair, he accepts her scoundrelism as the normal condition of women.

Something, probably Trafford's clean physical vigour, overcame her natural carelessness of destiny, that cold sensuality that made her think of her body as a thing to barter for sideboards. So she eloped with him, and henceforth mastered his life and beggared it. She wanted 'things'— old Dutch clocks and wonderful dinner-dresses and Chippendale chairs. And she claimed them from him because she was his wife and the mother of his child.

There is something sinister about a figure such as the great Christ who hangs on the cross athwart the Catholic Cathedral at Westminster. The blood about His brow, the distortion of His mouth, the tension of the body, the changeless attitude of pain, convey at last the sense of an eternal hunger. The lights of a thousand candles, all the incense of the pious, the daily worship of millions, have whetted Him to the remorseless acceptance of the lives of men and the reason of nations. Not till the roof of the world falls in will that hunger cease from feeding on the hearts of men; and then, amid the dust of the universe, one can imagine a God impatiently making a new world of worshippers. Perhaps it is because of this harsh lien on the world's love and sympathy that blasphemy is the one crime that all men commit before they die.

And women have taken for themselves the right to claim worship, by virtue of the suffering through which they pass to bring men into the world—although a casual glance at the worshippers might show them that they had done it carelessly and without exclusiveness—and of the beauty of their lives. There is no end to their hunger. They send men they do not know into the snowy wastes to trap silver foxes, and set the men they do know working at barren, profitable commercial muddles to buy the pelts. For in particular they demand material, inessential things. And they get them; but also they get hatred and curses that are the inevitable offerings to divinity.

Trafford had a genius for scientific research. 'I want research,' he moaned when delirium overtook him in Labrador, 'and that still, silent room of mine again, that room, as quiet as a cell, and the toil that led to light. Oh! the coming of that light, the uprush of discovery, the solemn joy as the generalisation rises like a sun upon the facts—floods them with a common meaning. That is what I want. That is what I have always wanted. . . .' Marjorie began her attack on his soul by disliking his work and putting a background of domestic dispeace to the splendid foreground of his laboratory. 'He went home about half-past five, and found a white-faced, red-eyed Marjorie, still dressed, wrapped in a travelling-rug, and crumpled and asleep in his study armchair beside the grey ashes of an extinct fire. . . . "Oh, where have you been?" she asked almost querulously. "Where *have* you been?" "But, my dear!"

he said, as one might speak to a child, "why aren't you in bed? It's just dawn." "Oh," she said, "I waited and waited. It seemed you *must* come. I read a book. And then I fell asleep." And then, with a sob of feeble self-pity, "And here I am!" She rubbed the back of her hand into one eye and shivered. "I'm cold," she said, "and I want some tea." ' That repulsive desire for tea is a masterly touch. It reminds one of the disgust one felt as a healthy schoolgirl when one saw the schoolmistresses drinking tea at lunch at half-past eleven. It brings home to one poignantly how disgusting the artificial physical weakness of women, born of loafing about the house with only a flabby mind for company, must be to an ordinary, vigorous man.

A little later he discovered that to furnish her house daintily with Bokhara hangings and brass-footed work-boxes she has spent every penny of his income of six hundred and frittered away a thousand of his capital. She avoids discussion by having a baby in a sentimental and rather pretentious way. Although she knows that his work is being cut out of his life as one might cut a living man's heart out of his breast, and that its place is being taken by popular lectures to the scientifically-minded of Pinner and such parts, she continues to ruin him by buying post-impressionist pictures and hoarding up bills. Finally she breaks his spirit by having another baby.

So he drops research and takes up the manufacture of synthetic rubber. For nine years he runs this business and plays tedious games with rubber shares, while Marjorie lets herself go with the price of his perdition in a great, beautiful house filled with the creations of genius and silly, chattering people. 'Look at this room,' cries Trafford in despair, 'this litter of little satisfactions! Look at your pretty books there, a hundred minds you have pecked at, bright things of the spirit that attracted you as jewels attract a jackdaw. Look at the glass and silver, and that silk from China!' He suddenly rebels. He takes Marjorie away to the heights of Labrador, where, between combats with lynxes and wolverines, sickness and famine, they brood on Life.

Marjorie, somewhat impertinently, uses her own worthlessness into the basis of a generalisation as to the worthlessness of all women.

[Quotes Bk III, ch. 4 'What are we women' to 'That's the man!']

Trafford confirms her suspicions.

[Quotes Bk III, ch. 4 'You're a finer individual' to 'you hardly begin to follow'.]

So they go home in a very good temper.

And Mr. Wells agrees with them. That is the terrible thing, for there is no author who has a more religious faith; nor one who speaks his gospel with such a tongue of flame. His first sin lies in pretending that Marjorie, that fair, fleshy being who at forty would look rather like a cow—and the resemblance would have a spiritual significance—is the normal woman; and the second lies in his remedy, which Marjorie discovers in a period of spiritual turmoil brought on by debt. 'A woman gives herself to a man out of love, and remains clinging parasitically to him out of necessity. Was there no way of evading that necessity?' she meditates sentimentally. 'Suppose the community kept all its women, suppose all property in homes and furnishings and children vested in them.... Then every woman would be a princess to the man she loved.' The cheek of it! The mind reels at the thought of the community being taxed to allow Marjorie, who could steal her lover's money and barter the brightness of his soul for brass-footed workboxes, to perpetuate her cowlike kind. I can see myself as the one rebel in this humourless State going forth night after night to break the windows of the barracks or Yoshiwara where Marjorie was kept in fat ease, and going to prison month after month until——

But 'all women!' 'Suppose the community kept all its women....' Heavens, I shall be inside too! I object to living under the same roof as Marjorie.

I wonder about the women who never come across any man who was worth loving (and next time Mr. Wells travels in the tube he might look round and consider how hopelessly unlovable most of his male fellow-passengers are), who are not responsive to the lure of Dutch clocks, and forget, as most people do, the colour of the dining-room wallpaper, who, being intelligent, can design a becoming dress in five minutes and need think no more about it. I wonder how they will spend the time. Bridge-parties, I suppose, and possibly State-facilitated euthanasia....

Let Mr. Wells and any other man who loathes the daughter of the horse-leech reflect a minute: 'What would happen to Marjorie if she had to fend for herself?' That is a very important reason why women should be made to work. Under present conditions Marjorie is a handsomely subsidised young woman. For she is to many the typical wife and mother, since she has not her more sensitive sister's objection to the monotony and squalor of domestic drudgery that men have thrust on the wife and mother. But supposing she had to work. How long could she stand it? The weaker sort of Marjorie would be sucked down to prostitution and death, the stronger sort of Marjorie would develop qualities of decency and courage and ferocity. It is worth trying. Not only because men ought to be protected from the monstrous demands of Our Lady of Loot, but because women ought to have a chance of being sifted clean through the sieve of Work.

67. Henry James to Wells

18 October 1912

Extract from letter to Wells, in *The Letters of Henry James*, ii, pp. 271–3.

This letter was James's last and most candid attempt to convince Wells that artistically he was taking the wrong course. Wells replied with a hasty and insincere apology (19 October). He records in his *Autobiography* that James also broached the topic of *Marriage* at one of their meetings, criticizing in particular the sketchiness of the courtship scene between Marjorie and Trafford. James evidently realized that his strictures were passing unheeded, and his disenchantment is expressed in a letter written on 24 October. Ironically, the recipient was Mrs Humphry Ward, herself an unashamed propaganda-novelist: 'Strange to me—in his affair—the coexistence of so much talent with so little art, so much life with (so to speak) so little living! But of him there is much to say, for I really think him more interesting by his faults than he will probably ever manage to be in any other way; and he is a most vivid and violent object-lesson' (ii, pp. 275–6). Eighteen months later he wrote 'The Younger Generation' (1914), his public denunciation of the Wells and Bennett novel, and this was followed a year later by Wells's satirical attack on him in *Boon*.

Meanwhile if I've been deprived of you on one plane I've been living with you very hard on another; you may not have forgotten that you kindly sent me *Marriage* (as you always so kindly render me that valued service;) which I've been able to give myself to at my less afflicted and ravaged hours. I have read you, as I always read you, and as I read no one else, with a complete abdication of all those 'principles of criticism,' canons of form, preconceptions of felicity, references to the idea of method or the sacred laws of composition, which I roam, which I totter, through the pages of others attended in some dim degree by the fond yet feeble theory of, but which I shake off, as I advance under your spell, with the most cynical inconsistency. For under your spell I do advance—save when I pull myself up stock still in order not to break it with so much as the breath of appreciation; I live with you and in you and (almost cannibal-like) *on* you, on you H. G. W., to the sacrifice of your Marjories and your Traffords, and whoever may be of their company; not your treatment of them, at all, but, much more, their befooling of you (pass me the merely scientific expression—I mean your fine high action in view of the red herring of lively interest they trail for you at their heels) becoming thus of the essence of the spectacle for me, and nothing in it all 'happening' so much as these attestations of your character and behaviour, these reactions of yours as you more or less follow them, affect me as vividly happening. I see you 'behave' all along, much more than I see them even when they behave, (as I'm not sure they behave *most* in *Marriage*) with whatever charged intensity or accomplished effect; so that the ground of the drama is somehow most of all in the adventure for *you*—not to say *of* you—the moral, temperamental, personal, expressional, of your setting it forth; an adventure in fine more appreciable to me than any of those you are by way of letting *them* in for. I don't say that those you let them in for don't interest me too, and don't 'come off' and people the scene and lead on the attention, about as much as I can do with; but only, and always, that you beat them on their own ground and that your 'story', through the five hundred pages, says more to me than theirs. You'll find this perhaps a queer rigmarole of a statement, but I ask of you to allow for it just now as the mumble, at best, of an invalid; and wait a little till I can put more of my hand on my sense. Mind you that the restriction I may seem to you to lay on my view of your work, still leaves that work more convulsed with life and more brimming with blood than any it is given me nowadays to meet. The point I have wanted to make is that I find myself absolutely unable, and still more unwilling, to approach you, or to take leave of you, in any projected light of criticism, in any judging or concluding, any comparing, in fact in any aesthetic or 'literary', relation at all; and this in spite of the fact that the light of criticism is almost that in which I most fondly bask and that the amusement I consequently renounce is one of the dearest of all to me. I simply decline—that's the way the thing works—to pass you again through my cerebral oven for critical consumption: I consume you crude and whole and to the last morsel, cannibalistically, quite, as I say; licking the platter clean of the last possibility of a savour and remaining thus yours abjectly

HENRY JAMES.

THE PASSIONATE FRIENDS

September 1913

68. Robert Lynd, review in *Daily News and Leader*

12 September 1913, 2

Robert Lynd (1879–1949), writer and journalist.

Mr. Wells's new novel in its form, at least, ought to please Mr. Shaw. It is a discussion as Mr. Shaw's ideal drama is a discussion. The hero and heroine talk and write review articles to each other except while they are entangled in the drama of a guilty love. Mr. Wells is less anxious to tell a story or to portray characters than to let us know what Stratton and Lady Mary thought about Imperialism or the world-wide subjection of labour or votes for women. Stratton and Lady Mary and all the rest of them are merely toy figures, like the figures in one of the author's war games, moved this way and that, not by any inward-compulsion, but by an outside intelligence. They have little reality except the reality of Mr. Wells's ideas. We feel that if we pricked them they would bleed arguments. In the last analysis they are simply collections of arguments for the abolition of international and sexual jealousies.

It would, of course, be unfair to saddle Mr. Wells with the responsibility for all the arguments his characters use. He represents rather the dramatic conflict of arguments that occur to him while he is trying to puzzle out, as he is always trying to puzzle out, what is wrong with the world. It is as though he were making a desperate effort to explain the Universe in prose, and the two lobes of his brain did not entirely agree on the matter. Bitterly conscious of the existence of some curse of original sin in the human race, he is eager to make it clear to himself and to us what this sin is which prevents men from being the splendid idealists who will build up the great World State—the republic of the brotherhood of man to which all the ends of the earth must come. His answer, as we seem to find it in the present story, is at least as old as Genesis. It is Eve who tempts Adam to his fall. Mr. Wells, however, would put it more subtly than that. Adam, in his view, is not the victim of Eve, but of the passion within him for mastering and subjecting Eve, and of the passion of all the other Adam for mastering and subjecting Eve. His jealousy, which is the ruin of the world, is merely this egoistic passion in action against the family of men.

The lay figure of a story which Mr. Wells dresses up in his assorted arguments is simple enough. Stratton and Lady Mary love each other as boy and girl. Stratton and Lady Mary love each other as young man and young woman. Lady Mary will not marry him, however, for he is only a clergyman's son with a career to make, and she sees a better chance of being her own mistress in a marriage with a rich financier which will give her the freedom that wealth gives, instead of hampering her with the bonds that are an essential part of a marriage for love. She is a character a little difficult to make out. Mr. Wells seems inclined to idealise her—to regard her as a type of womanhood to whom the society of the future must in some way conform. To most people, however, she will seem a clandestine and greedy person, a woman who demands all concessions but will make none, an egoist of sex beyond any other character in the book. She will not risk marrying her lover; neither will she let him go. When he returns from South Africa (where he has distinguished himself in the war) and is just on the point of falling in love with the 'angel in the house' sort of girl he afterwards marries, Lady Mary puts out her claw and makes him her own again. They discover before long that friendship apart from love is beyond their power, and Mr. Wells's hero seizes the occasion to expound his strong conviction of the impossibility of anything like comradeship between men and women at the present stage of civilisation.

Whether this is true or false—and it is probably both—the passionate friendship between Stratton and Lady Mary ends in disaster. Lady Mary's husband, who has up till then hardly opened his eyes, suddenly wakes up, becomes what is called a regular Turk, makes Lady Mary little better than a prisoner in his house, threatens divorce, and compels Stratton to agree to go and live out of England for the next three years. The chapters describing those three years of wandering are the fullest of argument of any in the book. They might be described as a continuation of *A Modern Utopia* and *The Great State*.*

* A volume of essays by Wells and others (1912).

One would have thought that such a prolonged Cook's Tour of sociological adventure would have effectually driven out the image of Lady Mary, but not a bit of it. When Stratton returns, marries his angel in the house, and begins his life-work of running a sort of peace stores for all the world, Lady Mary once more comes down on him with a letter, and there they are arguing away at it as volubly as ever. Love, it may be admitted, has now given place to debate, and they do not even meet, except once by accident when abroad. This meeting is the occasion of much expression of bewilderment about things in general, for Stratton and Lady Mary are both about as bewildered by life as a hen trying to dodge a motor-car. The meeting, however, is big not only with argument, but with fate. Lady Mary's husband, hearing of it, believes the worst and renews the threat of divorce. It is in order to save her lover from the disgrace of the divorce proceedings that Lady Mary suddenly puts an end to her life and, incidentally, to the story.

It is in its way an interesting story, for with all his versatility Mr. Wells has never yet succeeded in being a bore. It has few qualities but interest, however. It has a sort of glamour here and there, but it is curiously lacking in imaginative wonder. It is, so far as the poetry of life is concerned, dumb. Mr. Wells is fond of the word 'beautiful,' but beauty is just the thing which he seems to miss in the speech and actions of men and women. He is, we feel, born to prose as the sparks fly upward. When he attempts lyrical effects, as he sometimes does in the dialogue of his lovers, he only achieves a kind of oratory. On the other hand, he is splendidly, hotly, in earnest about the business of clearing up his mind—of clearing up his soul. He is as eager to explain things as if men needed a new creed every day with the morning paper. He reveals himself to us constantly as a drowning man clutching at Utopian straws, and he keeps on at the desperate game with such courage and resource that we cannot but admire him. One thing we cannot help noticing, however. He again and again announces a new vision of brotherhood, but never for an instant in his characterisation of men and women does he express that brotherhood, as Mr. Shaw, for instance, expresses it in *Androcles and the Lion*—surely by far the most moving of his plays. Great imaginative literature is not merely about brotherhood: it is brotherhood. Mr. Wells's work always seems to me to belong to the 'about' school of literature. That is, perhaps, why his solutions often appear so shallowly related to fact. His indictment of passion, in the present book, for instance, is only convincing as far as any of the old Puritan divines would bear him company. When it merges into a vision of that vague person of the future of whom he speaks as the 'sister-lover,' it becomes as unreal as a sentimental picture. This creature, we feel, is a speculation of the brain, not of the spirit. That is symptomatic of Mr. Wells's weakness as a prophet.

69. A. R. Orage, review in *New Age*

16 October 1913, n.s. xiii, 730

Alfred Richard Orage (1873–1934), journalist and editor of the *New Age* from 1907 to 1922. Orage was the leading radical editor of his day: Wells was at first a contributor to his magazine, but relations between the two men became increasingly strained. *The Passionate Friends* had already caused a quarrel between them, for Orage had attributed the non-arrival of a review copy of the book to a deliberate act on Wells's part. Hence the first sentence in the present review, which appeared in Orage's 'Readers and Writers' column over the initials 'R.H.C.', and was reprinted in his *Selected Essays and Critical Writings* (1935), ed. Herbert Read and Denis Saurat, pp. 100–2.

I have now read the copy of his *Passionate Friends* which Mr. Wells has had sent to the *New Age*. It is not a masterly work in any sense of the word, but, on the contrary, as loose and incontinent a production both in style and ideas as could well be produced by an habitual writer. Usually, as is well known, an author becomes more real, defined, and concrete as his discipline of thought and writing invigorates his mind. Ruskin, for example, who began as a windbag, ended by nearly writing perfect good sense; in time, he would have written, perhaps, as simply as Swift wrote or as passionately to the point as Demosthenes spoke. With Mr. Wells, however, the case is just the reverse. He began by writing of definite persons, things, and ideas, and he is now writing indefinitely of anything. In fact, he appears to suppose that indefiniteness is a virtue, a quality characteristic of the best intelligence. To obliterate the natural or acquired distinctions between the sexes, for instance, is for him a kind of duty to civilisation. When his heroine, the Lady Mary, talks of living her own life and of belonging to herself, not only does the fool hero, Stephen, assent to her claim of these male privileges; but Mr. Wells pleads for the view with an almost personal appeal. But such chatter on the part of a woman like Mary, incapable of supporting herself for a day, is chatter and nothing more; and if Stephen were not the 'complementary male' spoken of by Dr. Almroth Wright,* he would have either laughed at her or turned and left her. That, I hope and believe, is what young men are to-day doing with the apes of the wives of Ibsen's and Shaw's eunuchs and baby-husbands. But just as Mr. Wells is no longer able to discriminate between a man and a woman, and would have it that a woman can possibly be as 'free' as a man, so, I find, he is no longer able to discriminate between economic and spiritual affairs, between democracy and aristocracy, between one form of government and another, between Socialism and aimless amiable Social Reform. On all these subjects in the course of interminable digressions, Mr. Wells exfoliates to marvel, but he never by any chance drops a seed. I did not note in my reading a single observation fit to be placed at the head of an essay or demanding a moment's reflection to open it. This, which would be no defect if the story were continuous, is a damning defect in a story deliberately interrupted to admit reflections and observations. The book, as my readers will gather, irritated me. It did more, it disgusted me. There is not a sign of passion (which is intelligent single-mindedness) in *The Passionate Friends* from beginning to end. What Mr. Wells calls passion is nothing but lust. All the chief characters are as promiscuous as they can hang together. There is neither charm nor virtue in one of them.

* A reference to Wright's *Unexpurgated Case against Women's Suffrage* (1913).

70. Review in *Bookman* (New York)

January 1914, xxxviii, 554–7

Ward Clark, the reviewer, was one of a considerable minority of critics who failed to see any evidence of artistic decline in the discussion novels.

It has been said (applying a respectable canon of literary criticism) that Mr. Wells cancels his own claim to immortality by his very cleverness. He is so keenly alive to the present, so preternaturally 'modern,' that he misses the universal appeal. No matter how stimulating, how significant his books may be for us in 1913, they are bound to be out of the fashion by 1917.

Thus runs the argument, based, one is to suppose, on careful examination of the qualities that have in the past made for the permanence of literary reputations. One defect of the theory is that as a generalisation it won't work. Is the quality of contemporaneity fatal to lasting fame? It remains to be proved that Mr. Wells is more modern than was Meredith for his day, or Shakespeare or Homer for theirs. The unsupported dogma looks like a suspiciously feeble last resort. No one denies his interest for us here and now. To convict a man of his virtues—is this the way to deny him the glory he has earned?

Yet it is not a mere mean jealousy that would scan with suspicion a fame too easily bestowed. There are many such nowadays. It is right that the tough-minded should preserve an air of scepticism toward the towering reputations that we reviewers are industriously creating every day. It must be an extraordinarily dull novel of which in these days some enthusiast does not publicly predicate immortality.

It is the consciousness of this fact that imposes a certain restraint in dealing with Mr. Wells's latest book. For the present reviewer must in honesty record first that he has long been Mr. Wells's admirer, and that he thinks that in *The Passionate Friends* Mr. Wells has given us his finest, most notable work. If the high estimate placed upon this novel is to escape the reviewer's own reproach, he must attempt, however inconclusively, to state some definite reasons for the belief.

It has been said that no one denies Mr. Wells's interest for our own day. He is supremely the 'modern' novelist. No one else has shown such intense preoccupation with those questions in which every one of us, if he have a spark of intelligence, must feel a vital concern. We are aghast at the portentous changes that are taking place in our commercial fabric. We see the old comfortable social order breaking up before our eyes, and wonder what monster of socialism or anarchism is to take its place. The new disquieting note of feminism is heard, the first symptom of a revolt that may involve half the race. Science goes on its conquering way, compelling philosophy to remake itself because its old antagonist has achieved the impossible; and with science goes increasing discontent and misery. There is a new morality in the air, unformulated yet, but none the less threatening to the ancient standards. These tremendous problems are the stuff of Mr. Wells's thought. In the series of novels beginning with *Tono-Bungay* he has touched each of them in turn with his incisive intelligence. And if any one imagines that these are topics of merely momentary importance, he is in need of enlightenment from some supra-earthly source. History is making, it is true, with unprecedented rapidity; yet probably these big questions of 1913 will still be big questions a dozen or a hundred years hence.

Furthermore, Mr. Wells is not merely abreast of the times; he has repeatedly shown himself uncannily able to keep in advance of the crest of the wave. His prescience is extraordinary. Here is a trifle by way of illustration. In *The Passionate Friends* he speaks in his fictitious capacity of the remarkable school of Bengali poets and novelists, proposes a series of translations of their works into English. Now this book may have been written six months or a year ago. Who then outside of the narrowest literary circles had heard of this Eastern literary group? Who would have dared prophesy that they would ever become known to the man in the street? Yet pat on the publication of *The Passionate Friends* comes the announcement that the Nobel prize has been bestowed on the Bengali Tagore, and every one is talking about him. It is as though Mr. Wells had actually foretold the event.

But all this wonderful material of the present is, after all, the property of no one man. It is what he has done with this stuff of life, the ends to which he has fashioned the matter, that constitute his achievement. The importance of the ideas Mr. Wells has to offer us may be disputed, but hardly his superb gift of narration. If *The Passionate Friends* had no light to throw on the turbulent social whirlpool, if the characters could be imagined as detached from the common life of the day, it would remain a memorable story. Never has Mr. Wells made his craftsmanship count for more; never has he seemed less conscious of his art. He can even use triumphantly a device that in hands less sure would court failure as a hackneyed trick. How many novels have had for their basic scheme a retrospective recital of events by one of the chief actors in them? Mr. Wells not only uses the ancient device without disaster; he gives it an actual distinction, as of originality. *The Passionate Friends* is the life story of Stephen Stratton, written in middle age to leave for his young son. It is the story of a man who loved two women, who with honesty of purpose on the whole, steered close to total shipwreck, who yet by virtue of some big, unreasoning faith, managed to save some fragments of his life. Though there is the possibility, almost the necessity, of melodrama in the plot, in some way the characters manage always to dominate the situation. The Lady Mary Christian, Stephen's great love, is the finest, most complex, most baffling character Mr. Wells has created. She is the consummate flower of womanhood, and yet she is a rebel; and yet she weakens in her rebellion at the critical moment and smashes two lives to bits. Stephen, with all his weaknesses and heroisms, is her victim, but his love is comprehensible because she has both brains and charm. When she voices her inmost beliefs one hears, not the observations of a man on the Woman Question, but the authentic note of the modern woman who, striking out in blind protest against she knows not what, has given a new meaning to the word feminism. And even in this outburst she remains herself, an actual individual, while her end, shut in a dreadful coil of impossible circumstance, has the accent of grave, reserved tragedy. If it misses the inevitability of the highest tragedy, the failure is no more than relative.

Strangely enough, the 'note' of the book is one of hopefulness. Mr. Wells is an incorrigible optimist; the fact is one of the signal triumphs of the human spirit. No one has a clearer sight than he of the stupidity, the abysmal idiocy of the constitution of society; no one feels more intensely the maladjustments, the discontent, the misery of so many of us. But he starkly refuses to believe other than that something better is to come of all this. His first and last thought is always for finding a better way of doing the thing we have hitherto done badly. We scold the critic who is, as we say, merely destructive; we must then in decent consistency, recognise the critic of life who is inveterately constructive. Out of these fumbling attempts to do fine things that seem always to end in such utter failure he seeks to pluck some lesson that will serve to make the next attempt a little less a failure. He offers no solutions of insoluble problems, but he tries in all honesty to point a way wherein a partial solution may after innumerable attempts be found.

After all, perhaps the secret of Mr. Wells's success with a hackneyed literary form is that he has recorded a genuine confession. Make no mistake, this is real autobiography; not in the mere literal sense, but in the sense that it comes straight at first hand from the man's own experience and thought. The strongest impression that remains of *The Passionate Friends* is of the author's intellectual honesty. He may or may not be on the whole a true prophet; as to that there is room for difference of opinion. But however much he may offend your sober common-sense, outrage your taste, do violence to your moral standards, he will not pretend. He is of those men, and they are rare, who seek the truth with passion. He utters his own soul, and says: Here it is, this mixture of nobility and meanness, of high altruism and anxious egotistical vulgarity; at least, the authentic soul of a man. In this, as in much else, Mr. Wells has placed himself in the line of the Great Succession. If this passionate quest of the truth, joined to the wisdom of a man who has lived and the skill of one who has mastered a great craft, be not genius, then it is something so very like to genius that failure to see the difference may be more pardonable than refusal to see the resemblance.

THE WIFE OF SIR ISAAC HARMAN

October 1914

71. Walter Lippmann, review in *New Republic*

7 November 1914, 27

Walter Lippmann (b. 1889), political journalist, expresses the disappointment with which some of Wells's admirers realized that in fiction he was now largely a spent force.

Somewhere in *The New Machiavelli* H. G. Wells pictures himself surrounded by piles of manuscripts discarded in an effort to find a true account of his story. When I finished reading *The Wife of Sir Isaac Harman* I wondered whether Mr. Wells had not passed beyond the stage of rejecting any part of his own work as inadequate. For though this latest book is amusing and perhaps useful, it is a careless book written with comfortable facility out of the upper layers of his mind. You say to yourself, Wells has turned out another book. You cannot say to yourself, as you could of his earlier work, Wells has learned from fresh experience and Wells is giving of that experience. For *Tono-Bungay* and *The New Machiavelli* were wrung with tortured sincerity out of a man's own life, and they were scarred and shapeless with the effort; they seemed to stammer inevitably into Wells's famous suspension points with their own inner need for the elusive fringes of the truth.

Since he wrote *The New Machiavelli* Wells seems like a man who has retired to live in the country on the proceeds of his accumulated spiritual capital. Where formerly each book had been a fresh adventure and a new conquest, these later ones seem like creations from an armchair which cost little and give little. No doubt it is understandable that men should grow weary of danger, that arctic explorers should become lecturers and that old soldiers should write their memoirs, that Wells should plagiarize Wells. Few men who write have driven themselves as he has driven himself. The old Wells seemed to be living in a chronic crisis, in which there were immense visions and shattering disappointments, a gorgeous socialism breaking its heart over the actual facts. In the characters he created love was a pursuit in which the woman his hero desired was always just beyond the one he possessed. He was forever adjusting his hope of reality, trying almost in agony to find in England a home for his dreams. And because that struggle was relentless, Wells had come to typify the modern man, his weakness and his constant relapses, his tentative hope and his overwhelming tasks.

For what distinguished Wells among the Utopians is the fact that his Utopia was never finished and that every new experience amended it radically. He was not content to indulge his fancy or to clamor for freedom. He seemed to live in that dangerous region where freedom is being tried and vision embodied. He seemed to be buffeted from both sides, challenged by his dreams which revolted at the compromises of reality, and assaulted by reality which denounced the emptiness of all dreams. He seemed to spend himself in that struggle—the severest that a man can face; and he seemed to win by a constant renewal of effort in which he refused to sink either into placid acceptance of the world, or into self-contained satisfaction with his vision.

But in his later books there has been an evident slackening of effort, betrayed at first by a too great fluency of style, an increase of mannerism, a tendency to large rhetoric, and to plots which creak along by accident. Worse than that, his heroines have become distant and beautiful, they have moved up in society as heroines do, so that of late a Wells heroine to have a soul and to suffer must also have a title. Moreover, the villain has appeared, as the husband in *The Passionate Friends*, as Sir Isaac in this book. Now a villain is a device for shirking the issue; you ascribe all the difficulties to him, and your story can proceed. But he is fatal to the truth, as the earlier Wells would have proclaimed on every page.

Yet here is the villain drawn as an uncannily malignant figure who is responsible for modern commercialism and for the suffering of generous souls like the wife, Lady Harman. 'Poor Sir Isaac had lived like a blind thing in the sunlight, gathering and gathering, when the pride and pleasure of life is to administer and spend. . . .' And you take it from this book that only when he dies is freedom possible. At any rate, Lady Harman kisses the other man and the final note is a happy one. The earlier Wells, I think, would have begun the book there; he would have written the history of the marriage of well-meaning Lady Harman and well-meaning and inadequate Mr. Brumley. He would, in short, have faced the real problem of love and business and politics, which is not of black villains and of white heroines, but of maundering and confused human beings.

Wells has tried to write that book several times, but of late the effort seems too great for him, and so he writes instead these hasty, imitative, and somewhat querulous additions to the stock of the popular novel. There has perhaps always been in him a tendency to run away from his problem. His distressed heroes and heroines have fled to laboratories or gone up in balloons or committed suicide. He himself has fled recently from the business of reconstruction to a very thin picture of *The World Set Free*. Generally he has conquered this weakness or compensated it by a great mass of honest speculation and vivid experience, but in this latest book the flight has become precipitate amidst a wreckage of abstract nouns in the plural and absurdly simplified accounts of human motive. For the mere fact that Wells has written about marriage as if the wife were all innocence and the husband all villainy is in itself the most distressing commentary on this book.

72. Van Wyck Brooks on Wells's socialist imagination

1915

The World of H. G. Wells, ch. 1 ('The First Phase').

Brooks (1886–1963), writer and literary critic, was author of the earliest critical book on Wells, from which this extract is taken.

'I am, by a sort of predestination, a socialist' Wells wrote once. And everything one can say of him serves merely to explain, justify, qualify, illuminate and refine that statement.

First of all it implies a certain disposition and certain habits of mind, habits of mind which are all to be found in the first phase of his work, in those marvellous tales of Time and Space that won him his original sensational fame. It is this disposition behind them, this quality they have as of an inevitable attitude toward life and the world, which distinguishes them at once from those other superficially similar tales of Jules Verne. The marvels of Jules Verne are just marvels, delightful, irresponsible plunderings from a helpless universe. To the grown-up mind they have a little of that pathetic futility one associates with a millionaire's picture-gallery, where all sorts of things have been brought together, without any exercise of inevitable personal choice, because they are expensive. I don't know that the tales of Wells are better tales, but they have that ulterior synthetic quality that belongs to all real expressions of personality. Wells was never merely inventive; his invention was the first stage of an imaginative growth.

Now the quality that pervades all these early writings is what may be called a sense of the infinite plasticity of things. He conceived a machine that could travel through time, a man who found a way to become invisible, a drug that made men float like balloons, another drug that enabled men to live a thousand hours in one, a crystal egg through which one could watch the life in Mars, a man who could stop the sun like Joshua, a food that turned men into giants, a biologist who discovered

223

a method of carving animals into men, an angel who visited a rural vicar, a mermaid who came to earth in search of a soul, a homicidal orchid, a gigantic bird hatched from a prehistoric egg, a man who passed outside space. In short, the universe appeared to him like that magic shop of which he also wrote, where the most astonishing things may happen, if you are the Right Sort of Boy.

If all this implies anything it implies that things in general are not fixed and static, but that they are, on the contrary, infinitely plastic, malleable, capable of responding to any purpose, any design you may set working among them. The universe, it seems to assume, may be and quite possibly is proceeding after some logical method of its own, but so far as man is concerned this method appears to be one of chance. Obviously, man can do the most surprising things in it, can take as it were all sorts of liberties with it. The universe, in short, is like a vacant field which may or may not belong to some absent landlord who has designs of his own upon it; but until this absent landlord appears and claims his field, all the children in the neighbourhood can build huts in it and play games upon it and, in a word, for all practical purposes, consider it their own.

This idea of the relation between free will and determinism is the underlying assumption of Wells, as he explains it in *First and Last Things*:

[Quotes from Bk I, para. 9 and Bk II, para. 3.]

In a word, for all the purposes that affect man's need the universe is infinitely plastic and amenable to his will. Like every clean-cut philosophical conception, this clears the ground for practical conduct and a certain sort of direct action.

There was a time, no doubt, when he shared the old Utopian folly of expecting a sudden and unanimous change of human will. When the universe appears as unconventional as it used to appear to Wells, there can surely be no reason to think it impossible, after a comet has collided with the world, for the human race to become suddenly Utopian. Generally speaking, comets do not collide with the world, and in the same way men are slow to change. But certainly if Wells ever thought of humanity as merely a multiplication of one pattern, certainly if he has long since abandoned the idea of our all turning over a new leaf one fine morning, he has never lost his faith in free will as regards the individual. He has always believed in the personal doctrine of summarily 'making an end to things' as distinguished from the old-fashioned doctrine of 'making the best of things'; and there is nothing more modern about him than his aversion to the good old English theory of 'muddling through.'

Mr. Polly is a good example of his view of personal direct action, the getting rid, quickly and decisively, of a situation that has only sentiment to save it from complete demoralization. 'When a man has once broken through the wall of every-day circumstances,' he remarks at the moment of the Polly *débâcle*, 'he has made a discovery. If the world does not please you, *you can change it*. Determine to alter it at any price, and you can change it altogether.' Mr. Polly sets fire to his shop, takes to the road and repairs his digestion. Desertion of duty and the quick repudiation of entanglements make him healthy and sensible and give him a sense of purpose in things. And I know of nothing in all Wells that is described with more relish than that Beltane festival which occurs toward the end of *In the Days of the Comet*. The world's great age has begun anew, and the enlightened men of the new time revive the May Day of old in order to burn the useless trappings of the past. They heap old carpets on the fire, ill-designed furniture, bad music and cheap pictures, stuffed birds, obsolete school-books, dog-eared penny fiction, sham shoes, and all the corrugated iron in the world; every tangible thing that is useless, false, disorderly, accidental, obsolete, and tawdry to celebrate the beginning of things that are clean, beautiful, and worthy. Sceptical, hesitant, and personal as Wells has become, that indicates a strong primitive mental trait. Philosophy does not spring out of the brain; we hate the hateful things of our own experience, just as we think the things we desire. And though there are nine and sixty ways of being a socialist, they all unite in a certain sense of the plasticity and malleability of things human, a certain faith in the possibility of asserting order in the midst of disorder and intelligently cleaning house.

Inherent in this trait is another—detachment. You only become aware of confusion when you stand free of it, when you cease to be a part of it. And of all writers who have so immediately felt life I doubt if there has been one so detached as Wells. The mental detachment of his early tales is a detachment half scientific, half artistic; scientific as of one who sees things experimentally in their material, molecular aspect, artistic as of one conscious of moulding will and placed amid plastic material. Thus, for example, he sees human beings quite stripped of their distinctively human qualities; he sees men anatomically, as in that passage where the Invisible Man, killed with a spade, becomes visible again as a corpse:

225

[Quotes ch. 28 'Everyone saw' to 'dense and opaque'.]

Similar is a passage in 'A Story of the Days to Come,' where he describes an ordinary breakfast of our own day: 'the rude masses of bread needing to be carved and smeared over with animal fat before they could be made palatable, the still recognizable fragments of recently killed animals, hideously charred and hacked.' That surely is quite as a man from another planet, or a chemist after a long day's work in the laboratory, would view our familiar human things. And one recalls another sentence from *Kipps* where this detachment links itself with a deeper social insight and hints at the part it had come to play in Wells's later mind: 'I see through the darkness,' he says, toward the end of the book, 'the souls of my Kippses as they are, *as little pink strips of quivering, living stuff*, as things like the bodies of little ill-nourished, ailing, ignorant children—children who feel pain, who are naughty and muddled and suffer, and do not understand why.'

And just as he sees men and human things chemically and anatomically, so he sees the world astronomically. He has that double quality (like his own Mr. Bessel) of being bodily very active in life and at the same time watching it from a great distance. In his latest book he has figured a god looking on from the clouds; and there is nothing in his novels more stimulating and more uncanny than a certain faculty of telescoping his view suddenly from the very little to the very large, expanding and contracting his vision of things at will. You find the germ of this faculty in his early tales. Looking down as though from a balloon he sees the world as a planet, as a relatively small planet. In doing so he maintains at first a purely scientific set of values; he is not led, as he has since been led, and as Leopardi was led by the same imaginative experience, to adopt poetical values and to feel acutely the littleness and the powerlessness of man. His values remain scientific, and the absurdity he feels is the absurdity an astronomer must feel, that in so small a space men can vaunt themselves and squabble with one another. Race prejudice, for example, necessarily appears to him as foolish as it would appear to ordinary eyes among insects that happen to be swarming on a fallen apple. Once you get it into your mind that the world is a ball in space, you find a peculiar silliness in misunderstandings on that ball. This reflection has led to many views of life; in Wells it led to a sense of the need of human solidarity.

And solidarity implies order. The sense of order is one of those instincts exhibited everywhere in the writings of Wells that serve as preliminaries to his social philosophy. There is a passage in *Kipps* where he pictures the satisfactions of shopkeeping to an elect soul:

[Quotes Bk III, ch. 3 'There is, of course' to 'coloured silks'.]

De Foe knew a similar satisfaction and has pictured it in *Robinson Crusoe*. De Foe was himself a shopkeeper, just as Wells has been in one of his incarnations; and he knew that good shopkeeping is the microcosm of all good political economy. The satisfaction of a thoroughly competent man who is thrown on a desert island, and sets to work to establish upon it a political economy for one, is a satisfaction by itself. That certainly is a primitive relish, and it is one of the first gestures of Wells's sociology.

Now the sense of solidarity, the sense of order, implies the subordination of details, the discipline of constituent units. Only in his later works did Wells begin to consider the problems of the individual life; in his novels he has considered them almost exclusively, but always in relation to the constructive purpose of society and as what may be called human reservations from it. The telescope has been adjusted to a close range, and the wider relationships are neither so emphasized nor so easily discerned. Nevertheless it is still the world that matters to Wells—the world, the race, the future; not the individual human being. And if, relatively, he has become more interested in the individual and less in the world, that is because he is convinced that the problems of the world can best be approached through the study of individuals. His philosophy has grown less abstract in harmony with his own experience; but the first sketch of his view of human nature and its function is to be found crudely outlined in the scientific romances. How does it figure there?

The human beings who flit through these early tales are all inconspicuous little men, whose private existence is of no account, and who exist to discover, invent, perform all sorts of wonderful experiments which almost invariably result in their summary and quite unimportant destruction. They are merely, in the most complete sense, experiments in the collective purpose, and their creator has toward them just the attitude of an anatomist toward the animals upon which he is experimenting; not indifferent to their suffering as suffering, but ignoring it in the spirit of scientific detachment necessary to subordinate means to an end. 'I wanted—it was the only thing I wanted—to find out the limit of plasticity in a living form,' says Dr. Moreau in his confession; 'and the study has made me as remorseless as nature.'

Invariably these experiments in human possibility, placed in a world where charity is not so strong as fear, die quite horribly. Dr. Moreau is destroyed by the beasts he is attempting to vivisect into the semblance of men, the Invisible Man is battered to death with a spade, the Visiting Angel burns to death in attempting to carry out his celestial errand, the man who travels to the moon cannot get back alive. Does not all this foreshadow the burden of the later novels, that the individual who plans and wills for the race is destroyed and broken by the jealousy, prejudice and inertia in men and the blind immemorial forces of nature surging through himself? These are the forces that are figured, in the early tales, by that horrible hostile universe of nature, and the little intrepid men moving about in the midst of it. And the mind of Wells is always prepared for the consequences of what it engenders. The inevitable result of creating an imaginary world of malignant vegetables and worse than antediluvian monsters is that the imaginary men you also create shall suffer through them. You reverse the order of evolution and return men to conditions where life is cheap. An imagination which has accustomed itself to running loose among planets and falling stars, which has lived habitually in a universe where worlds battle with one another, is prepared to stomach a little needless bloodshed. The inflexible pursuit of an end implies the sacrifice of means, and if your experiment happens to be an invisible man you will produce the invisibility even though it kills the man.

Widen the range and this proposition logically transmutes itself into a second: if your experiment happens to be an orderly society you will produce order at the expense of everything that represents disorder. And from the point of view of a collective purpose, ends, motives and affections that are private and have no collective significance represent disorder. Now the whole purpose of Wells's later work has been to illuminate and refine this proposition. He has flatly distinguished between two sorts of human nature, the constructive, experimental sort which lives essentially for the race, and the acquiescent, ineffectual sort which lives essentially for itself or the established fact; and he gives to his experimental men and women an almost unlimited charter to make ducks and drakes of the ineffectual. Think of the long list of dead and wounded in his novels—Mr. Pope, Mr. Stanley, Mr. Magnet, Mr. Manning, Margaret, Marion—and you realize how much of a certain cruelty, a certain ruthlessness is in the very nature of his philosophy of experimental direct action.

Another primitive relish exhibited in these early tales is the delight of constructing things. The Time Machine, for example, is the work of a mind that immoderately enjoys inventing, erecting, and putting things together; and there is not much difference between constructing an imaginary machine and constructing an imaginary society. If Wells's early Utopian speculations are ingenious impossibilities, are they any more or less so than his mechanical speculations? One doesn't begin life with an overwhelming recognition of the obstacles one may encounter —one doesn't fret too much about the possible, the feasible, or even the logical. It was enough for Wells that he had built his Time Machine, though the logic by which the Time Traveller explains his process is a logic that gives me, at least, a sense of helpless, blinking discomfort— partly, I confess, because to this day I don't believe there is anything the matter with it. In any case it is the sheer delight of construction that fascinates him, and everything that is associated with construction fascinates him. He is in love with steel; he speaks with a kind of ecstasy somewhere of 'light and clean and shimmering shapes of silvered steel'; steel and iron have for him the transcendental charm that harebells and primroses had for Wordsworth. A world like that in *The Sleeper Awakes*—a world of gigantic machines, air fleets, and the 'swimming shadows and enormous shapes' of an engineer's nightmare—is only by afterthought, one feels, the speculation of a sociologist. It expresses the primitive relish of a constructive instinct. It expresses also a sheer curiosity about the future.

In a chapter of his book on America* Wells has traced the development of what he calls his prophetic habit of mind as a passage through four stages: the millennial stage of an evangelical childhood when an imminent Battle of Armageddon was a natural thing to be looked for; the stage of ultimate biological possibilities; the stage of prediction by the rule-of-three; and a final stage of cautious anticipation based upon the study of existing facts—a gradual passage from the region of religious or scientific possibilities to the region of human probabilities.

[Summarizes and quotes from ch. 1, 'The Prophetic Habit of Mind'.]

And the burden of his lecture *The Discovery of the Future* is that an inductive knowledge of the future is not only very largely possible, but is considerably more important for us than the study of the past. Even in the sciences, he says, the test of their validity is their power to produce confident forecasts. Astronomy is based on the forecast of stellar move-

---

* The Future in America (1906).

ments, medical science exists largely for diagnosis. It is this thought which determines the nature of his own sociology.

There is usually something inept in speaking of a man, and especially an artist, as interchangeable with any ism. Socialism, in the common sense of the word, is a classification of men. Individual socialists are as a rule something more than socialists; often they are socialists by necessity, or imagination, or sentiment, or expediency—their socialism is not inherent, not the frame of their whole being. In the degree that socialism is a classification, or a school of thought, or an economic theory, the individual socialist will, in practice, make mental reservations from it. Now my whole aim in this chapter has been to suggest that if socialism had not existed Wells would have invented it. It is not something which at a given moment or even after a long process of imaginative conversion or conviction came into his life. It is, in his own formulation of it, the projection of his whole nature, the expression of his will, the very content of his art. With one or two exceptions—works deliberately devoted to propaganda or exposition—even his purely sociological writings are subjective writings, personal and artistic in motive; socialism figures in them just as Catholicism figures in the masses of Mozart, or the brotherhood of man in the poems of Whitman, not as a cause but as a satisfying conception of truth. And just as, if one were to study the psychology of Mozart or Whitman, one would find habits of mind that inevitably produced the individual Catholicism of the one and the individual fraternalism of the other; so behind the socialism of Wells are certain habits of mind, certain primitive likes, relishes, instincts, preferences: a faith in free will, a sense of order and the subordination of details to design, a personal detachment, a pleasure in construction, a curiosity about the future.

These are innate qualities, which inevitably produced their own animating purpose.

73. Stuart P. Sherman on Wells and the Victorians

20 May 1915

'H. G. Wells and the Victorians', *Nation* (New York), c, 558–61; reprinted in an extended form as 'The Utopian Naturalism of H. G. Wells' in *On Contemporary Literature* (1917), from which the present extract (pp. 60–6) is taken.

Stuart Pratt Sherman (1881–1926), critic and professor of English at the University of Illinois, is here attacking the comparison of Wells and Matthew Arnold drawn by Van Wyck Brooks in his Introduction to *The World of H. G. Wells*. Here Brooks claimed that 'Wells on Education, on Criticism, on Politics and the nostrums of Liberalism, Wells even on Religion continues the propaganda of Arnold.' Sherman replies that a more plausible ancestor would be Shelley (Arnold's 'beautiful but ineffectual angel'). After contrasting the metaphysical assumptions of Wells and Arnold, their beliefs about education and the role of the state, he proceeds to their attitudes towards morality.

Nowhere, however, does the irreconcilable opposition of Wells and Arnold appear more distinctly than in their respective attitudes toward morality, and in particular toward 'sexual morality.' In the latter field, the Bosnia of the moral world, Wells has been an incessant dropper of bombs. Arnold, in general, maintained the despised Victorian 'reticence.' One recalls, nevertheless, significant passages in his letters expressing apprehensions for the future of France on the score of the 'social evil.' And one recalls his equally significant declaration that Dowden's *Shelley* makes one feel 'sickened for ever of the subject of irregular relations.'

To this humanistic moralist of the Victorians morality seems a settled and simple matter. He holds that in the course of some thousands of years of civilized society the elementary principles of conduct have been adequately tested, and are now to be unequivocally accepted. They constitute a standard of 'right reason' outside ourselves, to which we should vigorously subject our treacherous individual sensibilities. By adopting these principles the individual acquires a character, becomes a member of civil society, and performs the first duty of man, which is to perpetuate in and through himself the moral life of the race.

The zoological moralist of the Younger Generation holds that morality is a new, complex, experimental science with its work all before it and only a vague generalization fresh from Mr. Wells' laboratory to guide it. In order to get society upon a sound moral basis, says Mr. Wells, it is essential 'to reject and set aside all abstract, refined, and intellectualized ideas as starting propositions, such ideas as right, liberty, happiness, duty, or beauty, and *to hold fast to the fundamental assertion of life as a tissue and succession of births.*' How Sairey Gamp would have enjoyed that 'tissue and succession of births'! Upon this striking obstetrical truth Mr. Wells proposes to hang Moses and all the prophets. Then he will erect upon it the new morality.

Since life is fundamentally a tissue and succession of births, it appears to follow that the first duty of man is to perpetuate not the moral but the physical life of the race. Since 'we don't know what to breed for,' orthodox eugenics is all astray. Since scientific man-breeding, or zoological ethics, is still in its infancy, it behooves us to encourage all sorts of experimentation in procreation, cohabitation, the rehabilitation of natural children, the state subsidization of mothers, and perhaps also of lovers. In the new society, instead of the Victorian convention which precluded the married man from investigation in this field, we shall have freedom for various sex-associations, and, consequently, for enriching emotional discoveries in what are now the dull years of domestic fidelity and emotional hebetude. Mr. Wells is rather fond of turning the tables upon the naughty dramatists of the Restoration, who, as every one knows, exalted the bachelor at the expense of the married man. In *Ann Veronica*, for example, and *The New Machiavelli*, it is the bachelor who is the cad and the *cornuto*; it is the married man who knows how to strike the emotional diapason.

It may be objected that it is idle to promise a future in which a man may love any woman he pleases, since all history teaches that a man has his life-work cut out for him if he pleases any woman he loves. Mr. Wells does not care what history teaches. It may be pointed out that experimentation in irregular relations is not a novelty; that it is now, and always has been, widely practiced; and that the experience of mankind has generally proved it disastrous. Mr. Wells does not care what the experience of mankind has proved. If you assure him that it is not a question of social 'systems,' but of human nature, if you insist that irregular relations under any system quite regularly beget that 'vehement flame' of jealousy which the wise man of Israel says is 'cruel as the grave,' you do not abate his enthusiasm one jot. He is a man of imagination. He makes his beliefs as he wants them. If they clash with immutable things in this world, he creates another world. He has heard of jealousy; but he intends to abolish it. He intends to create a new society in which one can make love to another man's wife without exciting the jealousy of her husband. This is the inspiriting message of *The Passionate Friends*, which closes with these words: 'I will not be content with that compromise of jealousies which is the established life of humanity today. I give myself—to the destruction of jealousy and of the forms and shelters and instruments of jealousy, both in my own self and in the thought and laws and usage of the world.'

Precisely Shelley's idea when he magnanimously invited his wife to join him and Mary Godwin in Switzerland. And she, poor wretch, dumbly criticized his idea from the bottom of the Serpentine.

The defect in Wells's religion which distinguishes it from the religion of Arnold is exactly the defect in his morality, namely, the lack of any principle of control. Here again, he cries, we are in a field for free experimentation; nothing has been determined; 'religion and philosophy have been impudent and quackish—quackish!' And so, while for Arnold religion is something which binds and limits, religion for Wells is something which looses and liberates. Arnold rejects dogmatic theology, but he writes three books to justify the Hebraic faith in an Eternal, not ourselves, which makes for righteousness, and to extol the 'method' and the 'sweet reasonableness' of Jesus. Wells rejects dogmatic theology and all our inheritance from the Hebrews— except their turn for business organization; his substitute for 'morality touched with emotion' is a hot fit of enthusiasm for social progress excited by fixed meditation upon the Utopian projections of his own fancy.

For Arnold, the men of true religious insight are Jesus, Marcus Aurelius, St. Francis, the author of the *Imitations*, Spinoza, who all consent together that 'the Kingdom of God is within you.' Wells designates this conception in the case of Marcus Aurelius as 'a desire for a perfected inconsequent egoism.' There is something to be said for a religion which produces a perfected egoism like that of Aurelius. But

Wells, in the temper of Shelley and other social revolutionists, insists that 'salvation's a *collective* thing,' to be accomplished somewhere in the social environment, beyond the borders of the individual soul. The logical product of the sentimental altruism of Wells may be seen in the hero of almost any of his later novels—in the hero, for example, of *Tono-Bungay*, whom his creator quite accurately characterizes as a 'spiritual guttersnipe in love with unimaginable goddesses.'

With all its fervor for perfecting mankind in the mass, the religion of Wells somehow fails to meet the needs of the individual man. It helps every one but its possessor. He has struggled with this problem, but he has not brought to his task the resources of the religious sages; he has approached it with only the resources of the scientific perfectibilians. He has felt, as we all have felt, the dumb and nameless pain which throbs at the heart of our being as we march or mince or creep or crowd through the welter of cross-purposes, wars, poverty, dreadful accidents, disease, and death, which we call our life. If you ask him how to assuage that pain, he answers that we must apply scientific methods to make mankind pacific, intelligent, well, and wealthy. If you ask him why his hero, Trafford in *Marriage*, who is already wealthy, well, intelligent, and pacific, still feels the throbbing pain, he replies, 'That is because Trafford has a developed social consciousness, and cannot enter into felicity until there is a like felicity for all men to enter.'

Now, did Mr. Wells possess not the insight of the religious sages, but just the sober human experience of a pagan like Horace, he would know that though all men entered his earthly paradise of lacquered ceilings, white-tiled bathrooms, Turkey rugs, scientific kitchens, motor-boats, limousines, and Victrolas, still in their poor worm-infested breasts would dwell 'black care,' still would they remain spiritual guttersnipes in their scientific Elysium. And if Mr. Wells consulted Arnold or the spiritual physicians who have effectually prescribed for the essential malady of living, he would be told that inner serenity springs from self-collection, self-control, and, above all, from the Hebraic sense of personal righteousness, which is the beginning of religious wisdom.

Here and there through the works of Wells there is a glint of skepticism, a flash of self-mockery, which makes one wonder to what extent he himself feels the confidence of the young people who look to him as their saviour. But I have deliberately renounced inquiry into the essential sincerity of his radicalism. I have presented him in the rôle that captivates his admirers, not as an empty resonator for a bewildered and discontented multitude, but as a glowing, eloquent, sanguine leader of the generation which is pressing for a place in the sun. I have exhibited him rising in adorable, unworldly innocence to arraign a social system under which two and two make only four, and water refuses to run up hill, and a child cannot eat his cake and keep it, and fire will not refrain from burning, nor the lion and the lamb lie quietly together, nor sober people take seriously his fairy tales of science, sex, and sociology. If my analysis is correct, I have detached him from Arnold, and established his connection with Shelley. This service should be grateful to him and to his followers; for I have denied him the rank of a Victorian critic only that I might elevate him to the rank of a Georgian angel.

MR. BRITLING SEES IT THROUGH

September 1916

74. Unsigned review, *The Times Literary Supplement*

21 September 1916, 451

For the first time we have a novel which touches the life of the last two years without impertinence. This is a really remarkable event, and Mr. Wells's book, with all its many and obvious imperfections, is a proud achievement. It is a wonder to have been able, already, to absorb and re-fashion such an experience in a way that is merely imperfect, not false or base. After a plentiful crop of novels in which the mightiest blow that has ever fallen upon the world has been used for giving a fresh appeal to old vulgarity, the free sincerity of this book, with its unfailing distinction of tone, is beautiful enough even to cover its staring defects. If these are to be stripped bare it is easy to see that Mr. Wells himself has never written a novel more shapeless and wasteful than this. He starts a score of people and lavishes all his art on them, only to drop them, forget them, pick a few of them up spasmodically again, and drop them once more, as the tide of his dissertation gathers and spreads. Yet for this one reason his haphazard ways have not succeeded in destroying his book—the reason being that nothing in it is so true and fine as its tone, and that its tone never fails. It fills and rounds off the fragmentary drama, transforming it into a creation with which we have as yet seen, in this country at least, nothing whatever to compare.

Mr. Britling had in the summer of 1914 a ranging and critical mind which dragged him in many directions. He was untiringly discursive, intelligent, indignant; he rioted in ideas and bold generalizations; he talked even more than he wrote, and wrote, evidently, a great deal more than he read. He was a very stimulating and very modern sort of man.

236

His charming place in the country was the kind where the farmyard has become an Italian garden and the barn is used for dressing up and dancing in. His family circle were joyful and energetic young people, much exercised in the new romping culture, with its attractive flash of bare arms and bright colours. They were easy in temper and manner, promiscuous and friendly, slightly provincial, extraordinarily divested of responsibility and tradition. A young German tutor, who was one of the household, deplored and enjoyed their careless freedom. A gentleman from New England, arriving in their midst, was bewildered and charmed. Mr. Wells has often proved his mastery in the art of setting such a scene. He does not paint a picture, he surrounds you with exuberant life: he seems to follow no particular descriptive thread, he disdains any orderly succession of strokes; but light pours into his pages, figures multiply and sounds thicken, the quality of a whole order of existence is imparted before another man would have finished describing his heroine. Perhaps he a little presumes on his art; it is sometimes as though he were so sure of himself that he ventures on small fantastic escapades, arbitrary queernesses, like the strange and far-fetched names he so delights in, just to show how easily he can take them in his stride. None the less, his opening chapters once again prove him to be one of the very few of our novelists who can call out images of life with a liberal gesture. The chattering activity of the Britling circle, their nonchalant familiarity with ideas, stands out against the immobile, time-mellowed Essex village with a contrast that two years ago might certainly pass as typical.

On this pretty scene there breaks a very distant rumble of disturbance, a swiftly growing uneasiness, and then the fact of war. At first it affects the Essex village, on the whole, as a sudden desire to lay in food, a refusal on the part of the grocer to take cheques in payment, a stir and an uncertainty which enhance its taste of life. But the matter for the rest of the chronicle is the question how it affects Mr. Britling. It gives him in the first place a passionate desire to help somebody, something, somewhere; it carries him up to London to find one of the innumerable points where a sound man of forty-five is certain to be needed. It takes him two days to discover that the busy people are far too busy to think of getting anyone to help them; he returns to the country and to his thoughts. In the months that follow he has plenty of time to suffer under them and much to look on at, from his distance, before he 'sees it through.' It is not the war that he sees through; it is his occupied, rebellious, anguished mind, no longer discursive, but summoned to deal with a fact which has no proportion to any other fact, an incommensurable thing from another order of things.

He does it perhaps as thoroughly as the incessant labour of a year, to the autumn of 1915 (where we leave him), could achieve. He does it in a manner, with breaks and episodes and new turns of the vast screw, which is possibly interesting, possibly exasperating, possibly of deep and living beauty. He passes through storms of indignation, uncontrollable agonies, fears, elations, despondencies. He is constantly, perhaps generally, unjust; unjust, often, to his own country, in the fever of his desire that his country shall do honour to the huge opportunity before the world; and bitterness does not leave him until he has seen it through and reached a hope which leaps far beyond a victorious end to destruction and massacre. But if the author of this book is able to bring out of the crash of experience something that has the appearance of created form, it must not be pretended that criticism is ready to meet him on his own ground. Is the circle of thought round which Mr. Britling is led a circle truly described, a real fashioning in just terms of one man's one year, of one particular fragment of desire and sensation? It may be this, or it may be a volume of scattered and disjointed notes for a book which Mr. Wells has not written. We shall all be able to criticise it when our own notes fall into line; we cannot until then. But there is one faculty which the last two years have sharpened to the last perfection, and that is the power of recognizing a mean or vulgar touch on the subject of the war. It can be said absolutely that Mr. Wells's book is not this, nor ever within sight of it. Whether he masters his theme, through its many moods, is a question that drops. He knows the height of it, and so new, in the art of a novelist, is this knowledge that it may stand for the very matter of his book. He may or may not have written a great novel on the war; he certainly has written a beautiful one on the only tone we can endure in regard to it.

75. Randolph Bourne, article in *Dial*

28 December 1916, lxi, 563–5

Randolph Silliman Bourne (1886–1918), journalist and essayist, discusses Mr. Britling's conversion to belief in a 'finite God'.

How widely Mr. Wells's latest consolation for the war will be disseminated and absorbed by this Wellsian generation we have yet to learn, but one can at least register the gravity of the situation which his latest book creates. There is still a possibility that Mr. Britling may not be Mr. Wells himself but rather a mere ironic portrait of the very modern Briton *bouleversé* by the personal thrust of the war. If this is so, the 'seeing it through' to an end which materializes only in a Finite God is a touch of Wellsian humor only too deeply ironic. But Mr. Britling's ante-bellum vivacity, his self-conscious gayety of life with its tumbling ideas, its pianolas and hockey and automobiles, its careless, vital, intellectual women, its nonchalant air of wanting everybody to see very clearly that the modern Englishman is intensely getting much more out of life than anybody else in the world,—all this is too much of the very air that Mr. Wells breathes not to make one wonder at the risk he runs and the responsibility he will undertake in getting himself misunderstood. If Mr. Britling is not Mr. Wells, his reaction to the war, his conviction of the many aspects, protests, explanations that have to be set down very clearly and confidently in pamphlets of sonorous titles, makes him at least Mr. Wells's own brother. And the map-revising which takes place after the death of Mr. Britling's son seems to set us back into the old captivating intellectual serenity which always tried to fuse and steady and left the emotional tangles and defeats of life without bruising them.

But the old Wells magic is no sooner revised than a rude hand brushes over it and blots it out. This quick flop into religion, this opening of the flood-gates by the letter to the parents of the dead Heinrich, this unstemmable plunge into the emotional abyss, with never a recovery or hint of a recovery, takes the breath away in dismay.

Does it mean that the Mr. Britlings of England, quenched in personal sorrow, are beginning to find their consolation in this last and least reparable of idealisms? Have they no choice but to find God? It is true that, as a pragmatist, Mr. Wells may have hinted at his God in his *First and Last Things*. But no one took the pragmatists to mean any more than that if there was a God, this was the kind of God he was. To feel that there is a God, to feel that there must be a God, would have seemed a few years ago a jump too colossal for even a tender-minded pragmatist to make, except poetically or in wistful play. The question that staggers us in Mr. Wells's book is, Just how far is he dealing in wistful play? Which may lead the cynical to, Just how far does he deal in anything else?

What Mr. Wells is up to, however, is far less important than what the people who read him will think he is up to, and whether they will, in all sincerity, allow themselves to be influenced by the consolation which he makes his hero see through to. The American world has been, for a number of years, in the highest state of suggestibility toward Mr. Wells. So magical is his power of seeming to express for us the ideas and dilemmas which we feel spring out of our modernity and stamp us with a sort of cautious self-consciousness, that a great many of us would be in a high state of suggestibility toward Mr. Britling even if we were convinced that Mr. Wells did not mean him to be Mr. Wells himself. The discoverer of the Finite God has a great American following whom each successive book tends to sweep from their emotional moorings. For several weeks after these readings, they are not quite themselves. Their imaginative life is engaged on researches magnificent, on the turning of their personal relations into passionate friendships, on think-ing in large emotional international terms. But in a part of this following Mr. Wells is fortunate. There are those of us who feel a flimsiness in his fabric, a slight limp in his soaring, a little uneasiness in his facile content to reiterate the dilemmas of sex and *samurai* rather than to make hopeful stabs at a solution. He seems to acquire more and more a certain brave luminousness of phrase which, if dwelt on, shines so little deeper than itself.

We continue to be swept away, but we have an anchor somewhere to windward. The drop of the poison of distrust has upon us the altogether happy effect of inoculating us against disillusionment. We get all the thrill of Mr. Wells and we are never disappointed in him. This protection was never so much needed as now. If Mr. Wells has not capitulated at this all-testing crisis to an obscurantism against which he

always so bravely contended, he is at least willing to take the responsibility of his suggestive power. He is willing to see us follow him into
a consolation that is all the more insidious for his making it rush in and
overwhelm the rational and realistic consolation of intelligence which
Mr. Britling was setting for himself. He is willing to have that gallery
of people who are reading Mr. Britling this month and will be reading
him for many weeks to come set about the imaginative adventure of
substituting the Finite God for the Research Magnificent, or at least of
building their war-consolation out of a God—immensely pragmatic, I
admit, immensely diluted, almost a figure that one becomes pathetic
and tender about, yet unmistakably a God. The effect he would produce
on our minds is that somehow this Finite God would not be gainsaid.
The combination of horrors was too potent. No other consolation
would have staggered up to meet it. A year of butchery, tension, dread,
the sacrifice of the young Hugh and the young Heinrich, national and
personal calamity playing into each other in the vivid personal mind,
meeting, embracing, reinforcing each other,—but did this have to end,
even in the mind of the most self-consciously pagan and intellectual of
middle-class Englishmen, in this sentimental cosmification of his own
despairing struggle? One reacts to it as to a sort of wilful bankruptcy of
intellect.

Yet our reaction would be stronger if we were not in the habit of
not being disillusioned by Mr. Wells. For our slight distrust acts, as
everything else seems to act, to his glory and ratification. If we trusted
him, the shock of disillusionment would be complete, and we would
have no more of him. But distrusting him, we find ourselves giving
him the benefit of the doubt. Over here where we strain our imaginations to feel the personal shock of the war, and console ourselves with
the rightness of the cause and a nebulous vision of vast changes to come,
Mr. Wells tempts us to wonder if this consolation of his, were we
enmeshed in its claims, personally dragged in its terrible wash, would
be the only one for us too. And the number of Americans who, under
the spell of the book, will see, like a burst of light before their eyes, how
impossible it was for Mr. Britling or for any American spectator to
come to any other consolation,—this will be the index of what the war
is doing to our education, of how far it is setting back our struggle after
a modern and realistic philosophy of life.

For some of us the benefit of the doubt will not save Mr. Wells. It
was bad enough for the French and Germans to erect new tribal gods
to go out with their armies and smite the aggressor. It is bad enough to

have the American bishops put a God of Hosts into their Prayer Book to protect our soldiers and make them to 'wage war in righteousness.' But these are robust and inevitable expansions of the old primitive popular and national religions, as unsophisticated as the objectifications of desire which savage peoples use to inflate their ardor and endow them with a sense of power. These tribal Gods of Hosts collapse with the passing of battle. Only the ignorant are really moved. The intelligent use them only in metaphors of pious fervor.

A Wellsian Finite God, however, is far more plausible and dangerous. A personal god tends to linger long after the crisis which produced him has passed. He is always there to help and to be helped. For his struggles, as Mr. Britling rhapsodizes them, appeal almost to instincts of chivalry. Mr. Britling finds in him all the consolations he needs for personal calamity, and he objectifies him into a Captain of Mankind. And such a God seems sustaining as long as he is a mere cosmified Mr. Asquith leading him by the hand. But extend this succor to other fields of struggle. Are we to see Mr. Britling's God as a cosmified Mr. Asquith leading him by the hand to the victory of public right in Europe, or as a mystic Russia in the skies struggling hopefully along with her for the possession of Constantinople? The Finite God breaks down as soon as we get outside of our own private consolation, and we see the world again as contending powers controllable only as we get power sublimated into workmanship, and superstition into intelligence.

Mr. Wells does not disillusion us, and so we cannot be angry with him. But his plunge into the rubbish of Captains of Mankind, World-Republics, Religion as the first and last thing, will steel our hearts against such cheap and easy consolations for calamities against which there can be no consolation. There is one hope left for Mr. Britling—that he went back to his map-drawing. He may have faced his God frankly for what he was, the overwhelming need of his stricken hour, the object that his desire, crushed with his sympathy for European fathers and mothers in their stricken hour, built for his consolation. But, created for his need, its shining face passes slowly away, and Mr. Britling returns to the Better Government of the World, with its recasting of frontiers, its justice that shall demand no more sacrifice. There are the relentless realities the need for which will not pass away.

Otherwise Mr. Britling did not see it through. For those who live, the world is not livable except through triumph over the despair of death, and over a religion which is little more than an evasion of that despair. The only consolation permitted is to feel one's self cooperating with the intelligent forces that are making for the better ordering of the world. To be on the right track, that is salvation in the modern world. Mr. Britling with his maps was sound in instinct and purpose. His poring put him in the current of the world's hope. Past religion into creative intelligence, such effort should lead all who will resolutely seek such consolation. Nothing else is a seeing it through.

JOAN AND PETER

September 1918

---

76. Virginia Woolf, unsigned review in *The Times Literary Supplement*

19 September 1918, 439

Virginia Woolf's best-known references to Wells come in the essays of the 1920s in which she attacks Wells, Bennett and Galsworthy as didactic novelists and as 'materialists' whose external treatment of life condemns them to superficiality. But the critical references to Wells in these essays are brief, and original only in the finality with which he is classed as an Edwardian novelist. The present review, written half-a-dozen years earlier, appears to be the only piece by Virginia Woolf devoted to Wells alone. It was reprinted in *Contemporary Writers* (1965), pp. 90–3.

The moralists of the nursery used to denounce a sin which went by the name of 'talking at', and was rendered the more expressive by the little stress which always fell upon the 'at', as if to signify the stabbing, jabbing, pinpricking nature of the sin itself. The essence of 'talking at' was that you vented your irritation in an oblique fashion which it was difficult for your victim to meet otherwise than by violence. This old crime of the nursery is very apt to blossom afresh in people of mature age when they sit down to write a novel. It blossoms often as unconsciously as we may suppose that the pearl blossoms in the breast of the oyster. Unfortunately for art, though providentially for the moralist, the pearl that is produced by this little grain of rancour is almost invariably a sham one.

In the early chapters of *Joan and Peter* there are a great many scenes

244

and characters which seem to have been secreted round some sharp-edged grain which fate has lodged in the sensitive substance of Mr Wells's brain. Lady Charlotte Sydenham had some such origin; so, too, had Miss Phoebe Stubland; the sketch of Arthur Stubland was due to a disturbance of the kind, and certainly the schoolmistresses of St George and the Venerable Bede had no other begetter. We catch ourselves wondering whether Mr Wells is any longer aware of the grotesque aspect of these figures of his, burdened as they are with the most pernicious or typical views of their decade, humped and loaded with them so that they can hardly waddle across the stage without coming painfully to grief. The conscientious reader will try to refer these burlesques to some such abstraction as the Anglican Church, or the vagaries of aimless and impulsive modernism in the eighteen-nineties; but if you are indolent you will be inclined to give up playing your part in the game of illusion, and to trifle with idle speculations as to the idiosyncrasies of Mr Wells. But soon the very crudeness of the satire leads us to make a distinction, and directly we are satisfied of its truth our irritation is spent and our interest aroused. Mr Wells is not irritated with these people personally, or he would have taken more pains to annoy them; he is irritated with the things they represent. Indeed, he has been so much irritated that he has almost forgotten the individual. He is sore and angry and exaggerated and abusive because the waste, the stupidity, the senility of our educational system have afflicted him as men are, for the most part, afflicted only by their personal calamities. He possesses the queer power of understanding that 'the only wrongs that really matter to mankind are the undramatic general wrongs', and of feeling them dramatically, as if they had wronged him individually. Here, he says, we have two children endowed with everything that the world most needs, and let us see what the world will make of them. What education have we to offer them? What are we able to teach them about the three great questions of sex and State and religion? First, he gluts his rage upon Lady Charlotte and Miss Phoebe Stubland, much to the detriment of the book, and then the matter is seriously taken in hand by Mr Oswald Stubland, V.C., a gallant gentleman with imaginative views upon the British Empire. He had believed that the Empire was the instrument of world civilization, and that his duty in Central Africa was the duty of an enlightened schoolmaster. But when his health broke down he returned to the far more difficult task of educating two of the children of the Empire in the very metropolis of civilization. He started off upon a pilgrimage to the schools and colleges of England, asking imaginative questions, and getting more and more dismayed at the answers he received.

Don't you *know* that education is building up an imagination? I thought everybody knew that. . . . Why is he to *do* Latin? Why is he to *do* Greek? . . . What will my ward know about Africa when you have done with him? . . . Will he know anything about the way the Royal Exchange affects the Empire? . . . But why shouldn't he understand the elementary facts of finance?

This is a mere thimbleful from the Niagara which Mr Wells pours out when his blood is up. He throws off the trammels of fiction as lightly as he would throw off a coat in running a race. The ideas come pouring in whether he speaks them in his own person or lets Oswald have them, or quotes them from real books and living authorities, or invents and derides some who are not altogether imaginary. He does not mind what material he uses so long as it will stick in its place and is roughly of the shape and colour he wants. Fiction, you can imagine him saying, must take care of itself; and to some extent fiction does take care of itself. No one, at any rate, can make an inquiry of this sort so vivid, so pressing, so teeming and sprouting with suggestions and ideas and possibilities as he does; indeed, when he checks himself and exclaims, 'But it is high time that Joan and Peter came back into the narrative,' we want to cry out, 'Don't bother about Joan and Peter. Go on talking about education.' We have an uneasy suspicion that Joan and Peter will not be nearly so interesting as Mr Wells's ideas about their education and their destiny. But, after all, we know that Mr Wells is quite right when he says that it is time to bring them in. He would be shirking the most difficult part of his task if he left them out.

Like his own Oswald Stubland, Mr Wells 'belongs to that minority of Englishmen who think systematically, whose ideas join on'. He has 'built up a sort of philosophy for himself', by which he does try his problems and with which he fits in such new ideas as come to him. He is not writing about education, but about the education of Joan and Peter. He is not isolating one of the nerves of our existence and tracing its course separately, but he is trying to give that nerve its place in the whole system and to show us the working of the entire body of human life. That is why his book attains its enormous bulk; and that is why, with all its sketchiness and crudeness and redundancy, its vast soft, billowing mass is united by a kind of coherency and has some relation to a work of art. If you could isolate the seed from which the whole fabric has sprung you would find it, we believe, to consist of a fiery passion for the rights of youth—a passion for courage, vitality, initiative, inventiveness, and all the qualities that Mr Wells likes best. And as Mr Wells can never think without making a picture of his thought, we do not have youth in the abstract, but Joan and Peter, Wilmington and Troop, Huntley and Hetty Reinhart. We have Christmas parties and dressings up and dances and night clubs and Cambridge and London and real people disguised under fictitious names, and very bright covers on the chairs and Post Impressionist pictures on the walls and advanced books upon the tables. This power of visualizing a whole world for his latest idea to grow in is the power that gives these hybrid books their continuity and vitality.

But because Mr Wells's ideas put on flesh and blood so instinctively and admirably we are able to come up close to them and look them in the face; and the result of seeing them near at hand is, as our suspicions assured us that it would be, curiously disappointing. Flesh and blood have been lavished upon them, but in crude lumps and unmodelled masses, as if the creator's hand, after moulding empires and sketching deities, had grown too large and slack and insensitive to shape the fine clay of men and women. It is curious to observe, for example, what play Mr Wells is now constrained to make with the trick of modernity. It is as if he suspected some defect in the constitution of his characters and sought to remedy it with rouge and flaxen wigs and dabs of powder, which he is in too great a hurry nowadays to fix on securely or plaster in the right places. But if Joan and Peter are merely masquerading rather clumsily at being the heirs of the ages, Mr Wells's passion for youth is no make-believe. The sacrifice, if we choose to regard it so, of his career as a novelist has been a sacrifice to the rights of youth, to the needs of the present moment, to the lives of the rising generation. He has run up his buildings to house temporary departments of the Government. But if he is one of those writers who snap their fingers in the face of the future, the roar of genuine applause which salutes every new work of his more than makes up, we are sure, for the dubious silence, and possibly the unconcealed boredom, of posterity.

THE OUTLINE OF HISTORY

July and November 1920

77. E. M. Forster, review in *Athenaeum*

2 and 9 July 1920, 8–9, 42–3

A review of the first volume of Wells's *History*. Forster later made some brief but illuminating comments on Wells as a comic novelist in *Aspects of the Novel* (1927).

I

It's no good humming and hawing; at least it is, but before the operation begins the following sentence must be penned: A great book. The writer tries to outline the history of the world, from the epoch of igneous gas to the establishment of Christianity; he succeeds, and it is the first duty of a reviewer to emphasize his success. Whatever he may do in his second volume he has achieved a masterpiece in his first, and one desires to offer him not only praise but thanks. Unconvincing as a Samurai or a bishop, he has surely come through as a historian. A great book; a possession for ever, for the ever of one's tiny life.

But now let us lower the voice a little, otherwise nothing gets said. What, after reading the book, is one's main sensation? Perhaps that it wasn't so much a book as a lecture, delivered by a vigorous, fair-minded and well-informed free lance. He was assisted by a lantern—its assistance was essential—and bright and clear upon the sheet he projected the misty beginnings of fact. The rocks bubbled and the sea smoked. Presently there was an inter-tidal scum: it was life, trying to move out of the warm water, and subsequent slides showed the various forms it took. A movement also became perceptible among the audience; one or two of the prehistoric experts, discontented at so much lucidity, withdrew. Man, Neanderthalian, Palæo- and Neo-Lithic; man in Mesopotamia and Egypt; nomad man; man in Judæa (more experts go out), in Greece (still more), in India (exeunt the theosophists), in China (murmurs of 'me no likee') and in Rome. Over Rome there is a serious disturbance; the Public School masters rise to protest against the caricature of Julius Cæsar, while the neo-Catholics denounce the belittlement of the Pax Romana and the Latin Thing, and lumber out to drink beer. The lecturer, undeterred by these secessions, describes the origins of Christianity and loses the Anglican section of his flock meanwhile, though the withdrawal is quieter in this case, and due more to bewilderment than wrath. Finally the lights are turned up, and the room seems as full as ever: one can't believe that a single person has left it. Immense applause. The lecturer thanks the lanternist . . .

In praising so large a work, one must presumably begin with its arrangement. Arrangement is a negative quality, but a great one: it is the faculty of not muddling the reader, and Wells possesses it in a high degree. He masses his facts together, kith with kin, yet they seldom overlap chronologically: there is a little confusion as one crosses from prehistory into history, but really this is all. How masterly, for example, is the arrangement of the Roman and the Chinese Empires! One knew that they were contemporary and alike menaced by 'barbarians,' but here one sees China elbowing off the attack, and so generating a westerly movement with nomad tribes which is communicated across Asia and Europe, and finally overwhelms Rome. Maps and time-charts elucidate the process. How masterly again, and how necessary, is the emphasis laid upon the novelty of civilization! It is an episode, the latest in the career of Man, just as Man is only an episode in the career of the earth. 'Half the duration of human civilization and the keys to all its chief institutions are to be found *before* Sargon I.;' yet man is thousands of years older than the earliest institution, and millions of years before man there was life. With the help of time-diagrams this proportion is made clear: another triumph of arrangement. Arrangement seldom receives its due praise, though we suffer and whine as soon as it is absent. It is the oil that allows the machine to function. From it proceed the ease and the pleasure with which we read ahead.

Selection is of course a more controversial topic, and here the critics can get going if they think it worth while. Each of us can write two long lists: facts that Wells might have left out, and of facts that he ought to have put in. Here is an item from the first list: The Scythian expedition of Darius occupies too much space: Wells has been seduced into garrulity by the companionship of Herodotus, and in his account of the crossing of the Danube he even inflicts 'imaginative' touches that are unwarranted by his original. And here is an item from the second list: The Sicilian expedition of Athens occupies only a sentence; yet it is in the opinion of other historians a fact of the highest importance—pivotal, not merely dramatic—and Wells should at least show cause to the contrary. So might one go on, even adding flourishes of scholarship such as 'Surely Pompey's Pillar at Alexandria wasn't meant for a sea mark.' But is there any point in going on? Listen to the experts! They are beginning to argue over their beer. They are saying to each other: 'It's only in *my* period he breaks down—he's quite sound in yours.' There is not a man alive who could have selected from those millions of years so well, and we had better acknowledge this handsomely, and give the writer 'good' again.

A third merit is the style. The surface of Wells' English is poor, and he does not improve its effect when he tints it purple. But it does do its job, as the following example will show. He is speaking of the nomads (and, by the way, his sympathy with outsiders contributes largely to the balance of his historical outlook). He is wanting to describe their migrations, which combined a steady advance with a north-and-south movement between winter and summer pasturage. So he says: 'They moved in annual swings, as the broom of a servant who is sweeping out a passage swishes from side to side as she advances.' You may complain that the sentence is journalistic rather than literary. But hasn't it 'got' the nomads for you, and so fulfilled the aim of the historian? Similarly with the refilling of the Mediterranean in 30,000 B.C. and with the disaster that overtook the Mesozoic reptiles; such events, hitherto somewhat academic, will be intimate in the future, because Wells has written of them racily.

Arrangement, selection, style: so these make up the case for his *Outline*, and it is an overwhelming case. Now let us attempt to state the other side.

II

We indicated last week the chief merits of Wells' *Outline*. Now for the defects, and the first of them is a serious one. Wells' lucidity, so satisfying when applied to peoples and periods, is somehow inadequate when individuals are thrown on to the screen. The outlines are as clear as ever, but they are not the outlines of living men. He seldom has created a character who lives (Kipps and the aunt in *Tono-Bungay* are the main exceptions); and a similar failure attends his historical evocations. He has occasion in this volume to sketch about thirty eminent humans, from Akhnaton to St. Benedict, and only one of them sticks in one's mind. That one is Cato the Censor, and he is galvanized into life not so much by the author's insight as by his crossness. Cato is the type Wells cannot stand, and the result is a brilliant tirade such as might occur in *The New Machiavelli*. Of course he does not intend to produce a portrait gallery, and it is well that this is not his intention, for if it were his history would fail. As it is, the eminent humans appear as diagrams, lettered at their characteristic angles; the lecturer points to the lettering and then passes on. Often no harm is done; the case becomes serious when an individual has, so to speak, to be the epitome of his age, when he is required by the historian to focus all the unhappiness or joy or hope that surrounds him. Xerxes was such an individual at Salamis, as Æschylus and Herodotus both realized. But when Wells would also achieve this most necessary effect, he makes a disagreeable rattling noise and produces a passage like this:

We can imagine something of the coming and going of messengers, the issuing of futile orders, the changes of plan, throughout the day. In the morning Xerxes had come out provided with tables to mark the most successful of the commanders for reward. In the gold of the sunset he beheld the sea power of Persia utterly scattered, sunken and destroyed, and the Greek fleet over against Salamis. . . .

Over against such a sunset the only possible comment is, 'Don't do it again; it isn't your line.' But he does it again. Observe how he dramatizes a sorrow even more representative than Xerxes':

[Quotes Wells's description of the Crucifixion.]

Over against such a red twilight the only possible comment is a coloured illustration, and the publishers have provided one. There we may see the three crosses, so far more tremendous than the fantasies of Tintoretto, and we may reflect on the nemesis that attends the non-Christian who would write sympathetically of Christ. Wells' failure on Golgotha, however, is due to the same cause as his failure at Salamis. He cannot create individuals, and when he would use one to epitomize a great contemporary emotion the result is a mess. Arrangement, selection, lucidity of style, no longer assist him. He often tells us that individuals ought to merge themselves in something greater, and he has practised what he preaches, for we come away with no knowledge of the faces and hearts of his thirty dead leaders.

Thus, though his history 'lives,' it is in a peculiar way: by its fundamental soundness, expressed through brilliant parallels and metaphors; not by imaginative reconstructions of individual people or scenes. We see the nomads advancing into the Roman Empire like the housemaid's broom, but if Wells took one of the twigs of the broom and tried to describe its mentality he would at once become thin and sentimental. It is a history of movements, not of man. Nor is this its only weakness. As a rule the writer most admirably suppresses his personal likes and dislikes; there are none of the explosions that interrupt his fiction, and much dignity and coherence accrue. But in one direction he does break out. He has one little complaint against the past, which, try as he will, he cannot silence; he cannot pardon it for having been so ill-informed. Even in Mesozoic times ignorance is censured. He notes the uneducated tendencies of the reptiles, who might have averted extinction had they taken appropriate steps. He has, again and again, to deplore the incuriosity of Homo Sapiens, who will not study science, will not invent tippy labour-saving appliances. Man might have evolved the conditions of 1920 a thousand years earlier if only he had bucked up. The Chinese invented printing, but made no use of it owing to some mental blur. The Alexandrians had a library, but their books were shaped like pianola rolls, and consequently awkward to consult. 'One thinks at once of a simple and obvious little machine by which such a roll could have been quickly wound to and fro for reference, but nothing of the sort seems to have been used.' And the Romans were worst of all, ignorant of geography and economics, and not even developing the steam engine devised by Hiero; why, the legions might have rolled about in motor lorries! Irritability is better than reverence, but it does result in some absurdity and in a sort of Polytechnic glibness. Our curiosity is stimulated, our wonder never; the lecturer has no use for wonder. He doesn't know how life began, but there is nothing mysterious in its beginnings; he might know them and probably some day will, and the intertidal Palæozoic scum is no queerer than the beach at Southend; it is only less accessible to students. Compare such an attitude with that of Remy de Gourmont in his essay 'Une Loi de Constance Intellectuelle.' The account of early man there given may not be as learned or as brilliant as Wells', but it shows an instinctive sympathy with the difficulties of invention. The conscious kindling of fire, according to de Gourmont, was the highest mental achievement of our race, and he can strip us of our clothes and match-boxes, and set us to watch the awakened blaze, while Wells would only be annoyed that it wasn't kindled earlier. He confuses information with wisdom, like most scientists, so his judgments are sometimes very naïf, and though his intelligence is both subtle and strong, it cannot quite supply his lack of imagination.

And what is it all about, anyhow? What is the meaning of this evolution from igneous gas, through scum and Christianity, to ourselves and mustard gas? De Gourmont had his answer: 'Evolution n'est pas progrès. L'évolution est un fait, et le progrès un sentiment.' And Dean Inge, though he adds a proviso in favour of Hope, as a clergyman must, makes the same answer. Wells does not agree. His hand holds a lecturer's castanet, but his heart is Victorian, with a quite Tennysonian trust in the To-be. To him evolution is progress, and though a few events (e.g. the Punic wars) are condemned as purely toxic, he is on the whole inclined to give a good mark to everything that happens, on the ground that it makes the past a little more like the present. What of the present? He will tell us in Vol. II, but we may be sure that he will condone it by pointing to the future. There is no collaring these optimists. They asked for science in 1914, they got it, and in 1920 they still ask for science. Nor would one wish to collar them, for it is only an optimist who could attempt a history of this planet. To the rest of us it is a planetful of scraps, many of which are noble and beautiful, but there seems not any proof that it progresses. 'Seek no proof,' says Orthodoxy, as she gazes up to heaven through the bottom of her beer mug, but Wells will not go as far as that. He has the air throughout of adducing facts, of arguing that Science will do the trick if only we have enough of her. He sees that humanity is creative. He cannot see that there may be an incurable defect in us, a poison sucked from the Palæozoic slime, that renders us incapable of putting to good use what we have created. When he approaches this problem his manner becomes episcopal, and he introduces that curious but not unfamiliar figure, his 'God':

The history of our race and personal religious experience run so closely parallel as to seem to a modern observer almost the same thing; both tell of a being at first scattered and blind and utterly confused, feeling its way slowly to the serenity and salvation of an ordered and coherent purpose.

The religious experiences of Wells, like those of Mr. Britling, have been little more than a visit to a looking-glass in whose area he has seen an image of himself which imitates his gestures and endorses his deficiencies; if he feels his way to a chair, no doubt his reflection sits down too. But it is hard to see what consolation the human race can derive from this, or what parallels it can supply. It has indeed had another experience, but one that the writer despises or ignores: the experience of mysticism. The neglect of mysticism is, from the psychological point of view, the chief defect in the book, for mysticism may be selfish or erroneous, but it dwells permanently in the human mind, whispering, when least we expect it, that education, information, action, and history itself, are an illusion. It can be explained away—part of our original malaise, perhaps; but it cannot be weeded out; it is as ineradicable as death. Christ had it occasionally; by 'the Kingdom of Heaven' he meant sometimes (though not always) a Kingdom in Heaven. Buddha had it often. And Wells, by pooh-poohing it, has made of his two chief characters mere spiritual and social revolutionaries. Men want to alter this planet, yet also believe that it is not worth altering and that behind it is something unalterable, and their perfect historian will be he who enters with equal sympathy into these contradictory desires.

Such are the defects of the book; but, as the previous article indicated, they are entirely outweighed by its merits. A great book—a book to buy rather than to order from the library, and consequently one or two practical remarks may be in place. Price, moderate considering. Print and paper, excellent. Binding, strong but rather clumsy; in the copy under review the pages have been gashed by the fastenings. Coloured illustrations: tolerable when they reproduce photographs, vulgar when they attempt to be 'imaginative'; in the later instalments (not here reviewed) they are getting worse—there is an awful thing of the Crusades. Photographs: well selected, well reproduced—though here again there is a falling off in the later instalments, as regards number, size, clearness and appropriateness; it is to be hoped that the publishers are not going to skimp their enterprise as it proceeds. Time-charts, plans, maps, other drawings: these, by Mr. J. F. Horrabin, are admirable and invaluable; the scholar as well as the draughtsman has been at work. All the same, there should have been fewer sketches, and more photographs, of prehistoric implements, Greek vases, Indian gods, &c., because Mr. Horrabin's method tends to uniformity. And there shouldn't have been any fig-leaves: they are contrary to the whole spirit of such a book.

78. Edward Shanks on Wells's impatience

March–April 1922

Edward Shanks (1892–1953), poet and journalist. Shanks's discussion of *The Outline of History* occurs near the close of a general survey of 'The Work of Mr. H. G. Wells'. This article first appeared in the *London Mercury*, March–April 1922, v, 506–18, and was reprinted in *First Essays in Literature* (1923), pp. 148–70.

This is not the place, if I had the room and the competence, for an exhaustive criticism of Mr. Wells's political, moral, and religious ideas; but a general sketch of the character of his thought is necessary. Its predominating colour is that of impatience. He once delivered a lecture which he called *The Discovery of the Future*. One of the most remarkable things about him, as I have already noted, is that the past has no native roots in his mind; and it might be said that the future has taken its place. It is natural for a man so constituted to be impatient. He can foresee in an hour more than can happen in a century; and he demands that the procession shall be accelerated. He is perpetually in the position of a child on Christmas Eve: he finds that the hours go very slowly to Christmas morning. He has, indeed, through the mouth of one of his characters, Karenin in *The World Set Free*, preached patience with human slowness; but after all there are few points of view which he has not preached at one time or another. Karenin's effect on his listeners was doubtful: on his creator it has been quite negligible.

It would be interesting if an investigator would some day trace the rise of that nineteenth century rage for prophesying which culminated in the liberal vaticinations of Mr. Wells. The 'discovery of the future' was a good phrase. The nineteenth century discovered it almost as definitely as Columbus discovered America: until then it was thought of roughly as an unchanged continuation of the present. And, before Mr. Wells's *Anticipations*, prophecy was hardly organised or methodical: it was mostly a method of finding a locality for your Utopia. But Mr. Wells has prophesied more ardently, more often and more fully than any one before or since. His first book of forecasts, written about 1900, is still readable and in many ways has proved astonishingly correct. He foresaw the splashing out, instead of the spreading, of the great towns over the surrounding country-side. He foresaw the development of road-transport. So far as flying was concerned, he imagined slower than events have gone, but how much faster than any one else imagined! He pictured a different type of machine from any that has appeared; but his visualisation of aerial warfare turned out to be strangely correct.

Then after twenty years of looking forward over the history of the world from the moment in which he happened to be writing, he turned back and surveyed it from its beginnings. This wonderful book—which phrase I use without forgetting its defects—is certainly the work of a man whose chief interest lies in the future. Mr. Wells sets about all the past ages with just so much zest as he might find in tidying a cluttered writing-table. It would have been considerably better if in several places he had adopted a different point of view. But, in spite of its defects, it was very much better that *The Outline of History* should have been written than that it should not; and who else could have done it with so much chance of success and influence? This is among his perishable works, for others, it can hardly be doubted, will follow him and rewrite his history without his peculiar biases. But he has established the framework, as it has never yet been done, since, under the influence of Ranke, history took on the methods of science, multiplied its material a hundred-fold and passed out of the hands of men of letters and imagination.

The radical fault of the *Outline* is, of course, merely its impatience. One seems to hear Mr. Wells saying: You talk of your Greece and Rome! Poor fools, who had not even enough wit to invent the Penny Post! Mankind has been on the earth some twenty thousand years and even now (for to such details does his Utopia condescend) the practice is not universal of rounding the corners of rooms and the edges of floors and ceilings for convenience in dusting. It is an unfortunate fact that Mr. Wells often seems to find himself in the position of scold to the entire human race.

In an impatient man, a man always in a hurry, we are not surprised to find the allied defect of instability. Some one once said that it was Mr. Wells's habit 'to conduct his own education in public': he himself, I believe, invented the expression 'provisional thinking.' One sometimes wishes that he could educate himself a little more privately, that he would keep his provisional thoughts a little longer in his notebook. But he is a man of ideas; and when he has an idea to express he proceeds to express it with all his persuasive powers. A disciple would be hard put to it to ascertain his final views on the sex-problems he has so often solved. The just men made perfect by an unknown gas in a comet's tail admit a sort of group-marriage as a conceivable solution of some of them. The hero of *The New Machiavelli* seems to arrive at a comparative chastity by a process of trial and error. George Ponderevo's love-affair with Beatrice is a justificatory study in æsthetic sensuality. Peter's trials and errors with Hettie are severely reprobated. And, one may be allowed to observe, if the propagation of right ideas can do any good then the propagation of wrong ideas must do harm. All the ideas Mr. Wells has put forward on political and social topics cannot be right.

His defence might be that the good done by right ideas is greater than all the harm wrong ideas can ever do. It is perhaps at any rate a tolerable defence that he is a man of many ideas. His impatience, his restlessness, and his haste carry him incessantly round the modern world and nothing that is topical is alien to him: there is no subject which may not inspire him to demand of the thinking public that it should stop and think about it. Even where he causes repulsion, as his glib and facile assertions often do, that is of itself a stimulus to thought.

79. Evgenii Zamyatin, Wells's revolutionary fairy-tales

1922

Herbert Wells (Petersburg, 1922), translated by Lesley Milne.

Evgenii Zamyatin (1884–1937), author of plays, stories and the anti-Utopian novel *We* (1920–1). Trained as a marine architect, Zamyatin was an ex-Bolshevik who had a crucial influence on the immediately post-revolutionary generation of Russian writers. His outspoken individualism later brought him into disgrace, and he left the Soviet Union with Stalin's permission in 1931 and died in Paris. *Herbert Wells*, Zamyatin's most extended critical essay, grew out of his editorial work on Wells translations from 1918 onwards. He relates the English writer's work to his beliefs about revolution, modernity and the heretical role of the artist—and, by implication, to his hopes for a new Soviet literature. The present translation follows the first edition, published as a pamphlet by 'Epoka' in 1922, with some omissions which are indicated in the text. A revised version appeared as the introduction to Wells's collected works (Leningrad, 1924). Zamyatin's 1922 pamphlet also contains another, more pedestrian essay ('Wells's Genealogy') situating Wells's work in the traditions of science fiction and of 'socio-fantastic' fiction.

I

The laciest, most ethereal Gothic cathedrals are built none the less of stone; and the most fabulous, most absurd fairy-tales of any country are composed none the less of the earth, trees and beasts of that country. In the fairy-tales of the forest there is the wood goblin, shaggy and gnarled as a pine tree, with a laugh originating in the forest echo; in the tales of the steppe there is the magic white camel, flying like sand whipped up by the wind; in the tales of the polar regions there are the whale-shaman and the white bear with the body of mammoth bone.* But imagine a country where the only fertile soil is asphalt; and on this soil, thick forests—of factory chimneys; and herds of beasts of one breed only—motor-cars; and no spring fragrance apart from petrol fumes. This stone, asphalt, iron, petroleum, mechanical country is called twentieth-century London, and naturally it had to produce its own iron, motorized goblins, its own mechanical, chemical fairy-tales. There are such urban fairy-tales: they are told by Herbert Wells. They are his fantastic novels.

Today's huge, feverishly rushing city, full of roars, rumbles, buzzes, propellors, wires, wheels and advertisements is omnipresent in Wells. The modern city, with its uncrowned king—mechanism, either as explicit or implicit function—enters unfailingly into each of Wells's fantastic novels, into the equation of any of Wells's myths, and these myths, as will be seen, are nothing more nor less than logical equations.

With the mechanism, the machine—this is where Wells began. Even his first novel, *The Time Machine*, is a present-day urban myth of the flying carpet, and the fictitious tribes of the Morlocks and the Eloi are, of course, the two hostile classes of today's city, extrapolated and taken in their typical characteristics to the point of the grotesque. 'A Story of the Days to Come': this is the modern city shown through a monstrously exaggerating, ironic telescope; here everything rushes past with fairy-tale swiftness—machines, machines, machines, aeroplanes, turbine wheels, deafening loudspeakers, flashing advertisements. *The Sleeper Awakes*: again aeroplanes, wires, searchlights, armies of workers, corporations. *The War in the Air*: aeroplanes once more, droves of aeroplanes, balloons, herds of dreadnoughts. *The War of the Worlds*: London, London crowds, and that most representative urban goblin, bred on the asphalt, the Martian; a steel, hinged mechanical goblin with a mechanical siren so that he can whoop and howl as befits every goblin conscientious in the execution of his duties. In *The World Set Free*: an urban variant of the folk-tale of the magic grass, only the magic grass is found not in a clearing on midsummer night, but in a chemical laboratory, and is called atomic energy. In *The Invisible Man*, again chemistry: a present-day, urban, chemical cap of darkness. Even where Wells seems for a moment to betray himself and takes you out of the city into the forest, into the fields or onto a farm, you are assailed by the hum of machines and the smell of chemical reactions. In *The First Men in the Moon* you find yourself on a lonely farm in Kent, but it turns out

* These are the first of several references to Russian fairy-tales.

that 'dynamos occupied the cellar, and there was a gasometer in the garden.' And similarly, the isolated cottage in *The Food of the Gods* turns out to be an institute of experimental physiology. No matter how much Wells wanted to get away from the asphalt, it is on the asphalt that he is to be found, among machines, in the laboratory. The modern city, chemico-mechanical, entangled in wires—this is Wells's ground, and on this loom every thread of his work is woven, with all its fanciful and at first sight contradictory patterns.

The motifs of Wells's fairy-tales are in essence the same as those of all other fairy-tales; in him you will find the cap of darkness, the flying carpet, the magic grass, and the magic tablecloth, dragons, giants, gnomes, mermaids and cannibals. But the difference between his tales and our Russian ones, say, is as great as the difference between the psychology of a native of Poshekhonye* and the psychology of a Londoner: the man of Poshekhonye sits down by the window and waits for the cap of darkness and the flying carpet to come to him 'at the wave of a wand'; the Londoner does not trust in the wave of the wand, but trusts in himself; the Londoner sits down at the drawing-board, takes a slide-rule and calculates a flying carpet, or goes into the laboratory, lights the electric stove and invents the magic grass. The man of Poshekhonye is reconciled to the fact that his marvels are all in the never-never land at the other end of nowhere; the Londoner wants his marvels today, here and now. And therefore he chooses a sure path for his fairy-tales: a path paved with astronomical, physical, chemical formulae, a path beaten out by the cast-iron laws of the exact sciences. This sounds very paradoxical at first: exact science and fairy-tale, exactitude and fantasy. But it is so, and has to be so. After all, myth is always, whether explicitly or implicitly, connected with religion, and the religion of the present-day city is the exact sciences, so that there is the most natural connection between the latest urban myth, the urban fairy-tale, and science. I do not know if there is any branch of science too important to find reflection in Wells's fantastic novels. Mathematics, astronomy, astrophysics, physics, chemistry, medicine, physiology, bacteriology, engineering, electronics, aviation: almost all Wells's tales are constructed around brilliant, unexpected scientific paradoxes; all his myths are as logical as mathematical equations. And that is why we of today, we sceptics, find this logical fantasy so compelling, why it grips us so fast, and why we have such faith in it.

* A region of Russia which, as described by Saltykov-Shchedrin, became symbolic of all that was backward and stagnant under the Czarist regime.

Wells leads the reader into the atmosphere of the marvellous, of the fairy-tale, with exceptional cunning. Cautiously, gradually he leads you from one logical step to the next. The transitions from step to step are quite imperceptible; suspecting nothing, you step trustfully on, climb higher and higher. . . . Suddenly, you look down and gasp—but it is too late: you have already believed in what seemed from the chapter-heading to be absolutely impossible, completely absurd.

Take at random any of Wells's fantasies: *The Invisible Man*. What nonsense! How can we, people of the twentieth century, be made to believe in such a childish fairy-tale as an invisible man? But wait: what, in general, is invisibility? Invisibility is nothing more than the simplest, most real phenomenon, subject to the laws of optics; it depends on the capacity to absorb or reflect rays of light. A piece of glass is transparent; the same piece in water is invisible. And if the glass is ground to a powder, the powder will be white in colour, opaque and very clearly visible. One and the same substance, therefore, can be both visible and invisible: everything depends on the state of its surface. You may say, 'Yes, but man is a living substance.' But what of that? In the sea, starfish can be found which are almost transparent, and some sea larvae which are completely transparent. You may say, 'Yes, but sea larvae and man are two quite different things.' But do you know that nowadays in medicine completely or partially transparent preparations of the human body are already in use? I can even give the name of the inventor of these preparations—a German, Professor Spalteholz. And once we can make one hand transparent, we can also make two hands transparent, and if two hands, then the whole body as well. And if we have achieved this transparency in a dead man—perhaps we shall achieve it in a living man too? After all, transparency, invisibility—and a living organism—are concepts which in no way exclude each other, this we have already seen. And consequently. . . . And you are already thinking, 'Well, after all, maybe in fact. . . .'—you are already caught, you are already coupled to a logical train, and it will carry you along the rails of fantasy wherever Wells wants to take you.

In just the same way Wells will make you believe in *The Island of Doctor Moreau*—in the learned doctor who turns animals into people by means of skilful operations; in a sleeper who wakes after a hundred years; he will make you believe in 'Cavorite,' a substance which forms a screen against the earth's gravitational pull, and that in a Cavorite sphere—no further explanation required—you have an excellent mode of travel to the moon; in the invention of 'Herakleophorbia,' a food which increases the growth of men, plants and animals to gigantic proportions; he will make you believe that it is possible to travel not only in space but in time as well; he will make you believe in a war with the Martians, in a country of the blind, in the new accelerator, in the adventures of Mr Plattner in the fourth dimension, he will make you believe that any of his fantasies is not fantasy at all, but reality, if not of today, then of tomorrow.

If it comes to that, how can anyone in our time—a time of the most improbable, most incredible scientific wonders—say that this or that is impossible? Thirty years ago you would have laughed at a man who spoke seriously of the possibility of flying from London to Paris, from Paris to Rome, or from New York to Australia. Thirty years ago it was only in fairy-tales that you could read of things that nowadays we can read about in the newspapers: of the wireless telephone, of speaking into a receiver in London and being heard in New York. Thirty years ago no one would have believed it possible to see through opaque objects, but nowadays any grammar-school boy can tell you about X-rays. And who knows, perhaps in another thirty years—in ten—in five—we may look with the same indifference at a machine setting off for the moon as we do now at an aeroplane, a scarcely perceptible black dot in the sky.

The Wellsian fantasy is perhaps fantasy only for today, and tomorrow it will already be commonplace. We can say this with all the more certainty since many of Wells's fantasies have already come into existence; because Wells has a strange gift of prophecy, a strange gift for seeing the future through the opaque curtain of the present. But that is not in fact true: there is nothing more strange in this than there is in a differential equation which allows us to predict where a projectile, launched at a given speed, will fall; or in the second-sight of an astronomer who foretells an eclipse of the sun at a certain hour on a certain day. This is not mystical, but logical—only a logic more daring, more long-range than usual.

Let us think ourselves back into the old London—into the London of twenty-five years ago. Not long ago, it would seem, but those twenty-five years are as a century; it is all so different from nowadays. Cabs amble peaceably along the streets; imposing, top-hatted coachmen carrying long whips sit on their high boxes. Horse-drawn omnibuses rumble past, hooves clopping on the cobbles. In the sky a jackdaw lazily flaps its wings, not a cloud in sight; the blessed reign of Victoria, everything in the world has settled firmly in its place and is slowly ossifying; there will be no more wars, revolutions, catastrophes. . .

And through this peaceful, quiet existence perhaps only Wells could see even then the turbulent, runaway present. While the first motor cars were still barely crawling along, and their chief function was to amuse the street urchins, Wells in *Anticipations* was already giving an exact description of today's rushing London street, full of taxis, buses and motor lorries—a street where there are as few chances of seeing a horse as there are of seeing a man in a top hat nowadays in St. Petersburg.

In the sky also Wells could see something very different. Then it was only the most extreme fantasts who were dreaming of aeroplanes. Somewhere in America the ancestor of today's aeroplane—Hiram Maxim's machine—was still making clumsy trial runs along its rails. But in the novel *When The Sleeper Wakes* Wells could already hear the hum of aeroplanes high in the sky, could already see battles between aircraft squadrons, and airports everywhere on the ground. That was in 1893.* And in 1908, when the prospect of a European war was still not a topic for serious conversation, Wells could already discern monstrous, unprecedented storm clouds in the seemingly cloudless sky. This was the year in which he wrote his *War in the Air*.

[Quotes selections from ch. 8, 'A World at War'.]

And amid all this thunder of a collapsing civilisation—familiar details like these: air battles, aeroplanes, zeppelins, night raids, panic, the blackout, a sky lacerated by searchlights, the gradual disappearance of books and newspapers; newspapers replaced by absurd, contradictory rumours; and finally, people returning to savagery, expending all their energies in a primeval struggle with hunger and cold in the chilly, dark ruins of houses. . . . All this is recounted by a man who seems already to have experienced our times. Thirty years ago the novel was fantastic—now it has become naturalistic.

The theme of an impending world war and an unprecedented worldwide upheaval clearly haunted Wells, for he returns to it more than once. Take his wonderful tale *The War of the Worlds* (1898). If we read it now, after a world war and a revolution, how many familiar voices can be heard from beneath the fairy-tale masks. The battle with the Martians, for example:

These canisters smashed on striking the ground—they did not explode—and incontinently disengaged an enormous volume of a heavy inky vapour, coiling and pouring upwards in a huge and ebony cumulus cloud, a gaseous hill that

---

* Other examples of Zamyatin's inaccurate dating have been silently corrected.

sank and spread itself slowly over the surrounding country. And the touch of that vapour, the inhaling of its pungent wisps, was death to all that breathes.

Where is this from? From a fantastic novel written twenty years ago—or from some newspaper of 1915–1916, when the Germans first released their poison gas?

And another world war—in the novel *In the Days of the Comet*—and a prediction that this war will end with a radical change in human psychology, with a universal brotherhood of man. And once more a world war, the ultimate war, in *The World Set Free*. Here even the combination of warring powers is precisely marked out: the central European powers attack the Slav Federation, and France and England engage in its defence. In *The World Set Free* all the self-consuming force of the old civilisation is given in one concise, concentrated symbol—atomic energy. It is that energy which with terrible force binds together the atoms of matter, which makes atoms into strong steel and which is released in the mysterious conversion of radium into other elements. Wells imagines that the same has happened with atomic energy as with aeroplanes: having mastered atomic energy, man has used it less for constructive than for destructive ends. During the universal war described in *The World Set Free*, atomic bombs have destroyed whole cities, whole countries—have destroyed the old civilisation itself. And on its ruins there begins the construction of a new one, on new principles.

The work of reconstruction is taken in hand by a World Congress which creates a single World State. The Congress abolishes parliamentarism in its old form—separate parliaments for each state—and, after a short period of arbitrary organisational rule, announces world elections to one single world government. The Congress introduces one single monetary unit for the whole world, works out a lingua franca,—a single world-wide language—raises the level of development of the backward agricultural class and reforms agriculture itself on collective principles. The Congress frees the world from economic oppression and at the same time assures full freedom of enquiry, criticism and movement. The Congress itself then gradually reduces its own power to zero. And a free, anarchic system of government comes into existence, introducing the epoch known in Wells' fantastic universal history as 'the epoch of florescence'. The overwhelming majority of citizens are artists of all kinds, the overwhelming majority of the population is occupied with the highest sphere of human activity—art.

Such are the last predictions of Wells. These are the horizons which he opens in the last of his fantastic novels, the last of his fairy-tales.

In all these prophecies the reader has doubtless already managed to discern one further characteristic of the Wellsian fantasy—a characteristic inextricably linked with the city, that stone soil in which Wells has his roots. After all, present-day urban man is inevitably *zoon politicon*, a social animal; and from this stems the social element which is woven, almost without exception, into each of Wells's fantasies. Whatever tale he tells, however far removed at first sight from social problems, these are questions with which the reader will unavoidably be confronted.

Take even *The First Men in the Moon*, a subject apparently as distant as possible from the earth and all its works. You fly with the heroes of the novel in their Cavorite sphere, you land on the moon, travel in the lunar valleys, descend into lunar caves. . . . And suddenly, to your surprise, you see that on the moon there exist the very same social diseases as on our earth. The same division into classes, ruling and ruled, but the workers here have already turned into a species of hunch-backed spider, and outside working hours they are simply put to sleep and stacked in the lunar caves like firewood, until they are needed again.

In *The Time Machine* you hurtle with the author 800,000 years into the future—and again you find there those same two worlds of ours: the twilight world of the working class, and the daylight world of the leisured. Both classes have degenerated, the first from excess of work, and the second from excess of idleness. And the class conflict has taken on cruel and brutal forms. In 800,000 the degenerate descendants of the oppressed classes simply devour their 'bourgeoisie', like beasts. In the ugly images of the cruel mirror held up by Wells's fantasy we again recognise ourselves, our times, and the consequences of these diseases in the civilisation of old Europe.

The Sleeper has slept through two hundred years, he awakes—and what does he see? Again the same present-day city, the present-day social system, only the gulf between black and white is a hundred times deeper; and the workers, under the leadership of the awakened Sleeper, rise up in mutiny against the capitalists. We open 'The Days to Come'— the sharpest and most ironic of Wellsian grotesques—once more a magnificent parody of contemporary civilisation. And finally, *The War in the Air* and *The World Set Free*—a detailed analysis of the epoch preceding a world war, an epoch when millions were being spent on battleships, zeppelins and guns, an epoch when in the cellars of the old civilisation's palace great stacks of explosive had accumulated, and on top, however strange this may seem now, people were calmly living, working and playing—on top of dynamite. Wells demonstrates with force and conviction that a world war is the only natural conclusion to be drawn from the whole syllogism of the old civilisation; in these novels loudest of all, he calls men to their senses, calls on them to remember that they are not Englishmen, Frenchmen, or Germans, but people, and calls on them to reconstruct life on new principles.

These principles have not as yet been identified by name. But the reader has doubtless already filled in the unspoken word: these principles, of course, are socialist. Wells is a socialist. That is indisputable. But if any party ever thought of using Wells as a seal to its programme, that would be as ridiculous as trying to use Tolstoi or Rozanov to affirm Orthodoxy.

I have no intention of comparing Wells to Tolstoi, but all the same, Wells is first and foremost an artist. And an artist—whether greater or lesser—is always a heretic. The artist, like Jehovah in the Bible, creates for himself his own particular world, with its own particular laws; creates in his own image and likeness, and not in anyone else's. And that is why a real artist will never settle into the already created, seven-day, rigidified world of any dogma. He will inevitably leap outside the articles of such a dogma; will inevitably be a heretic. Or else he does not have his own world, his own lineaments—and then he cannot be counted an artist.

Wells, I repeat, is above all an artist, and for that reason everything in his world is his own, and his socialism is his own, Wellsian brand. In his autobiography* we read:

I have always been a socialist, but not a socialist according to Marx. . . . For me, socialism is not a strategy or a conflict of classes: I see in it a plan for the reconstruction of human life, for the replacement of disorder by order.

The aim of the reconstruction is to introduce into life an organising principle—*ratio*—reason. And therefore, in this reconstruction, Wells allots a particularly important role to the class of 'able men,' above all to educated, learned technicians. He proposes this theory in his *Anticipations*. The idea acquires an even more curious and, it must be added, more heretical colouring in his *Modern Utopia*, where the leaders of the new life are the 'Samurai,' and the new world is presented to us as a society constructed to a certain extent on aristocratic principles, led by a spiritual aristocracy.

* The document referred to here is Wells's Introduction to the Russian edition of his novels (1912). The second and third quotations (see below) are taken direct from this, while the first appears to be a free paraphrase of the same source.

There is yet another feature of Wells's socialism, a feature perhaps more national than personal. Indubitably, socialism is for Wells a way of curing the cancer which has eaten into the organism of the old world. But medicine knows two ways of combating this disease: one way is the knife, surgery, a way that will, perhaps, either cure or kill; the other—slower—way is radiotherapy. Wells prefers this bloodless way. Here are a few more lines from his autobiography:

We English are a paradoxical people, at once progressive and constructive and intensely conservative of traditional forms, so that we have changed continually and yet never had any really dramatic and fundamental revolutions . . . never any definite overthrowing of the established order, never any 'beginning again' such as almost every European nation has experienced.

Wells's red banner is not coloured with blood. It is coloured with the joyous dawn of a new human day, which Wells can see breaking through the darkness of a world war. Human blood, human life—for Wells these are inviolable, because he is, above all, a humanist. And this is what lends his words such trenchancy and conviction when he speaks of classes cast into the pit of hopeless toil and want, when he speaks of the hatred of man for man, of war and the death penalty. In Wells's eyes no-one is guilty, there is no evil will: the evil is inherent in life. People can be pitied, can be despised, but they must be loved: they must never be hated.

Clearer than anywhere else—in that clear relief which even the blind can read—this thought is imprinted on his novel *In the Days of the Comet*. The hero is a young worker-socialist, with a squarely primitive mode of thought: he is convinced of the existence of 'callous insensate plots— we called them "plots"—against the poor.' He is full of primeval hatred: his chief thought is of vengeance on the evil conspirators. But later on in the novel Wells the humanist makes his hero confess: 'You will consider these notions of my youth poor silly violent stuff; particularly if you are of the younger generation born since the Change.' This revolution is itself accomplished under the influence of the 'green vapour' of a comet which has collided with the earth. It consists in man's organic loss of the ability to hate, kill; organically, inevitably people are brought to love. And the same humanism informs *The War in the Air*. It is enough to watch with the author—through the author's eyes—the scene in which one of the German airmen is executed. And again in *The Island of Doctor Moreau*, where Dr. Moreau becomes the victim of his own cruel experiments. In *The Invisible Man* the hero is a Utopian of genius, but Wells cannot forgive him his crime of murder. And again in *The Time Machine*, in the cruel caricature that Wells gave in the image of his cannibal Morlocks.

This is what we find when we enter those whimsical buildings, Wells's fairy-tales. There, side by side, are mathematics and myth, physics and fantasy, project and prodigy, story and socialism. If from the cloud-capped towers we descend to the lower floors, if from Wells's fantastic novels we pass on to his realistic novels—to the middle period of his work—we will no longer find these strange, paradoxical combinations: here Wells has both feet firmly planted on the ground, in the solid world of three dimensions. And only in his latest novels, written in days when the three-dimensional world was whirling in the vortex of wars and revolutions, did Wells take off once again, and leave reality behind, so that we meet once more a fusion of ideas at first sight strange and unexpected.

II

When, eight years ago, I saw an aeroplane in flight for the first time, and the machine came down on a meadow, when the man that had flown climbed out of his canvas wings and took off his strange, goggle-eyed mask—I, I remember, was somehow disappointed. The bird-man, clean-shaven, plump, red-faced, turned out to be exactly the same as all the rest of us; he could not manage to take out his handkerchief—his hands were numb with cold—so he wiped his nose on his sleeve. And the same sensation—something akin to disappointment—will inevitably be felt by the reader when, after Wells's fantasies, he opens his realistic novels. 'What, is this Wells too?' Yes, Wells too, only not in an aeroplane, but on foot. The man that had flown turned out on the ground not to be so sharply distinguishable from other English novelists. And if before, after two pages, without even reading the signature you could say 'That's Wells,' now you have to glance at the name. If before, in the sphere of the scientific-fantastic, socio-fantastic novel, Wells was the only one, now he has become 'one of.' Certainly, one of the greatest, most weighty and most interesting English writers, but all the same, only 'one of.'

The reason, no doubt, lies in the fact that Wells, like the majority of his English fellow-writers, pays considerably more attention to plot than to language, style, the word—all those things that we have come to appreciate in the most recent Russian writers. He did not create his own Wellsian language, his own Wellsian style, nor did he have time: he had to hurry on and write those forty volumes that he has written. What was his own, original, exceptional, lay in the plot of his fantastic novels; and as soon as he descended from the aeroplane, as soon as he took up more customary plots, the greater part of his originality was lost.

The headlong, aeroplane flight of the story in Wells's fantastic novels, where everything whistles past the eyes and ears—faces, events, thoughts—this headlong flight makes it physically impossible for the reader to examine details of style. But the relaxed, unhurried pace of the realistic novel allows one to sit down from time to time, to look closely at the narrator's face, at his dress, his gestures, his smile. An impression of something familiar. But what? Another close look and it is clear: Dickens—Charles Dickens—he is Wells's illustrious ancestor. The same slow delivery, sometimes too slow for today's reader; the same complicated, Gothic periods; the same manner of giving a full, complete projection of the hero in all dimensions, often beginning from his very first appearance in the world; the same technique of repeating some sharp line so as to etch the image of the character on the reader's memory; and finally, as in Dickens—the constant smile. But in Dickens this is affectionate humour, the smile of a man who loves people, irrespective of what they are, who loves them in spite of their faults. In Wells the smile is different: he loves man and at the same time hates him—for not being man, for being a caricature of man—a narrow-minded money-grubber. Wells loves with a piercing love that is mingled with hate, and therefore his smile is a smile of irony, his pen often turns into a knout, and the weals it leaves are not quick to heal.

Even in his most innocently amusing and witty tales, written, it would seem, for a twelve-year-old, a more attentive eye will see that same love-in-hate. Take *The Food of the Gods*: from the miraculous food chickens grow as large as horses, nettles like palm-trees, rats more terrible than tigers, and finally people grow into giants the size of bell-towers. You read of the prince who stands below and looks up with horror through his monocle at his giant bride, afraid to marry her 'so as not to be put in a ridiculous position'; that is funny. You read of the tiny policeman who tries to arrest a giant and grabs him down below, by the leg; and that is funny too. You read of the scores of comic collisions between the giants and the pygmies, and the searchlight of Wells's irony silhouettes ever more clearly the pitiful figure of the obtuse pygmy, who clutches at his accustomed, comfortable life, in terror before the coming, powerful giant Man—and already it is more than simply funny. Or take *The War of the Worlds*: a world-wide catastrophe, all has collapsed in ruins, and amid the din you suddenly hear the voice of a pious clergyman: 'Oh dear, all our Sunday schools have been destroyed!' Or take the magnificent grotesque 'Story of the Days to Come': you are strolling about the streets of twenty-second century London, and before you flashes an advertisement on the pediment of a church: ' "The Sharpest Conversion in London, Expert Operators! Look Slippy!" . . . "All the Brightest Bishops on the Bench tonight and Prices as Usual." "Brisk Blessings for Busy Business Men." '*

This ironic warp is still clearer in the fabric of each of Wells's realistic novels. High society ladies whose basic component is the whalebone in their corsets; fiercely prudish old maids; wooden-headed schoolteachers; bishops who would have dismissed Christ from his post on the grounds that He was poorly dressed and used language unsuitable for a prince of the Church; the merchant on 'Change, sincerely convinced that it was the Lord God who inspired him to buy Pacific Ocean shares. . . '. Most likely England is appalled when she looks into this cruel mirror of angry love. And the blade of Wells's irony seems nowhere to flash so bright as in *Tono-Bungay*, the best of his realistic novels. 'I've met not simply the titled but the great. On one occasion— it is my brightest memory—I upset my champagne over the trousers of the greatest statesman in the Empire. . . '. This we read on the first page of the novel, and throughout, to the very end, irony stalks on every page, in every adventure of the unforgettable Mr. Ponderevo, that genius of advertisement and charlatanism.

The world knows Wells the airman, Wells the author of fantastic novels; these are translated into all the European languages, and even into Arabic and Chinese. And probably only a few people in the general reading public know that Wells the fantast is exactly one half of Wells: he has written precisely thirteen fantastic novels and thirteen realistic. . . .

[Proceeds to list them and to describe the autobiographical content of the early realistic novels.]

From the end of the nineties, after *The Time Machine* and *The War of the Worlds*, Wells the shop-assistant and Wells the schoolteacher at once became the popular writer. The wheel of chance turned a hundred and

---

* The source of this quotation is in fact *When the Sleeper Wakes*.

eighty degrees towards him, and of the consequences of this he was to write:

Success with a book—even such a commercially modest success as mine has been—means in the English-speaking world not merely a moderate financial independence but the utmost freedom of movement and intercourse. One is lifted out of one's narrow circumstances into familiar and unrestrained inter-course with a great variety of people. One sees the world. One meets philoso-phers, scientific men, soldiers, artists, professional men, politicians of all sorts, the rich, the great, and one may make such use of them as one can.

Wells broke out of his narrow circle, the field of his operations was greatly widened, and this was immediately reflected in the mirror of his realistic novels: the personal, autobiographical element in them dis-appeared, and crowds of people of the most different social positions began to pass through them—'philosophers, scientific men, soldiers, artists, professional men, politicians of all sorts, the rich, the great.' Wells did not forget his past, however, and he often climbs up to the brightly-lit, comfortable top storeys only to take their happy and care-free inhabitants down into the cellars, to the hungry and needy (*The Wife of Sir Isaac Harman, The Soul of a Bishop*).

Wells's realistic novels become a sociological observatory, and his pen, like that of a seismograph, systematically notes down every move-ment of the social soil in England at the beginning of the twentieth century. In the early 1900s the soil of John Bull's island is still extremely firm and steady, and, correspondingly, the notes of the Wells seismo-graph give curves of very local, narrow scope: the problems of the family and marriage, of education, the suffragette question (*Marriage, The Passionate Friends, The Wife of Sir Isaac Harman*). More general, radical social problems lie dormant as yet somewhere far below the surface, and are as it were statically reflected in Wells's novels. But gradually the underground rumbles become more audible, in the immovable soil there appear fissures reaching down to the very core, and through them surges the fiery red lava of unprecedented wars and revolutions. And, starting with *Mr. Britling*, this world-wide earthquake becomes the sole theme of Wells's novels. And so gradually from autobiographical works Wells's novels turn into a chronicle of the life of contemporary England.

If for a moment we step aside and contemplate Wells's realistic novels from a distance, so that the eye sees only the fundamental lines and is not distracted by detail, then from here, from this distance, it becomes clear: the architect who built his castles in the air in the scientific fairy-tales, and the architect who built the six-storey stone blocks in the realistic novels, is one and the same Wells. As in his fantasies, so in his realistic works we find the same unceasing assault on the old European civilisation; the same red reflexes of the peculiar Wellsian socialism; the same humanism; the same refusal to brand anyone as guilty; and the same petroleum and asphalt city with its flashing advertisements.

And suddenly, on the asphalt pavement, amid the incense of petrol fumes, the red banners, the patent medicines and the bowler-hatted gentlemen you meet ... God. The socialist, mathematician, chemist, motorist, aeroplane pilot, suddenly starts speaking of God. After scientific fantasy, after the most real reality, suddenly the tract *God the Invisible King*; the novel *The Soul of a Bishop*—about the religious revolution in the soul of an Anglican churchman; the novel *The Undying Fire*, not a novel in fact, but a debate on the subject of God; and the novel *Joan and Peter*, the hero of which conducts a dialogue with God.

At first this strikes you as impossible. But then, on looking more closely, you recognise the same Wells as before: the eternal heretic, the eternal aviator, daring to rise to the very bluest infinity, to the outer-most limits of the universe. It is only recently, in the last few years or so, that Wells has turned to the theme of God. This apparently unexpected turn took place with the beginning of the war, the beginning of the European revolutions, and they explain everything. All that has happened is that the whole of life has torn away from the anchor of reality and has become fantastic; all that has happened is that the most fantastic of Wells's predictions have come true, fantasy has tumbled down onto the earth. And naturally, the indefatigable aviator must fly still higher, still further, to the uppermost reaches of the sky—and there, in the distance, the hazy image of God rose before him. An apparently absurd war, the apparently unjustifiable destruction of millions of lives, posed before many the tormenting question: Why? What for? Is not the whole of life simply a futile chaos? And of course this was a question which Wells could not evade either.

He answers it, as was to be expected, in the negative: No, life is not futile, life still has a meaning, an aim, and a wisdom. And it turns out that long before, in 1901, he had written in his *Anticipations*:

Either one must believe the Universe to be one and systematic, and held together by some omnipresent quality, or one must believe it to be a casual aggregation, an incoherent accumulation with no unity whatsoever outside the unity of the personality regarding it. All science and most modern religious systems presuppose the former, and to believe the former is, to any one not too anxious to quibble, to believe in God.

And so, on the foundations of rationality, on the *telos* of all existence, Wells builds a temple to his God—and alongside, on the same foundations, erects his scientific laboratories, his socialist phalansteries. And, in this light, it no longer seems surprising that Wells should turn to religious themes. . . .

[Summarizes *The Soul of a Bishop, The Undying Fire* and *Joan and Peter.*]

Thus from his latest novels we can discover one more item in the Wellsian formula: God. And if we integrate this formula we shall see that even in his religious constructions, Wells remained the same Wells. Of course, his God is a London God, and of course the most fitting incense to Him is the smell of chemical reactions and of aeroplane exhaust. Because the omnipotence of this God lies in the omnipotence of man, of human reason, of human science. For this is not the oriental God, in whose hands man is only an obedient tool; this is a western God, who demands of man primarily activity and work. This is a God acquainted with the British constitution; he does not rule, he only reigns. And the banners of this contemporary God, of course, are not gold or silver, but red; this God is a socialist.

The dry, compass-drawn circle of socialism, limited by the earth, and the hyperbola of religion, stretching into infinity—the two are so different, so incompatible. But Wells managed to breach the circle, bend it into a hyperbola, one end of which rests on the earth, in science and positivism, while the other loses itself in the sky. This amazing art of passing with logic intact through the narrowest of paradoxes, we have seen already in Wells's fairy tales, where he managed to fuse fantasy and science into one. And now it seems that Wells would simply not have been Wells if he had not written these three novels about God. . . .

[Discusses *Joan and Peter* and *Russia in the Shadows.*]

III

The aeroplane—for me the whole of our contemporary life is focussed in this word, and in this same word I find the whole of Wells, the most contemporary of contemporary writers. Man has taken off from the ground and risen apprehensively into the air. From the giddy height of the aeroplane he can survey unbounded distances, take in with one glance whole nations, continents, this whole lump of caked mud—the earth. The aeroplane hurtles on; kingdoms, kings, laws and faiths disappear from sight. Still higher—and far away glitter the pinnacles of an amazing tomorrow.

This new skyline, these new airman's eyes—they are common to many of us who have lived through the past few years. But Wells has long since had those eyes. They are what give him his penetration of the future, these vast horizons of space and time.

Aeroplanes—flying steel—that, of course, is a paradox, and the same kind of paradox recurs in all of Wells's novels. But the seemingly paradoxical aeroplane is logical throughout, to the last rivet; and in the same way Wells is logical throughout, to the last rivet. The aeroplane, of course, is a marvel, mathematically calculated and petrol-fed; and Wells's marvels are just the same. The aeroplane, daring what previously only angels were allowed, is a symbol of the revolution taking place in mankind; and all Wells's writings are about this revolution. And, rising higher and higher, the aeroplane of course inevitably presses on into the heavens; and just as inevitably Wells pressed on into the heavens. I know of nothing more urban, more up-to-date, more contemporary than the aeroplane, and I know of no writer more contemporary than Wells.

THE WORLD OF WILLIAM CLISSOLD

September–November 1926

80. Conrad Aiken, review in *Atlantic Monthly*

November 1926, cxxxviii, 'Bookshelf', 20

Conrad Aiken (b. 1889), poet and novelist.

In a somewhat petulant preface to *The World of William Clissold*, a preface directed at reviewers, Mr. Wells makes it clear that he wants his new *magnum opus* to stand or fall as a novel—a 'full-dress novel.' Why not, he says in effect, introduce into a novel the history of the hero's opinions, the history of his full awareness—social, religious, economic, political—of the complicated environment in which he finds himself? This sort of awareness undoubtedly plays an enormous part in the life of any educated or reasonably intelligent being. Why, then, leave it out? Or, if it *is* introduced, why must the critic be in such haste to assume that it is merely the *author's* awareness, not the hero's? It appears that Mr. Wells has been annoyed by the persistence with which his critics have identified him with his Britlings and Clissolds; he draws up a list of his 'characters,' a little angrily, as if to say that in such diversity it would be absurd to see uniformity. And nevertheless the critics have been right. For as one looks back over Mr. Wells's long and honorable record as a novelist one fails to recall a single vivid or credible character. They are all alike—and all alike in being rather colorless automata, mere puppets by which their manipulator has sought to demonstrate his successive attitudes toward a changing world.

The truth is that Mr. Wells is not in one sense, and that perhaps the finest sense, a novelist at all. In *The World of William Clissold*, an enormous book enormously documented, he entirely fails, in spite of the masses of information he gives us as to the nature and views of Clissold, to bring him alive. It is no use arguing, as Mr. Wells argues, that in any character-creation there must be elements of self-projection. True enough. But there is something more—there must be an extremely subtle selection and synthesis of those elements, an æsthetic and psychological envisagement of them as a unit, without which they will never take recognizable shape as the thing we call a character. Mr. Wells has always failed at this, and he fails again. He lacks insight, he lacks psychological subtlety, he never once gives us one of those little scenes which are the very pulse of the novel—those scenes in which the hero's action flowers visibly out of his thought, or his thought flowers visibly out of his action. For the most part, Mr. Wells is content with the explanatory method. When he does, now and then, give us a 'scene,' it is as often as not unreal and unconvincing. One does not believe in a single one of Clissold's various mistresses; and the dialogue, in which Mr. Wells tries to make us hear them, is not infrequently ridiculous.

One is compelled once again, therefore, to accept Mr. Wells as a skillful tractarian, one of the most skillful alive, who knows admirably how to make ideas interesting. As a survey of the modern world from a 'liberal' point of view, and as propaganda for a World State to be evolved (and already evolving) on an economic rather than on a political basis, a World State in which the individual will to a fuller extent than at present surrender himself to the service of mankind, *The World of William Clissold* is impressive. The range of Mr. Wells's mind is encyclopædic. He covers everything, he leaves nothing out—his novel is a 'liberal' education in itself. If one struggles through these eight hundred pages of biology, sociology, economics, and disquisitions on sex, it is because Mr. Wells is himself interesting on these subjects, and not because he has succeeded in his 'full-dress novel.'

81. Mary Colum, review in *Saturday Review of Literature*

13 November 1926, iii, 289–90

Mary Colum (d. 1957), Irish critic and journalist.

The World of William Clissold, let me state at once, is likely to remain news for some time, though it contains nothing that is really new, though its value as literature is almost nil, but it is remarkable because it is an emporium of most of the things that Wells has been teaching and preaching and writing of since he began. The book, in other words, is important because it is a Wells book, and Wells is important because of his enormous influence, not on the best minds, but on a large number of the intelligent minds of his own time. His influence was, perhaps, largely due to the time of his arrival on the literary scene; he came after the Victorian period, and announced with enormous assertiveness that life was a grand adventure, that people need no longer believe in Hell or Matrimony or God or the Aristocracy or the Royal Family, and that Socialism was the open and inevitable gate to a better world. The great Victorians by their exhausting greatness and their exhausting discoveries, the lesser Victorians, by their primness and repressions, and their Puritanism, had taken the gusto out of life. Then Wells came along with a gusto that has remained with him still and told everybody that life was not meant to be lived as a painful duty but as a gorgeous adventure. He gave the younger generation of twenty years ago the exact tidings they wanted to hear; he also gave them opinions which they need not have the trouble of translating into convictions by passing them through the fires of any searing emotions or meditations. Whether it was that I was born a little too late in the last century to be a Wells enthusiast, or that I grew up in the hard intellectual conflict of the Irish revival, whose leaders taught that life was mostly not so grand for the sensitive and high of heart, but could indeed be a most lonely adventure which in those who thought out new ideas needed a steely courage instead of a heady optimism for its living—whichever of these two influences counted most with me, I have to admit that I can read Wells's later novels with only a moderate amount of patience. His own acceptance of what a novel ought to be composed of is, in a manner, responsible for this.

His preface to *The World of William Clissold* is both an account of his theories of novel-writing and a protest against its being reviewed by the class of book-reviewer to which I belong. He declares that this preface is a 'protest against certain stock tricks of the book-reviewer and certain present vulgarities about books—they concern the treatment of opinion in works of fiction and what is called "putting people into novels." ' More than three-quarters of *The World of William Clissold* is taken up with discussions of opinion; it contains, as he says, 'religious, historical, economic, and sociological discussions.' Does that make it anything but a novel? he asks. Perhaps not. But we can assure Mr. Wells that we could make him a present of all the opinions in the entire world for his emporium, and it would hardly make a pin's difference to literature, for nearly the whole of life would be left for other writers to deal with. Mr. Wells has, in fact, never yet shown how literature can be made out of opinions. The theme of *Tess of the D'Urbervilles* might be called sociological by gentlemen who go in for cataloguing ideas, but it is the human experience, the human tragedy, and the human passion, bare of all opinions, bare of all discussion, which makes *Tess* a great novel. 'Is it not as much life to meet and deal with a new idea as with a new lover,' he asks.

It is not. First of all, because an idea by itself is not life of the kind that can be put into a novel, whereas a lover most intensely is, and secondly, because it requires far more creative power to deal with a new lover in a work of fiction than with a new idea. He shows the direst dislike to such as might be reckoned on to call this book an autobiography and he points out certain superficial differences between his own life and that of William Clissold. According to his emphatic statement this book is not an autobiography. It is my belief that the reader and not the author is the best judge of this. Among the real people whom Mr. Wells introduces is Dr. Jung, the psychoanalyst. Now, if Mr. Wells, instead of making Dr. Jung an automatic figure could have really got into his consciousness the philosophy the great Doctor stands for, he would know that an author might not be able to tell whether his own book was an autobiography or not, and that a reader with a certain knowledge of psychoanalysis could prove that it was. *The World of William Clissold* is not the whole and complete autobiography of Mr. Wells, but it is perhaps a larger part of it than if it were written in the first person over his own name, because far less self-conscious than such a work would naturally be.

William Clissold, like the usual Wells hero, marries young; he divorces his wife and during the rest of his career indulges in varied sex-adventures for which love, as a rule, appears to be left out; in fact, with extraordinary crudity, he gives us his notion of love as 'something that may come into a sexual relationship.' We have seen this hero under various names such as Mr. Remington or Mr. Britling get a little older and older, but always with the illusion, no matter what his age, that he can be an object of passionate love to a young woman, until we now arrive at William Clissold, who, at the age of sixty, really believes that a woman of thirty is gloriously enamoured of his *beaux yeux*. Perhaps one of the reasons why Mr. Wells prefers dealing with ideas to dealing with lovers is that he cannot deal with lovers—his lovers have gradually become the biggest bores and the most fatuous old fools in contemporary literature. Like certain other Wells heroes he starts as something in science; he gives up the pursuit of pure science and becomes an industrialist, a holder of patents and an exploiter of secret processes, but, as we are assured, he has always been a taker of moderate profits. Like Mr. Wells, Mr. Clissold makes the fatal mistake of trying to think in terms of a world. When Mr. Wells left the territory of Kipps and Mr. Polly, and Dr. Moreau, and took the world as the place for the gyrations of his mind, his mind was unequal to the effort. As the historian of Mr. Polly and Kipps and Dr. Moreau, he had an unique gift; as the historian of the world and the world of William Clissold he becomes merely a generous-minded, highly intelligent Main streeter whose intelligence never reaches the point where it becomes intellect, but always remains on a plane where ideas can easily be reduced to platitudes.

In *The World of William Clissold* he struggles to explain the ideas that moved our elders and contemporaries, and the ideas that he thinks will move our descendants. It is a sort of outline of opinion. We are brought through the golden age of Socialism in England, when Karl Marx shocked so many remarkable minds into motion, and made, as Bernard Shaw has told us, a man of him. Mr. Clissold is somewhat vindictive about Socialism, about Karl Marx, and about the Fabian Society which

Wells once adorned. In his sixtieth year Mr. Clissold finds his Socialism little more than 'an old label on a valise.' Socialism, he tells us, is gone out of his world, having borne a narrow-souled, defective, and malignant child, Communism. What is called the Russian experiment fills him with resentment; he gives the impression of a man who simply so much dislikes the ideas the Russians have that he will not bother trying to understand what lies at the root of the order that they are imposing on their world, be it for good or evil. He calls Karl Marx 'the maggot of his decayed Socialism,' and says he poisoned and embittered the whole Socialist idea by arousing class-hatred. Without any interest in either Socialism or Communism, I am yet shocked into resentment by the unfairness of his treatment of Karl Marx and the present Russian system. It is unexpected in a gentleman who stands for a more generous ordering of the world.

All this is of course of interest to the historian of the future, as well as the skill with which he describes the dawn of advertisement in England, when the psychology of making people buy things by persuading them they wanted them whether they did or not first came into use. There are also the usual Wellsian discussions about Paleolithic man and the Ancient World and an elaborate discourse on Finance from which we gather that nobody understands anything about money, least of all, financiers and bankers, and that it has a helpless, uncontrolled manner of tearing through the world, making everybody its slave. If this be the case, wouldn't it be a simple way out of the muddle to give all the money in the world to Mr. J. P. Morgan, and Mr. Otto Kahn, and a selection of the several Baron Rothschilds, and let the rest of us get on as well as we can without it? It seems to me that this as a financial idea is as profound and revolutionary as Mr. Wells's.

Some of the most vigorous writing in the book is on the subject of birth-control and the sexual integrity of women. He attacks the romantic tradition of womanhood, which made of any spiritless creature a good woman if she conformed to the herd-code of chastity—a code which, as Shaw showed long ago, might mean in practise a life of abandoned lust, provided she was married to the man she lived with, whereas a woman of the highest sexual integrity and asceticism might be made an outcast for living without a legal tie with the man she loved. As to birth-control, he gives the threadbare arguments against filling the world with the unfit and against exhausting women with child-bearing, and has the usual complacent assumption that all who are against artificial birth-control are against the higher progress of the world.

Might the progress of the world not be more fitly advanced by a crusade in favor of self-control instead of unrestricted birth-control and the unrestricted self-indulgence that comes in its train? And might not the super-race that Mr. Wells tells us of and that Higher Man of his be more likely to come from a civilization in which self-control rather than artificial birth-control held sway?

Mr. Clissold attacks universities as places which put the repressive training of the young above freedom of thought, and he announces that 'we must be prepared to cut out this three or four year holiday at Oxford or Cambridge and their American compeers from the lives of young men we hope to see playing leading parts in the affairs of the world.' 'The only good thing I've heard in favor of a university gown is that it is better than a tailed coat for cleaning chalk off a blackboard.' Now this may be Mr. Wells's idea of humor, but as an argument against universities it looks suspiciously like what in the teaching of Karl Marx he called bitter class animosity. It looks, in fact, merely like the animosity of the non-university man against the university man.

None of his discussions seem to me to bring any clarity of thought, or even largeness of vision to vital questions. When he has finished his discussions of biological, financial, economic, and all the other questions that he prides himself on dealing with in this book, we evermore come out by the same door as in we went. His book is a huge emporium, like a Main Street department store, where you can buy almost anything; the populace can clothe itself there, but the fastidious will clothe themselves somewhere else. Similarly, for original or unique thinking or a large creativeness, you will have to go to somebody else than Mr. Wells. There is, to be sure, hardly any current question he leaves untouched in this book. Assertively and pedagogically he tells us things about the future, about man, about life, about the past, not with a delicate clarity of someone revealing a mystery which he has spent himself on discovering, but with the loud emphasis of somebody who has not had the pain of discovering anything, but only the need to excitedly shout other peoples' discoveries from the market place in words unsubtle enough to get over to the multitude, in a literary style that is frequently appalling, and too often with a resentful determination to get even with opponents.

82. H. L. Mencken, review in
American Mercury

December 1926, ix, 506–8

As Mencken recalls here, the publication of *Joan and Peter* led him
to write a punishing obituary of Wells as an artist ('The Late Mr.
Wells', 1918). But he soon retracted somewhat, and his review of
The World of William Clissold was the second article he had
written under the title 'Wells *Redivivus*'.

Long ago, as time runs in literary science—to wit, in December, 1918—I
printed a melancholy article upon the engulfing of H. G. Wells the
novelist by H. G. Wells the publicist and seer. The former, I argued,
was a charming fellow, full of spicy observation and waggish reflection;
the latter was only a bore. The title of that article was 'The Late Mr.
Wells,' and it was later reprinted in a book. All I can say now, re-reading
it in the light of *The World of William Clissold*, is that it seems to have
been a bit premature, not to say injudicious. For I overlooked completely
the probable effect of the fats, carbohydrates and proteids of Wells the
novelist upon the metabolism of the cannibalistic Wells the seer. I
assumed that the latter, as in *The Future in America* and *God the Invisible
King*, would go on being a bore.

This assumption, as connoisseurs will recall, was given a severe blow
in 1920, by the publication of *The Outline of History*. It is now completely blown up by *The World of William Clissold*. In this book the
novelist and the seer finish their process of mutual digestion. They
become one and indivisible, as a Christian and a holy wafer become one
and indivisible. And they become, likewise, extraordinarily meritorious.
It is not only a good book; it is an amazing book, and I confess that I
have read it from cover to cover with eager and constantly rising
interest. There are, to be sure, weak spots in it, as there are in Holy Writ,
but taken as a whole it is unquestionably a sound and brilliant performance. I can imagine no other English novelist writing anything
comparable to it, and no American of any sort. It is at once the confes-

sion and the defiance of one of the most remarkable men of our time. Summing up at sixty, he puts the world as he has seen it in its place.

In a longish preface, printed before the title-page, Wells protests somewhat violently against the common critical error of confusing him as an individual with the characters in his books, and in the pages that follow he is at pains to make this distinction clear, sometimes by the naïve device of having Clissold discuss and attack the known ideas of Wells. His sensitiveness on the point, I suspect, has its rise in the notorious tendency of certain literary gossips to concern themselves with his private affairs, and especially with his affairs of amour. He is credited by these gossips with a great enterprise in that department, and no doubt they will seek, as usual, to identify the prototypes of the ladies loved by William Clissold. But that inquiry need not concern us here. As he says himself, a novelist, in the last analysis, must always dredge most of his material out of his own experience: he needs imagination, obviously, but it is useless without observation.

If Wells, in his journey through this world, has ever actually had dealings with such women as Sirrie Evans, the Helen whose surname I disremember, and Clementina Campbell, then I can only offer him my respectful felicitations. For they must have been extremely amusing and instructive gals, and out of his conferences with them has come a series of character studies of the first rank. There is little of dull normalcy in Sirrie, Helen and Clementina. They are all, as the Victorians used to say, handsful. They fetch Clissold by their striking and often abominable strangeness. But Wells somehow reduces them to the natural order of femininity. They become laboratory animals in an elaborate and immensely illuminating investigation of the ways of their sex. It is not, however, their specially sexual character that is under scrutiny. There is little of sex, indeed, in the ordinary sense, in the book: Clissold is a psychologist rather than a lover, though he once describes himself grandly as a rake. The lights are always upon their ways and means as persons, individuals, units of human society. I can recall no more penetrating discussion of sex in general, nor of its social implications, including marriage.

The book, thank God, has no plot: Clissold simply lives and dies. Nor is there any visible hortatory purpose in it, despite its constant concern with grave matters of social organization, statecraft, education, morals, and human destiny. Clissold is the intelligent modern of Wells' old adoration—the fellow who has had a sound grounding in exact knowledge, but has branched out into the regions of speculation. The type is admirable, and essentially new in the world. The Greeks, for all their intellectual adventurousness, never produced it, nor even, indeed, came to any suspicion that it could exist. They tried to formulate history without statistics, science without experiment, and ethics without psychology. The modern man is something quite different. If he lacks the daring of the Greeks, then he at least has vastly more information. No college professor of today is so stupid that he doesn't know more than Aristotle. No school-boy can read even Thucydides without occasionally coughing behind his hand. This increase of sheer enlightenment, in Wells' view, is gradually producing a type of man who is at once a philosopher and a man of the world—a sort of super-Goethe, purged of romantic illusion, and capable of visioning progress over long periods and against all imaginable obstacles, even the obstacle of human imbecility.

Wells himself is obviously a shining example of that type, or, at all events, of its forerunner. He is thoroughly the modern man. Certain vestiges of Victorian sentimentality, to be sure, are still in him. There are moments when his concept of progress becomes merely meta-physical, mystical, maudlin. He glimpses tantalizing visions of a perfected humanity that is scarcely to be distinguished from the pre-Darwinian God. But that is only now and then. In the main he sticks to facts—and his store of them is so immensely greater than that of any other contemporary novelist that he stands in a class all his own. Having imagined something, he is able to prove it. The proving, as I long ago contended, sometimes hobbles him as artist—but an artist pure and simple could not have written such a book as *The World of William Clissold*. We must be content to take the bitter with the sweet. In order to get the Wells of that extraordinary work, and of *The Outline of History*, we must make some sacrifice of the Wells of *Mr. Polly* and *Tono-Bungay*.

Taking the man as he stands, it must be manifest that he is one of the most remarkable personages in the England of today. There is a stimulating and abounding aliveness about him. He has his finger in a multitude of pies. His fancy is bold and original. He is the complete antithesis of the stolid, unimaginative, muddling Briton of tradition. It seems to me that his speculations, even when a touch of extravagance gets into them, have a solid value—that in the midst of his most daring imaginings he often comes very close to the ultimate truth. Read, in *The World of William Clissold*, his chapter on sex. Read his several interpolated essays on money. Read what he has to say about government, marriage, education—especially education. There is here a profoundly enterprising, competent and original mind, and I believe that it will put its marks upon the thought of the next generation. I have, in my time, damned Wells as much as most. I formally damn him again. But I see no way for the human race to escape him.

83. J. M. Keynes, review in *Nation and Athenaeum*

22 January 1927, xl, 561–2

John Maynard Keynes (1883–1946), economist, is (like Shaw and Jung) one of the 'real persons' who figure in Wells's novel and whose influence William Clissold acknowledges.

Mr. Wells and his publisher having adopted an ingenious device by which his newest book has been reviewed three times over, perhaps it is too much to write about it again at this late date. But, having read the reviews first and the book afterwards, I am left seriously discontented with what the professional critics have had to say. It is a weakness of modern critics not to distinguish—not to distinguish between one thing and another. Even Mr. Wells's choice of form has confused his reviewers. They fail to see what he is after. They reject the good beef which he has offered the British public, because mutton should never be underdone. Or their delicacies are sharpened against his abundance and omnivorous vitality, the broadness and coarseness of the brush with which he sweeps the great canvas which is to catch the attention of hundreds of thousands of readers and sway their minds onward.

Mr. Wells here presents, not precisely his own mind as it has developed on the basis of his personal experience and way of life, but— shifting his angle—a point of view based on an experience mainly different from his own, that of a successful, emancipated, semi-scientific, not particularly high-brow, English business man. The result is not primarily a work of art. Ideas, not forms, are its substance. It is a piece of educational writing—propaganda, if you like, an attempt to convey to the very big public attitudes of mind already partly familiar to the very small public.

The book is an *omnium gatherum*. I will select two emergent themes of a quasi-economic character. Apart from these, the main topic is women and some of their possible relationships in the modern world to themselves and to men of the Clissold type. This is treated with great candour, sympathy, and observation. It leaves, and is meant to leave, a bitter taste.

The first of these themes is a violent protest against Conservatism, an insistent emphasis on the necessity and rapidity of change, the folly of looking backwards, the danger of inadaptability. Mr. Wells produces a curious sensation, nearly similar to that of some of his earlier romances, by contemplating vast stretches of time backwards and forwards which give an impression of slowness (no need to hurry in eternity), yet accelerating the Time Machine as he reaches the present day so that *now* we travel at an enormous pace and no longer have millions of years to turn round in. The Conservative influences in our life are envisaged as Dinosaurs whom literal extinction is awaiting just ahead. The contrast comes from the failure of our ideas, our conventions, our prejudices to keep up with the pace of material change. Our environment moves too much faster than we do. The walls of our travelling compartment are bumping our heads. Unless we hustle, the traffic will run us down. Conservatism is no better than suicide. Woe to our Dinosaurs!

This is one aspect. We stand still at our peril. Time flies. But there is another aspect of the same thing—and this is where Clissold comes in. What a bore for the modern man, whose mind in his active career moves with the times, to stand still in his observances and way of life! What a bore are the feasts and celebrations with which London crowns success! What a bore to go through the social contortions which have lost significance and conventional pleasures which no longer please! The contrast between the exuberant, constructive activity of a prince of modern commerce and the lack of an appropriate environment for him out of office hours is acute. Moreover, there are wide stretches in the career of money-making which are entirely barren and non-constructive. There is a fine passage in the first volume about the profound, ultimate boredom of City men. Clissold's father, the company promoter and speculator, falls first into megalomania and then into fraud, because he is bored. Let us, therefore, mould with both hands the plastic material of social life into our own contemporary image.

We do not merely belong to a latter-day age—we are ourselves in the literal sense older than our ancestors were in the years of our maturity and our power. Mr. Wells brings out strongly a too-much neglected feature of modern life, that we live much longer than formerly, and, what is more important, prolong our health and vigour into a period of life which was formerly one of decay, so that the average man can now look forward to a duration of activity which hitherto only the exceptional could anticipate. I can add, indeed, a further fact, which Mr. Wells overlooks (I think), likely to emphasize this yet further in the next fifty years as compared with the last fifty years;—namely, that the average age of a rapidly increasing population is much less than that of a stationary population. For example, in the stable conditions to which we may hope to approximate in the course of the next two generations, we shall somewhat rapidly approach to a position in which, in proportion to population, elderly people (say, sixty-five years of age and above) will be nearly 100 per cent., and middle-aged people (say, forty-five years of age and above), nearly 50 per cent. more numerous than in the recent past. In the nineteenth century effective power was in the hands of men probably not less than fifteen years older on the average than in the sixteenth century; and before the twentieth century is out the average may have risen another fifteen years, unless effective means are found, other than obvious physical or mental decay, to make vacancies at the top. Clissold (in his sixtieth year, be it noted) sees more advantage and less disadvantage in this state of affairs than I do. Most men love money and security more, and creation and construction less, as they get older; and this process begins long before their intelligent judgment on detail is apparently impaired. Mr. Wells's preference for an adult world over a juvenile, sex-ridden world may be right. But the margin between this and a middle-aged, money-ridden world is a narrow one. We are threatened, at the best, with the appalling problem of the able-bodied 'retired,' of which Mr. Wells himself gives a sufficient example in his desperate account of the regular denizens of the Riviera.

We are living, then, in an unsatisfactory age of immensely rapid transition in which most, but particularly those in the vanguard, find themselves and their environment ill-adapted to one another, and are for this reason far less happy than their less-sophisticated forbears were or their yet more-sophisticated descendants need be. This diagnosis, applied by Mr. Wells to the case of those engaged in the practical life of action, is essentially the same as Mr. Edwin Muir's, in his deeply interesting volume of criticism, *Transition*, to the case of those engaged in the life of art and contemplation. Our foremost writers, according to Mr. Muir, are *uncomfortable* in the world;—they can neither support nor can they oppose anything with a full confidence, with the result that their work is inferior in relation to their talents compared with work produced in happier ages,—jejune, incomplete, starved, anæmic, like their own feelings to the universe.

In short we cannot stay where we are; we are on the move,—on the move, not necessarily either to better or to worse, but just to an equilibrium. But why not to the better? Why should not we begin to reap spiritual fruits from our material conquests? If so, whence is to come the motive power of desirable change? This brings us to Mr. Wells's second theme.

Mr. Wells describes in the first volume of *Clissold* his hero's disillusionment with Socialism. In the third volume he inquires if there is an alternative. From whence are we to draw the forces which are 'to change the laws, customs, rules, and institutions of the world'? 'From what classes and types are the revolutionaries to be drawn? How are they to be brought into co-operation? What are to be their methods?' The Labour Movement is represented as an immense and dangerous force of destruction, led by sentimentalists and pseudo-intellectuals, who have 'feelings in the place of ideas.' A constructive revolution cannot possibly be contrived by these folk. The creative intellect of mankind is not to be found in these quarters but amongst the scientists and the great modern business men. Unless we can harness to the job this type of mind and character and temperament, it can never be put through,—for it is a task of immense practical complexity and intellectual difficulty. We must recruit our revolutionaries, therefore, from the Right, not from the Left. We must persuade the type of man whom it now amuses to create a great business, that there lie waiting for him yet bigger things which will amuse him more. This is Clissold's 'Open Conspiracy.' Clissold's direction is to the Left—far, far to the Left; but he seeks to summon from the Right the creative force and the constructive will which is to carry him there. He describes himself as being temperamentally and fundamentally a Liberal. But political Liberalism must die 'to be born again with firmer features and a clearer will.'

Clissold is expressing a reaction against the Socialist Party which very many feel, including Socialists. The remoulding of the world needs the touch of the creative Brahma. But at present Brahma is serving Science and Business, not Politics or Government. The extreme danger of the world is, in Clissold's words, lest, 'before the creative Brahma can get to work, Siva, in other words the passionate destructiveness of Labour awakening to its now needless limitations and privations, may make Brahma's task impossible.' We all feel this, I think. We know that we need urgently to create a *milieu* in which Brahma can get to work before it is too late. Up to a point, therefore, most active and constructive temperaments in every political camp are ready to join the Open Conspiracy.

What, then, is it, that holds them back? It is here, I think, that *Clissold* is in some way deficient and apparently lacking in insight. Why do practical men find it more amusing to make money than to join the Open Conspiracy? I suggest that it is much the same reason as that which makes them find it more amusing to play bridge on Sundays than to go to church. They lack altogether the kind of motive, the possession of which, if they had it, could be expressed by saying that they had a creed. They have no creed, these potential open conspirators, no creed whatever. That is why, unless they have the luck to be scientists or artists, they fall back on the grand substitute motive, the perfect *Ersatz*, the anodyne for those who in fact want nothing at all—Money. Clissold charges the enthusiasts of Labour that they have 'feelings in the place of ideas.' But he does not deny that they have feelings. Has not, perhaps, poor Mr. Cook something which Clissold lacks? Clissold and his brother Dickon, the advertising expert, flutter about the world seeking for something to which they can attach their abundant *libido*. But they have not found it. They would so like to be Apostles. But they cannot. They remain business men.

I have taken two themes from a book which contains dozens. They are not all treated equally well. Knowing the Universities much better than Mr. Wells does, I declare that his account contains no more than the element of truth which is proper to a caricature. He underestimates altogether their possibilities—how they may yet become temples of Brahma which even Siva will respect. But *Clissold*, taken altogether, is a great achievement, a huge and meaty egg from a glorious hen, an abundant outpouring of an ingenious, truthful, and generous spirit.

Though we talk about pure art as never before, this is not a good age for pure artists; nor is it a good one for classical perfections. Our most pregnant writers to-day are full of imperfections; they expose themselves to judgment; they do not look to be immortal. For these reasons, perhaps, we, their contemporaries, do them and the debt we owe them less than justice. What a debt every intelligent being owes to Bernard Shaw! What a debt also to H. G. Wells, whose mind seems to have grown up alongside his readers', so that, in successive phases, he has delighted us and guided our imaginations from boyhood to maturity.

84. Geoffrey H. Wells on Wells's failure

February 1926

'The Failure of H. G. Wells', *Adelphi*, iii, 609–21.

Geoffrey H. Wells (no relation to H.G.), author of a Wells *Bibliography* (1926) and of the first biography of his namesake— *H. G. Wells: A Sketch for a Portrait* (1930). Written in consultation with its subject, this indispensable book appeared under the pseudonym 'Geoffrey West'. The following article is a concise statement of the critical position elaborated in West's biography.

At the beginning some explanation of my title seems necessary; it must be made clear that its application is intended in a limited if fundamental sense. Wells has, of course, his detractors, but few responsible critics will be found to deny that he is in any meaning of the term a great man. Anatole France has described him justly as the greatest intellectual force in the English-speaking world, and Wells himself writes truly of the Atlantic Edition of his works that 'there is in the ultimate reckoning something said in these volumes that was not said before, and something shaped that was not shaped before.' The ninety books and pamphlets which preserve the bulk of his writings represent an activity and an achievement unequalled by any other living author, a range of inquiry, criticism, entertainment, suggestion and information which is remarkable. It is an achievement, too, more enduring than many of his critics seem to care to acknowledge, for quite apart from the mere organised 'knowledge' and the astounding wealth of creation, he has written some of the finest passages in modern prose, and possesses a quality of imaginative intuition which again and again lifts his work to a poetic plane. Wells is indisputably a great man; if he has failed he has failed greatly, and even his failure sets him high above the topmost success of ordinary men.

I can best make clear the sense in which I impute failure to H. G. Wells by stating my perhaps peculiar personal connection with his work. On my eleventh birthday I was given a copy of *The First Men in the Moon*—the most potent present I have ever received. I began to read Wells at once, and since then I have read practically everything he has written over and over again. He gave me, even so early, a certain standard of good writing which brought me through a morass of otherwise unguided youthful reading to some appreciation of literature; from him I took presently the germs of any interest I have in politics and sociology and philosophy. He has been to a great extent, in default of anything better, my education. There is no man living to whom, fundamentally, I owe so much, nor any great writer for whom I have so steadfast a personal affection. And yet, at the end of it all, I seem to have come only to a sense of dissatisfaction; I have been forced to a persuasion that for myself at least his knowledge, his perception of the world and of man, the sum of his experience, leads only into an impassable desert of futility and distress and spiritual death, and that all his Promised Lands are but mirages—lifeless visions created within his own brain to hide from himself the barren wastes which lie before him. I have done my uttermost to understand Wells, to accept him and to live by him, and this is the end. A personal matter it may seem, yet I have found traces of the same dissatisfaction, in various degrees, in other readers of Wells, and it is in essence, I am convinced, a fundamental criticism of him as a great man and a great writer.

Since this is to be essentially a criticism of Wells's work as a whole, it is necessary to outline, though briefly, his progress and achievement, to follow roughly a few main threads. Within my limits of space there can be little pausing to account for occasional inconsistencies, turnings aside or bendings back, but for myself I have left nothing unconsidered, and I can find no discrepancy which invalidates what is set forth in the following pages.

In Wells's earliest work we find two distinct divisions of interest. There are the scientific romances, in which are explored, with wonderful imaginative power and daring, a few of the material possibilities of the universe. 'I found,' he writes of his short stories of this period, 'that, taking almost anything as a starting-point, and letting my thoughts play about it, there would presently come out of the darkness some absurd or vivid little incident more or less relevant to that initial nucleus.' The longer tales must have been conceived in very much the same manner; the circumstances are the primary thing, and the characters for all their living reality remain little more than puppets to display those circumstances. Prendick, Griffin, Bedford, and the Time Traveller could have changed places without altering their stories in any major degree. But in *The Wheels of Chance* and *Love and Mr. Lewisham* the characters themselves to a very large extent are the circumstances. These are the two divisions, and I think that if all things are taken into consideration, and particularly the fact that at the height of his first popularity he turned, disregarding a financial loss, to the writing of *Love and Mr. Lewisham*, it may be said that Wells's real interest was rather in the 'studies of personality' than in the romances, that he was engrossed, as every artist must be, in the study of the eternal mystery of man, of the potentialities and failures of the individual being. We may find confirmation of this interest in the tendency of the romances toward satire. In both divisions the fundamental question is, 'What is man?' In one it is answered with ever more penetration, ever more bitterness, and ever wider vision, from the view-point of distant worlds, in the other ever more sympathetically, ever more comprehensively, from that of a man among men. In one the arbiter is the cold reasoning intelligence, in the other the intuition; in both there is with every volume an imaginative advance, an increase in depth and certainty, a keener apprehension of a reality. And as that apprehension deepens the pain of the world, its disorder, its waste and want, oppress him more and more. He has looked at the present world from the far limits of past and future, from without and from within, and the burden of its distress has come upon him. So much is, it seems, explicit in his turning to the practical suggestions of Fabianism and socialism generally, and in the writing of *Anticipations* and *Mankind in the Making*.

The work of the first years of the new century makes apparent a kind of welding of the two divisions. The romances approach more and more nearly to novels, while the novels frequently have a touch of imaginative adventure foreign to the earlier ones. But there is another even more essential change. The interest in the individuals, in the 'personalities thwarted and crippled by the defects of our contemporary civilisation,' increases; Wells discovers more fineness in, he has more sympathy for, particular men than Mankind. And at the same time his 'admirable' man becomes more and more the scientifically trained reasonable man. The intellectual man. Mankind to-day moves to self-destruction—that is the message of *The War in the Air*. Mankind must change, or not so much change as give full development to its finest potentialities—that is made clear in *In the Days of the Comet*. The primary step toward this change must be the conscious development by men and women of these potentialities in and for the service and guidance of their fellows—that is the vital essence of *A Modern Utopia* and *First and Last Things* (and, incidentally, of *The Food of the Gods*).

All these books reveal a preoccupation with an unreasonable world and a search for a way out, a way to something socially and materially better, to a world of men and women like ourselves but educated and organised. He finds that way out in the assertion of the reasonable, the intellectual man, who alone can save mankind from self-annihilation. At last, in *Tono-Bungay*, he shows the completely reasonable man in conflict with his world. Again, in *The History of Mr. Polly*, he shows, in a quite different mood and key, a quite different kind of man also in conflict with his world. These two books are, not only to myself but by general consent, Wells's finest works; they appeared in 1909 and 1910 respectively, with between them only *Ann Veronica*, a fragmentary and shapeless story.

After *Mr. Polly* a change is immediately noticeable in a series of novels—from *The New Machiavelli* to *The Research Magnificent*—which have been called, not altogether unjustifiably, Wells's Prig Novels. Their heroes have it in common that 'through their voluntary actions they proposed to enlighten the collective mind and stir up the collective will.' They are not content, as was George Ponderevo, merely to be critical. But there is another difference, stated clearly in *Marriage* when Trafford tells his wife: 'I've always felt you're a finer individual than me, I've never had a doubt of it. . . . And yet—I'm a deeper and bigger thing than you. I reach up to something you don't reach up to.' In *Tono-Bungay* Wells had striven for the vindication of the man as individual; now he says that there is something finer, to put away one's self in the service of mankind. The element of priggishness in these men, their creator says, was 'derived from their failure to realise that the impulse to serve mankind comes from a source outside of and greater than one's individual good intentions.' Still another change, too, is noticeable, in method rather than matter, a tendency to discuss rather than to present, to explain and expound—inevitably to the detriment, and even to the forcefulness, of the work. In *Mr. Britling Sees it Through*, where comes the first clear statement that 'Religion is the first thing and the last thing, and until a man has found God and been found by God, he begins at no beginning, he works to no end'—that statement is made clear rather than convincing, while *God the Invisible King* and *The Soul of a Bishop* are even less satisfactory. Many of these later novels seem designed less to render life than to discuss explicitly some social or intellectual problem; they are concerned less with life than with living. Wells the artist gives place to Wells the philosopher and Wells the historian, both aspects, fundamentally, of Wells the journalist. And if the later books are better I find them so more from a decrease in the fervour of the journalist than from any increase in the impulse of the artist; the best in them is but a repetition of the best in the earlier books. There has been neither artistic nor intellectual progress; the central ideal of *Christina Alberta's Father* is the ideal of ten years before—that of the rejection of the self in the service of God—somewhat elaborated, formulated indeed a little further from reality.

Tono-Bungay and *Mr. Polly* remain Wells's most satisfying achievements. They are still his closest contact with reality, the outposts of his soul's adventure. Forward from them he has not gone—it is the purpose of this essay to attempt to suggest why he has not.

Many of Wells's books reveal traces of an inward conflict between intuition and 'reason,' but for the present it is convenient to take one volume, written only just before or even during, the critical period, in which it is very clearly expressed—*First and Last Things*. We find in it again and again, usually in isolated sentences, a certitude of mystical statement. 'Things move to Power and Beauty; I say that much and I have said all that I can say.' 'To me Beauty is a final, quite indefinable thing. Either you understand it or you do not. . . . There is something that shows suddenly . . . it is right, it is commanding, it is, to use theological language, the revelation of God.' And this is the last sentence in the book: 'In the ultimate I know, though I cannot prove my knowledge in any way whatever, that everything is right and all things mine.' 'In the ultimate *I know*'—yet he seems unable to carry his knowledge over, to make it a working knowledge. The truth is, as *Tono-Bungay* and other books make clear, that he has chosen the intellectual attitude, and therefore has to reject all that he cannot rationalise. This negative rejection is naturally more difficult to present in brief quotation, but much of the section on metaphysics is devoted to explaining Wells's scepticism of the mind as a reliable instrument for the discovery of truth—with the inference that beyond the mind there is no other instrument. 'I figure the mind of man as an imperfect being obtaining knowledge by imperfect eyesight, imperfect hearing, and so forth. . . . Of everything we need to say: this is true but it is not quite true.' At the final point he is prepared to throw the intellect overboard and to say without hesitation that he knows, but by far the greater part of *First and Last Things* is, in its nature, the exposition of a rationalistic attitude. 'I am, in relation to religious and moral questions, an agnostic.' In this book the two sorts of apprehension are allowed to exist, rather strangely, side by side; it is in *Tono-Bungay* that the final test is made, that for the first time a man's whole world and being are submitted to the judgment of the intellectual consciousness.

It is to some extent this rigidity of treatment, this unrelenting judgment, which makes *Tono-Bungay* the amazing story that it is—one of the few books in modern English fiction which can be described as 'thought-adventure' without hesitation or qualification. It is thought-adventure and nothing else. It has sex in it, but no 'love-interest,' it has conquest, but no victory; it is essentially the quest of George Ponderevo, the personification of the intellectual consciousness, for a reality which will stand against all his tests. Again and again, without cessation, he applies them to every level and phase of society, and society smashes about him. Life breaks down at that inhuman questioning, until at last there seems nothing left. In the last chapter, one of the most wonderful passages Wells has ever written, is focussed the whole spirit of the book. The reticent prose drives on like the destroyer it tells of; it comes very near to poetry, it exalts and moves beyond all rational explanation.

[Quotes Bk IV, ch. 3 'I and my destroyer' to 'England passes'.]

This is the book itself! George Ponderevo, himself the destroyer, has passed by and darkened the old lights, has found these prides and devotions but empty things, and goes beyond them out to new horizons. Into darkness he goes, into darkness. . . . There is not in all modern literature, one might say, so exact an image of the progress and the end of the intellectual consciousness.

But that is not the end. On the next page, the last in the book, we find something of which there has been no hint at all before.

[Quotes Bk IV, ch. 3 'But through the confusion sounds another note' to 'dreams that have no words'.]

I am forced to see this last page as a repudiation, a confession of failure, of the intellectual consciousness. Its utmost power has discovered no ultimate reality beyond this worthless material reality; this is the inevitable victory of the intellect, and in the moment of victory there comes defeat. This victory is unbearable, a thing which the soul cannot admit; in the vital hour Wells fails, and has to take refuge in a conception which, whatever it is, certainly has nothing to do with the intellectual consciousness.

I doubt, indeed, whether that last page was not forced in quite against the original design. The value of *Tono-Bungay* to me lies in its effort to find a final reality; in it man the individual carries the banner of the intellectual consciousness to the last barrier—it is only when he is beaten back that his deeper self cries out an instinctive knowledge. But, despite that last cry, Wells could not allow himself to see in the failure of George Ponderevo the failure of the intellectual consciousness. His attitude had divided him against himself; he had no self certain enough to stand alone in its own strength. He had therefore to see in that failure the failure of man the individual. From that intolerable loneliness which was George Ponderevo's end he flies, and the later books almost without exception are a record of that flight to something stronger and more enduring than anything he finds within himself. He comes at last, inevitably, to the idea of God; to the idea of God rather than to God himself.

For *God the Invisible King* is not the book of a man who knows God; it is that of one tortured by a need for him. Wells must have God, and his God must *be* God. No longer the collective intelligence of mankind, the Mind of the Race, but God, 'a Being in himself,' 'as real as a bayonet thrust or an embrace.' God is a person, he insists, and then takes away from him every quality that constitutes personality in all but the most esoteric meaning of the word. One must believe that he has had some kind of religious experience, but he destroys it by the very act of trying to make it real to the intellectual consciousness through a process of formulation. There is a lack of real spiritual quality in Wells—for that comes utterly and necessarily from the depths of the united self, and that self Wells has rejected.

Few things are more significant in the later books than this rejection. 'Between God and the believer there is no other way, there is nothing else, but self-surrender and the ending of self.' All his heroes, from Trafford to Preemby, come to that. 'That cherished personal life which men and women struggled to round off and make noble and perfect, disappears from the scheme of things.' Wells is, in fact a Romantic who has rejected the Romantic tradition, even as he is an artist who has rejected art. 'Our fundamental beliefs, our rules of conduct, we must all make for ourselves,' he says, but at the same time rejects the complete for the partial judgment. One measure of his rejection may be found in his attitude to art; to take a particular case, his attitude to Shakespeare. 'What did Shakespeare add to the world's totality? Some delightful plays, some exquisite passages, some deliciously observed characters. He was a great playwright, a great humorist, the sweetest laughter in the world. . . . But if he had never lived, things would be very much as they are . . . Shakespeare's "thought" amounted to very little. He added no idea, he altered no idea, in the growing understanding of mankind.' And elsewhere, again with reference to Shakespeare: 'Great art exists for joy. The joy in literature is its only justification. . . . Written and made poetry is not necessary for everyone. There are many who can take the grandeur of history, the splendour of the stars, the majesty of natural law, the ripple in the water, and the beauty of a flower without the help of the poet.' Surely Wells doesn't know in the least what he is talking about! Yet to the intellectual consciousness, strictly applied, art perhaps can be no more than this, and it may well seem absurd to consider Shakespeare as more than the entertaining playwright, the jolly soul, to find in his works, indeed, 'man's final lore.' It is all one, though, with Wells's declaration of himself as not artist but journalist; as one, that is, who sees with a contemporary rather than an eternal vision.

This is not to say, of course, that his work has not a very great immediate value, but the larger part of it must in time, I think, except for extracts and fragments, fall into oblivion. Of many of his books it may be said, as he himself says of *The Outline of History*, that it is 'a book of to-day—with no pretensions to immortality. It is the current account.' Even to-day his own interest seems more in the journalist than in the artist; it is the logical conclusion of that which has gone before, and yet I cannot believe that it was a chosen conclusion. No man who was in himself, from the very depths of himself, an artist, could ever turn happily to journalism, and that Wells was at one time an artist to those very depths there is at least one book to prove. Not *Tono-Bungay*, though that might seem proof enough, but that top of all his endeavour, the book which followed so close upon it, *The History of Mr. Polly*.

It stands alone. There may be in other volumes pages and parts— even large parts—which seem to come close to it. Some chapters of

Kipps, the first quarter of *Bealby*, pages of *The Dream*. But *Mr. Polly* alone is completed all in one mood, it alone sustains its quality to the end, pure gold; in it alone there is no bitterness, the artist is triumphant. As in the last page of *Tono-Bungay*, so here, after that great battle, Wells turns back to the instinctive vision, the pure artistic knowledge which has always existed deep within him, but before had only been allowed to express itself in paragraphs and pages of the earlier romances and novels. *Mr. Polly* is what it is because it is neither what Wells thinks nor what he believes, but what he knows; he is true to the experience of his profoundest being. In some of the later books, *Christina Alberta's Father*, for example, he may seem superficially far more completely himself, but in *Mr. Polly* he is much more actually so. Being what he was, what he had made himself, he could not hold to that vision, and the book remains, uniquely, just a promise of what he might have achieved had he been finally and continuously true to himself, as *Tono-Bungay* is a promise of what he might have achieved had he been true to the intellectual consciousness.

Wells fails to satisfy the deepest instincts, I think, because he has been divided against himself. He has rejected his truest knowledge for the judgment of the intellectual consciousness, and at the same time has lacked the courage (for it needs a final tremendous courage) to follow to its bitter end the path of the intellectual consciousness. Yet he had to find some way out, and since he could go neither forward nor back had at last to discover a faith which had only a sentimental and not a fundamental authority. That this faith, at least subconsciously, fails to satisfy him is, one may suggest, made obvious in his impatience, his instability, his inability to 'brood over experience,' his desire (as Freeman remarked of Remington) for 'experiences rather than experience.' ('Much more to me,' he writes in *First and Last Things*, 'than the desire to live is the desire to taste life.') It is made obvious in his revolt against 'the clothes we wear and the food we eat, the houses we live in, the schools we have, our amusements, our money,' and so on. Inwardly realising his failure to fulfil himself, he has to deny himself as artist, and to get on with the work as mere journeyman, building for the day. He can no longer wait, as Dostoevsky waited, 'his hour when he should have found a means of expressing himself in the language of the imagination.'

His genius was always (if the distinction may be allowed) a comic rather than a sublime one. It is a form of genius which does not penetrate less deeply or less essentially to the eternal reality, but it is a more restricted genius, less able to rise above its limitations. Shakespeare's was both comic and sublime, and he rose—how splendidly the later plays show—above the insistent questioning of the intellectual problem. But in that Wells has failed, and it is difficult now to believe that after all these years he may still reverse his defeat and emerge victorious. We have much to thank Wells for—his fine and brilliant thought, his visioning of a material hope, his advocation of many splendid causes, the astonishing imaginative effort which produced *The Outline of History*, the entertainment of the early books, the plenitude of character creation—most of all for those two enduring volumes, *Tono-Bungay* and *Mr. Polly*. But he remains, despite this, a failure; a great man must be judged by his progress, by his fulfilment. Wells has turned back from the final reality, from the facing of the final truth, and to do that, whatever the rest may be, is failure.

85. John Holms, Wells under scrutiny

July 1927

Calendar of Modern Letters, iv, 142–52, reprinted in *Scrutinies* (1928), an abrasive collection of critical essays edited by Edgell Rickword.

John Holms (d. 1934), critic and socialite.

Mr. Wells has written a great many books on a great many subjects, subjects for the most part of the first importance to civilized man. A list of his works to date is commonly printed before the title page of each new addition to the tale, and to a prospective reader, unacquainted with their contents and with the cultural peculiarities of our era, this astonishing array of titles promises nothing less than the encyclopædic life work of a creative and philosophic mind of the first order. To select the more important of his activities, Mr. Wells, the list informs us, besides a great quantity of fiction, has produced sociological, educational, philosophical, theological, historical, and prophetic works. Since it is impossible in a short essay to deal with these in turn, it will be more convenient and useful to commence with Mr. Wells' fiction, for which he is most widely and deservedly known; in which his more specifically creative talent is exercised; and in which we may expect the fruit of a comprehensive mental activity, its quality and its significance, to be presented in its most conclusive and valuable form, related to and interpreting an organized conception of human life.

Mr. Wells' first love was science, which also supplied the stimulus for his earliest imaginative work. It seems clear, indeed, from the start that it was not the pursuit of knowledge that primarily attracted him, but the dramatic possibilities offered by science and the scientist to a romantic journalist, whose view of the laboratory only differed from that of the man in the street in the possession of a somewhat more specialized knowledge, and of an exceedingly vivid and fluent imagination of an adolescent type. It was, in fact, like the man in the street's, a view, which is how an object looks from outside; and Mr. Wells' imagination was affected by this view in two ways. The naïve delight in the practical achievements of science that distinguishes the savage and the adolescent European became for Mr. Wells a permanent obsession. The conditions of scientific work and the disinterested labour of the scientist provided for his awakening religious instincts the moral ideal unattainable by self and the object of worship they required. Since the love of truth, in short, was not sufficient to keep Mr. Wells at the laboratory bench (where, as he believes, truth is to be found), undivided reverence for the love of truth was the least he could profess instead. So genuinely a religious procedure deserved, and attained, success; the demands of truth satisfactorily complied with, Mr. Wells was free 'to sweep in with wide strokes the canvases designed to carry millions upwards and onwards', in the words (I quote from memory) of an eminent economist in a recent article on *The World of William Clissold*.*

But, before tracing the development of Mr. Wells' scientific religion, the fruits of his practical interest in science deserve mention. He was the first to exploit its journalistic possibilities, and a stream of spirited and entertaining short stories, fantasies, and novels, based on some newly-acquired piece of biological or psychological knowledge or recent scientific speculation, appeared and delighted the public, who felt that a fairy story with a scientific explanation might come true. At the same time, however, Mr. Wells himself appeared in print, a Mr.

* Holms is misquoting a phrase from the first paragraph of Keynes's article (No. 83).

Wells very similar in physical appearance to the Mr. Wells we know; a Mr. Wells who has retained, indeed, his physical likeness to his creator, with whom he has grown old; and with whom we are familiar under the names of Mr. Lewisham, Mr. Polly, Kipps, Mr. Ponderevo, Mr. Preemby, and many others. These creations of Mr. Wells' genuine and vivacious comic talent, or, more accurately, since Mr. Wells can create only himself, these variations on a central comic perception, are well enough known to need no description. Mr. Wells' humour and comic sense owe a great deal to Dickens, but the figure of his invention is essentially his own. It is a small scale figure, and its implications are not profound, but, as the begetter of an authentic comic creation, which is to be found in none of the pages of his contemporaries, Mr. Wells leaves us no option but to consider him as an artist. Mr. Wells, as Plato, has not a high opinion of this order of creative imagination and, as a comple- ment to the Republic of the future, has written a short history of the past of a world in which art and literature are non-existent, with the exception of some able paleolithic drawings and neolithic pottery of the Periclean age itself, and of the works of an artist of considerably later date, Leonardo da Vinci, who foresaw the steamship and aeroplane. In these circumstances it will be interesting to see how Mr. Wells puts on the New Man, and sublimates the artist in the interest of his religion, which is the religion of science, of the subjection of the universe to man by hard, clear, remorseless thinking, in the words of Mr. Wells, or, to put it more simply, by the capacity to discover and adhere to the truth.

Leaving aside his scientific romances, Mr. Wells exploited the discovery of himself as a comic figure in several books of minor but authentic value, of which *Mr. Polly* is, perhaps, the best. Mr. Wells' religion, beyond a vague socialism, had not yet taken shape; and in common with other works of talent, these owe their value to the instinc- tive and consistent fidelity of their author to what we may call artistic truth, to distinguish it from the scientific truth to which he was shortly to transfer his adherence. *Tono-Bungay* marks the first step in his regeneration; and, appropriately enough, the old man and new man, struggling in Mr. Wells' breast, issue forth in uncle and nephew, Edward Ponderevo and George: the one destined to a flare of creative ecstasy and an ignominious end; the other, freeing himself with difficulty from the old man's toils, to emerge as the first incarnation of Mr. Wells' religion, to herald the salvation of man by science through the invention of starker and speedier destroyers, and, incidentally, triumphing over his lowly birth, to love and lose a lady of high degree.

Since this novel is the testament of Mr. Wells' conversion, and contains in uncle the gist of what he had written, in nephew the gist of what he was to write, it is worth some consideration. Mr. Wells' readers will recall how the rising tide of Tono-Bungay floats Uncle Ponderevo on the sole plank of a talent for publicity from a small chemist's shop to a fantastic affluence that finally turns his head and involves him in forgery and disaster. Besides containing many admirable comic scenes, the whole forms a spirited extravaganza, based on a substantial and accurate criticism of life, until we reach Mr. Ponderevo's downfall; which might, indeed, have occurred, but since a satirist's business is with the typical, is a regrettable lapse into convention. I am unacquainted with the ingredients or the history of Beecham's pills, but it seems to be the rule that, if bankruptcy is to supervene at all in such successful affairs, it is left to the next generation to incur it. However, let us leave Uncle Ponderevo, who represents life as Mr. Wells sees it, and turn to George Ponderevo, the spokesman of life as Mr. Wells would like it to be. George's reflections at the close of the volume are worth quoting at length, as an early summary of Mr. Wells' religious faith, the substance of which, with admirable and unrecognized consistency, he has repeated but not improved upon in every succeeding book. So characteristic are they in fact that George's concluding words may be found by the incredulous reader printed, presumably with Mr. Wells' consent, opposite the title-page of each volume of his collected works; and shorn to the simplicity of Greek they are echoed in the motto to William Clissold: 'We are all things that make and pass, striving upon a hidden mission, out to the open sea', concludes George; *panta rei* concludes William.

[Quotes *Tono-Bungay*, Bk IV, ch. 3 'Through it we dodged' to 'out to the open sea'.]

Before commenting, perhaps unnecessarily, on this passage, some sentences from Mr. Wells' preface to *William Clissold* may be recalled:

And one other question may be glanced at here before this note concludes. There is much discussion of opinion in this book. Does that make it anything but a novel? Is it not quite as much life to meet and deal with a new idea as to meet and deal with a new lover? Must the characters in our English and American novels be for evermore as cleaned of thought as a rabbit is of its bowels, before they can be served up for consumption?

Since Mr. Wells invites us then to the banquet of thought, we may accompany humanity in the person of George Ponderevo into the great spaces of the future, to windy freedom and trackless ways. What carries him to this happy destination is a destroyer, used by Mr. Wells (a shorter name than Ponderevo) as a symbol of Science, or Truth, because, as he tells us, it is irrelevant to most human interests. The significance of a destroyer is presumably destruction, which it is surprising to find Mr. Wells considers as irrelevant to human interests. But, apparently, Mr. Wells' prophetic élan would flag without the imaginative stimulus of the killing of men in unfamiliar lands. Or, perhaps, Mr. Wells really means to suggest that Science, or Truth, is destructive to humanity which, if George is to be admitted as an exemplar, is at least an arguable opinion. But no, Mr. Wells sees it as the heart of life, as the one enduring thing. He sees it also as austerity, as beauty, which is surprising too, both in view of the prose wherein he celebrates it and of the final consummation he suggests for it, which is the windy freedom of the unknown. It is a pity, moreover, that, having referred to a Kiplingese surpassing in turgidity and degeneracy his own, Mr. Wells did not invent a sample of it for our astonishment. Finally, to cut a silly business short, it is instructive to observe that Mr. Wells omits from his symbolism the most evident essential, which is the due and necessary return of the destroyer from windy freedom to her moorings in the Thames; though this consideration would interfere, it is true, with the inspired and cloacal imagery of his peroration.

One other quotation—chosen at random, for it is a matter on which he feels keenly and lays frequent emphasis—will fitly conclude this example of Mr. Wells' thought. Mr. Barnstaple, in *Men Like Gods*, is learning the principles of Utopian Society.

And that brought him to the fourth Principle of Liberty, which was that Lying is the Blackest Crime. Crystal's definition of Lying was a sweeping one; the inexact statement of facts, even the suppression of a material fact, was Lying. Where there are lies there cannot be freedom. . . . Lying the Primary Crime! How simple that is! How true and necessary it is! That dogma is the fundamental distinction of the scientific world state from all preceding states.

What then we have to discover is how the author of George Ponderevo's meditations, selected as characteristic of many thousands of pages written by Mr. Wells, of which at once the most accurate and charitable definition is an 'inexact statement of facts', can, at the same time, be sincerely persuaded that Lying is the Blackest Crime. Stated in these terms, indeed, so common a phenomenon scarcely demands

classification. The principles of religious psychology are always illuminating, however, since they are simple, profound, and universal. To
adopt Mr. Wells' formula, one or two of them might run as follows.
The first Principle: Since service, not self, is the goal of life, truth is for
others' consumption, not one's own; therefore, II: It is at once nobler
and more useful to proclaim truth than to observe it; and a third may be
added for the benefit of artists: Represent what you would like to see,
not what you see. It would be gratuitous to pillory Mr. Wells for
adherence to such commonly accepted principles were it not that he
flies the flag not of religion, but of science, which deserves a better
advertisement. Moreover, he would still prefer, he tells us with some
acrimony, that his novels should be considered and judged as the works
of an artist; and since the distinction between art and imitation, between
the Old and the New man, between Uncle Ponderevo and William
Clissold is one of truth, some elementary discussion of the subject is
unavoidable.

The pre-eminent aspect of reality for Mr. Wells, as for others, is
himself and his own experience; an exact statement of the facts of this
reality seems, therefore, of pre-eminent importance if we are to believe
Mr. Wells that Lying is the Blackest Crime. And, indeed, Mr. Wells'
exact perception of one category of facts about himself bore appropriate
fruit in comic creation, which happened to be his particular method of
accepting and assimilating the important piece of reality represented by
himself, and thereby reality as a whole. This reality was a comic one,
it may be added, because Mr. Wells, observing human life in the person
of himself, perceived as its first and essential characteristic the discrepancy
between desire and fulfilment, between pretension and performance,
between noble ideals and ignoble practice, which it is the function of
the comic artist to perceive as essential reality and exploit. Such was,
and is, we must believe, the reality as Mr. Wells sees it, since this is the
only reality he has communicated to us. Man, however, is created to
create himself; and in *Tono-Bungay* Mr. Wells began the necessary
substitution of the world he would like to see and the Mr. Wells he
would like to see for the world and the Mr. Wells he saw. Whatever
Mr. Wells now describes, whether it is a woman, a love affair, society,
a statesman, himself under many aliases, the world as it is, was, or will
be, we are sure of being told, not what Mr. Wells sees, which since he
is a man of talent might be of interest to others, but what he would
like to see, which is of no interest to anyone but himself. For the world
Mr. Wells would like to see and has described for us, in place of the

world he sees, in many books, resembles all such worlds in being the image of the sometimes vulgar, sometimes puerile desires and vanities of the average sensual man, more or less envious, more or less callous, and more or less dishonest.

The discrepancy between what Mr. Wells sees and would like to see is most evident, as is to be expected, despite his efforts, when he is describing matters in which his desires are most closely engaged, such as the relations between the sexes, and social life. The snobbery of social reformers is a historical commonplace, but what is amusing in the private life of a revolutionary is inharmonious in a novel; and Mr. Wells' Tennysonian feats in this line can only be equalled by his master, on whom, indeed, he has modelled his style so closely that the two, discounting the exigencies of blank verse, are frequently indistinguishable: 'I was there from college, visiting the son—the son a Walter, too—with others of our set, five others; we were seven at Vivian Place'. The resemblance in fact goes farther, and Mr. Wells' scientific religion, besides his social aspirations, is closely paralleled in the poet. 'Mechanophilus' ('In the time of the first railways') in style and thought, is a remarkable anticipation of George Ponderevo:

Now first we stand and understand, and sunder false from true, and handle boldly with the hand, and see and shape and do. Dash back that ocean with a pier, strow yonder mountain flat, a railway there, a tunnel here. . . . Far as the Future vaults her skies, from this my vantage ground to those still-working energies I spy nor term nor bound.

Only Lord Tennyson or Mr. Wells could have signed the phrase 'and handle boldly with the hand', so obscure in the context. Mr. Wells' treatment of the relations of the sexes, in which also a strong if modernized Tennysonian flavour is discoverable, suffers proportionately with his treatment of society. Mr. Wells, as many men, would like women to be what he calls mates, if not precisely because this would afford a simpler means of gratifying his desires than is available among women possessing the psychological characteristics that distinguish them at present, but, at any rate, because this would be some kind of a solution for the present physical and spiritual complications of sexual love, and in particular a welcome relief from the burden of masculine responsibility. He would also like woman to be gracious, austere, like 'a black princess waving a sword', and so on, which is uncommon in reality. Down go Mr. Wells' love scenes accordingly as he would like them to be, and as, one must conclude, he persuades himself they have been in his experience. My dear! is the usual cry of one mate to the other. My dear! signifying a world of gracious and austere implications and urgencies. The disadvantage of premising women to be something they are not, however, is the liability to a righteous indignation when forced to discover what they are; and this Mr. Wells cannot always avoid letting slip into his books, with an effect that is not only artistically but morally distasteful. To mention a recent example, despite Mr. Wells' singular claim to dramatic irresponsibility for his characters in the preface to *Clissold*, the quality of the writing dealing with the characters of Clissold's wife and mother reveals a vindictiveness and insensibility for which William cannot, unhappily, be held responsible.

Nevertheless, if Mr. Wells' preference for describing what he would like to see is incompatible with the novelist's function of communicating the reality he sees, the artist's loss, it may be argued, is the prophet's gain, whose function is the communication of a reality superior to the actual. What we have not seen, however, we cannot communicate; a vision is something seen, and the prophet differs only from the artist in perceiving another kind of reality. What we would like to see, on the other hand, we dream about; and Mr. Wells has so long been occupied in dreaming of what he would like to see that he has had no time to see either the reality of this world or another. The Utopias of a writer whose fundamental sense of reality is comedic cannot in any case be expected to carry more conviction than any other worlds of wish-fulfilment achieved by the suppression of reality. On this definition, Mr. Wells has for a long time written nothing but Utopias, and his descriptions of the world as it will be do not differ from his descriptions of the world as it is, in his novels, or as it was, in his history, except in so far as he can indulge his personal predilections unhampered by any necessity of relating them to reality. In these circumstances, it is not surprising that the world depicted in his Utopias is even less prepossessing than that of his novels, though it must in justice be admitted that Mr. Wells evinces some dissatisfaction with his Utopias himself, and usually provides them with a further outlet among the stars, where it is to be presumed that our desires, if not fulfilled, will assume the graciousness and austerity regrettably denied them in the small breeding-ground of a single planet.

But, indeed, it is evident that to accord Mr. Wells, despite his protestations, the harsh treatment due to a thinker or an artist is to do him an injustice. Many men write nonsense, which many others are glad to read, and nobody is possibly the worse. Moreover, Mr. Wells does not always, even latterly, write nonsense, and as an educational publicist he has no rival. *The Outline of History*, in spite of obvious and lamentable errors in taste, in accuracy, and in proportion, could have been achieved so successfully for its purpose by no other contemporary. Such gifts, if not of the highest quality, are both rare and useful; and no purpose would be served by depreciating them, had their owner never given evidence of possessing others. But, since Mr. Wells' progression to quasi-religious publicist has been by way of the artist, it seems worth demonstrating from his own works that a page of comedy contains more actual truth than a library of exhortation to that end; and that an exact statement of the facts of experience conveys a more lively notion of dignity and freedom than the most high-minded spate of imaginary Utopias, love affairs, and discussions, bestrewn with the painful adjectives under which Mr. Wells at once conceals and reveals his dissatisfaction with human nature in himself and others.

86. Freda Kirchwey on Wells as the ideal father

28 November 1928

'A Private Letter to H. G. Wells', *Nation* (New York), cxxvii, 576.

Freda Kirchwey was editor of the *Nation* from 1932 to 1955.

Dear Mr. Wells:

Although you do not know me from Eve and as likely as not would disown me if you met me, I am, as you English would say, by way of being one of your daughters. Only in the most figurative sense, of course. Actually I have an excellent father who offered me a cigarette and your novels at almost exactly the same time—when I was about sixteen years old. I imagine he knew I was likely to adopt you as a sort of secondary parent and was willing enough to share the job.

I recall riding in a night train from New York toward the Adirondack Mountains and reading on the way a new novel, *Ann Veronica*. Beside me was seated a stout, gray dignitary who knew my family. 'Does your father allow you to read that sort of book?' he asked me. 'I read them first,' I said, 'and then I decide whether to allow him to.' You can see that the Wellsian influence was already at work. By adopting a new father at that viscous age I took shape gradually in his image: pert, undignified, irreverent, headlong, hopeful, ready to alter everything including myself into almost anything different.

And not only I. By the same process, a whole generation of cocky, iconoclastic young men and women came into being. Of course, you were not our only father. Mr. Wells. There were others, particularly Mr. Galsworthy and Mr. Shaw. Together you formed a sort of Unholy Trinity, a symbol of all that seemed daring and wicked and promising in those pre-war years. So much of us was bound up in you and your creeds that when Virginia Woolf with her thin sharp knife quite recently unfleshed your bones, we felt the blade along our own nerves and shrank slightly—even while we admired her deft and hardy courage.

But you were the most energetic and intimate of our fathers. You covered so much ground. You opened so many doors. You delighted and excited and angered us. You offered us all the world in tempting cans with lively labels: Socialism, Free Love, Marriage, Education, World Organization, and H. G. Wells's Patented Feminism—Very Perishable. Down they went. And gradually, on this varied if not always digestible diet, the children grew older.

You know what happened; it often happens to the better sort of fathers. You stayed just exactly the same age; but we grew up. For long periods we stopped associating with you; then we would run into you again. 'He hasn't changed in ten years,' we would say admiringly; or, 'He doesn't seem a day older. How does he do it?' The war came; and there you were being intelligent, hopeful, inquiring about the war. The Russian Revolution burst—and you were there as the sparks descended. You launched a religion or two and unhorsed a couple of rather worn-out deities. You wrote a history of the universe. You condensed it. You sniffed the smoke of the General Strike, and wrote *Meanwhile*. Then, not long ago, you began to map the future, the whole future, to visualize more completely the organizing of the race, the creation of a social purpose, the international control of the collective interests of mankind. In short, you wrote a book on What to Do About Everything, and promised several more to follow. And in the midst of this project you took time out to write a very pleasant sort of novel or fantasy with sermons attached, called *Mr. Blettsworthy on Rampole Island* which brings us down past the execution of Sacco and Vanzetti.

So here you are, right to the minute, with ideas, humor, plans, romances, charts, slogans, energy, erudition, religion, science, hope. . . . And where are we—the generation you so obviously and inescapably begot? Some of us are dead—because people didn't listen to you before the war began. The rest of us have grown skeptical. We smile paternally every time a new book by you appears and we read one of them now and then if it isn't about religion. We smile and then we go on as we are—expecting little, doing less, seeing and understanding somewhat more. We have lost most of the brash impetuosity and expectant eagerness that characterized our pre-war years. We are not even as pert as we were. War and revolution and peace have combined to make us wary of programs and dubious of collective purposes, especially those developing from the enterprise of 'stronger and better men' than we. We are the Mr. Blettsworthys of your world, Mr. Wells. You tell us, out of the mouth of your latest personal spokesman, Mr. Graves, that 'this world is full now of enterprise. Confused, conflicting, disorganized, aimless, if you like, but here it is. . . .' We grant the enterprise; it has created an exciting and in some ways a pleasant world. But how much of it is being spent on organizing the equitable distribution of rubber and oil and cotton and coal or in intelligently planning for peace? Such organization may be attempted one day, if the Western World holds together, but not, we suspect, because wise and strong people 'are feeling their way; making their plans.' Rather because great pressures produce slight shifts.

Still, don't let's argue about that; it would take all night. Let us agree to differ. Let us admit that you are young and we are old and the generation that is just behind us is older still. Let us admit that, from your point of view, your children didn't turn out very well. The truth is, I've been disagreeing with you ever since I adopted you. First about feminism; then about marriage; then about religion. And now about everything. (Particularly, I think you did the natives of Rampole Island a serious injustice; only the seamy side of primitive customs seems to attract your attention.) All in all, I should say that this state of universal disagreement between us proves that you are the ideal father.

August 1927

87. T. E. Lawrence, unsigned review in *Spectator*

25 February 1928, cxl, 268–9

The author of *Seven Pillars of Wisdom* wrote this review while serving in the Royal Air Force as Aircraftman T. E. Shaw. It appeared over the initials 'C.D.', which stood for 'Colin Dale', the name of the Underground station, Colindale, next to Hendon Aerodrome. Reprinted in *Men in Print* (1940).

One thousand one hundred and fifty pages of H. G. Wells's short stories for 7s. 6d. It is amazing value for money. Probably they are renumbered stereos of another edition, otherwise Messrs. Benn could hardly have done it. It is nearly as difficult to see how Wells did it. In this collection are sixty-three stories, none negligible, some very long. My memory vaguely suggests to me others not here included. Besides this decent life-output for a short-story writer Wells has the achievement of his massive *History*, and a shelf of novels, and miscellaneous prose-work, literary or political. His drafts would tell us if this huge production is due to industry or to a happy fluency. His writings let us into so many workshops and laboratories that we would like to see his own.

This sudden bulk of tales seems a chance to distinguish the profile of H. G. Wells, the prose artist. In his mature novels we cannot see the writer for the dust of his manly activities. He preaches and argues and attacks, has theories and practical programmes, tries to get something done. This rôle of politician and sociologist he imposes upon the primal artist. Indeed, he spares little admiration for pure writing which he thinks a fad of emasculate amateurs. Yet he cannot keep out of his work that secret rhythm which its sentences (bare of relative clauses, and dependents, and adjectives, and participles) hold somewhere in their structure. So that any person with an ear and knowledge of letters, after about six lines, says 'Wells,' and is right every time. At his highest he writes magnificently; and deliberately always; never falling below adequacy: only the stuff of the novels is too contentious to show us a clean edge. In these shorter pieces he is determined to entertain and to relieve his imagination of a burdening idea: there is no ephemeral moral underlying them.

It would be scientific to date each tale, and consider Wells as a growth, like an oak-tree. The publishers have grouped them, irrelevantly, to give their bulk palatable variety. If we undo their work, and classify each sort apart, we are in a position to examine the complete phenomenon of H. G. where he stands full-high, as an entertainer. Then we see at once that the futurities—those jugglings with the time-sense for which he is very famous—are only a scrap of his collection. There are five such stories, depending primarily on the time-sense, and three others into which it enters. Not much, in sixty-three. There are only four stories radically concerned with mechanisms, another notorious side of his invention. To me this quantitative insignificance of his most reputed side came as a shock. Nor did these seem his very good stories. They date. Man-made things grow queer to our eyes, sooner than the queer shapes of ourselves. Wells lasts better where he deals with human nature, which varies as slowly as the structure of men's bodies. The best of us would be as good (after a year's apprenticeship) as the best Cro-Magnon men, if our time were suddenly put back.

The next thing to come out, overwhelmingly, was the standpoint of the student of biology. The trend or evidence of science everywhere obsesses the mind which wrote: but it is a humble mind, prepared to hold everything as possible—the genuine, unmixed humility of the student-investigator on the threshold of science. There is not a trace of the professorial mood and no presumption of deep knowledge. There are five stories which declare themselves aloud as the trial or apprenticeship pieces of the laboratory student beginning to write, with the materials provided by his class-rooms and text-books. Only, as it happens, they are not his first work!

A true-blue biologist would see man only in his place in nature. Wells must have been engrossed in the problems of personality before he came to study science. Five of these stories deal with aberrations of personality. Aberrations—yes: but not one queer man amongst them. His queerest things are done by ordinary people. Six stories deal intensely with Nature, the Huxleian Nature; only H. G. is an alienist among biologists. For him the aberrations of Nature, its sports and freaks, its violent rejections of the norm—these are the fascinations.

The student of life shifts his gaze from the eye-piece of his microscope to universal nature. Six stories deal with world-exchanging, with transmutations of spheres or entities. In them the author is heavy with material, and takes a very long time to get off the ground. He has not the nature to be happy in blind space. He cannot be tremendous. He likes to anchor his strangenesses to some familiarity, to make concrete his vision by focussing it on the light outlining the back of a woolly rhinoceros, on the control levers of an indescribable machine. Yet he does not really describe even the levers, he makes us think he has described them. The method slips into the grotesque in his sub-oceanic story 'In the Abyss.' Perhaps his own imagining is not often very strange and he feels uneasy when he loses sight, for long, of earth and pavements.

Thirty-one stories, so far: and he has finished with the stars. Half of this collection is of the earth and of mankind, familiar. In them he is on common ground with his peers; and we look eagerly for adherences and affiliations. In two instances there is a trace of Wilde; and here and there a little of the *Yellow Book* carefulness of step. Good schools of prose, these, for a man having no preoccupation with the graceful; who does not even, like Butler, try to say his say at its very plainest. Later there is a hint of Kipling, and two essays in the fatuous which remind me of *Three Men in a Boat*; but these reflections are not the manner—Wells remains an integer as stylist—but a situation or setting. He has never belonged for more than a moment to fashion or movement or clique. What a panorama, what diversity of literary modes fill the backward gaze of a man who began writing in the end of the eighties, and is still a producing artist, with mind yet unfixed, to-day! Homer was more near to Peisistratus than 1886 to us.

Of these thirty-two entertainments twelve seem to be just entertainments. Perhaps no one else could have written them; but perhaps it would not have mattered if Wells had been lazy on their day. Six others partake of the age of overseas adventure, which followed the decline of Kipling. They are excellent. Three or four throw a passing glance at magic, that toy for tired intellects. One story, 'The Door in the Wall,' is a very lovely thing, and seems rather by itself—like a gloss on an E. M. Forster fragment.

'An intimation of beauty,' say the publishers: half the tales deserve that heading. See, for example, how horror flowers under Wells's hands. There are six stories of the succession of Poe; they are too good to be called Grand Guignol, so compact are they with painful beauty and strength and passion: 'The Cone,' 'The Reconciliation,' 'The Lord of the Dynamos.' Besides these are a few parables, for a quiet close to the set. One is a satire, not very acute; another, 'The Pearl of Love,' seems to me a fancy to be proud of. Its full cup of sentiment does not brim over, nor its rich prose become precious.

In such analysis of the forms of these sixty-three stories the grave rare comeliness which is their common denominator has been neglected; and Wells himself, the writer, has slipped through the meshes of my thinking. Always he does. We take for granted so above-board a man. He seems to show himself fully, and we forget he is only showing us what he pleases. Generalizations about H. G. must needs be tentative; for they cannot be maintained against challenge.

As regards his characters, the greatest in this volume is 'I,' who colours the whole with himself. There seems not one queer *soul* in the sixty-three. Wells deals more with events and externals than with motives, and uses lay figures as pegs for his costumes. It is easier to arrange the necessary incidents on a stock character—a character which the author has used so often that he need not explain it to himself or to his readers. Wells sees his men as a part of things, and is tempted to make matter as mobile as man. He knows that there is no wonder in the machinery of the senses, but only incompleteness in them. His descriptive work lacks colour. The sense he most calls upon is the visual one. Yet his exactest picture will not make into a drawing. The generalness of his landscape is surprising. You don't catch breath with 'That's Surrey, that's its picture.' The bay of page 355 might be Devon or California, or Malaya. You can feel it, and yourself in it, but it does not take hold of you with any sharpness of its own. Probably Wells would remove, as a blemish, any detail which did take the reader's attention from the business of the story. He is wonderfully adequate, as craftsman, over all his unexampled range. For exact subordination of means few English writers better earn the attribute classical—in respect to his short stories. In the novels, his men and women sometimes mutiny and exceed his plan: it was nearly inevitable with the fierceness of characterization demanded by the novel of twenty years ago.

He angles throughout for a wide public. To most writers, after their beginning book, there comes this fork in the road—whether to care first for what is to be bound between their covers, or for the suffrages of all the people outside. Wells would not have us think him interested in form (though incidentally an invisible H.G. takes good care of what Mr. Wells would disregard), and his characters are meant to mean something to most people. Not for him the lofty solitary soul, but the gregarious fellow, clubbable either in pub or in Athenaeum. The tales have almost no recognizable women. They are not touched in, except for Elizabeth in 'The Days to Come.' Yet even Elizabeth you would not know in the street, as you know Altiora Bailey.

Doubtless it is deliberate, this drawing upon the untapped resources of the readers' minds. It saves space in development. The sudden subtlety of a plain-faced man is like to be overwhelming. Wells will operate for pages in a quietude as fine as Jane Austen's, and suddenly fling in a rarity, like a whale's *bulla*, and make it justify tragedy. Yet even the tragedy is controlled.

Perhaps in the end we should come back to his student ambitions for the secret of Wells's individuality as a short-story writer. The interest in biology has mated happily with his concern for the mass of human nature to make him a general practitioner in the diseases of creation: his consciousness of life as an organism has made him the cosmic doctor. One-third of this volume is extracted from the case-book of his practice and details the patients' ills and treatment: aberrations of nature, of matter, of personality. There is a complete absence of quackery and of specialist absorption. Alienist was, perhaps, too strong a word for him, since for alienists often no normal man exists: whereas Wells is sure of the sane core within his creation.

THE WORK, WEALTH AND HAPPINESS OF MANKIND

February 1932

88. F. R. Leavis, review in *Scrutiny*

May 1932, i, 80–3

F. R. Leavis (b. 1895), literary critic and editor of *Scrutiny* from 1932 to 1953. This review appeared in the first number of *Scrutiny* and incorporates a characteristic statement of the magazine's position.

'Few people' notes Mr. Wells on page 199, 'can be trusted to cut and arrange their own toe-nails well.' He is describing, with the detail that this extract suggests, the particular advance of civilization represented by the beautician's parlour. 'Museums are littered with the rouge cups, trays, manicure sets, mirrors and pots for greases and messes, of the pretty ladies of Sumeria, Egypt and Babylonia, and thence right down to our own times; but never can the organization of human adornment have reached the immensity and subtlety shown by these American figures.' No, there may be archness, but there is no irony in Mr. Wells's account of the up-to-date ritual. 'But, you will say, this is a very exceptional woman, and indeed this is a superfluous section to insert in a survey of world economics!' Wrong! Before long, Mr. Wells implies, many more hundreds of millions a year will be spent on these things, and in a Utopia not very remote (if we will listen to Mr. Wells) *every* woman will enjoy the advantages of rouging, face-lifting, massage, pedicure, manicure, greases and messes even more scientific. This fairly represents the essential triviality of a large part of *The Work, Wealth and Happiness of Mankind.*

And yet Mr. Wells's directing idea—'the re-orientation of loyalties through a realisation of the essential unity of our species'—is not trivial. To this he has devoted his life with a noble disinterestedness. So I reminded myself when, having first thought of replying to the editors of *Scrutiny* that Mr. Wells is, at this date, not worth reviewing, I started on this his latest book. We may find it hard to like or respect him, but he is doing work that needs doing and that at the moment seems terribly urgent. Yet we must also remind ourselves that the more his kind of influence seems likely to prevail (and the process of civilization works with it) the more urgent is drastic criticism. If he belongs to the past it is only in the sense that it has long been impossible to discuss him seriously except as a case, a type, a portent. As such, he matters. More and more the disinterested power in the world seems likely to be Wellsian. Mr. J. M. Keynes hailed *The World of William Clissold* as a distinguished and important book. So the essential points are perhaps worth making once again.

Mr. Wells energizes tirelessly on behalf of a 'world-machine, planned and efficient, protecting and expanding human life. . . .' And, if there is not a speedy approximation to such a machine the un-Wellsian preoccupations of some of us will, it is plain, soon cease to trouble us or the world. But once the machine is smoothly running, what then? What is this 'expanding,' this 'richer,' life, what are these infinite 'possibilities,' that Mr. Wells promises us, or rather, the species? Roger Bacon knew (according to Mr. Wells) that if men would listen to him, 'Vision and power would reward them. Steamship, aeroplane and auto-mobile, he saw them all, and many other things.' Steamship, aeroplane and automobile, and many other things, have already rewarded us. Does 'expanding life' mean more and more 'vision and power' of this kind? Mr. Wells notoriously thinks it the duty of the civilized man to own or use the latest products of civilization, and I knew a French friend of his who thought this sense of duty vulgar. But it is plain that what Mr. Wells says of Edison might be adapted to himself: to him 'the delights offered by the luxury trades must have seemed extraordinarily stupid.' He has found fulfilment in his life's work. He can find his Utopia satisfactory because he has found his actual life satisfactory.

But there are some of us to whom the satisfactions of Edison and Mr. Wells, when offered as ultimate ends, seem insufficient. And Mr. Wells is not unaware of this perversity of human nature. He even devotes the twelfth, and last, volume of his ideal World Encyclopædia to 'beauty.' 'In it aesthetic criticism would pursue its wild, incalculable, unstandard-ized career, mystically distributing praise and blame. . . . The artist in his studio, the composer in his music room and all the multitude who invent and write down their inventions, have hardly figured in our world panorama, and even now we can give them but a passing sentence or two. They are an efflorescence, a lovely and purifying efflorescence on life.'—In this essay on the Happiness of Mankind, we can give them but a passing sentence or two. Mr. Wells, of course, believes that if we look after the machinery, they will look after themselves. But the perverse among us persist in urging that looking after the machinery should mean seeing that it works to desired ends, and that a world that gives no more attention to the 'lovely efflorescence' than Mr. Wells does is likely not to know what it desires; the efficiency of the machinery becomes the ultimate value, and this seems to us to mean something very different from expanding and richer human life.

Mr. Wells, however, is not interested in this kind of question. And it is for this reason that his book, for all its wealth of information, has a total effect of triviality: the energy that made it seem to the author worth writing is indistinguishable from a schoolboy immaturity of mind. Mr. Wells is praised for his interest in the world, but he is not interested enough. 'The story of New Zealand is particularly illuminating,' he notes. It is: I know someone who is enquiring why New Zealand has developed nothing in the nature of a distinctive literature. But Mr. Wells's notion of an educated man is one to whom such questions wouldn't be worth troubling about.

Yet inadvertently (he is not an athletic thinker) he admits their importance—and unwittingly passes judgment on himself. 'One peculiar value of the "Five Towns" novels of Mr. Arnold Bennett lies in the clear, convincing, intimate, and yet almost unpremeditated way in which he shows the industrialized peasant mentality of the employing class in a typical industrialized region, The Black Country, waking up to art and refinement, to ampler personality and new ideas'—The Wellsian man *will* wake up to 'art' and 'refinement' and 'ampler personality' and it will be in Mr. Arnold Bennett's way—a way that, we know, ended in the Imperial Palace Hotel. In spite of Edison's asceticism the inventor, the researcher, the man who gets things done, will seek his guerdon of the 'luxury trades.' And perhaps even Mr. Wells does not find his work and his Vision quite self-sufficing. Perhaps his interest in beauty-culture is significant. And it is perhaps permissible to suggest that specialized sexual charm counts for more in his scheme of things than a mature mind could think worthy; Mr. Wells will not blush.

But he might, perhaps, blush if one pointed out the falsities of his book in matters of fact. Take, for instance, his naïve account of beauti-cianry: he pays here, as the articles on the Beauty Racket published recently in the *New Republic* might bring home to him, involuntary tribute to the power of advertising that he acclaims elsewhere. Again, he has swallowed with completely uncritical innocence the official Ford legend. Let him read *The Tragedy of Henry Ford* by Jonathan Norton Leonard. This book is just out, but so much was already common knowledge that Mr. Wells cannot be acquitted of complicity—he was not an unwilling gull. This may seem a severe verdict. But read him on the 'ultra-scholastic education' that the 'citizen' gets from news-papers, radio, cinema, and so on (pp. 745ff.): 'On the whole, it is sound stuff he gets.' I know that Mr. Wells's criteria are not mine; but even by his own what he lets out elsewhere is enough to brand his complacency as something worse.

We can respect him as we cannot respect Arnold Bennett, but it is significant that, for all his disinterestedness, he is not safe from the Arnold Bennett corruption.

RETROSPECTIVE AND OBITUARY

89. T. S. Eliot, Wells as journalist

New English Weekly, 8 February 1940, xvi, 237–8

Eliot wrote this article during the 'phoney war' period when a
discussion of the Rights of Man initiated by Wells (and fore-
shadowing the United Nations Human Rights Convention) was
taken up eagerly by the British and foreign press.

No one can have failed to observe that since the beginning of this war
two men, whom we had thought of as slowly and unwillingly retiring
from public life, have emerged into a glare of prominence. I mean Mr.
Churchill and Mr. Wells. They must be nearly contemporary; they
were both men of celebrity, I remember, when I was a freshman. Both
have spoken and written a great deal in the last thirty-odd years; neither
possesses what one could call a *style*, though each has a distinct idiom:
that of Mr. Wells being more like a durable boiler suit, and that of
Mr. Churchill more like a court dress of rather tarnished grandeur from
a theatrical costumier's. I do not know what they have in common,
except that at an age when one would expect them to be withdrawing
to the contemplative life, they are embarking on new and furious
careers. I do not speak in disparagement: I do not suggest that either of
them ought to retire—on the contrary. Nobody needs retire until the
world is so changed that he has nothing to say to it. The interesting
thing is that the world has not changed; that Mr. Wells and Mr.
Churchill can go on because there is still a public for them to direct—
and because there is no one else to direct it. The situation is so odd that
it is worth a moment's consideration.

My own generation does not seem to have produced either a great
demagogue—such as have been Mr. Churchill and Mr. Lloyd George—
or a great journalist—such as have been Mr. Wells, Mr. Shaw and Mr.
Chesterton. I am not, in this context, using either term, 'demagogue' or

'journalist,' in any but the most favourable sense. Of men highly gifted for journalism—in this most favourable sense—there have been several. For instance, Mr. Wyndham Lewis, Mr. Middleton Murry and Mr. John Macmurray all have the necessary fluency, earnestness and desire to influence as large an audience as possible; and Mr. Lewis, at least, is unquestionably a writer of as great genius as Mr. Wells. Yet none of them has ever been listened to by more than a minority public; and as for the men of my time who have been able to capture a large audience, I believe they are all, by comparison with Mr. Wells, pygmies. By individual comparison of gifts alone, ample reason can be found for Mr. Wells's success. Mr. Wells started as a popular entertainer, and his advantages of education gave him the opportunity to exploit 'popular science' for a generation all ready to suspend disbelief in favour of this form of romance. To this paying activity he brought imagination of a very high order: some of his short stories, such as 'The Country of the Blind,' and certain scenes from his romances, such as the description of sunrise on the moon in *The First Men in the Moon*, are quite unforget-table. Later, he employed remarkable gifts as a recorder in chronicles of the sort of society in which he took his origins. Through being a popular entertainer, he found an opening as a prophet—the nearest parallel in the last few years is Miss Dorothy Sayers. None of my contemporaries of a distinction at all comparable to that of Mr. Wells has started by this popular appeal of entertainment. And I think that this is more than a personal difference; it is the difference of a generation.

The world into which Mr. Wells—and the late Arnold Bennett—arrived (the same world, really, as that of Lord Stamp) was a world of 'getting on.' For the ambitious youth of literary gifts and humble origins, the first thing—sensibly enough—was to make a living by giving the public its entertainment; when one had got sufficiently established, then one might be free, either to devote oneself to a work of literary art, or to preach openly to a public which is docile and respectful to success. In the course of this rough experience Mr. Wells probably learned a number of things about writing—about 'putting over' ideas to the large public—which his juniors have never learnt. He also suffered, because of his period, in a way in which younger men have not suffered. He exhibits, for example, a curious sensitiveness about his origins: in a recent contribution to the *Fortnightly* he rebukes the younger generation for grudging him in middle age the modest competence which is no more than his due in consideration of his straitened youth. I cannot help comparing him here with the man whom

I consider the greatest journalist, in the best sense of the term, of my time: Charles Péguy. Péguy was a peasant, and makes you feel that he took a deep pride in his origins. But the difference between Mr. Wells and my own generation is of another kind. I cannot think of any good English writer of my generation who is either sensitive because of being humbly born, or who puts on airs because of being well born: the distinction is of no interest among writers. Perhaps it is partly that we have found ourselves in a position in which 'getting on' was always out of the question. There was nowhere to get to. That kind of success, for a serious man of letters, is no longer possible.

The serious journalism of my generation is all minority journalism. That is more than a difference between Mr. Wells and my contemporaries; it is a difference between the worlds into which they were born. The crowd of season-ticket holders is still there—it is bigger than ever—reading Mr. Wells's latest in the first class as well as the third class compartment: he tells them what they are ready to accept, and part of what he says is true. His great imaginative gifts, and picture-book method, make very real to his public the situation that he describes; and as he does not reason, or draw upon any kind of wisdom inaccessible to the common man, he imposes no great strain upon the minds of his readers. And as his proposals are always in world terms, he does not ask of his readers individually any great exertion from which they would flinch. On the other hand—and this is perhaps something to be mentioned in common with Mr. Churchill after all—he is capable of a kind of bluntness which is far too rare among the loud-speaker voices of our time. Like Mr. Churchill, he is capable of putting his foot into it again and again; and this capacity for rudeness is more endearing, in the long run, than the cautious, diplomatic politeness of the people who are so careful never to put their feet into anything. There is something very refreshing about Mr. Wells's violent hostility to Christianity in general and to the Catholic Church in particular; and his words about the American attitude towards the war, and our attitude towards America, in the Fortnightly article already cited, are worth all the suave palaver and exasperating preachments to which other publicists treat that country.

There is, I believe, no place for a modern Wells to educate the public in more modern opinions. Our public is not yet in existence. We can only hope to provide thought of a very different kind and very different tendency, formed in very different categories, for a small number of thinking people prepared for new 'dogma' (in Demant's phrase). This is not to maintain an attitude of aloofness, but a realistic view of the limits of our possible effectiveness. We can have very little hope of contributing to any immediate social change; and we are more disposed to see our hope in modest and local beginnings, than in transforming the whole world at once. On the other hand, though the immediate aims are less glittering, they may prove less deceptive: for Mr. Wells, putting all his money on the near future, is walking very near the edge of despair; while we must keep alive aspirations which can remain valid throughout the longest and darkest period of universal calamity and degradation.

90. Leading article, *The Times Literary Supplement*

17 August 1946, 391

Wells had died on 13 August.

It is a poorer world without H. G. Wells. Perhaps only the middle-aged or those on whom the years bear more heavily will know how truly and how astonishingly he enriched it. For more than any other man, Mr. Shaw alone excepted it may be, it was Wells who created the popular intellectual climate of the English generation which came immediately after him, who gave inquiring purpose and direction to current thought in the era bounded by the last years of the long Victorian glory and the early years of confidence and doubt after the return of peace in 1918. Wells and Shaw: these were the educators, the prophets, the master minds of expectant youth, and not in this country only. There was a time when Wells spoke more clearly than any other man to the youth of the world.

The magic faded. The single conviction that possessed Wells lost its spell, and the more impatient, more emphatic tone of voice in which he preached salvation through the orderly planning of the progress of mankind did not secure greater attention for him. The world moved on. Yet the mind that had conceived the magnificent scientific fantasies, dreamed of an 'Open Conspiracy' to avert the threatened destruction and doom of society, and reinterpreted history from the very beginnings of life for the benefit of a world community in the making, still retained its irresistible stimulus. The torrent of ideas was never subdued in Wells. It poured forth from him in a prodigal and intoxicating flow of improvisation. And with the ideas went a rich, vital, humorous and essentially common humanity. The Wellsian novel of ideas is less or more than a novel, sometimes a good deal less, but even at his most expository or disputative level his delight in idiosyncratic character, his relish for comic incident and the warmth and sly humour of his human sympathies are almost always present. They give something of endearing quality to the creator not of Kipps alone but also of Mr. Britling and even of William Clissold.

Today it is not difficult to recognize his limitations as an artist and as a thinker. His most original work, without question, consists of the scientific romances, whose daring of fancy, often of amazingly prophetic fancy, has never been surpassed or, indeed, equalled. It is not originality, however, which distinguishes what must surely be, in spite of all its modesty of intent and in spite of all Wells's own protests in later life, the work which gives him the securest title to the affections and gratitude of posterity. When time has taken its toll of Wells it is Kipps, Mr. Polly, the Ponderevos and the others who are likely to remain. There is the imagination that outlasts change and chance. The rest is all too vulnerable to the years. Wells, it need hardly be said at this time of day, is a popularizer and educator rather than a thinker, and as such he belongs somewhat narrowly to his time and place. Boldly conceived though they are, *The Outline of History* and *The Science of Life* do little more than infect one with the author's own tireless curiosity of mind. Even so, moreover, they exhibit the fatal touch of philistinism in his thought and his still more fatal utopian positivism. Wells's faith in knowledge and reason, in brief, excluded too large, too central a part of human experience. He was for all that a very great figure of his epoch, a formative influence upon the mind and imagination of countless men and women, of society itself, and our debt to him cannot but be sincerely and gratefully acknowledged at this fateful moment of history in which we live and which in some measure he foresaw.

91. John Middleton Murry in *Adelphi*

October–December 1946, xxiii, 1–5

John Middleton Murry (1889–1957), literary critic, pacifist and editor of the *Adelphi* from 1923 to 1948.

When H. G. Wells's *Mind at the End of its Tether* appeared last November, its curious incoherence warned us that his mental grip was failing. Nevertheless, his death on August 13, 1946, at the age of 79, came with a shock. England without H. G. Wells, to many of us, will hardly be England. 'Heavens, *what* a bourgeois!' Lenin exclaimed of him after a long and famous interview. Translated out of Marxian into English that reads: 'Heavens, *what* an Englishman!'

But he was the Englishman of an age when England was undergoing a profound transition—that social upheaval which had its first large-scale political manifestation in the Liberal triumph of 1906. The speed of the change was indicated by the fact that the unprecedented triumph of the great Liberal party was the immediate prelude to its complete collapse. Of this social upheaval—accelerated by two senseless and exhausting wars—H. G. Wells was, in some sort, the embodiment. He had moved with startling speed from existence under the shadow of the great aristocratic country house, through apprenticeship to a draper's, to a scholarship and a brilliant degree* at the new Imperial College of Science at South Kensington, and thence to an immediate, dazzling and entirely deserved success in imaginative fiction, based on a combination of sheer literary genius and a unique apprehension of the possibilities of applied science. *The Time Machine*, written in a few weeks in 1895, gave him an international reputation: and within a few years he had become the chief representative of English literature upon the European continent. In every bookshop in France you would see, in the early years of this century, the impressive rows of his translated works. It grew apace: for he was magnificently prolific. I believe it was on the immense sales of his early scientific stories and romances that the success

---

* In fact Wells's performance was far from brilliant—he failed his Finals at the first attempt.

of the great French publishing house, the Mercure de France, was mainly founded.

Both nationally and internationally Wells was a portent. Nationally, his meteoric rise repeated that of Dickens sixty years before: and even in his early books there was a touch of a kindred comic power in sympathetic delineation of English urban 'types.' This he was to develop eventually—as Mr. Lewisham and Kipps, Mr. Polly and Ponderevo succeeded Bert Smallways—into a kind of fiction which, for many, will remain his greatest achievement. Like Dickens he had swiftly ascended through all the social strata of England: but it was a very different England from that of Dickens—an England on the brink, it seemed, of a triumphant emancipation. There is an atmosphere of confidence and gaiety, a sense of illimitable vistas (well symbolised by his prodigious addiction to dots for punctuation) in Wells's earlier work which expresses the temper of his time. *Anticipations . . . Mankind in the Making . . . New Worlds for Old . . . The New Utopia . . .* such were his signature tunes. Of the ascent to emancipation which they celebrate, Wells was himself the exemplar. Science was the beneficent power which had unloosed the social fetters from his feet. He was the spoiled child of the new freedom.

It was an intoxicating progress, and the generation to which I belong shared the intoxication. No small part of the quality of our experience of life in the ten years before 1914 came from the exciting question: 'What would Wells do next?' Neither Shaw nor Chesterton—brilliant expositors of new angles of vision though they were—came near to this intimate centrality which Wells occupied in our experience. He was, so to speak, consubstantial with the generation whose aspirations he at once kindled and defined. At the same time, he transported us into a realm of fantasy and felicity. Heavens, how we laughed! *The Adventures of Mr. Polly* must have been thrown off almost between two trains: 'a giddy parergon.' But it was a masterpiece, drawing one irresistibly on to a condition in which the scheme of things entire was dissolved in laughter.

'The grave and reverend signiors with the palatial bokos' were shocked by him. I well remember how, on the pale green *Westminster Gazette* on which I worked, Wells's books became tabu. They were not to be reviewed, because Wells had dealt unpardonably in *The New Machiavelli* with the respected figures of Beatrice and Sidney Webb. So, too, an audible silence descended upon the cultivated when he described the style of Henry James as like 'a hippopotamus trying to pick up a pea.' Probably he did overstep the mark; but then he was always overstepping the mark. He was exuberant and irrepressible: things came into his head, as they did into Mr. Polly's, and they were too good not to go into his books: and if he thereby offended against decorum, that was essential to his function and himself. The contradiction between his intellectual passion for 'a new order' and his irrepressible irreverence was probably unresolved to the end. It was part of his Englishness—the impishness which is generally called Cockney, but is by no means peculiar to Londoners. It is more affectionate and kindly than the American urge to debunk everything: it sees through things and yet is inclined to leave them as they are.

This combination of intellectual impatience and tolerance—most satisfyingly expressed in the Wells who projected himself into Mr. Polly—caused him to appear in real life as something of a snob. There is nothing more English than a snob: and there are very few Englishmen of genius in whom a streak of snobbishness has not manifested itself, from Shakespeare downwards. It was evident in writers so different as Hardy and D. H. Lawrence and Arnold Bennett besides Wells himself. It is natural enough: the refinements of culture are maintained by social privilege, and men who have stormed society by the power of genius alone are isolated, conscious of being in, not of, the elect: at once critical of, and luxuriating in, their new environment. But in Wells the discrepancy was peculiarly marked: for, unlike many men of genius, he was an intensely social and gregarious person; he was also a very generous one. So that he was forever throwing his younger and more modest friends into contact with the socially eminent and secure, to whom he showed a greater deference than the younger felt themselves, or felt that their hero ought to feel.

Thus one had the impression of some essential insecurity or volatility in Wells. This impression was oddly reinforced by his ill-controlled and squeaky voice; which hardly seemed the utterance of a whole man. But, at the bottom, I suppose this appearance of insecurity was due to the fact that he did epitomise, at every level of experience, an age of revolutionary transition. If we, who were his younger and admiring friends, were a little disappointed in him as a person, it was probably an inevitable consequence of the rôle he filled for us. A living epitome of an age of transition does not make a comfortable friend. Rousseau did not.

He belonged to the rare type of men—rare even among men of genius—who become national and international symbols. Far more than Shaw, Wells was a figure in the European mind. He lent himself to the necessary simplification that international eminence requires: his early work fixed a European image of Wells which none of his subsequent achievements could seriously modify. He was the prophet of the future in which science was the key to liberty. In this rôle, he represented the last manifestation of a united Europe: the last intellectual effort of a common culture, a common belief in a common emancipation. 1914 drew down the curtain on that heady vista. Naturally, Wells was exasperated at so stupid and outrageous a denial of his plans. His initial judgments on the causes of the first world-war were accordingly as resentful and circumscribed as those of other Englishmen. No doubt they helped to form Lenin's judgment of him. But what was condemnation in Lenin's eyes, should not be so in ours. We English *are* bourgeois; it is our achievement, not our failing. We have evolved a pattern of bourgeois life so radically tolerant that the proletariat can be absorbed into it. If the rest of Europe—Germany and France in particular—could have followed our example Europe might well have remained a political and cultural unity today.

To claim Wells as the last prophet of bourgeois Europe is to claim a good deal more for him than that he was the prophet of a lost cause. It was a cause that might have won. The mistake Wells made is the mistake that all Englishmen make. They do not understand how different England is from the continent, how the cleavages which cut across European societies are mitigated in this country. The diffused Christianity which is still so potent an element in British politics acts here as a solvent of political intransigence. Christianity on the continent is still, in the main, one term of an antithesis. Liberal still means secularist; and Socialists are assumed to be materialist and anti-clerical. Indeed, at the present moment, the possibility of any unity at all, even in Western Europe, appears to depend on the doubtful possibility of a genuine alliance between democratic Catholics and moderate Socialists. The alliance between the bourgeoisie and the Christian Church against the working-class is an evil legacy of the French Revolution.

Wells, the Englishman, was immune from all this. He cheerfully indulged, in true English fashion, in his own private reconstruction of the Christian religion; and in his novels he expressed, with a genius and gusto all his own, the peculiar British tolerance, that guys and guards. He had an undisguised contempt for the clumsiness and brutality of revolution, and a passionate but impatient faith in the power of education. To this task, of educating the human race, when he had come to less superficial conclusions concerning the causes of the first world-war, he devoted himself in an astonishing series of compilations which began with the *Outline of History*. It was a unique and heroic enterprise: and if the world wobbled steadily on towards disaster it was not his fault. He had done more to stop the rake's progress than a legion of men.

To say that Wells ignored human limitations may be true. But if it is intended as a criticism of his work and aims it badly misses the mark. What conceivable advantage would have accrued to him or the world if he had not continued to rebel against human stupidity? He would not have conceived more Kippses, more Mr. Pollys. He could write such books precisely because he felt pretty confident that things were going well. He was mistaken; he was too sanguine. Perhaps: but he was not unwise. Those who pretended to superior wisdom, and gave up hope, merely showed proof of less vitality than he. He delayed his complete pessimism to the end of his life, when he had done all that he could to open men's eyes and enlarge their vision.

It is easy, and fashionable, to condemn Wells for having believed in a terrestrial millennium. But to believe in the moral necessity of a rational world-order, and in the capacity of mankind to achieve it, is not really inordinate. The alternative is despair. You may call this despair Christian hope if you like; but the alternative to a rational world order remains universal catastrophe. If you are seriously preparing for that evil day, well and good. But how many of those who presume, on religious grounds, to condemn Wells's hard-working meliorism are seriously preparing for anything at all—even for the last Judgment, in which they profess to believe? Nor will it do to argue that the only way to avoid disaster is to return to the Christian faith. Christians professed do not behave more sensibly, more humanely, more imaginatively than the rest of their fellowmen. They are just as recalcitrant to the new demands made upon man's behaviour, just as blind to the necessity of a reconstruction of his habitual morality, just as besotted by nationalism as the non-Christian. Perhaps on an average they are even more retrogressive than their secularist fellows, because they pride themselves on having achieved already something that sounds like the *unum necessarium* of today, but is in reality only a phantasm of it. They claim to be actual members of a supra-national society. If they behaved accordingly, we should be at least half-way towards an escape from the terrible calamity that threatens us all. But what do they do to show the reality of their membership of the supra-national society? They bomb one another, they starve one another, they torture children. There is a Catholic party at the head of the French State today. The part of

Germany it occupies is mainly Catholic too. It is the most damnably oppressed of all the zones of occupation.

If I am called upon to choose between Wells's humanism, his impatience, his exasperation and even his final despair, and the religion of those who condemn him for the superficiality of his faith in reason and education and enlightenment, I am on his side, with all my heart and all my mind and all my soul. They deceive themselves who assert, or even imply, that there is a Christian alternative to the Wellsian faith. There is only one alternative to it—that is an acceptance of the inevitability of mundane catastrophe. Christians may be capable of this; but so may non-Christians. The Christian may call his attitude hope; the non-Christian will call his despair, or indifference, or acceptance. But neither the hope of the Christian, nor the despair of the non-Christian, will determine their behaviour. In so far as they have understanding and charity and imagination they will try to build against the evil day; they will teach the truth they know and do the good they can.

Wells had a great genius, perhaps the greatest natural genius that has been manifest in our day. Had he stuck to writing novels, what a legacy he would have left to posterity! But he could not help reading the writing on the wall, when it appeared in 1914. It took him some time to decipher the message; but when he did, he wasted no time in trying to rouse his countrymen and the world into awareness of its predicament. The new freedom which applied science had given to mankind, except it was controlled by a new order, could only lead mankind to new disaster: the potentiality of disaster coextensive with the potentiality of freedom. In didactic fiction, in essays, in encyclopaedic histories, in pamphlets—pleading, angry, cocky, depressed—in a prose style which for sheer vitality will hardly be surpassed, he toiled to open men's eyes to their condition. Just as it is a narrow and circumscribed judgment which condemns him for his rationalism, so it is a partial and parochial vision which accuses him of squandering his magnificent gift as a creative writer. His greatness—and he *was* great—consisted in his power to respond to the challenge of the times. Even though he came to despair of it—*bene meruit de re publica*.

92. Jorge Luis Borges on the first Wells

1946

Jorge Luis Borges (b. 1899), Argentinian poet and short-story writer. This essay, which was written at the time of Wells's death under the title 'El Primer Wells', is reprinted here from *Other Inquisitions 1937–1952* (University of Texas Press, 1964), pp. 86–8. The translation is by Ruth L. C. Simms.

Harris relates that when Oscar Wilde was asked about Wells, he called him 'a scientific Jules Verne.' That was in 1899; it appears that Wilde thought less of defining Wells, or of annihilating him, than of changing the subject. Now the names H. G. Wells and Jules Verne have come to be incompatible. We all feel that this is true, but still it may be well to examine the intricate reasons on which our feeling is based.

The most obvious reason is a technical one. Before Wells resigned himself to the role of a sociological spectator, he was an admirable storyteller, an heir to the concise style of Swift and Edgar Allan Poe; Verne was a pleasant and industrious journeyman. Verne wrote for adolescents; Wells, for all ages. There is another difference, which Wells himself once indicated: Verne's stories deal with probable things (a submarine, a ship larger than those existing in 1872, the discovery of the South Pole, the talking picture, the crossing of Africa in a balloon, the craters of an extinguished volcano that lead to the center of the earth); the short stories Wells wrote concern mere possibilities, if not impossible things (an invisible man, a flower that devours a man, a crystal egg that reflects the events on Mars, a man who returns from the future with a flower of the future, a man who returns from the other life with his heart on the right side, because he has been completely inverted, as in a mirror). I have read that Verne, scandalized by the license permitted by *The First Men in the Moon*, exclaimed indignantly, '*Il invente!*'

The reasons I have given seem valid enough, but they do not explain why Wells is infinitely superior to the author of *Hector Servadac*, and also to Rosney, Lytton, Robert Paltock, Cyrano, or any other precursor

330

of his methods.* Even his best plots do not adequately solve the problem. In long books the plot can be only a pretext, or a point of departure. It is important for the composition of the work, but not for the reader's enjoyment of it. That is true of all genres; the best detective stories are not those with the best plots. (If plots were everything, the *Quixote* would not exist and Shaw would be inferior to O'Neill.) In my opinion, the excellence of Wells's first novels—*The Island of Doctor Moreau*, for example, or *The Invisible Man*—has a deeper origin. Not only do they tell an ingenious story; but they tell a story symbolic of processes that are somehow inherent in all human destinies. The harassed invisible man who has to sleep as though his eyes were wide open because his eyelids do not exclude light is our solitude and our terror; the conventicle of seated monsters who mouth a servile creed in their night is the Vatican and is Lhasa. Work that endures is always capable of an infinite and plastic ambiguity; it is all things for all men, like the Apostle; it is a mirror that reflects the reader's own traits and it is also a map of the world. And it must be ambiguous in an evanescent and modest way, almost in spite of the author; he must appear to be ignorant of all symbolism. Wells displayed that lucid innocence in his first fantastic exercises, which are to me the most admirable part of his admirable work.

Those who say that art should not propagate doctrines usually refer to doctrines that are opposed to their own. Naturally this is not my own case; I gratefully profess almost all the doctrines of Wells, but I deplore his inserting them into his narratives. An heir of the British nominalists, Wells condemns our custom of speaking of the 'tenacity of England' or the 'intrigues of Prussia.' The arguments against that harmful mythology seem to be irreproachable, but not the fact of interpolating them into the story of Mr. Parham's dream. As long as an author merely relates events or traces the slight deviations of a conscience, we can suppose him to be omniscient, we can confuse him with the universe or with God; but when he descends to the level of pure reason, we know he is fallible. Reality is inferred from events, not reasonings; we permit God to affirm *I am that I am* (Exodus 3:14), not to declare and analyze, like Hegel or Anselm, the *argumentum ontologicum*. God must not theologize; the writer must not invalidate with human arguments the momentary faith that art demands of us. There is another consideration: the author who shows aversion to a character seems not to understand

* In *The Outline of History* (1931) Wells praises the work of two other precursors: Francis Bacon and Lucian of Samosata [author's note].

him completely, seems to confess that the character is not inevitable for him. We distrust his intelligence, as we would distrust the intelligence of a God who maintained heavens and hells. God, Spinoza has written, does not hate anyone and does not love anyone (*Ethics*, 5, 17).

Like Quevedo, like Voltaire, like Goethe, like some others, Wells is less a man of letters than a literature. He wrote garrulous books in which the gigantic felicity of Charles Dickens somehow reappears; he bestowed sociological parables with a lavish hand; he constructed encyclopedias, enlarged the possibilities of the novel, rewrote the Book of Job—'that great Hebrew imitation of the Platonic dialogue'; for our time, he wrote a very delightful autobiography without pride and without humility; he combated communism, Nazism, and Christianity; he debated (politely and mortally) with Belloc; he chronicled the past, chronicled the future, recorded real and imaginary lives. Of the vast and diversified library he left us, nothing has pleased me more than his narration of some atrocious miracles: *The Time Machine, The Island of Doctor Moreau, The Plattner Story, The First Men in the Moon*. They are the first books I read; perhaps they will be the last. I think they will be incorporated, like the fables of Theseus or Ahasuerus, into the general memory of the species and even transcend the fame of their creator or the extinction of the language in which they were written.

Appendix: other items of criticism

The following list contains a selection of the more interesting critical articles published during Wells's lifetime. Book reviews, political articles, biographical features and reminiscences are not included.

1900 'A Novelist of the Unknown', *Academy* (23 June 1900), lviii, 535–6.

1902 Arnold Bennett, 'Herbert George Wells and his Work', *Cosmopolitan Magazine* (August 1902), xxxiii, 465–71. Reprinted in *Arnold Bennett and H. G. Wells* (1960), ed. Harris Wilson, 260–76.

1904 Frank Blunt, 'M. H. G. Wells et le Style', *Nouvelle Revue* (15 September 1904), xxx, 186–92.

1904 'H. G. Wells and his French Critic', *Westminster Gazette* (27 September 1904), 3.

1904 Marcel Réja, 'H. G. Wells et le Merveilleux Scientifique', *Mercure de France* (October 1904), lii, 40–62.

1908 'The Ideas of Mr. H. G. Wells', *Quarterly Review* (April 1908), ccviii, 472–90.

1911 Firmin Roz, 'Romanciers Anglais Contemporains: M. H. G. Wells', *Revue des Deux Mondes* (1 August 1911), xl, 612–41.

1912 René Séguy, 'H. G. Wells et la Pensée Contemporaine', *Mercure de France* (16 February 1912), xcv, 673–99.

1914 Henry James, 'The Younger Generation', *The Times Literary Supplement* (19 March, 2 April 1914), 133–4, 157–8. Reprinted in *Notes on Novelists* (1914), 314–61, as 'The New Novel'.

1914 Francis Gribble, 'H. G. Wells', *Everyman* (19 June 1914), iv, 295–6.

1915 Stuart P. Sherman, 'The Realism of Arnold Bennett', *Nation* (New York, 23 December 1915), ci, 741–4. Reprinted in *On Contemporary Literature* (1917).

1917 Maurice Simart, 'Herbert George Wells Sociologue', *Mercure de France* (16 March 1917), cxx, 193–221.

1917 Wilfrid Lay, 'H. G. Wells and his Mental "Hinterland" ', *Bookman* (New York, July 1917), xlv, 461–8.

1917 Frederic Harrison, 'A Very Invisible God', *Nineteenth Century and After* (October 1917), lxxxii, 771–81.

1918 H. L. Mencken, 'The Late Mr. Wells', reprinted in *Prejudices: First Series* (1921), 22–35.

1922 Marc Bloch, 'H. G. Wells, Historien', *Revue de Paris* (15 August 1922), xxix, 860–74.

1924 Virginia Woolf, 'Mr. Bennett and Mrs. Brown', reprinted in *The Captain's Death Bed and Other Essays* (1950), 90–111.

1925 Henry Seidel Canby, 'Outline of a Journalist', *Saturday Review of Literature* (24 January 1925), i, 473–5.

1925 J. B. Priestley, 'H. G. Wells', *English Journal* (February 1925), xiv, 89–97.

1925 Virginia Woolf, 'Modern Fiction', in *The Common Reader* (1925), 184–204.

1927 Wilbur Cross, 'The Mind of H. G. Wells', *Yale Review* (16 January 1927), xvi, 298–315.

1927 Arnaud Dandieu, 'Wells et Diderot', *Mercure de France* (15 March 1927), cxciv, 513–36.

1928 'The Wells and Bennett Novel', *The Times Literary Supplement* (23 August 1928), 597–8.

1931 David Ockham, 'People of Importance in their Day: H. G. Wells', *Saturday Review* (20 June 1931), cli, 896.

1932 D. S. Mirsky and Christopher Dawson, 'H. G. Wells and History', *Criterion* (October 1932), xii, 1–16.

1934 Odette Keun, 'H. G. Wells—The Player', *Time and Tide* (13–27 October 1934), 1249–51, 1307–9, 1346–8.

1936 Ford Madox Ford, 'H. G. Wells', *American Mercury* (May 1936), xxxviii, 48–58. Reprinted in *Mightier than the Sword* (1938), 145–65.

1938 Christopher Caudwell, 'H. G. Wells: A Study in Utopianism', in *Studies in a Dying Culture* (1938), 74–95.

1941 George Orwell, 'Wells, Hitler and the World State', reprinted in *Collected Essays, Journalism and Letters* (1968), ii, 139–45.

1946 V. S. Pritchett, 'The Scientific Romances', in *The Living Novel* (1946), 116ff.

Bibliography

A bibliography of secondary works bearing on Wells's contemporary reception.

BERGONZI, BERNARD, *The Early H. G. Wells* (1961): quotes reviews of the scientific romances.

CANTRIL, HADLEY, *The Invasion from Mars* (1940): a sociological study of the effects of Orson Welles's 1938 broadcast of *The War of the Worlds*.

DICKSON, LOVAT, *H. G. Wells: His Turbulent Life and Times* (1969): quotes reviews and traces Wells's publishing history with Macmillans.

HILLEGAS, MARK R., *The Future as Nightmare: H. G. Wells and the Anti-Utopians* (1967): studies Wells's influence on Zamyatin, Huxley, Orwell and others.

HYNES, SAMUEL, *The Edwardian Turn of Mind* (1968): narrates the Fabian Society and *Ann Veronica* episodes in Wells's career.

LEVIDOVA, I. M. and PARCHEVSKAYA, B. M., *Herbert George Wells: A Bibliography of Russian Translations and Critical Literature in Russian 1898–1965* (Moscow, 1966).

PARRINDER, PATRICK, *H. G. Wells* (Writers and Critics series, 1970).

RAKNEM, INGVALD, *H. G. Wells and his Critics* (1962): a comprehensive study of Wells's reception with full bibliographical apparatus.

Wells's Published Books

This list excludes posthumous works. Pamphlets of less than a hundred pages have generally been omitted.

1893
Textbook of Biology
Honours Physiography (with R. A. Gregory)
1895
Select Conversations with an Uncle
The Time Machine
The Wonderful Visit
The Stolen Bacillus, and Other Incidents
1896
The Island of Doctor Moreau
The Wheels of Chance
1897
The Plattner Story, and Others
The Invisible Man
Certain Personal Matters
Thirty Strange Stories (New York)
1898
The War of the Worlds
1899
When the Sleeper Wakes
  (revised as *The Sleeper Awakes*, 1910)
Tales of Space and Time
1900
Love and Mr. Lewisham
1901
The First Men in the Moon
Anticipations
1902
The Discovery of the Future
The Sea Lady
1903
Mankind in the Making

Twelve Stories and a Dream
1904
The Food of the Gods
1905
A Modern Utopia
Kipps
1906
In the Days of the Comet
The Future in America
1908
New Worlds for Old
The War in the Air
First and Last Things
1909
Tono-Bungay
Ann Veronica
1910
The History of Mr. Polly
1911
The New Machiavelli
*The Country of the Blind,
  and Other Stories*
1912
The Great State (essays by Wells
  and twelve others)
Marriage
1913
Little Wars
The Passionate Friends
1914
An Englishman Looks at the World
The World Set Free
The Wife of Sir Isaac Harman
The War that Will End War

1915
Boon
Bealby
The Research Magnificent
1916
What Is Coming
Mr. Britling Sees It Through
The Elements of Reconstruction
1917
War and the Future
God the Invisible King
The Soul of a Bishop
1918
In the Fourth Year
Joan and Peter
1919
The Undying Fire
1920
The Outline of History
Russia in the Shadows
1921
The Salvaging of Civilisation
1922
Washington and the Hope of Peace
The Secret Places of the Heart
A Short History of the World
1923
Men Like Gods
1924
The Story of a Great Schoolmaster
The Dream
A Year of Prophesying
1925
Christina Alberta's Father
1926
The World of William Clissold
1927
Meanwhile
1928
The Way the World Is Going
The Open Conspiracy
Mr. Blettsworthy on Rampole Island
1929
The King Who Was a King

1930
The Autocracy of Mr. Parham
The Science of Life (with Julian
   Huxley and G. P. Wells)
1931
*What Are We To Do With
   Our Lives?*
1932
*The Work Wealth and Happiness
   of Mankind*
After Democracy
The Bulpington of Blup
1933
The Shape of Things to Come
1934
Experiment in Autobiography
1935
Things to Come
1936
The Anatomy of Frustration
The Croquet Player
1937
Star Begotten
Brynhild
The Camford Visitation
1938
The Brothers
World Brain
Apropos of Dolores
1939
The Holy Terror
*Travels of a Republican Radical
   in Search of Hot Water*
The Fate of Homo Sapiens
The New World Order
1940
The Rights of Man
Babes in the Darkling Wood
*The Common Sense of
   War and Peace*
All Aboard for Ararat
1941
Guide to the New World
You Can't Be Too Careful

1942
The Outlook for Homo Sapiens
Phoenix

1943
Crux Ansata

1944
'42 to '44

1945
The Happy Turning
Mind at the End of Its Tether

Index

The index is divided into three sections: I. H. G. Wells's works; II. Wells's themes and characteristics; III. General.

II. WELLS'S THEMES AND CHARACTERISTICS

III. GENERAL